THE MANTLE OF THE PROPHET

THE
MANTLE
OF THE
PROPHET

RELIGION AND POLITICS IN IRAN

ROY MOTTAHEDEH

PANTHEON BOOKS NEW YORK

All rights reserved under International and Pan-American Copyright
Conventions. Published in the United States by Pantheon Books, a
division of Random House, Inc., New York, and simultaneously in
Canada by Random House of Canada Limited, Toronto.
Originally published in hardcover by Simon and Schuster, New
York, in 1985.

Library of Congress Cataloging-in-Publication Data

Mottahedeh, Roy P., 1940–
  The mantle of the prophet.
  Includes index.
  1. Islam and politics—Iran. 2. Shīʿah—Iran.
  3. Iran—Politics and government—1941–1979. I. Title.
  BP192.7.I68M67 1986   955′.053   86-15092
  ISBN 0-394-74865-4

  4   6   8   9   7   5   3

Manufactured in the United States of America

First Pantheon Paperback Edition

Grateful acknowledgment is made to the following for permission to reprint from previously published materials:

Bibliotheca Islamica, Inc.: Excerpt from *The School Principal* by Jalal Al-e Ahmad, translated by John K. Newton. Copyright © 1974 by Bibliotheca Islamica, Inc., Box 14474, University Station, Minneapolis, MN 55414.

E. J. Brill: Excerpt from *Satan's Tragedy and Redemption: Iblis in Sufi Psychology* by Peter J. Awn. Copyright © 1983 E. J. Brill, Leiden, The Netherlands. Reprinted by permission.

Mazda Publishers: Excerpts from *Iranian Society: An Anthology of Writings* by Jalal Al-e Ahmad and *Gharbzadegi* by Jalal Al-e Ahmad, translated by John Green and Ahmad Alizadeh, copyright © 1982 by Mazda Publishers. Reprinted by permission.

Mizan Press: Excerpt from *Islam and Revolution: Writings and Declarations of Imam Khomeini*, translated and annotated by Hamid Algar. Copyright © 1981.

New York University Press: Excerpt from *Taziyeh: Ritual and Drama in Iran* edited by Peter J. Chelkowski. Copyright © 1979 by New York University Press. Reprinted by permission of New York University Press.

State University of New York Press: Excerpt from *The Life of Ibn Sina: A Critical Edition and Annotated Translation* by William E. Gohlman. Reprinted by permission of the State University of New York Press. Copyright © 1974 State University of New York.

Robert Wells: Translations of material by Jalal Al-e Ahmad from Ph.D. thesis, "Jalal Ale Ahmad" by Robert Wells, 1982.

CONTENTS

To My Mother
Mildred R. Mottahedeh

NOTE TO THE READER

FROM THE beginning of 1978, when I became aware of the riots and protests which would eventually lead to the Iranian revolution, I knew, as someone who had devoted a good part of his life to the study of premodern Iran, that I was witnessing something both familiar and new in Iranian history. It was familiar because the ethos that motivated its leaders, the now-famous ayatollahs of the Shiah Muslim world, was not dissimilar to the ethos that had motivated comparable specialists in Muslim law a thousand years ago. It was new because, during the last two centuries, this religious ethos had undergone an internal intellectual revolution that had passed unnoticed by all except a handful of legal specialists within the Shiah Muslim tradition itself.

During the late spring of 1978 a professor at the University of Tehran came to visit me in Princeton, New Jersey, where I teach. He had studied for many years at the seminaries in the shrine city of Qom at which traditional Shiah learning is taught; after that he had become interested in gaining a secular education and had

parted (with a certain relief) from the company of mullahs and
ayatollahs. Traditionally-educated religious leaders were much on
our minds at that time because they were directing the movement
of protest that had swollen in a few months from the provincial
outcry by some seminarians in Qom to a clamor heard throughout the Iranian nation and even then heard from time to time by
the world beyond Iran.

As we walked through the hybrid Gothic architecture of the
university, I asked my friend about his early education: How did
one study to become a mullah? He told me that in the Shiah seminaries such as those in Qom a student began by studying grammar, rhetoric, and logic. From that moment I knew I wanted to
write this book.

Grammar, rhetoric, and logic comprise the *trivium*, the first
three of the seven liberal arts as they were defined in the late
classical world, after which they continued to constitute the foundation of the scholastic curriculum as it was taught in many parts
of medieval and Renaissance Europe. So basic were the subjects
of the *trivium* that people who had passed on to more advanced
levels of learning considered an elementary knowledge of all
three commonplace and therefore of little importance; hence our
word "trivial." I realized (and subsequent study confirmed) that
my friend and a handful of similarly educated people were the
last true scholastics alive on earth, people who had experienced
the education to which Princeton's patrons and planners felt they
should pay tribute through their strangely assorted but congenial
architectural reminiscences of the medieval and Tudor buildings
of Oxford and Cambridge. Here was a living version of the kind
of education (with its tradition of classroom disputation and of
commentaries and super-commentaries on long-established "set
texts") that had produced in the West men such as the saintly and
brilliant theologian Thomas Aquinas and the intolerant and
bloodthirsty grand inquisitor, Torquemada, and in the East thinkers such as Averroës among the Muslims and Maimonides among
the Jews.

I spent the next two years reading the curriculum mullahs read
and interviewing Iranians (and one or two Iraqis) who had studied
this curriculum in the traditional seminaries. The "Ali Hashemi"

in this book is a real person whose wish to remain anonymous I have scrupulously respected. All the events in the narrative of Ali Hashemi and his friends are based on the lives of Iranians as described to me by Iranians. I believe in the good faith of my informants, and have often found evidence external to their accounts that confirms what they said.

The passages between the accounts of Ali Hashemi's life, which try to present an extended reading of the history of Iranian culture insofar as it applies to the lives of the principal characters, are based on a reading of the primary sources for Iranian history that is as accurate as my time and abilities allow. The reader may notice a difference in tone between these analytic passages and those that narrate the life of Ali and his friends. Naturally the characters of the narrative tell of their own lives with an inward-looking voice that I neither can nor wish to imitate in the historical sections of the book, where events are told in my own voice and from my own perspective.

The non-Iranian reader should be aware that no presentation of the history of Iranian culture, and, in particular, no presentation of its religious tradition, can please all Iranians. In the past five years, as Iran has moved through a political and cultural revolution with dramatic and often violent aftermaths and entered a long and bitter war with its neighbor Iraq, many thousands of Iranians have been executed, tens of thousands have died in battle, and hundreds of thousands have chosen to live in exile. Any consensus on the meaning of the Iranian past has been torn up by the deeply felt disagreement among Iranians over the meaning of the Iranian present.

As a result of this disagreement, some Iranians will feel that the account of the mullah who stands at the center of this book's personal narrative is not reverential enough; he has experienced doubts and shifts of attitude that they will think atypical of Shiah men of religion. Others will think the portrait altogether too reverential; they will protest that a mullah who has attended a secular university and who is so broad in his interests and so liberal in his views is no typical mullah. To some degree both parties will be right. But I am not giving an account of an archetypal mullah, and as a historian I could not do so in good conscience. In preparing this book I talked with real Iranians, not archetypes, and the book reflects what they said. Nevertheless a number of significant details and episodes have been transferred from the lives of some informants to the lives of others in order to preserve their anonymity; attempts to identify any character with a specific living Iranian are almost sure to fail. All these changes have been checked and corrected by Iranian friends with a view toward preserving the book's faithfulness to the characters of the individuals it portrays. The reader may also notice how little is told of the adult family life of the figures prominent in the personal narrative. My Iranian friends were reluctant to speak about such matters, and I have respected their reticence. Ali Hashemi's silences reflect his character as much as does his own narrative of his life.

This book is, in some sense, the story of all of us in the last part of the twentieth century—a time in which we have seen a revival of religious enthusiasm and a reassertion in so many societies of the demand that religion play a role in politics. In another sense it is the story of most of the Third World, where disappointment at the yield of a generation or more of nationalism, Westernization and socialism has fostered a return to older and more deeply rooted values. But it is most particularly the story of Iran, a land with over two millennia of consciousness of itself. Love for its heritage informs everything I have written here.

PROLOGUE

ALI HASHEMI only half listened to the radio after lunch on February 11, 1979. He knew that however the fighting came out in Tehran, he would feel better if he could plant something in his garden. In other parts of Iran a man like Ali, who was wealthy, in his late thirties, and a learned mullah, would never be seen, even by his family, bent over a plot of seedlings with a spade. But in Qom it was different; in the ancient families of the town, especially in the ancient families of sayyeds, or descendants of Mohammed, the men, regardless of their callings or wealth, took pride in at least occasionally working the land with their own hands. Besides, there seemed to be no point in listening to the radio carefully. After briefly reporting on the two o'clock news that the central police station was on fire, the army had withdrawn to barracks after heavy fighting during the morning, and a crowd of revolutionaries was moving up Kakh Avenue to seize the office of the Shah's prime minister, the radio dissolved for about two and a half hours into musical selections, none of them introduced or identified. Then suddenly it was silent for three or four minutes.

Ali had put down his portable radio on one of the brick paths in the courtyard garden where he was working. When it became silent he stuck his spade in the earth, stood up, and listened. He noticed that Hamid, who came at this season to prune the trees in the gardens of the house, had stopped sawing. Ali's older brother, who had been reading an accounting ledger in a room that opened onto the courtyard, walked up to the radio and stared at it. Ali decided to walk closer too, and at this point Hamid let himself down from the lower branches of the pine tree he had been pruning and, still carrying his saw, approached the brothers very slowly, almost tiptoeing, as if he expected the radio to explode.

Suddenly Ali heard the words of a deep-voiced man, undoubtedly a mullah from his intonation and his pronunciation of Persian words of Arabic origin. The mullah, a little breathless but dignified nonetheless, said: "This is the true voice of the Iranian nation. The ill-omened regime of the Pahlavis is finished, and an Islamic government has been established under the leadership of Ayatollah Khomeini." At this point the speaker, obviously at a loss for what to say next, cleared his throat and hemmed a few times, then said abruptly: "We ask the Imam to send instructions to the radio station." Then there was a burst of whispering. Finally he announced excitedly: "We hope to receive messages from Ayatollah Khomeini and Ayatollah Taleqani. Please keep listening; they will be broadcast as soon as possible."

The telephone rang. Ali turned off the radio while his brother ran to answer the phone in a nearby room. A few seconds later he reappeared, calling to Ali: "My God, the head of the Manzariyeh army base has just come into town and surrendered to Ayatollah Montazeri. In a minute people will be pouring into the streets. I'm going down to check the warehouse."

Ali wanted to go as soon as possible to the shrine and the Faiziyeh, the theological college where he had taught until it had been closed by the government in 1975; he wanted to see the faces of his students, and he knew they would have questions for him. He asked Hamid to water the planted seedlings and to put the unplanted ones in the shade; then, since he was going out into the streets, he grabbed his mullah turban and put on his long black aba.

For the rest of that day Ali's greatest problem was to walk in a dignified manner. He would start to skip, to jump, to run, then stop himself. He was almost airborne, like the fast-moving winter clouds that flew high over Qom, and his responsibility to his students and his fellow mullahs only barely managed to keep him on the ground. His fellow Qomis, usually divided in their feelings toward mullahs, Shiah men of religion (mullahs ran the theological colleges, the town's biggest industry, but they also imported some of the town's biggest nuisances—their students), on this day were showering every passing mullah with compliments. On the way to the shrine people shouted at Ali, "Through your blessing we are saved." As he went past them they called out a variation on a standard Persian farewell, "May God never let the shadows of the mullahs grow less for us." The throngs of people, in their excitement to speak to—and often embrace—their fellow Qomis, even those they hardly knew, were moving so slowly that Ali had to hide his impatience.

As he approached the larger streets near the shrine and the *madresehs*, the theological colleges, he sensed the relief of the town, its consciousness of release. Since January 1978, when several theological students had been killed in a demonstration over an article denouncing Ayatollah Khomeini, the bazaar of Qom, in a show of sympathy with the protesters, had been shut for all except a scattered forty days. For nearly fourteen months only the bakers, butchers, and men who sold produce off barrows in the streets had operated on a normal schedule. Qomis had been dependent on the distribution of food and clothing through local mosques, and the town had been filled with a certain sense of duress.

Today the sense of release was total. On the previous day the Qomis themselves had occupied the headquarters of SAVAK, the secret police, and the chief of the municipal police had gone to Ayatollah Montazeri, the representative and former student of Khomeini, to say that he would obey Montazeri's orders. Even the signs of the fourteen months of duress spoke the language of victory. As Ali passed the cavelike bombed-out building that until a

year ago had housed the Qom branch of the shah's Resurrection
party, he remembered the passage in the Koran that described the
Prophet Mohammed's words of comfort to a companion when the
two of them were hidden in a cave, hunted by enemies determined to kill them: "He said to his companion: 'Have no fear, for
God is with us'; then God sent down upon him His divine tranquillity, and strengthened him with his hosts which you did not
see, and humbled to the depths the word of the unbelievers. But
the word of God is exalted to the heights; for God is all-powerful,
all-seeing."

In fact, everywhere the word of God seemed exalted to the
heights. The very words of the posters on the buildings he passed,
words that by their anger showed how vulnerable the opposition
had felt throughout the struggle against the government, now
looked like triumphant proclamations: "Those who follow the
slain Imam Hosain will gain victory over the tyrant Yazid who
slew him"; and "The blood of martyrs has prevailed over the
sword."

Ali reached the crossroads, about two hundred meters from the
shrine, where a police station stood, not far from two hospitals.
Even though Ali had heard that Ayatollah Montazeri had sent his
representatives to supervise the police, he wasn't prepared for
what he saw now: a knot of policemen in their nattiest dark-blue
uniforms, with military-style caps, bowing slightly to a middle-
aged mullah, who looked at them with cautious approval as he
stood outside the police station.

It was then that Ali felt he could dare to believe it had really
happened. How many times had he seen the police bowing in the
same way to a bureaucrat, "Engineer" so-and-so, just down from
Tehran in his spanking new European suit, getting out of his
spanking new car for a day's business in Qom under police escort.
But the police bowing to an ordinary mullah in his turban and
robe?

It was like the departure of the Shah one month earlier; nobody
had believed it could happen, and even if they had seen it on television, deep down nobody fully believed that it had happened.
The disappearance of even the caretaker regime left by the Shah
had been like the final collapse of Solomon, who had been obeyed
after his death as long as his body stood. Solomon—according to

the Koran—had set the genies, the occult spirits of the world, to work for him; and after his death they worked on, still believing he was alive: "Thus, when We decreed death for [Solomon], nothing gave any sign of his death to them; yet a small worm of the earth was gnawing at his staff. So when [finally] he fell, the genies saw plainly that if they had known the unseen, they would not have tarried in the humiliating torment [of their subjugation]." In front of the police station Ali suddenly knew that for weeks, maybe even months, while he (and so many others) had feared the stroke of Solomon's cane, the cane was rotting and Solomon was already dead. But of course the Shah's dead regime could not be compared even to the dead body of a prophet such as Solomon; if it were comparable to anything mentioned in the Koran, it would be the body of Pharaoh, the enemy of God's prophet Moses.

As Ali approached the area near the shrine he saw that the floodlights illuminating its golden dome and other prominent features had been turned on as usual before sunset. But that was almost the only thing that was usual about what he saw and heard in the next few minutes. Students training to be mullahs, who usually labored so hard to seem dignified, were actually jumping in the air and waving their hands almost as if they were dancing, an activity so repugnant to mullahs and their students that the students would have fled in terror if their teachers had suggested the possible resemblance.

Neither Ali nor any other mullah teacher had any desire to spoil the joy of their students. They felt that an age of Iranian history, the age of worldly "Engineers" in their European suits, had been rolled up and a new age was theirs to unroll. Some of the students were shouting such slogans as "In the springtime of freedom we deeply miss our martyrs." But the noise they made was overwhelmed by the loudspeaker system of the shrine, which was—surely for the first time in history—merely broadcasting what came over the radio from Tehran. Message after message of local support by police brigades and army units, from such towns as Beidokht and Andimeshk, which Ali could place only vaguely on the map, were broadcast, together with new slogans for listeners to chant.

Some of Ali's students began to approach him, each bowing

slightly and waiting to ask a question. "Haji Agha, Khomeini has made Islam live again. You studied with him in Iraq; what sort of teacher is he?"

Questions of this sort were comparatively easy to deal with or to postpone for less public discussion. So were the questions from certain naïve students (not great favorites of Ali) who were preoccupied with temptations to moral corruption: "How long will it take to remove all the filth put in people's heads by magazines like *Today's Woman?*" and the like. But the difficult questions were the ones he himself was undecided about after months of thinking. One student, practically in tears with emotion, said, "Haji Agha, do you think that if we bring the Koran to the people, if we fill them with the spirit of Hosain and tell the young people the true history of Islam in their schoolbooks, we can bring about the 'return' very soon after our beloved revolution?" Ali told him, "Removing Pharaoh was only the first step; we may have to wander for a time until God's promise is fulfilled."

Ali, of course, like most mullahs in Qom, had read the book his student was referring to, *The Return to Ourselves* by Ali Shariati and, like most mullahs, he had longed for the masses to accept the book's message—that with a return to true Shiah Islam, Iran would be free from the shackles of political and psychological subjugation to the West. But he knew that the Qom of his early youth, a small town of walled gardens where a tradition of learning was maintained by his mullah father and his father's friends in a spirit of quiet heroism, had already disappeared and could never return. He rejoiced to see the two black flags of mourning for the martyrs of the revolution removed from the two minarets and a green banner tied to the top of the golden dome to signal the victory of Islam. But as he knew for certain the past could not return, he felt surprisingly uneasy about what this banner might mean for the future and, more especially, for him, for his responsibility as a learned mullah and as a descendant of the Prophet, a man entitled to wear the Prophet's color green.

Eventually the crowd became so thick that, as one says in Persian, "a dog wouldn't recognize its master," and Ali felt that he was not doing his students or fellow townsmen any good by participating in the crush. Besides, he felt hungry; he had forgotten lunch because he had worked so hard at distracting himself from the radio with gardening.

As he reentered the inner garden courtyard at home he could still hear shouting in the large avenue two blocks away and the indistinct words of someone preaching on the loud-speaker system in the great mosque that sat a kilometer away, face-to-face with the shrine. There was a smell of rain in the air, always welcome in the dry climate of Qom.

His brother had come back and was laughing with an excitement that seemed almost as strange for an important textile merchant of the bazaar as dancing seemed for the student mullahs. "All the desert between Qom and Tehran will be covered with crops by this summer. Just imagine it! It's going to be a terrific year for business. I'd better go out and pay some calls on some friends."

The sun had not yet set but was low enough so that the shadow of one wall of the courtyard had covered all except a thin strip of the garden. Ali noticed that the shadow was reaching out to touch the spade he had stuck in the ground next to the seedlings, and he went over and picked it up. Then he noticed the gardener Hamid, standing in the shaded part of the courtyard just under the tree he had finished pruning. Hamid was holding the saw in his hand and dividing his attention between Ali and the tree. Not the least remarkable thing about the day was that Hamid had apparently continued pruning throughout the vast celebration of the late afternoon. Hamid finally decided to give Ali his entire attention.

"God be blessed, sir, Islam is victorious. Of course, I'm sure ten years from now I'll still have this saw in my hand. But it's a great day, sir, a blessed day. You have studied with Khomeini, and you are a respected teacher in the Faiziyeh. I expect they'll need you in Tehran. With all due respect, sir, you and I are too old to become Tehranis. You and your family have been working the soil of Qom for generations, sir; you'll always be happiest when you return to Qom. I hope you have a chance to finish planting the seedlings soon; they won't survive long in that flat."

CHAPTER ONE

THREE THINGS had inclined Ali Hashemi to become a mullah: his father was a mullah, Ali was clever at religious studies, and he was born and raised in Qom. For thousands of students who arrive there each year, Qom is the highest seat of religious learning in Iran. For the tens of thousands of pilgrims who come in all seasons it is a town dominated by the great religious shrine that lies at its center. Ali Hashemi, who in 1979, in the year of the Revolution, became thirty-six, studied at Qom and has always revered the shrine. But for him Qom has always been something simpler and bigger: it was the first place he knew and almost all he would know until he was nineteen.

Ali did, of course, visit other places as a child. He remembers, for example, that when he was six he made the two-hour car trip north from Qom to Tehran for the first time. But except for a vague impression that the capital city was far bigger and noisier than Qom, the one scene he clearly remembers from this visit could easily have taken place at home. He recalls sharing his father's pleasure when they caught sight of his father's friend, a venerable mullah, seated in a chair near some cypress trees in a hospital garden.

Ali has a far earlier memory. The trees in his very first memory are the small fruit trees that are grown with such solicitous care in the difficult soil and hot climate of Qom. Ali, who was then about three, was at one of the smaller shrines, one called in Persian "the Gate of Paradise," with his mother. It was afternoon. A flock of green finches had landed on the trees of the orchard that surrounded the small brick building of the shrine. Ali remembers that a woman bent with age was bringing a pitcher of water and people were saying, "The birds are pilgrims too."

There can be no doubt of the season of his next memory because he can still see in the background the red and white flowers that grow on pomegranate trees, flowers whose fragrance in spring somehow resembles the taste of the fruit that is picked in the fall. He and his brother were being led to a corner of the garden behind his father's house, where his mother sat in front of a short leafy bush and held a newborn baby in her arms. He suddenly understood something he had been told on other occasions. He, his older brother, his father, and his newly born brother were all wearing green sashes; and Ali knew that they were all sayyeds, descendants of the Prophet. It didn't matter that the baby kept its eyes shut; Ali liked his younger brother and felt sure his younger brother liked him.

· · ·

Perhaps it is an accident that the Prophet's color, green, is the same as the color of vegetation, but in the painfully cultivated oasis of Qom it seems altogether appropriate. Just as Mediterranean Christians have for centuries marveled that their bare hillsides can produce bloodred grapes for use as a sacrament, Iranians have for centuries loved the enclosed green gardens that their labor has won from the dry soil of their country. The ancient world knew that Iranians loved such walled-in green spaces, and the Greeks adopted the word *paradeisos*, borrowed from *pairidaeza*, an ancient Persian term for an enclosed garden. The authors of the Greek New Testament adopted the same word for "the abode of the blessed." How fitting that green should be the color of the descendants of Mohammed, who, through the Koran, brought true Muslims the promise of a heavenly garden "underneath which rivers flow."

From its foundation the history of Qom has revolved around attentive concern for gardens and respectful care for people such as Ali who are descendants of Mohammed. When the Muslim Arabs conquered Iran in the seventh century, they seem to have found no important town on or near the present site of Qom, only scattered villages along an unpredictable and often brackish river. It was the new beliefs and new power of the Arabs that would eventually create the wealth that made a substantial town possible.

At first, however, the Arab conquerors were too few to govern their vast empire. In the Qom valley, as in many other communities in western and central Iran, as long as the local landlords forwarded taxes to the barrack towns of the Muslim Arabs in southern Iraq, the region was left to govern itself. But it was not as easy for the Arabs of southern Iraq to find a *modus vivendi* with their fellow Arabs of neighboring Syria. Through the quarrel between these two groups of Muslim Arabs, reverence for the descendants of Mohammed found a permanent emotional home in southern Iraq, and, indirectly, the quarrel was the cause of the foundation of Qom.

The quarrel had begun just about the time when Iraq became the capital of the Arab Muslim empire. Twenty-four years after Mohammed's death, Ali, his son-in-law and first cousin, had moved the capital there. The Arabs of southern Iraq had conquered most of Iran in the preceding generation, and they felt their pride of place was justified when this new leader of the Muslims moved the center of government from the holy cities of Arabia to the barrack towns of Iraq. But the Syrian Arabs disputed Ali's leadership, and when Ali was assassinated a few years later, the Iraqis grudgingly acquiesced to the transfer of the capital to Syria. In their hearts, however, many Iraqis continued to mourn for Ali and the time of his rule, and eventually they became known as "the partisans of Ali," *shiah Ali*, or simply the Shiah.

With the death of Ali these Iraqi Arabs transferred their allegiance to Ali's sons, the only grandchildren of Mohammed and the ancestors of all the sayyeds now alive, including Ayatollah Khomeini, King Hassan of Morocco, King Hussein of Jordan, and Ali Hashemi. After a generation of Syrian rule, one of these grandsons, Hosain, was encouraged by the partisans of his family to challenge the Syrians and raise the banner of revolt in southern Iraq. Hosain advanced from Arabia to southern Iraq, where "the partisans of Ali" might be expected to help him; but few of them did. In the deserts of that province Hosain, surrounded by troops loyal to the Syrians, watched some of his family and followers die of thirst, fought a series of desperate engagements, and was killed.

The Iraqi "partisans of Ali" grieved bitterly that Ali's son and the last surviving grandson of the Prophet should be killed in such misery and that they themselves should have done so little to save him. The death of Hosain became for the Shiah a focus of religious emotion comparable to the "passion" of Jesus in Christianity. The drama of his martyrdom is still reenacted yearly in processions and passion plays in Shiah communities from Lebanon to the Malabar coast of southern India. If many Iraqi Shiah of the seventh century grieved and plotted further rebellions, some few left and took refuge in the Qom valley of Iran.

To men from the burning heat of Arabian deserts the parched valley of the Qom River did not seem forbidding. Besides, the dryness and comparative insignificance of the Qom valley kept away more important administrators obedient to the Syrians. But these Iraqi Arabs were far from retiring in their treatment of the Zoroastrian Iranians then living in the Qom region. From central Asia to Provence the Arabs of Islam's first century were feared for their military virtues. At first the Iranian landlords helped the Arabs settle in the valley, but the landlords soon found that they were unable to prevent them from seizing water rights and even the land itself. The Arabs, however, gave something in return: their concentration of military and economic power allowed them to extend irrigation, grow cash crops, and thereby establish the town of Qom, the first sizable settlement in the region. Gradually most Iranians accepted not only the economic but also the spiritual domination of the Arabs and became Muslims. Again there was exchange: the Arabs, while preserving their genealogies, gave up their native language and became speakers of Persian like the people around them.

At the beginning of the ninth century the great-great-great-grandson of Hosain, who was recognized by most of the Shiah as their leader, died in eastern Iran in a place that was subsequently called Mashhad in his honor—literally, "the martyr's tomb." At about the same time his sister Fatemeh died in Qom. Ordinarily the tomb of a sister of even the most important descendants of Hosain would have been a place of only local pilgrimage. But as the people of Qom were Shiah, they treasured their shrine and treated Shiah visitors to the shrine with respect; and the town gradually expanded from the Arab settlement toward the shrine.

• • •

As a small child Ali was usually pleased when the visit of a relative or a friend of the family provided an excuse for a visit to the shrine because its inner room was always redolent of the fragrance of the huge sandalwood box that enclosed Fatemeh's tomb. He would walk with his mother near the river, past the religious colleges and the Great Mosque, to the imposing gateway through the high wall of the shrine. Inside the gate was a vast courtyard, in the center of which was a large round pool of clear greenish water, full at all seasons, unlike the Qom river, which seemed to live in states of feast or famine.

Once inside the courtyard, Ali's mother would slow down. Ali was glad not to have to rush across the courtyard, which was paved with large cobblestones and many gravestones, all aligned to face toward the central building of the shrine. Occasionally a *rowzeh-khan*, a preacher and teller of edifying stories, would approach Ali's mother. She was indistinguishable from all other women in the courtyard because all wore the chador, the black smocklike outer garment that covered them entirely except for a part of their faces. But as his mother was a native of Qom and the wife of a mullah, she did not want to pay a fee like a tourist to have the *rowzeh-khan* lead her in prayer.

Ali was less interested in the enormous gold dome and the four flanking minarets of the central building than he was in the intricate pattern made by the pieces of mirror cut to fit the honeycombed surface inside the three great arches on the front of the building. Just as interesting was the very thin and very ancient candle seller, with his perpetual ten-day growth of white beard, who stood in his skullcap, grayish collarless shirt, wrinkled brown jacket, and baggy gray trousers just inside the entrance to the central building. After Ali and his mother had bought a few candles and handed their shoes to another old man for safekeeping, they came to a door that divided the world of sunlight from a darker interior. His mother would say, "Hold onto my chador," and together they would kiss the doorposts.

Immediately the leisurely pace of the courtyard ceased. As they walked through an anteroom they could hear the sound of weeping and praying from the next room, which was built around the tomb. At the door of the tomb chamber they would kiss the right-hand doorpost and, if the rush of exiting pilgrims did not prevent them, the left-hand doorpost as well. Once inside the tomb chamber his mother bowed toward the sarcophagus, then lit her candles from candles already burning in a special room to the side.

Sometimes the crowd of pilgrims made it hard to catch a glimpse of the tomb itself through the high and massive silver grating around the sarcophagus, but Ali could always smell the sandalwood of the coffin-shaped box that covered the tomb. The determined pace set by the pilgrims at the door of the antechamber grew faster as they joined the outer circles of pilgrims moving counterclockwise around the tomb, and the inner circles whirled so rapidly that some people seemed trapped near the grating by the press and the speed of the movement. The noise was most intense nearest the grating; some cried, "O holy sinless one," others threw coins through the grating and tried to kiss it in passing, and many wept.

Often Ali's mother would stay in the outer circle because she had not made a vow and had no reason to get close to the tomb, but she too almost invariably wept. Ali wanted to weep as well and felt it was strange that he could not weep easily, but usually after circling the tomb a few times his throat became choked and he began to cry. Eventually they pulled away from the crowd, backed out of the room facing the sarcophagus, and kissed the doorposts as they came to them. When they had recovered their

shoes and gone outside Ali was always pleased to see new pilgrims strolling across the courtyard under a sky that had hardly
changed since they had left it. He always felt it would be a better
outing if he convinced his mother to walk home a different way.
And if she was not in a hurry she would say, "You little devil,"
and indulge him.

· · ·

To secularized Iranian intellectuals Qom is something very
alien and very familiar. It is familiar because as children they were
taken there by grandmothers and pious aunts to visit the shrine
and, in many cases, to visit family burial places. It is familiar because at home the same grandmothers and pious aunts would pay
rowzeh-khans, just like those who approach pilgrims at Qom, to
visit the family home and deliver a sermon that was really a lament, for his talk would be quickly drawn to the sufferings of
Hosain, and the rowzeh-khan would dwell on such suffering while
his entirely female audience would weep without restraint. It is
familiar because the secularized intellectuals had seen turbaned
mullahs like those around the shrines and seminaries of Qom at
weddings, had listened to them preach at funerals, and had probably even had them as teachers in courses of religious instruction at
state schools.

Yet Qom is alien as only something familiar but unacceptable
can be. It is not only that Qom is a tourist trap, complete with
photographers who take pictures of you and your wife with your
heads poking through a painted backdrop that shows you both in
dress of the most traditional piety. It is also a tourist trap in which
piety is used to milk you at all levels, from the rowzeh-khans to the
beggars. The latter, knowing the high religious merit of giving
alms, pop up near the graves of your ancestors crying pious
phrases at you and sticking out their hands. In the view of the secularized intellectual Qom not only milks the living, in the persons
of over a million pilgrims a year, it also milks the estates of the
deceased, for, in spite of the rising cost of burial at Qom, thousands of cadavers arrive each year from all over Iran to join the
hundreds of thousands already buried there. Since it contains the
tombs of so many of the privileged, even many rulers of the Shiah
dynasties of Iran, one might expect parts of graveyard Qom to be
well kept up, but, in fact, outside the shrine much of graveyard

Qom is a shambling ruin. The fields of graves, set close together in the ground facing in the same direction, are littered with cracked fragments of the stone and brick grave markers. The mausoleums more often than not have lost their roofs and become nesting places for storks (called by Iranians Haji Lak-lak—"the pilgrim who cries *lak-lak*").

To the secularized intellectual it seems altogether appropriate that traditional Shiah learning should have taken as its home a vast necropolis. To him the six thousand or so students are devoted to a form of learning as antiquated as the mullah clothes they wear, a learning as arid as the climate of Qom itself. For Qom is dry even by the standards of Iranian towns, and outsiders usually have been less struck by the success of the Qomis in creating green and fertile islands than they have by the ocean of dust and desert that surround these islands. A contemporary poet, Naderpour, sees Qom as:

> *Many thousand women*
> *Many thousand men*
> *Women, scarves on their heads*
> *Men, cloaks on their shoulders*
> *A golden dome*
> *With old storks*
> *An unpleasant garden*
> *With a few isolated trees*
> *Empty of laughter*
> *Silent of speech*
> *With a half-filled pool*
> *With green water*
> *Many old crows*
> *On piles of stone*
> *Crowds of beggars*
> *At every step in the road*
> *White turbans*
> *Black faces.*

• • •

It never occurred to Ali on his way home from the shrine that one could accept or reject the tombs and turbans of Qom. The tombs were facts of life like the seasons or the sun; and as for the turbans, his father wore one, and so, he hoped, would he in time. Home, nevertheless, was very different from the street, which belonged to no one (not even the municipality, to judge from the way it was maintained). Like the shrine, Ali's home was completely enclosed in a wall; and, like the shrine, it was a world in itself. But while the shrine had several huge courtyards to introduce you to its purpose, home offered a small but precise introduction, an octagonal gatehouse, one of whose doors opened on the street. Although the gatehouse was neither street nor home, it was cooler than the street and foretold the fresher air inside.

The first door on the right inside the gatehouse led to a gatekeeper's room, which was not used in Ali's time. Since Ali and his brothers had decided that a dangerous snake lived in a hole in its wall, for some months they would dare each other to enter and would take turns racing in and out. In contrast, the second door on the right was a familiar friend. It led to a stable that in his father's youth had housed the kind of white donkey usually owned by mullahs of his father's and grandfather's station. The stable consisted of two stalls, and Ali sometimes followed the servant who went to fetch the firewood stored there and pretended to support the back end of the bundles of branches that the servant carried back to the house.

The rest of the doors led to the two principal sections of the house, called in Persian the *andaruni*, "the inside," and the *biruni*, "the outside." As a small child Ali seldom visited the *biruni*, which was exclusively for his father and his father's male guests, but when he did, he was always struck by its resemblance to the "inside." Not only was the house divided into two but everything inside the *andaruni* and *biruni* was divided into twos. Each of the two sections was built around a garden, and each garden was clearly divided in two. As you entered there was a right-hand side and a left-hand side, each mirroring the other: if there was a cypress planted near the end of the right-hand side, there was sure to be a cypress at the end of the left-hand side as well. There were two long rooms on each side of the *biruni*, and at the end were two small rooms, all of them two steps above the level of the garden. Ali came to admire his grandmother's apparent rebellion against the rule of two; shortly after her husband's death she had prevailed on Ali's father to have three plaster arches built at the end of the garden in the *biruni* in front of the two small rooms, with openings that bore no relation to the two French doors that opened into these rooms.

The total isolation of the more public "outside" from the "inside" part of the house was one rule of division in two that no one dared violate. There was no opening, not even a window, that joined the *andaruni* and the *biruni*. Ali was surprised that his grandmother never insisted on knocking a hole through the wall to save the servant from carrying tea, food, charcoal, and whatever from the kitchens in the *andaruni* all the way out to the gatehouse and then in again to the kitchenless *biruni*.

The "inside" or *andaruni* had a right- and left-hand garden with a square pool in the center, like the *biruni*, and Ali knew this pool intimately. It was Ali's ambition to see all of the goldfish in the pool at once—which might happen if they all came to the surface when he threw crumbs in a space between the water lily leaves or if they formed a school and all came to one edge of the pool together. Ali cannot remember his father fabricating any kind of story except to frighten his son from leaning over the pool. If he saw Ali put his hand in the water he would run over, pull Ali back, and in an angry and embarrassed tone say, "*Vay, vay*, don't you know that the pool monster feasts on hands, you little devil?"

Occasionally there would be enough water to turn on the fountain, which was just a metal knob on a marble square slightly above water level at the center of the *andaruni* pool. The water would burble from a small pierced metal ball and the pool would overflow along grooves in the middle of each of its four sides into the four channels that ran the length of the garden and divided it into four parts. Ali remembers his grandmother's great pleasure on these occasions. She would place melons to cool in one channel of the pool and direct the servant as to where and for how long to release water from the channels into the four garden plots they separated. Finally she would sit down with Ali by the side of one of the channels and they would bathe their feet in the water.

In the *biruni* the trees and flowers were set out neatly in pairs with a strict sense of symmetry. In the *andaruni* the jasmine

bushes, the cypresses, and the flower beds were also in pairs or
sometimes in fours, but the quince and pomegranate trees stood
without matching companions, and in Ali's view made the *andaruni* even more private. When he and his grandmother sat with
their feet in the water, Ali would look at the tops of the cypresses
bending slightly in the wind, and even the portion of sky enclosed
by the buildings and wall seemed private and familiar.

Sometimes, when it was very hot and dry, Ali went with his
mother, father, grandmother, and brothers to a basement room
that also had a pool; but unlike the garden pool, it was very long
and narrow and was lined with blue tiles. There were no windows
in this basement, only narrow openings filled with a latticework of
small ceramic tiles of the most intense blue, which allowed air but
little light to enter. To Ali even the murmur of the thin jet of water
at the center of the room seemed blue. As the family sat there
without talking, only occasionally coughing and putting their
hands or feet in or out of the water, Ali knew they all respected
the blueness and silence as much as he did.

Hot weather was also the occasion for sleeping on the roof.
Mattresses and mosquito netting were carried to the roof shortly
after the last light of day, and Ali envied his elder brother, who
was allowed to keep a flit-gun and a swatter inside his netting.
After a little stirring the night would be remarkably silent, especially considering the large number of people sleeping on nearby
roofs, all of which were about the same height. In the dry, clear air
the stars were amazingly distinct, and the more Ali looked at
them, the brighter they seemed. But unlike the private and familiar garden sky of the *andaruni* in daytime, the night sky seemed
immense and disinterested, and the stars extraordinarily distant.

When they slept on the roof they usually woke with the call to
prayer, but the two servants, Kazem and his wife, always woke up
earlier, and Ali watched them on their accompanying roof fanning
the samovar they had already lit in order to prepare tea. After his
father prayed they would move into the proper sleeping rooms of
the *andaruni* to try and sleep an hour or two longer. If Ali woke
inside before the others, he would study the two semicircular
stained-glass windows that were above the curtained French
doors and seemed for ten minutes or so to be on fire when the

morning sun struck them. At regular intervals there were yellow hexagons separated by squares or, viewed differently, by blue and green triangles that fitted together to form squares. If you followed the blue or green, each color formed a series of straps, one color disappearing under the other and reappearing at regular intervals. When he began to learn to draw the letters of the alphabet, Ali told his older brother he wanted to draw the design and then try to design something similar. His brother smiled and said such designs were craftsmen's work.

Ali remembers that if his grandmother slept late, his mother would wake her by shuffling her feet on the carpet next to her or by coughing or clearing her throat. In fact, it was amazing how often the only protection for privacy was foot-shuffling and the clearing of throats. In particular, Ali remembers that no one approached the outhouse, which had no lock on its door, without coughing and dragging his feet to give any occupant a chance to clear his throat or cough in reply. Actually, as Ali realized when he left home, for those permitted into the *andaruni* everything was to some degree public, and you had privacy only insofar as you were able to feel private in your mind. In winter they would all sit around a charcoal brazier placed under a low table, which in turn would be covered by an enormous quilt. You could pull the quilt up to your neck or just keep it over your legs; you could read or talk; you could drink tea or sleep. At some time or other all these things would be done simultaneously around the brazier, and it was clear that those who read or slept considered themselves and were considered by everyone else to have the right to follow a private line of conduct different from that of the half dozen or dozen people a few feet away from them.

Very early in life Ali learned that, unlike his brothers, he needed more than privacy in company—he needed seclusion. Later he would walk to one of the small disused shrines on the outskirts of Qom, but as a child he found that when his mother and grandmother were busy, no one minded if he went under a bush and, as he very much liked to do, watched others closely from his seclusion or just tried to understand things that people had said. Once under such a bush he saw the war of the ants. He instantly knew the cause of the war and the nature of the parties.

The red ants, whose bite (he had been told) was slightly poi-
sonous, were Sunnis, the party among Muslims that rejected the
claim of the descendants of Ali, and they were attacking the black
ants, who were obviously Shiah, since black as well as green was a
color worn by people like Ali Hashemi's father who claimed descent from Ali. He remembers admiring the black ants for the
justness of their cause and their individual heroism; but as the
battle continued, he began to admire the orderliness and steadi-
ness of the slower-moving red ants. As far as he could tell, neither
side won.

Around his sixth birthday Ali stopped going to the bathhouse
with his mother and started to go with his father. It wasn't the
only important change at that time in his life; learning to pray,
learning to write, and learning to sit quietly with his father's
friends were just as new and took more hours each week than a
visit to the bath. But somehow he remembers the change at the
bathhouse best: one week he was with a lot of talkative, sweating,
half-naked women, the next week he was sitting with a lot of sol-
emn, half-naked men while his father explained to him that in this
bathhouse, as in so many others in Iran, a painter had put a picture of the devil on the ceiling. He had done so because the devil
was supposed to torture men in a place of fire and steam like the
bathhouse. The real devil, his father added, was Satan, the enemy
of God. Ali asked why God hadn't destroyed Satan if he was
God's enemy. His father smiled, wiped his face with a towel, and
said he was a very clever boy, a real little devil himself.

It wasn't that his mother had less time for him, it was that his
father seemed to have so much more. He had often watched his
father pray and had tried in private to raise and lower his hands,
bend forward, kneel, and touch his forehead to the ground in the
same way that his father did. It was hopeless. Besides, his father
spoke the prayer in Arabic, and Ali couldn't remember more than
a word or two of what his father said. Some months after he
stopped going to the bath with his mother, his father noticed Ali
imitating his movements while he prayed. When he finished his
prayer he took Ali's two hands in his own hands and said, "God
likes us to begin our prayers by saying in our heart or out loud, 'I
intend to pray.' 'I intend to pray' means 'I want to pray.' "

Ali said, "But I do want to pray—I want to be like you."

His father smiled and rubbed Ali's chin. "All right, I know you want to be like me. Learn part of the prayer in Arabic and you'll be ready to do it like me when you are old enough to know what it means to say 'I intend.' "

Looking back, Ali thinks it incredible that he should have had his first taste of Arabic—the true language of revelation and religious learning—devouring whole sentences then and there in front of his father, without any fanfare or ceremonious introduction. His father's translation of the Arabic sentences word for word from Arabic into Persian helped hardly at all, but the words of each sentence linked themselves to each other in a chain that never broke. The trouble was that sometimes Ali got the sentences themselves in the wrong order, and sometimes he developed new ways of saying Arabic words which amused his father very much. Twice in a prayer he had to repeat the shortest chapter of the Koran:

> In the name of God, the Merciful, the Beneficent;
> Say: He is God the One,
> God the Eternal.
> He does not beget and is not begotten;
> And there is none like unto him.

These twenty or so words in Arabic seemed to enter Ali almost at one swallow, but when he recited them back to his father two days later, for the Arabic word *samad*, "Eternal," he said *shamad*, the Persian word for "mosquito netting." "Dear son, if you have to speak Persian instead of Arabic in your prayers, at least compare God to something more substantial like *namad* [felt], which is a little stronger and more solid than mosquito netting."

Ali felt it suited his new importance as a member of the world of men to take more interest in shopping expeditions and to insist on carrying things home. Most days of the week his father went to the store, either to buy something his mother had forgotten or something his father suddenly yearned for, like cucumbers, which are for Iranians the archetypal fruit, as apples are for Americans. On instruction the greengrocer would pull things from the jumble of open crates on the ground. Ali's father would then place his purchases in an enormous handkerchief he had brought along, tie it at the four corners, and hand it to Ali.

Ali, to his disappointment, was not allowed to accompany the maid when she went on her daily trips to the large open-air market for fruits and vegetables because, his mother said, "It's dirty, it's noisy, and anyway you can't understand the way farmers talk." Apparently the farmers themselves were not dirty, even if their market was, because two or three times a year they came to the house with donkey loads of fruits and vegetables such as onions, pomegranates, and melons, which would then be piled in the cellar, usually with straw between the layers.

Shopping with his mother in the central bazaar, however, more than made up for missing the open-air market. The bazaar seemed immense. And because it was covered and somewhat dark, expeditions to the bazaar had a solemnity that other forms of shopping lacked. From the outside the bazaar, with its great gates, which were opened in the morning and closed at night, seemed bounded and defined. From the inside it appeared boundless and inexhaustible. It was a place of manufacture as well as sale, and it seemed more like a labyrinth because of its endless turnings, its abrupt changes from retailer to workshop and from alley to avenue. For example, the quiet street where cloth merchants sat among their bolts of material opened onto an avenue where the clatter from the coppersmiths sometimes made it impossible to talk.

To enter the bazaar was to enter a world of slow formalities and quick wits. It was also a world of old, even ancestral, loyalties. In general it was loyalty that directed his mother's steps. Whether it was in the small lane of the jewelers or the spacious barrel-vaulted central avenue of the cloth dealers, his mother always went to the same merchant in any section, a reliable friend of the family.

She did not just march up to the shop of the "reliable friend" and ask for what she wanted. She always walked around a bit so that the merchant should know that she gave her custom with some thought. But no woman could really have made up her mind what to buy just by examining the entrances to the shops. Merchants in those days paid little attention to arranging any sort of display at the front of the shop. In any case, at such shops as the draper's, if display had told the customers what was available, it would have destroyed the occasion for that gradual disclosure of merchandise and those leisurely demonstrations of politeness that made shopping worthwhile. The draper would offer Ali's mother a four-legged stool, set slightly inside the front of his narrow, deep shop, and ask first about her health and then, with his hand on his heart, about her husband's health. He would then easily persuade her to have tea, which an apprentice brought in small glasses on a round copper tray. Finally there was the excitement of discovery as she spotted bolts of cloth or as they were produced for her from the deep interior of the shop at the orders of the owner.

For Ali, shopping in the bazaar lost its genteel and ruminative character when he was six. He was about to enter the state elementary school. Ali, who had up to that time usually worn the lounging pajamas beloved by very young boys and older men in Iran, now went with his father to the tailor to have two pairs of shorts made in a dull gray color that the Ministry of Education decreed appropriate for small children. Ali and his father walked through the bazaar just as the apprentices were sprinkling the passages from improvised watering cans to lay the afternoon dust. They climbed a dark staircase to a second-story shop overlooking the barrel-vaulted central avenue of the bazaar. The tailor, who sat behind a massive sewing machine on an elevated area to one side of his shop, had just partially unwound himself from his cross-legged position to rise a foot or so for a customer who had entered immediately before Ali and his father. When he saw that a prominent mullah had come into his shop, he unwound himself completely and, with his hand on his chest, made a slight bow. Ali wondered whether the needles and straight pins stuck into his vest accounted for the slightly pained look in the tailor's large birdlike eyes.

An older apprentice was bringing a pair of scissors almost half as tall as Ali from a flat table in the center of the room. Another apprentice, hardly a year older than Ali himself, entered with a tray of tea for the tailor and his customers. He tripped on a stool that had been moved near the door and fell sideways, dropping the tray, which tumbled forward and scattered the glasses onto the brick floor. With a hoarse cry the tailor started toward the boy from across the room and roared, "Fatherless, godless child, dirt be on your head!" and struck his ear with the flat of his palm. The apprentice had been crying from the minute he tripped, but after he was struck he gave one yell and just lay gulping for air, emitting a thin, high whine. Ali noticed the purplish mange on the child's scalp under his very short hair and saw the scabs on his legs through his torn pajamas. Everyone tried to go about his business without looking at the boy except for the tailor, who was shouting at his older apprentice to clean up and announcing to no one in particular, "Boys are little devils. They play the devil every waking hour."

When Ali and his father left the room after a few measurements and explanations, the boy had stopped whining but was still breathing hard. Ali was never sure why his father did not take him back to the tailor with the birdlike eyes. For years afterward whenever he was in the bazaar Ali would feel certain that ahead of him he had spotted the apprentice who was close to his own age. Then, as he drew near, he became uncertain that he really knew what the boy looked like, and he would turn away.

· · ·

The bazaar and the mosque are the two lungs of public life in Iran. Bazaars, like mosques, shrines, and private houses, look inward, psychologically and architecturally, and more often than not they present blank and unexplaining walls to the streets outside. Bazaars and mosques have a public character that is the antithesis of the privacy of houses; but, as the shared spaces of people who enter them, like houses they look inward. Two men meeting on the street meet merely as two men, but for over a thousand years the bazaar has been recognized by Islamic law as a special arena of human life, and in law as well as in common understanding two men meet there as "two men in the bazaar." As such they share certain moral and even legal obligations—for example, to buy and sell with a shared knowledge of the current market price. Information about prices is, in fact, the quickening breath that sustains the life of the bazaar, and the mechanism by which these prices adjust to new information on supply and demand is so refined as to seem almost divine. "God sets prices," according to a saying ascribed to the Prophet Mohammed, and most medieval Islamic jurists agreed that an unseen hand that operated with such efficiency must be the hand of God.

Not only prices but men's reputations are set, reset, and continually adjusted in the bazaar as information flows through networks of reliable friends. All society is a catchment area for the information to which the unofficial brokerage of the mosque and the bazaar will ultimately give a common "market price." In this sense the bazaar is not just an economic arena, it is a region of the human spirit. As such it is the lineal descendant of the Greek agora and the Roman forum. The Greeks and Romans went to their markets not only to buy and sell but also to conduct their public political life and even to hold their public festivals. The bazaar was seldom the guardian of political life that the forum or agora had been, but the bazaar was and often still is the assessor that sets the valuations politicians must use when they trade.

When political life comes to a boil, the bazaar is not just the public assessor of values—it becomes a direct arena for political expression. At such times, in the classic Persian expression, the bazaar is "in disorder," which means that people come and go in an agitated way and seem close to violence and riot. When the bazaar boils over, it simply shuts. Streets of shop fronts barred by heavy shutters testify to the determination of merchants not to let normal life continue until the common concern is dealt with.

Moments at which the Tehran bazaar closed punctuate the last two centuries of Iranian history. In December 1905 the governor of Tehran punished two sugar merchants by the bastinado—caning of the soft soles of the feet—which is a repellent and persistent feature of Iranian penal practice. The sugar merchants were punished for not lowering their prices as ordered, although they insisted that high import prices gave them no choice. The bazaar closed. In fact the whole capital closed down, following the lead of the bazaar; unrest and dissatisfaction with the Qajar government that had been growing for years now came into the open. Many merchants and mullahs took sanctuary in nearby shrines and refused to return until the shah met their demands for some voice in the government. The first Iranian revolution had begun.

In the summer of 1960 the government announced the results

of elections to the parliament, still—in theory—elected according to the constitution established in 1906 during the first Iranian revolution. A completely honest election to the parliament was a fond dream, never yet experienced by any generation of Iranians. But the elections of 1960 were so blatantly rigged that even some of the winners were embarrassed, and an unusual season of limited freedom of expression allowed a few elder statesmen to say that the government had insulted the electorate. The bazaar closed. The elections were canceled.

If the bazaar was the precinct of public discourse, the mosque was virtually the only precinct in which personal opinion could be publicly proclaimed. The market appraised ideas through thousands of informal discussions; in the mosque, at least once a week, opinion formed a part of the formal service of prayer. Not that informal discussion was a stranger to the vast courtyards of mosques. When the bazaar shut, mosques filled as people sought the public space where exchanges of rumor and report could continue after the alleys and avenues of the bazaar were deserted.

People gather in the mosque every day for the five obligatory prayers, but they are free to pray instead in their homes or shops or anyplace not considered defiled or inappropriate from the point of view of Islamic law. Attendance at the mosque for Friday noon prayer and certain religious festivals, however, is a religious obligation, and bazaars have always shut for the Friday prayer and for at least half a century have shut for all of Friday. The service begins with a sermon in which the preacher prays for the community of Muslims and sometimes for the ruler. Sermons are also given at funerals, at dedications, and whenever preachers find an opening, and in this sense in the world of Islam the orator moved out of the market and into the place of prayer.

Sermons are sometimes the occasion on which the congregation becomes "disorderly," like the agitated throngs of the bazaar, and sometimes this disorder ends in riot. The disorder may arise from anger at what the preacher says as a spokesman for the government; it may arise from sympathy for his criticism of the government; and it may arise simply because the solidarity expressed by praying in unison gives the congregation a sense that it can act together, although its members had been previously unwilling to act alone.

In the first Iranian revolution the preacher and the mosque played their roles along with the market. When the sugar merchants were bastinadoed on December 11, 1905, and the mullahs and merchants withdrew the next day to a nearby shrine and subsequently to the shrine of Shah Abdol-Azim, the shah gave in after a month of stalemate and promised to meet their principal demands. The protestors returned to Tehran in triumph. Half a year later the shah had not fulfilled most of his promises. A popular local preacher denounced the government: "Iranians! Brethren of my beloved country! How long will this treacherous intoxication keep you slumbering? . . . Lift up your heads. Open your eyes . . . Behold your neighbors [the Russians] who two hundred years ago were in much worse condition than we. Behold how they now possess everything . . . Now we are reduced to such a condition that our neighbors to the south and north already believe us to be their property. . . . In the whole of Iran we have not one factory of our own, because our government is a parasite. . . . All this backwardness is due to autocracy, injustice, and want of laws . . ."

On July 11, 1906, the government arrested the preacher. A crowd of theological students descended on the police station of Tehran, and a shot from a policeman killed a student who was a sayyed, a descendant of the Prophet. The next morning thousands of theological students and people of the bazaar accompanied the sayyed's body in a cortège from the principal bazaar to the central mosque. The shah sent his crack troops, the corps of Iranians with Russian officers called the "Cossack" Brigade, to prevent the cortège from joining the mullahs who had already gathered in the mosque. They fired on the cortège near the mosque and killed twenty-two as well as injuring many more. The first blood of the Iranian revolution of 1906 had been drawn.

CHAPTER TWO

FOR ALI, entering the state school in 1948 was a great break from the privacy of the *andaruni*, the slow formalities of the *biruni*, and the ruminative trips to the bazaar. School was a long, methodical, and rather public exercise in learning what his teachers had decided was the proper place for things. Things in their proper place were things in order, even if the reason for that order was unclear to either teacher or pupil. There was only one proper place for him to stand in line, one proper place to write things in his notebook, one proper way to answer a question. Not only had his teachers and the Ministry of Education decided to create order by assigning everything its proper place, they had also decided that disorder would instantly arise if no one had a final say as to what order was truly correct. The final say belonged to the teacher and to the textbook, which the teacher followed so carefully that he had learned it by heart. If the third-grade teacher and text said that Qandahar was the second-largest city in Afghanistan and the fourth-grade teacher and text said that Herat was, then Qandahar was right in the third grade and Herat in the fourth.

Ali arrived for his first day of school clinging to his mother's chador. It was seven o'clock, a full hour before school began. The school yard was an enormous, dusty, and unfriendly version of the inside garden at home, with high walls that separated the interior from the street. Its one entrance faced a two-story building along the back wall, and on the right and left were one-story buildings with French doors opening into the courtyard. There were a few tall trees planted at regular intervals across the yard.

His mother led him to a short, stocky man who was walking up and down impatiently on the bottom step of the two-story building. The short man was holding a stick behind him and bowing slightly to a thin gray-haired man, who gave a far deeper bow in reply. Ali's mother explained that she had brought her youngest son, a son of Sayyed Mohammed Hashemi, to enter the first grade. The man pointed to one of the French doors and smiled at Ali, who felt really afraid for the first time. His mother took him to the room and placed him on one of the wooden benches in front of desks facing the blackboard. She kissed him and told him that he should be brave like his father and like his namesake and ancestor, Ali, the Commander of the Faithful, the cousin and son-in-law of the Prophet. Then she left.

Ali rested his head on the desk before him and looked at his bare knees and the brick floor and watched his tears fall on the bricks. He hoped nobody would come to class; he would sit quietly until his older brother would find him at the end of the school day and take him home forever. Then he heard footsteps and saw a man who looked like Kazem, the servant at home, entering with a broom and a watering can. The man nodded at Ali, opened his completely toothless mouth in a smile, and began to lay the dust, just as the apprentices did in the bazaar. Finally, he swept the corners quickly, then left. A strong smell of earth and wet brick rose from the ground, the smell of the late-afternoon bazaar and of the basement pool at home. Ali looked out of the window and saw that a pair of trees in the schoolyard were cypresses, which bent in the gentlest wind like the pair of cypresses in the rear of his own garden at home. Children were lining up by height, facing the stairs of the two-storied building. Ali's older brother waved through the window and in a loud whisper said, "Come on, silly, take your place in line." Ali ran out and saw that

most of the boys had closely cropped heads. He found his place
near the middle of the line.

The man with the stick shouted, "Quiet!" and all the yard became still except for the noise of the servant sweeping the last
classroom. A very tall man with a grayish cast to his face started to
speak. He was standing a step higher than the man with the stick,
who looked at him with the same timid attention as the boys were
showing. The tall man began: "Ferdowsi, our great national poet,
says: 'He who knows is powerful; thanks to his knowledge the old
man's heart is young.' This is written on the building behind me
and in your schoolbooks. Remember it. You have come here to
learn. You can learn only if you are obedient, orderly, and clean.
Bring your own drinking cup to school. You may bring your
lunch, your own notebooks, pencils, and pencil sharpener and
nothing else. No whistles, no flashlights, nothing. The head of
every boy must be cropped at the start of each school year unless
his parents have arranged permission for him to keep his hair. A
doctor will come next week to vaccinate all boys who do not have
vaccination cards. The vice-principal is in charge of discipline."
The short man with the stick turned slightly and—to make sure
they recognized him as vice-principal—gathered his bushy eyebrows in a knot and frowned at the boys. "If you do not obey your
teachers you will be sent to see him. Prepare your assignments on
time. Write neatly in your notebooks. Always wash your hands
before coming to school. May God give you success in the coming
year."

The teachers began to applaud, and Ali and the other first-
graders did their best to imitate them. Some of the older boys
were really puffing from their efforts at vigorous and prolonged
applause. Each class then marched into its room and received the
schoolbooks for the year.

The teacher wrote a large vertical mark on the board. "This is
the first letter of the alphabet. We write it for 'ah,' our long Persian *a*. Repeat after me: 'Ah.' "

"Ah."

"Very good." The teacher made another long vertical mark:
" 'Ah.' Repeat."

"Ah."

After many "ahs" in chorus the blackboard was nearly covered
with vertical marks. Then the teacher went around the room, and
Ali stood in his turn and said, "Ah." The teacher said "Very
good" to him, as he had to others, and Ali knew he would like
school.

The only problem was that Ali already knew how to write. On
the second day Ali brought his two blank notebooks to school,
one for practice and one for clean copies. On the preceding day of
school the teacher had them write "Papa gave water"—a Persian
sentence with four long "ahs" and only two other letters—at the
top of the page. They had already learned that the school nick-
name for their teacher, a serious and earnest young man, was
"Very Good, But." This morning "Very Good, But" came behind
each student and looked in each notebook. He said, "Very good,
but . . ." repeatedly, wrote corrections above their model sentences, and said they had an hour to copy "Papa gave water" on
every line to the bottom of the page. He then stepped out of the
French doors into the yard.

Ali had learned to read and write from his father almost as
quickly as he had learned his Arabic prayers; he really was, as his
mother kept telling him, his father's son. He finished his ten
copies of the sentence in a few minutes, then looked at the students around him. Almost all of them were copying the first word,
"Papa," in long, wavy columns down the page before attempting
the other words. Outside the class "Very Good, But" stood smoking a cigarette and talking with several other teachers who had
conveniently given writing exercises for the same hour.

Ali looked back at his book. At the top of page one it said in
Arabic, "In the name of God the Merciful, the Beneficent." He
wrote these words at the top of his notebook, as he had seen his
father write them at the top of every letter he started. He turned
the page. Whereas the page with "Papa gave water" had only a
drawing of two cypresses and their wavy reflections in a pool,
presumably Papa's source of water, the next page had three
drawings, one of pomegranates, another of loaves of flat bread
half hanging over the side of a table, and the third of a set of teeth,
a drawing that struck Ali as extremely funny. The third page had
a picture of a woman, identified as "Mama," leaning over a naked

child. Mama seemed half naked herself: her arms were uncovered almost to the shoulder, and her short hair showed her long neck. Ali copied the sentences on these two pages, in which Mama and Papa gave away pomegranates and bread and Papa was said to have no teeth. Then the teacher came in and collected the notebooks.

The next day of class the teacher called the roll and looked closely at each student with his "Very good, but" expression as he handed each clean-copy notebook back. He hardly glanced at Ali, however, but said, "Hashemi, I am keeping your notebook. Pick it up after the last class." For Ali, the next few hours were a little like the first visit to the men's bathhouse, when he felt pleased to be with his father but afraid that he might not be accepted by the other bathers. He had seen his older brother show his father homework on which the teacher had written "Bravo!" in the corner. With pleasure he pictured the pages of his exercises covered with "Bravos!" and with terror pictured the notebook covered with corrections and saw his teacher telling him that he was arrogant, or "full of face," as one says in Persian.

When the bell rang between classes Ali took advantage of the break to carry his cup down the stairs to the spigot on the side of an underground cistern. The change to the cool, damp stairwell made him feel giddy, and he crouched against the wall as an older boy dashed up the stairs with a ewer full of water for the outhouse in the schoolyard. Ali filled his cup, took several swallows, and lost almost all of the remaining water climbing back upstairs. He remained giddy throughout the next class while writing "bread" and "pomegranate" in his practice notebook under the teacher's supervision.

After the last bell the students no longer belonged to the school, and Ali's classmates seized their freedom by making as noisy and disorderly an exit as they could. Ali stayed seated, then walked forward to the teacher, who was busy making marks in an attendance book and did not look up. Ali stared at the scene on the side of the teacher's pen box, in which three men with turbans, bending slightly like poplars, sat under trees bending in the same direction. Finally the teacher looked up and spoke. "Whose son are you?"

"Sayyed Mohammed Hashemi's."

"Then you are the son of a learned gentleman. Your cousin was the son of a gentleman and had to repeat first grade." Ali remained silent. "You know how to write."

"Yes, sir—my father taught me." The teacher looked at him for a bit longer, then smiled.

"Bravo. I think you are too small to go into second grade. Later maybe you can skip a grade. Meanwhile be obedient and do only what you are told to do."

"Yes, sir."

Ali heard and obeyed. For the next eight years he committed every textbook to memory, filled every notebook according to instructions, and answered every teacher by quoting the teacher's words back to him. Even though he actually skipped two grades, his notebooks continued to be filled with "Bravos!" and his report cards, which he had to take home three times a year, always stated that the school was extremely satisfied with his conduct and had designated him "first student" in his class. His father, following the well-established formula, wrote in the blank space for the compulsory return message: "We are very grateful to the authorities of the school. He behaves himself at home as well."

It needed vigilance to be thought well behaved. The easiest way was to become a monitor. After the first few grades each teacher chose a student monitor, someone who was good at his lessons and also had an air of authority or was even a little bit of a bully. Many of the boys craved this job, but Ali didn't and was glad that his distracted and bookish nature disqualified him. To him it was strange that others should covet such a position because his authority reflected the suspicious authority of the teacher. The teacher was surrounded by a kind of awe that the students both felt with a sort of reverence and longed to see punctured. Sometimes a longing to ridicule the teacher would swell up in the class, and yet the rare boy who expressed it could expect no support from the other students.

Teachers sensed the disrespect and ridicule that lay just under the reverential obedience of their students and they were extremely touchy. One time an upper-school teacher said, "In lower school you will learn five thousand verses by heart, in upper school fifteen thousand." Ali asked, in a completely innocent display of his mastery of arithmetic, "Do they require forty-five thousand in the university?" and the nearsighted boy who sat next to him started to laugh convulsively with fits of snorting as he tried to cover his mouth and nose. The teacher pointed at the boy who had laughed and said, "Get lost—you're absent for today and tomorrow"—which meant that he would have to report to the man with the stick in the main building for two days.

The nearsighted boy knew that he would probably get more than the usual beating on the palms; he might even get a beating on the soles of his feet. He went to the door and turned around. "By God, we did nothing, sir." (He used the "we" under which Iranian schoolboys seek camouflage.) "We swear to God we are not disrespectful. We are not impolite. You cannot throw our corpse into the street." The teacher seemed unable to answer. The whole room was silent for a minute as everybody stared at the boy. They had never before heard anyone speak to a teacher like that, and Ali never again heard such a speech in school. The boy hadn't even said "Forgive me."

Just as the teacher seemed about to speak the boy rushed out of the door. "Hashemi, you mannerless child!" the teacher shouted at Ali, "copy your entire geography book three times. The rest of the class will copy this week's geography lesson three times." Then he went slamming out into the courtyard with his hand clasped over the cigarette package inside his jacket pocket. The nearsighted boy transferred to another school, and no one in Ali's class was ever quite sure if he was brave, rude, or simply a fool.

The teacher could hardly have chosen a more annoying punishment from his standard arsenal. Ali would have far preferred having his knuckles squeezed over a pencil or getting a slap on the face or twenty raps from a ruler on the palms of his hands. Geography was to him a subject of unrelieved tedium. Practically its only interest was the wonderfully accurate maps some teachers could draw freehand on the blackboard, a talent that seemed to prove the teachers had memorized the textbooks more thoroughly than their students ever could and were therefore qualified to teach. Geography started with the oceans and continents, moved to the great mountain ranges and rivers of the world, and then contracted its focus to Iran. In treating Iran it started with major topographical features, climatic regions, mineral resources, and so forth; it then treated small features province by province, then district by district.

Ali didn't think some of his teachers knew any better than he did what it meant to say that wildfowl abounded in the lagoon off the Caspian port of Enzeli or that shrimp were plentiful in the Persian Gulf—no wildfowl or shrimp had ever been seen in Qom. Teachers of geography, as of most other subjects, further validated their position by dictating their notes, and practically the only allowable interruption was to say, "Excuse us, sir, we have lost our place." At examination time the oral portion of the exam often consisted of the teacher's reading the topic sentence of one of his own lectures—for example, "Sugar beets are grown in all except one province of Iran"—and waiting for the student to reproduce the rest of the lecture, complete with statistics, word for word.

The only subject in which Ali was not easily "first student" was mathematics. Multiplication tables were no problem; they required the same persistence as did memorizing the other parts of the school text. But from fourth grade on, the math teacher dictated word problems, in which a merchant in the bazaar was pictured as buying or selling pencils, apples, and oranges; and from seventh grade the merchant began to deal in cloth and bricks and earned both simple and compound interest. Ali could solve such problems but only by continually urging himself to concentrate. The only word problems that held his attention were problems that involved the garden pool: it was empty and being filled by two channels, one, for example, pouring water in at ten liters an hour, another at forty liters an hour; how long, with a leak of five liters an hour, would it take the pool to fill? Ali imagined himself amazing his grandmother and the servant Kazem by his accurate forecast of a real pool filling in the *biruni*, after which he would triumphantly release the goldfish in the brimming pool to cries of "Bravo!" from members of the family.

One fellow student, Parviz, didn't seem to need dramatic settings to solve his word problems; on the contrary, for him pictures became numbers, organized so that they instantaneously yielded answers. Parviz was a very quiet student, thin and somewhat taller than most of the other boys. Much of the time he looked as if he were squinting slightly, but apparently he never needed glasses. His squint and his gaunt looks made him seem perpetually hungry, and Ali, who had seen him eat slowly and methodically, could picture him at his father's bakery slowly and methodically eating his way through a pile of flat loaves of bread like a tethered goat systematically cropping the circle of grass within its reach.

From the fourth year of school, when grades in mathematics began to be important, Parviz was always "second student" and began to sit next to Ali. Ali noticed that Parviz's notebooks were usually made of the flimsy light-yellow paper called "straw paper" and had been sewn and ruled by hand. Somehow he and Parviz were gradually drawn into an alliance. When Ali was stuck on a word problem Parviz would say, "Add the apples first," and get him untangled. Parviz required similar help for composition. For Ali, turning the subjects set by the teacher into polished essays was a matter of minutes, not hours. When asked to write an essay on the sea, Parviz would look oppressed and ask Ali in the schoolyard how he was to write about something he had never seen. Ali had never seen the sea either, but if he suggested, for example, that Parviz should describe the effect of light on the surface of the sea, based on his experience of the garden pool, Parviz would catch the thread and write compositions remarkable for the unusual but somewhat odd way in which he developed the subject. Ali found it as easy to develop the subject with a beginning, middle, and an end as it was to discover the images he would need to illustrate his essay. It all came to him effortlessly: the sun hitting the waves of the sea in good weather, the fisherman braving the sea in the service of Iran and its people, the storm, the small boat in peril, the heroism and rescue of the fisherman, the conclusion capped with a well-loved and beautifully ordered Koranic proof text for God's providence in creating the sea among His great works: "In the creation of the heavens and the earth, in the alternation of night and day, in the ships that flow through the sea for the profit of mankind, in the water that God sends down from heaven and with which he gives life to the earth after its death, in the beasts that move on the face of the earth, in the changes of the winds and in the clouds compelled to serve between heaven and earth, surely in these there are signs for those whose minds can understand."

At the end of the school day, when, like the clouds "compelled to serve between heaven and earth," the students of their class would march in a single line away from school, Parviz and Ali would take their places in line next to each other. Parviz would drop out of the line early, since his home lay near the school in a neighborhood of unusually convoluted narrow streets between houses of mud brick. Parviz seemed to know that Ali wanted to follow him home but seemed unable to do anything except look back with his hungry squint as he broke step to leave the line.

Strangely, the occasion for Ali to visit Parviz's house came during a holiday, not after school. The year Ali was twelve, one of the two dates for the death of Fatemeh (both were commemorated) fell late in autumn. Ali hadn't played with other boys in the street since the time when a gray-haired mullah had shouted at him, "Don't play in public; you are a gentleman's son." Ali was walking vaguely in the direction of school when he saw Parviz looking hungry and carrying a stack of dishes. Ali immediately knew that Parviz was distributing samanu, a kind of sweet made and distributed in Qom only in fulfillment of vows. Parviz, who was looking even more serious than usual, brightened at the sight of Ali and said, "My mother vowed that she would distribute samanu among the sayyeds. Here: thanks to your ancestor, I have a dish for you." To Ali, samanu, which is made from germinated wheat laboriously ground on a hand mill and boiled till it has the consistency of moist halvah, was the most unpleasant thing he had ever tasted, with the possible exception of the roots of his mother's rhubarb stalks, that he had tried when he was seven.

"I am unworthy. Besides, I can't stand the stuff. I'll show you the houses of my more worthy relatives and you'll be finished in fifteen minutes."

Parviz said, "We're lending each other bread" (which is the Persian equivalent of "You scratch my back and I'll scratch yours"), and they both laughed.

After distributing the dishes they drifted back to Parviz's house, walking Indian file on the shady side of the narrow streets, which

were divided by gutters running down the centers. Parviz knew
that Ali was already reading some of the first Arabic books taught
to mullahs. He timidly asked questions about them, then said:
"You know, I don't believe in vows. If God knows something
should be done, why does he need to be persuaded by the gifts of
a poor woman like my mother? My father always quotes the proverb, Even if I vowed to redeem my life with alms, if need be, my
son and I will eat the alms first. I agree with him."

"Vows like obligatory prayers or contracts are valid only if
formed intentionally, and, like contracts, if formed with intention,
they must be fulfilled," said Ali in a formal tone as if he were
quoting a text he had learned by heart. "Look, if we learn to say 'I
intend' before we do a good deed, our hearts get used to doing
good deeds. As Muslims we must believe that God cares for the
intention, not for what we actually get to do. What if, for some
reason, God lets us die before we do anything? As Muslims we
believe we should bear witness before God that we intend to do
something before we do it."

"I can solve other problems without having to say 'I intend.'
Anyway, what do I know? I'm not learned."

Entering Parviz's house was like entering one of the manufacturing sections of the bazaar. The center of the noise and activity
seemed to be the three mothers, each of whom managed her own
family's side of the square courtyard. Parviz's mother was cooking another batch of *samanu* in an enormous pot placed on bricks
next to the Aladdin brand kerosene stove, which had apparently
been abandoned because of its small capacity. The mother presiding over the rooms on the left was washing clothes with a large
bar of soap in a brass tub placed next to the central pool. She had
deliberately turned her back on the mother belonging to the rear
apartment, who was shouting vaguely in her direction. The rear-
apartment mother was coming down the outside ladder from her
roof, where she was drying tomatoes and fenugreek on newspapers, but she had stopped her descent a few rungs from the top
in order to look over her shoulder and comment loudly on the
scene. She warned "those who poured soapy water on other people's flowers" that God might see and forgive but neighbors
wouldn't. And she also warned those sweating over pots of *samanu*

that while sayyeds might not know the difference, God knew that eating the cook's sweat was not part of the vow.

Like the people in it, the courtyard lacked the geometry and discipline of the garden Ali knew at home. On the street side, where nobody lived, there was an outhouse on the right but none on the left. While the family on the left grew flowers, the family on the right didn't. The families on the right and in back preferred to cook outside; the family on the left had set up their kitchen inside. People showed less respect when they spoke to each other, and the women seemed to have less of a proper sense of shame: No one's face was really covered except for a girl a few years older than Ali and Parviz who was preparing the stalks of fenugreek for drying and had covered herself completely as a protection against the insults dropped on her by the woman on the ladder.

When Parviz's father entered, the women made an effort to cover up, and the woman over the tub continued washing with the edge of her chador in her teeth. He ordered one of the children to sprinkle his family's side of the courtyard to lay the dust, and Parviz went to get him his water pipe to smoke under a wooden awning. His first words to Parviz were, "I need you." There was a long hush while the courtyard waited for Parviz to speak. Parviz sat in silence and concentrated all the energy of his face on sharpening his squint. "My apprentice is a fool," he continued. "I have a right to order my only son to come to the bakery. You've learned how to write and keep accounts. A few more years of school and you'll be worthless in the bakery, and when I'm dead you'll be a beggar. You think you're a sayyed and the son of a teacher like your guest? Crows were never whiter for washing themselves."

As soon as this conversation began, Parviz's mother removed the pot from the outdoor hearth and shoved the bricks inward to contain the fire. Holding her chador tightly over her face, she walked with determination toward the awning and sat immediately behind the place where her husband had put his shoes. "I'll go from door to door and take in laundry. I'll put sawdust in your flour. I'll send my daughters to clean in other people's houses. You think I care about disgracing myself when my son has a chance to work in a government office? My son who can add in his head as fast as you can on the abacus?" The conversation was so well rehearsed that Parviz's father had finished exhaling the smoke just as his wife stopped to let him speak.

"A clerk! That's all I need, a miserable clerk for a son, who is rude to people until they bribe him."

Parviz had started to move quietly away as soon as his mother sat down, and Ali followed him. Within seconds they were out in the street together and walking toward the river. "As the expression goes, it's the same soup and the same bowl," said Parviz. "In about fifteen minutes my father will say, 'We'll see, we'll see,' and that's the end of it for the day."

"You never said what your mother made her vow for."

"She said she would distribute *samanu* to sayyeds every year for three years on this date if I passed the exam at the end of lower school and continued into high school."

"Bravo! You are living proof that vows work. I vow to have a lamb slaughtered and given to the poor on this day every year for three years if you pass the secondary school final exam and continue at university."

"Okay, we'll see. But if I need to, I'll come and eat the entire lamb myself."

Parviz had grabbed a pomegranate on the way out of his house. Ali produced a pocket knife and they split it. They sat near the river and spat out bits of the inside skin toward the nearly dry riverbed, whose stones were littered with clothes and carpets that women had washed in the small remaining trickle of water. Ali, having made his vow, couldn't help feeling like a conspirator; and, to his surprise, he rather liked the feeling.

· · ·

Iranian secular education began in the barracks and never quite lost its fascination with the drillmaster and the military parade. Napoleon, tempted by the fantasy of imitating Alexander the Great, sent military instructors to Iran to prepare the Iranians to help him in a great campaign from Europe through the Middle East to British India. The army of Napoleon never came, but Iran's northern neighbors, the Russians, having expanded their empire right up to the borders of Iran, never left. After two disastrous wars with Russia the Iranians determined to build an army on the

European model and began to send Iranians to Europe and to import European instructors (and physicians) to Iran. Some Iranian students died abroad; some came back and were of no use to the government; and finally, in 1851, the Iranian government decided to house the study of European sciences under one roof. The government founded a Polytechnic College, staffed by Austrian and Prussian instructors (all of whom taught in French). Inevitably the college had a military bent: three of the six instructors taught the "sciences of cavalry, of infantry, and of artillery."

The graduates of the Polytechnic did not defeat Russia. But the shah and his ministers saw that the new education provided other benefits for the central government. Graduates of the new education were as surely men of the regime as were the scribes who had been trained by apprenticeship in the old chanceries. They were indebted to the government, and in many cases they had skills that only the government could buy. They were an instrument of centralization, a new elite, the manipulators of new techniques by which the central government could more effectively dominate and tax the country.

The Iranians, however, learned more from their French-speaking instructors than the calculation of cannonball trajectories and double-entry bookkeeping. They learned the nineteenth-century European ideologies of nationalism and progress. A "people" should unite themselves in one nation-state, whose government belonged to the people and expressed their common interests. This sense of common interest, and the sacrifices it demanded, could reach the masses only through education, which had to be removed from the hands of backward priests, who had more loyalty to the church than the nation. (Here, in the translation of the European progressive model, "mullah" for "priest" seemed perfect to the Iranian audience, since until 1851 the mullahs had provided virtually all the organized education available in Iran.) Following this model, the Iranian people, mobilized by education and ready to sacrifice for a government that belonged to them, would become a real nation, which would owe its independence to its strength rather than to the accident of geography that made it a buffer between czarist Russia and British India.

By and large the nineteenth-century shahs of Iran, who had

achieved an astonishing and ongoing combination of greed and near-bankruptcy, did not approve. Telegraph lines, roads, and Maxim guns enabled them to collect more taxes. Notions of popular sovereignty did not. The new Iranian intellectuals met in secret societies, where they were joined even by liberal mullahs, to read banned Persian newspapers printed in Calcutta, London, and Istanbul.

By the end of the century some of these intellectuals demanded a "fundamental law" for the state, a constitution that described the limits of the government's power. A typical figure of this generation was Mostashar ad-Dowleh, who from 1882 to 1896 divided his time between middle-level government posts and prison. He was a sincerely religious Muslim, and his experience as Iranian consul in Tiflis, St. Petersburg, and Bombay caused him to add to his religious beliefs a devotion to railroads, education, and the creation of a code of laws guaranteed by a constitution. "It is self-evident," he wrote, "that in the future no nation—Islamic or non-Islamic—will continue to exist without constitutional law. . . . The various ethnic groups that live in Iran will not become one people until the law upholds their right to freedom of expression and to the opportunity for education." Like-minded Iranian intellectuals were fewer in number than were the liberal constitutionalists in Egypt and Turkey, their cause less hopeful. In 1906, in the explosion of the people's feelings that followed the arrest of the popular preacher and the killing of the sayyed on July 11 they carried off the first successful constitutional revolution in the Middle East.

It is far easier to understand why the shahs lost than to understand why the constitutionalists won. The government's financial and moral bankruptcy was absolute. Iranian merchants, now involved in international commerce, expected more and got less; the routes of commerce were unsafe, and the merchants themselves were raided for ready cash by government officials desperate to recou the expenses of buying their offices from the shah. The mullahs, both as traditional spokesmen for the oppressed and as members of an elite threatened by the government's weakness before foreigners and by its flirtation with foreign learning, felt that Iran's future as an Islamic state was in doubt. When the explosion came, large numbers of people knew what they did not want: they did not want unpredictable oppression, a shah free to raise ready cash by selling foreigners economic concessions for everything from tobacco to phonograph records, and a country whose central government was too weak to protect their products from foreign goods or their religion from alien encroachment.

In the first half of 1906, after the sugar merchants were bastinadoed and protesters had withdrawn from Tehran to the shrine of Shah Abdol-Azim, there was a general feeling that reform meant the establishment of a "house of justice" to implement Islamic law throughout Iran. But when the government failed to carry out its promise to establish this institution, and the sayyed was killed on July 11, many mullahs, accompanied by some merchants and craftsmen, left the capital and took sanctuary in Qom. Still more merchants and craftsmen took refuge in an even safer sanctuary, the enormous compound of the British legation. The vast crowd in the legation was surprisingly orderly. It produced its committee of elders to supervise its affairs, and as the crowd already numbered some fourteen thousand, after the first week the committee admitted only students and teachers from the Polytechnic and the recently formed schools of agriculture and political science.

With their arrival the men of new education had their first chance to teach a nation, and they succeeded beyond the fondest imaginings of earlier generations at the Polytechnic, who had labored through French textbooks on mining and artillery. Unlike many of the protesters, the students of the new education did know exactly what they wanted. According to one Iranian participant, once inside the British legation the students transformed the gathering into "one vast open-air school of political science" and changed a sentiment of loathing for the corruption, weakness, instability, and simple injustice of the old order into a demand for a written constitution giving authority to an elective assembly. On August 5, 1906, Muzaffar ad-Din Shah gave in. In October the newly elected National Assembly convened; in December the constitution was written and rushed to the desperately sick shah for his approval; and on December 30, only a few days before his death, the shah finally gave the newly drafted constitution his signature.

Isa Sadiq, the foremost historian of modern Iranian education, who was eleven years old when the constitution was ratified, remembered how the events of 1906 brought honor and fame to the supporters of the new education. Isa himself experienced the transformation and witnessed some of the dramatic events that surrounded it. His father was a merchant who, like so many leading men in the bazaar, strengthened his ties with the religious establishment by marrying the daughter of a prominent mullah. However, his father had liberal friends who persuaded him to send Isa to one of the schools that taught the new learning, and in addition to a good dose of Arabic grammar and traditional religious subjects (including Aristotelian logic), he studied French, mechanics, Western-style geography and Western-style mathematics.

Foremost among his father's liberal friends was a close neighbor, a preacher, a certain Jamal ad-Din of Isfahan, a mullah in style of dress and learning but in fact a man whom Isa believed to have little or no faith in formal religion. The warmth, openness, humility, and, above all, eloquence of this tiny man, with his black eyes, black turban, and wispy black beard, charmed little Isa. Whenever Jamal ad-Din preached in a nearby mosque Isa joined the throngs who came to listen and who struggled to kiss the preacher's hand, his shoulder, and his cloak. Jamal ad-Din was an outspoken supporter of the revolution, so outspoken that the shah had him imprisoned in 1908. He was strangled in confinement.

On December 26, 1909, Isa Sadiq entered the Polytechnic. Some tradesmen who despised the new learning teased him on the way to school. But Isa was a classic good boy. He redoubled his efforts, and by mastering his curriculum of solid geometry, algebra, geography, physics, chemistry, cartography, and—inevitably—French, he became "first student" in a class of students many of whom were undoubtedly his elders. Through an open exam he won a place in a group of students the government decided to send to France, and toward the end of October in 1911 he entered a lycée in Versailles.

He spent every waking minute in study because, as he candidly says in his memoirs, he not only loved learning but wanted the respect given to men of learning. He was also still upset at his discovery that Russian troops controlled some of the provinces of Iran he passed through on his way to Europe, and he was motivated by a sense of mission for Iran. Finally, he studied hard because he thought that success at school might somehow allow him to help his father, who had suffered business losses as a result of the disruption of a revolution that sometimes smoked, sometimes burned, but never came to a conclusion. Isa was a good boy who knew why he wanted to be good.

In France he was lonely. Of the French books he read he most liked the sad ones: *Atala*, *Renée*, and above all the translation of Goethe's *The Sorrows of Young Werther*, which he read several times. His French composition teacher managed to convince Isa that he was learning the superior logic of the French mind, and in his memoirs Isa admits that he felt impatient the rest of his life with people who were not "logical." In January 1914 he passed his *baccalauréat*, a milestone in his life. Until this point he had felt that Europeans, like his French schoolmates who ridiculed Islam and called him a savage, were half right to look down on Iranians. Now he had passed "their" exam along with their best students, and had excelled in mathematics, as would so many talented Iranians who studied abroad in the next seventy years.

He then started to study mathematics at the University of Paris, where he first became aware of the temptations of French life. "I derived pleasure from watching the cheeks of moon-faced French women," he wrote; but whenever he neared the "precipice" of involvement, a cry arose within him and he drew back. Actually, he was too busy for any plunges over the precipice. The Iranian government, on the edge of bankruptcy as usual, was not sending money regularly. Thanks to a shortage of teachers after the start of the First World War, Isa got a post at a lycée teaching math and English (which, as a passionate self-improver, he had picked up through extracurricular study in Versailles).

The following year he got a better job. He became the instructor in the Persian language at Cambridge, in England, under the supervision of E. G. Browne, the greatest Persianist of the European tradition. He was fascinated by the style of English universities, with their gowns, parietal hours, their un-French encouragement of student-teacher friendships, and especially the un-Iranian interest of their students in such voluntary associations as rowing clubs and debating societies, which "accustomed them to cooperation and joint efforts." He was, of course, diligently improving himself. In his spare time he studied higher mathematics with the famous G. H. Hardy and managed to learn German. He began to meet the "right" people; in 1917 he met Bertrand Russell and the poet laureate Robert Bridges.

Isa also began to worry about improving others. He wanted to found a university like Cambridge in Iran but decided that the tradition of Darwin, Milton and Newton could come into existence only through the efforts of thousands of scholars over many centuries. He began to feel that education in Iran had to be built from the ground up, and his new interest in education led him to observe elementary and secondary schools in the Cambridge area. He also decided to educate the British public and wrote letters to the *Manchester Guardian* in which he criticized Russia's role in Iran. Finally the foreign secretary, Sir Edward Grey, told him that he was disturbing relations between the Allies and should stop such correspondence or leave England.

Isa had had enough of Europe anyway; he went back to Paris, passed his *licence* (roughly, an M.A.) in 1918, and returned to Iran. His first assignment was to organize elementary and secondary education in the town of Rasht and in the surrounding province. Rasht was the great entrepôt of Iran's trade, where, as the schoolbooks said, "seafowl abounded." In this position he became aware, like many intellectuals of his generation, that the Constitutional Revolution was winding down into anarchy. The surrounding province was dominated by Kuchek Khan, an enormous man who made himself even more imposing by his semi-Russian guerrilla uniforms and Castro-like fullness of mustache, beard, and hair. He was an idealist, perhaps something of a patriot, but his two most important lieutenants were committed Marxists, and the English saw him as a tool of Soviet Russia.

In the summer of 1920 Kuchek Khan captured Rasht and imprisoned Isa Sadiq. Kuchek Khan's lieutenants, after explaining the progressive ideals of their leader on all issues and especially education, offered Isa the Ministry of Education in their provisional government. Isa sat in silence a few minutes. He then expressed his "boundless thanks" for the kind offer but said that he could not believe in the nationalism of a movement that had foreign (in this case, Soviet Russian) advisers. He told Kuchek Khan's deputies, "I prefer honor to life" and that as he had accepted a post from the government in Tehran, to accept a post in another government would be the end of his "honor." They released him.

He returned to a Tehran in which the central government, still enmeshed in Cabinet crises, seemed unlikely ever to regain control of its provinces from such men as Kuchek Khan. Then one morning in February 1921, his cook told him at breakfast that the Iranian "Cossack" Brigade had entered Tehran. Isa Sadiq telephoned the Ministry of Education and got no answer. He then went out into the street, where he saw a mounted patrol of Iranian "Cossacks," a brigade that had long since lost the czarist Russian officers who had trained them but had retained the karakul hats and long tunics laced with rows of cartridges that the Russian Cossacks had passed on to them. Newspapers had stopped appearing; Isa's neighbors had no idea who the commander of the "Cossacks" was or what the "Cossacks" wanted.

The next day a proclamation appeared on walls all over the city with the arresting beginning: "I command." It was signed: "Reza, head of the Cossack Brigade of His Imperial Majesty, and Supreme Commander." Within a month a new Cabinet was formed in which Reza was minister of war; and the new minister of education put Isa Sadiq in a high post in his ministry. It was now clear how wise Isa had been to reject Kuchek Khan and to behave as the *bon élève* he had been trained to be.

Slowly but surely the majority of men of the new education acted as Isa Sadiq had done and looked for places in the new order. The "man on horseback" had arrived. For the liberal intellectuals he was not exactly made to order; but, then, almost nothing had been made to order for them since they had created the constitution in 1906, and in retrospect that seemed something of a freak. Reza was indeed commanding, as a man on horseback should be—a physical giant of the center (or right, depending on your perspective), to match Kuchek Khan, the giant of the left.

Vita Sackville-West, who knew him in this period, wrote: "In appearance Reza was an alarming man, six foot three in height, with a sullen manner, a huge nose, grizzled hair and a brutal jowl; he looked, in fact, what he was, a Cossack trooper; but there was no denying that he had a kingly presence." In 1926 he became king in fact and crowned himself Reza Shah. He was the kind of autocrat whose total command gave his rule an egalitarian tone: he dumped pots of inferior food on the heads of cheating army quartermasters in front of the recruits, and when horses defecated at parades, fear of his disapproval made great landowners and generals fall to their knees to clean the ground before he came.

The Iran of which Reza Shah became king was a huge country—roughly the size of the United States east of the Mississippi—with a population of merely twelve million. The great majority of these twelve million were peasants who lived in the tens of thousands of scattered villages, most of which were bought and sold in their entirety by great landlords. Great landlords had bailiffs to represent them in their villages and had carefully cultivated friends to represent them in the king's "court," that strange miscellany of royal relatives, panegyric poets, entertainers, physicians, and official "wise men" that was a persistent feature of Iranian life. The chiefs of "tribal" peoples (most of them only partly nomadic—they had more or less fixed summer and winter pasturage areas) also cultivated their friends at "court." The kings (and, after 1906, the parliaments) of Iran had found that while they could sometimes use coercive force on some of these landlords and tribal chiefs, without the quiet assent of the majority of them and the active support of at least some of them, the central government in Tehran could guarantee little more than the obedience of its panegyric poets. But local strong men needed the government too. By occasional use of terrifying violence the government could keep sufficient order for local elites to survive both their ever-renewing quarrels with each other and the threat of insubordination from those below them.

The central government was aided in its attempt to exert authority by a bureaucratic elite that was, by the time of Reza Shah, a mix of old bureaucratic families and men of the new education. This bureaucratic elite included high generals as well as high financial officials, and these generals often became governors of provinces. A central government that guaranteed order and didn't tax arbitrarily also usually got support from the important men of the bazaar, who were very conscious both of their need to be apolitical enough to survive regimes and of their ability to paralyze the economy of any regime that made economic life unbearable for them. By the time of the accession of Reza Shah to the throne, differing cultural orientations had appeared among these elites, particularly the high civil servants and the great merchants and landlords. Some were more interested in Western objects and habits than others, although there was seldom a clear correlation between wealth, profession, and the phenomenon called "Westernization."

In the cities, below the great merchants and high bureaucrats, were "the middle sort of people" such as the shopkeepers, the artisans, the bookkeepers, and the government clerks. And below the "middle sort" were the laborers, sometimes seasonal workers who moved between the city and the village, sometimes permanent dwellers in the city such as sweepers, menial workers, or those workers in the "unrespectable" professions. These groups were the least likely to have differing orientations toward Western culture—which for them largely consisted of luxury objects—unless they had gone to one of the few missionary schools or had lived for a while in a Muslim region of the Russian empire or the like.

Intermixed with all these groups were the mullahs, the Shiah men of religion. Many of them were from mullah families, some from mullah families of great wealth. Some were extremely poor men who worked as farmers because their villages could not support nonworking mullahs. In the cities the mullahs drew a significant part of their income from pious endowments, often set up by wealthy men specifically to support them. The most respected of these mullahs were called ayatollahs. Ayatollahs often intermarried with the families of the great merchants and occasionally with those of the landlords, but they seldom formed alliances with those merchants and landlords who were culturally "Westernizing." Intermarriage between ayatollahs and the new intellectuals produced by the new education was even rarer.

In the changes he brought about in the fifteen years of his reign Reza Shah gave the new intellectuals such as Isa Sadiq some of what they wanted. He reconquered Iran for the central government. Before the end of 1921 the head of Kuchek Khan, in whom the Soviets had lost interest, was on display in Tehran; there was room for only one giant in Iranian politics. In succeeding years Reza achieved order in all the provinces, expelled foreign troops, and compelled foreign governments to treat Iran as an equal, if a very touchy equal—he once broke diplomatic relations with France because a cartoon in a French newspaper made a pun on *chat* (cat) and "shah." At his order the new men built the symbols of progress and national unity that they had been dreaming of for over a half century. They blasted tunnels through the rings of mountains that surround the Iranian plateau, laid stable beds of gravel and cement through the unstable deserts that lie at the plateau's center, and built the Trans-Iranian railroad that the sometime Iranian consul Mostashar ad-Dowleh had dreamed of half a century earlier.

Yet Reza Shah was in no way "one of them." His education was slight, and when they mention his speeches in their memoirs, the men of the new education speak with evident foot-shuffling and embarrassment of the extreme "simplicity" of his way of talking. He accepted many of their goals: a new legal code, which they wrote for him; factories for light manufacturing, which they ran for him; and progress toward the emancipation of women, most especially through the abolition of the chadors, which they abhorred. But all these measures were carried out with a brutality that made the new men uneasy even if they argued that some brutality was necessary. In mid-July of 1935, angry crowds thronged into the courtyard of the shrine in Mashhad, the burial place of Imam Reza, the brother of the Fatemeh who is enshrined in Qom, and for the Shiah the holiest spot in Iran. They came to hear preachers attack the policies of Reza Shah. When they did not disperse, Reza Shah's troops mounted machine guns on the roofs overlooking the courtyard and opened fire. Over one hundred people were killed. Three soldiers who had refused to fire were shot. No further hostile religious demonstrations of any significance took place in Reza Shah's reign.

The shah and the new intellectuals now lived in an uneasy symbiosis. Some of the new intellectuals refused to betray the ideals of 1906 and refused to take their places in the national forced march even if it was going in a direction they wanted. These men went to prison, into exile, or committed suicide, as did the author of Reza Shah's new law code. Most, however, accepted places in the new order, where they were well paid. They were to become a kind of ruling class, less subject to the shah's interest in building a personal fortune than were the landlords and large merchants. Maybe, they reasoned, the shah would build a nation in which the diffusion of the new education and the new techniques would make Iranians spontaneously adopt the ideas that they now accepted out of obedience.

Isa Sadiq seems never to have lost this hope. His faithful service to the new regime in the late twenties was soon rewarded when he caught the attention of a professor at Columbia University in New York, who invited him to do graduate work in a program at Teachers College for foreign specialists in education. Isa arrived in New York in the fall of 1930 and, ever the good student, finished his Ph.D. thesis by the time he left in the fall of 1931. On his return to Iran he wrote *One Year in America,* an altogether engaging book, in Persian, which reflects the author's mixture of curiosity and intelligence and his capacity for being fascinated by mind-numbing masses of detail.

Isa was given a room in Columbia's International House, and he devotes two full pages of the opening chapter of his book to a description of the cafeteria in this remarkable institution, taking the reader from the stacks of trays through the steam table to the automatic change machine. He dutifully lists the advantages of the cafeteria system; for, though, as he explains, "I am an Iranian, and used to having others do things for me," first, self-service created a real equality among students, and, second, it allowed him to choose what he wanted to eat. He goes on throughout his book to list, count, and describe everything: the number of bulbs in the light fixtures on the tables at the Teachers College library, the dimensions of the Holland Tunnel, and the three hundred and seventy-three displays by firms at the meeting of the National Educational Association in Detroit.

When Isa's teachers took him on school trips to see how the minds of American children were being molded, he immediately knew what his teachers thought were the "lessons" of American education for the non-American world. In the Jackson Avenue School in Hackensack, as in so many other schools, he sat through school assemblies, watched the meetings of student councils and PTAs, attended classes for slow learners, and visited the school nurse's office. He understood the patriotic and collectivist effect of school songs and school celebrations of the birthdays of national heroes. He understood how hands-on experience in laboratories and technical schools created a more capable labor force and furthered the alliance of American industry with education.

Isa sensed that this system of education was related to the style of American middle-class home life, where he found American husbands in charge of repairing major appliances and children eagerly selling the *Saturday Evening Post*. After the communalism of Iranian home life, he was impressed to find that each American child had his own room, his own closet, his own desk, and his particular household chore. He also, incidentally, thought American education intellectually rather shallow but knew that, like newspapers and radio, even intellectually shallow education could create a kind of national consensus, as did the mixing of social classes in schools and the mixing of elites in colleges.

Isa had not lost the knack of meeting the right people. He met John D. Rockefeller, Jr., Nicholas Murray Butler, the president of Columbia University, Admiral Byrd, and Harry Emerson Fosdick (whose Sunday school at Riverside Church he dutifully observed). His greatest coup came in 1931 when he went to Albany and had a long interview with the then governor of New York, Franklin Delano Roosevelt. FDR asked him about the future of communism in Iran, the degree of Russian influence, the extent to which Iran was economically dependent on the outside world, and if Iran ran deficits on its budgets. Isa asked FDR how the governor had come to know so much about Iran, and FDR explained that his maternal uncle Delano had gone to Iran in 1926 as head of the Opium Commission and his nephew was deputy ambassador in Tehran. According to Isa, the governor said, "Both have so praised Iran to me that I want to travel there myself."

In the final paragraph of *One Year in America*, in which he describes his ship sailing out of New York harbor, Isa allows himself virtually the only purple passage in his book (except for the section in which he describes how "my soul flew in the world of love to the beloved homeland" when listening to Persian music in a house in Flushing). As he stood on deck, "The sorrowful rays of the moon appeared in the East—that very same East which, with its thousands of deficiencies, was drawing my enraptured heart toward itself and might, perhaps, separate me forever from the pleasures of Western life." How many men of the new education had left and would leave the West with such feelings of "two-heartedness," as ambiguity is called in Persian.

During one humid New York summer before setting sail Isa had written his Ph.D. thesis, *Modern Persia and Her Education System*, which Teachers College immediately published. Isa Sadiq's nationalism, his common sense, and his receptivity to the ideals of John Dewey's Teachers College shine through this book. Isa Sadiq believed that the Iranian nation limped under unnecessary burdens of the past; after his successful travels through Versailles, Cambridge, and Morningside Heights, he "knew" that Iranians could cast these burdens aside and adopt the more useful ideas of the West without loss. Iranian history, he explained in his thesis, "shows a striking aptitude for national reconstruction, it shows the power of the Persian man to assimilate a foreign race and, rising above it, to impose its cultural superiority." Iran was filled with foreigners working for the government: "There are Belgians in the Customs and Finance; Americans in the Railroad; French in Education, the Pasteur Institute and the Wireless Telegraph Service; Germans in the Arsenal, Mines and Banks." Iran needs to train its own "technical leaders," and, once having trained them, to trust them fully and dismiss foreign experts. Iranians, he explains, have quite specific goals: they want to make Iran strong, healthy, wealthy, and wise (especially in the techniques of the modern world) because "they aspire that Persia have a place of honour among the nations of the world." In a sense it was the need for national honor that, more than anything else, had sustained Isa through the years of estrangement in foreign lands.

Iranians could best accomplish this, he felt, if they adopted a new educational philosophy, the philosophy he (like his teachers at Columbia) believed to be embodied in the self-service-cafeteria line at the International House and in the PTA of the Jackson Avenue School. Iranians, he complained, were totally unaware of John Dewey's "theory that education and school are life themselves, that the child is *living* in school and that the best way to prepare him to participate in adult life is to ensure his participation in the life that is around him." Iranians must see and respect their children as individuals with capacity for different kinds of original thoughts so that democracy and creativity might be fostered among them. Iranian teachers "must abandon the emphasis on memorization and cramming . . . [The pupils] must use the materials themselves; they must be put in a position to understand, to think, to judge and to criticize . . . Their opinions must be given consideration . . . They must never be ridiculed . . . The inductive method is the only one worthy of displaying the power of man . . . The Persian who encourages the proper utilization of a laboratory deserves much of his fatherland."

On his return to Iran he was amply repaid for "his loss of the pleasures of Western life": he began a career that carried him through the direction of the Tehran Teachers College and a position as head of the University of Tehran to six terms as minister of education and a lifetime appointment to the Iranian Senate. He owed his success not only to a good brain and his doctorate from Columbia Teachers College but also to his clear understanding of who ran his country. In his thesis he had written: "The whole history of Persia bears out . . . [that] whenever there has been a great leader . . . Persia has risen to the pitch of glory and zenith of power . . . The regeneration of Persia under the leadership of Reza Shah Pahlavi is another striking fact that proves that only great men have been able to lead the Nation toward its destiny." And he probably meant every word of this. There is no doubt that for him the Aristotelian logic he had learned in elementary school, the French logic he had learned at the lycée, and the celebrated American pragmatism of Teachers College all argued that if Iran were to become strong and take "a place of honour among the nations," intellectuals would have to cooperate with the regime. Neither side, the regime or the intellectuals, ever fully understood what the other wanted. Reza Shah and after him his son, Mohammed Reza Shah, wanted Iranian experts who would employ their skills as civil servants and loyal entrepreneurs, accepting the discipline necessary to "build the nation" under central leadership. The intellectuals wanted to use their French logic, their American pragmatism, and their inborn Iranian ingenuity to decide what kind of nation they wanted to build. One of the few goals they agreed on was education. The success and proselytizing of men such as Isa Sadiq eventually created a kind of frenzy for education among the Iranian upper and middle classes which the government was eager to encourage and pay for.

In 1811 the Shah of Iran had sent two students to England so that "they shall study something of use to me, to themselves, and their country"; only one ever saw Iran again, the other died in London of tuberculosis. In 1930, when Isa Sadiq went to the United States, there were at most a few hundred Iranians studying abroad. By the 1960s Iran was sending abroad more students for a country of its size than practically any other in the world; and this high proportion was maintained through the seventies. In America alone in the academic year 1969–70 there were over five thousand Iranian students; in 1974–75 there were over thirteen thousand; and by 1978–79 there were over forty-five thousand.

But the growth of foreign education was not even a patch on the growth of domestic education. In his thesis Isa Sadiq laments that in 1929, out of a population of about twelve million, there were just over a hundred and ten thousand students at all levels in the schools of the new education. By the mid-seventies there were more employees in the Ministry of Education than there had been students in 1929. Over seven million students studied in elementary and secondary schools, and a literacy corps reached hundreds of thousands of adults in the villages. In 1935 Reza Shah opened the University of Tehran, the first university in Iran; by the academic year 1977–78 the government had twenty-one universities and had hired the staffs for several more universities still to be built. Some of the faculties at the University of Tehran, particularly in technical subjects, maintained standards that matched the best universities anywhere in the world.

As with Isa Sadiq, education proved to be the common road to

royal advancement. Cabinets were studded with Ph.D.'s; and for a
student with family connections, a certificate of graduation from
practically any institution of higher education guaranteed a bureaucratic post. By the 1970s the regime had the money to buy the
services of graduates too cynical, too revolutionary, or too poorly
connected to get civil service jobs. Not only were there jobs for
the idealistic in the literacy corps but for ex-revolutionaries who
disavowed armed struggle against the shah's regime there were
jobs in the dozens of research institutes that the government established to accommodate them.

If education was the rare child born of the shared enthusiasm of
the intellectuals and the regime, it was a child that in many ways
defeated the hopes of both parents. The huge budgets allotted for
education bought the services but seldom the gratitude of Iranian
intellectuals. Thousands of Iranians acquired Ph.D.'s, but too
many Ph.D.'s were from unknown American universities that accepted hundred-page theses on such subjects as "The Future of
Iranian Education." Iranians continued to excel in math and physical sciences, but too many among the large Iranian contingents at
MIT and Cal Tech never returned to Iran, or else returned to find
laboratory equipment impossible to purchase and universities
closed every other year because of student demonstrations. Dem-
onstrating against the government was a rite of passage without
which Iranian university and even high school students felt their
education incomplete. They did not see themselves as special men
of the regime like the nineteenth-century students of the Polytechnic. On the contrary, they felt that the regime had been taken
from them.

For the intellectuals the education that emerged was more the
child of a ministry than of the liberal philosophy they had hoped
to nourish. It still smelled suspiciously like a creature of the barracks, with its emphasis on order and marching and its brutal
physical punishments. Its ethos was a strange mixture of nineteenth-century French and mullah education. Iranian textbooks
presented chopped-up bits of literary classics and set themes for
composition, and teachers demanded enormous feats of brute
memorization. Isa Sadiq either forgot or, more likely, despaired of
promoting his earlier interest in American hands-on education.

Iranian high school students learned how to draw microscopes and how to write letter-perfect descriptions of the way in which microscopes worked, but the microscopes in Iranian schools usually remained locked up as property too valuable to be put in students' hands.

The pool of Iranian skilled laborers and technical experts that Isa Sadiq wanted to create in order to replace "the Belgians, Americans, French and Germans" poured forth from the high schools and universities; but the foreign experts nevertheless stayed. Iranian professors at MIT might be at the forefront of laser research, but in Iran they could not find reliable staff to maintain a research lab; Iranian village mechanics could create cast-metal replacements for almost any part of a car, but the Iranian army mechanics could not be convinced that regular maintenance was necessary to keep a fleet of trucks running. Besides, secretly the government always thought the foreigners knew better.

In two respects, however, education decisively transformed Iran in ways that both the government and the intellectuals wanted: it created a deep nationalism and it killed the Koran school, the *maktab*. Isa Sadiq remembered his conclusions about the effect of the patriotic songs he had heard in Hackensack and Detroit. He and his contemporaries introduced school songs, patriotic holidays, and nationalistic themes in textbooks, all of which made an ancient love of Iran into a modern nationalism. The death of the *maktab* was even more dramatic. For a thousand years the staple of elementary education in Iran was the Koran school, the *maktab*, run by mullahs or pious elderly men or women, in which the rudiments of reading, writing, and business arithmetic were taught as well as some fundamentals of religion. Isa Sadiq reported thirty-six thousand *maktab* pupils in 1929 but admitted that the figure was inaccurate since many *maktabs* "are in the teachers' houses or in remote villages inaccessible to school inspectors"; in fact, there must have been tens of thousands more. The Koran was taught every day and formed the symbolic (though not always the actual) heart of the *maktab* curriculum. The teachers of the *maktab* usually lived on the modest fees they collected. The competition with compulsory, free, and universal education drove the *maktab* from Iran even as a supplementary school of religious instruction. Reza Shah also closed the missionary schools and the schools of the Jewish, Christian, and Baha'i minorities. By mid-century there was essentially one form of education in Iran, and if it required a few courses on Islam, it was nevertheless secular education, and it belonged to the state. Of the religious schools only the *madreseh*, the Islamic college, survived.

CHAPTER THREE

ON THE morning before his first day in the *madreseh* Ali spent a long time on the roof trying to stare down the stork in a nest on the neighboring house. The stork would put forward first its right, then its left eye, and its only reaction to all distractions, even the noises of Kazem banging the ashes out of the samovar, was to look a little haughtier and to raise a few feathers on its head. When Ali's older brother came to take Ali to the front door of the house, Ali asked him: "What is the stork thinking?"

"He's asking himself, What is that little boy who's staring at me thinking?"

"Now I will start thinking, Why is the stork thinking What is the boy thinking? And the stork will start thinking . . ."

"Yes, dear Ali, it's an infinite regress. Save it for the teacher at school. My friend is waiting for you at the gate."

Ali knew at first glance that Mohammed's friend, who was about fifteen, looked the part of a *madreseh* student, with his turban, black mullah coat, and bits of woolly beard, while Ali himself looked like what he was, a ten-year-old boy with only a dark-blue frock coat and a shaming lack of beard. But he was wearing a green turban, which, even though it had only two loops, still, by its color, distinguished him as a sayyed, in contrast to his companion, who had only the white turban of an ordinary person, however large it may have been.

They walked out of the alleyway in front of the family home onto the road that led to the river. As it was one of those September days, not uncomfortably hot, when the sky was full of lamb's-tail clouds, everyone seemed to be moving with a certain liveliness, maybe even a certain hope that the cooler days of autumn were not far away. Ali now found himself in his second staring contest of the day, this time with a camel loaded with burlap bags of melons, which was walking at the same pace as Ali and grumbling savagely. When the camel started to spit, Ali's companion speeded up, and they soon reached the square near the river which opened onto both the shrine and the Faiziyeh, the greatest *madreseh* in Qom.

The gate into the Faiziyeh led into a rectangular courtyard which in size was to the courtyard at home as the lion is to the cat. The courtyard had a large pool in the center; and each of the four paved avenues that led up to one side of this pool was as wide as the facing side of the pool. The remaining area of the courtyard was occupied by four parterres, each the size of the garden at home. But they were very open, with no trees except a few tubular pines that had been pruned so that they could grow to great heights while remaining thin and responsive to the slightest breeze. Otherwise, most of the space in the parterres was planted with petunias (called in Persian satin-flowers because of their texture) mixed with occasional watermelons, apparently the product of seeds spat out by students eating inside the *madreseh*. The courtyard was surrounded by two stories of student rooms, uniform in size, with their doors and windows set with perfect symmetry in recessed arches.

The openness and regularity of the courtyard's designs filled Ali with hope. In its overall pattern it seemed a public form of home which still remained somehow private, not only to the scores of student boarders who lived in the apartments that formed its walls but also to the teachers and nonboarding students who walked in the Faiziyeh as if at home. The tiles that covered the surfaces of the walls facing the courtyard were a light yellow, something between eggshell and egg yolk in color, with elaborate interlaced patterns in blue and turquoise which reminded Ali of the glass windows at home. At the center of each of the four sides of the courtyard was an arch two stories high enclosing magnificent honeycomb patterns of stalactites, also covered with tiles. On his first day Ali particularly noticed the dark-blue peacocks drawn on the tiles at the foot of each side of one of these arches. From the beak of each peacock an identical abstract design sprouted that transformed itself into plants and interlaced straps and polygons that crisscrossed as they moved upward until the two columns of design met at the apex of the arch. The peacocks, Ali noticed with relief, seemed to be staring at each other and not at him.

His companion brought him to a classroom that was in the lower story of another of the tall arches. Most of the students fourteen and under were wearing light-tan and light-brown frock coats; the older students wore the aba, a black coat, split down the front and furnished with full sleeves, which is the characteristic dress of mullahs everywhere. The students were sitting cross-legged in a semicircle around a teacher who sat on the second step of a movable set of stairs and smoked a cigarette with quiet concentration. When the teacher turned to face the class Ali noticed that there were two white streaks in his beard, evenly placed near the corners of his mouth. He was holding a truly gigantic copy of the prescribed book, so much bigger than Ali's own copy that Ali was at first afraid that his fifteen-year-old companion had dumped him in the wrong class.

The teacher put out his cigarette in a brass tea-glass coaster, cleared his throat, opened the gigantic book, and began: "In the name of God, the Merciful, the Beneficent. Yesterday we read the opening discourse of *Mullah Abdollah's Commentary*, in which he explains why the text underlying his commentary is called 'The Ultimate Rectification of Speech in Writing About Logic.' As Mullah Abdollah explains, the author of the underlying text, Taftazani, believed that no one could write a summary briefer than his 'Ultimate Rectification of the Essentials of Logic.'

"Today we reach the introduction, in which Taftazani says"—

and the teacher read in Arabic—" 'If knowledge is assent to a relationship, then it is verification; otherwise, it is representation.' " (The teacher clapped the enormous book shut and began to speak in Persian.) "There are two kinds of knowledge, and today we will discuss the difference between them. Sometimes we understand a thing without judging it, and such understanding is a simple, *not* a compound act. It is called 'representation,' because we make a picture for ourselves in our mind, a 'representation.' When I say I 'know' this book before me, or 'know' Zaid or the servant of Zaid, I know each of these by a simple act of immediate knowledge, a mental representation in which I exercise no judgment.

"Other times, we judge and we make a relation between two things. To use the example mentioned in the *Commentary*, my knowledge that 'Zaid is standing' is composed of two things, about which I have made a mental judgment. I have judged that Zaid has the status of someone standing." (Here the teacher turned his right hand to point upward, perhaps to represent Zaid standing. Ali's mind raced home to Kazem, "the servant of Ali and his family," and Ali wondered if Kazem would be offended if he knew that Ali was comparing him to someone in a book.)

"Consider." (The teacher now held the enormous book upright with a hand on each side.) "In analysis of the activity of the mind we have these elements: the subject 'Zaid,' the predicate 'standing,' and the relationship between the two. But maybe we also have a fourth element, judgment, which makes it possible to ask: 'Is Zaid standing or not?' After our mind has pictured the subject 'Zaid,' the predicate 'standing,' the possible relation that we express in Persian by the verb 'is,' we judge whether the predicate is true of the subject; because we can also say, 'Zaid is not standing.' We make a positive or negative judgment of the possible relationship.

"Yes. *But* another approach denies that we have four elements. According to this approach we have just subject and predicate, and our mind judges whether this subject belongs with this predicate or not. So we envisage only two things, and the third element, judgment, decides that yes, 'Zaid is standing,' or no, 'Zaid is not standing.' In any case, whether there are three or four elements, this knowledge is not like my simple, straightforward knowledge of Zaid or this book. It is compound knowledge, composed of more than one element, and we call it 'a verification.' " (The teacher briefly raised the book in front of him, apparently for emphasis. Years later when Ali taught in a *madreseh*, one day he found himself manhandling the text, instinctively following the example of his admired teacher of logic.)

One of the thirty-odd students spoke in the deliberately deep voice of a fourteen-year-old: "A problem. You said that knowing 'the servant of Zaid' is to know a piece of simple knowledge, a 'representation' in the mind. But it is compound knowledge, a 'verification,' since it involves a relation between two things: 'Zaid' and 'servant.' Then why do you and the commentary call it simple knowledge?" A student in a very shiny new tan frock coat on the other side of the class was nodding his white turban in energetic agreement. Ali knew the answer because he had thought of the question the night before and seen its irrelevance. Yet his mind kept racing home to Kazem, whose relation to the family, he knew, could never be explained by saying "the servant of Ali" or "the servant of Ali's father," and he wanted to tell Kazem that he was not trapped inside any logical cage either as a "representation" or a "verification."

The teacher finally put the book down and smiled so that the bottom ends of the two white streaks in his beard tilted outward. "A good problem. But notice that 'verification' occurs in situations in which a real judgment takes place. If I said, 'The servant belongs to Zaid' or 'The servant does not belong to Zaid,' then I have made a judgment, a verification about a relationship. But be careful—when we say, 'Zaid's servant,' has our mind judged something or just understood a relation? If our mind has understood an object with a relation, this is still simple knowledge, a direct image in the mind, a representation, just as the case would be if I said, 'the Qom River.' If I say, 'The standing Zaid is laughing,' then we understand that here 'standing Zaid' is a representation, which in this instance we are not judging, as we would be if I had said, 'Zaid is standing.' In a judgment we gather together things that existed separately in our mind. We create 'composed' or 'compound' knowledge, because we say one thing is the same as, or includes, the other, as when we say, 'Zaid is the father of Amr' or 'Zaid is a man.' As the Arabic maxim says, such knowledge is 'gathering and piecing together things dispersed.' " Almost everyone, including the student who had raised the difficulty, nodded in agreement.

Another pupil said: "But the opinion that a relation is a prior element can't be correct for negative propositions. If you say, 'Zaid is not standing,' it is merely a denial of the existence of such a relationship."

The teacher smiled again and looked downward for a moment. "You have to imagine a relation in order to deny it. If you had read a little farther in the margin, you would have found the answer. You are here to learn to reason, not just to learn to read. Think about the basic text and basic commentary on your own, and master it by asking about it in class. Otherwise, you will get caught in the houses of the genies." (Ali understood the joke even though he had not attended *madreseh* before: *madreseh* students called the checkerboard truth tables in the margins of their logic books "houses of genies.") "Then, when you have grown a trunk for the tree of your knowledge, look at the margins of your book, read the commentaries on the commentary, and sprout leaves and branches. But this tree draws its water and food from questions. Remember the Arabic proverb, The lesson is only a letter, yet repetitions should be a thousandfold. If you don't ask, my lessons themselves will dry up and wither."

The teacher now opened his book and read Mullah Abdollah's commentary on the sentence of Taftazani, which said in a very few lines in Arabic what the teacher had said in many more words in Persian. Ali had read the commentary very carefully the night before and had slowly convinced himself that he understood it completely. He was impressed by how right he had been about the meaning of nearly every part of the text and commentary. But he was also impressed by how very clear the book seemed after the teacher's explanation and defense of the commentator, and how thorough, careful, and convincing he found the book's approach. As he left the class at the end of the hour he no longer felt that his father and brother, who had until now been teaching him at home, were merely humoring him when they told him he had a real taste for mullah learning. As he went away from the class he watched the lamb's-tail clouds appear over one wall of the *madre-seh* and disappear far away over the opposite wall; even the absence of spreading trees and bushes did not bother him. Dense gardens belonged at home, but the huge, open courtyard of the *madreseh* allowed Ali to see and be seen in a world to which he wished to belong.

By the third day Ali had begun to see his teacher as more than a black beard with two white streaks. The teacher wore a black turban and therefore was, like Ali, a sayyed, a descendant of the Prophet who was entitled to wear either green or black on his head. His Persian was nearly perfect, but like so many people from Azerbaijan whose native language is Turkish, his Persian sometimes sounded slightly bookish. Once or twice he seemed to be quoting straight out of the *Golestan* of Saadi, the thirteenth-century literary classic so many Turkish Azerbaijanis learned by heart in order to master Persian, the principal language of Iran. Even though he was not yet old, he was somehow a very gray man, with a gray pallor and gray hair appearing at the sides of his turban, and there was even a grayish cast to his brown eyes. Yet he was old enough so that if he had been really clever, he would no longer be teaching one of the required books to fourteen-year-old *madreseh* students.

Ali did not wish him any cleverer. His explanations proved that he had every part of the text so thoroughly in his mind that he could always anticipate future difficulties and reexplain the significance of past texts as only someone could who had made the full meaning of the book entirely his own. His good gray head with its black eyebrows and black-and-white beard seemed so deeply involved in the text he taught that Ali felt his teacher spoke the inner mind of the enormous book he carried.

On this day Ali felt more daring and actually sat a little closer to the teacher than he had before. He knew that some classes were boisterous, with students shouting "Prove it!" and "How do you know?" and the like, and the relative decorum of his logic class gave him courage. The teacher began: "In the name of God, the Merciful, the Beneficent. In the underlying text Taftazani says" (and he read in Arabic): " 'When a word signifies everything that it was devised for it is called "full denotation." When it signifies a

part of what it was devised for it is "partial denotation." And
when it signifies something outside the concept but accompanying it, it is "connotation." ' " (As usual, he closed the book.) "Our
discussion today is about words and their relation to the things
they signify. Now, when we use the word 'dwelling' for all that
word can cover, including the building, the ground on which
it stands, the courtyard, everything—that is full denotation. And
if you use the word for one part of these things—for example, just
for the building—that is 'partial denotation.' If you apply it to
something associated with this concept but not part of it, then it is
'connotation' or 'implication.' For example, if you have bought a
dwelling, you have also by 'connotation' or 'implication' bought
the right of way to your dwelling." (The teacher finally put the
book down completely and put his hands forward.)

"Now, it is not enough for two things to be associated with each
other in the outside world. They must be associated in our minds
as well. And there must be no intermediates between the denotation and the connotation. Let us say that a man buys a dwelling
with the implicit understanding that this home has rights to
drinking water; then, when he takes possession, the city's water
supply fails and the ditch outside his door dries up. The buyer
cannot cancel the contract of sale *because*"—here the teacher
pointed the forefinger of his right hand upward—"the contract
implied *only* that he had rights to drinking water, not rights to demand the existence of water in order to fulfill the right to drinking
water. The possession of a dwelling is here"—he made a box with
his hands on the ground to his right—"and the existence of a supply of drinking water is here"—he now made a box on the ground
to his left. "These are not immediately associated with each other
in our mind and become associated with each other through
something intermediate here." (He formed a box directly in front
of himself.) "The thing in between, the thing really implied by the
dwelling, is the right to get water from the ditch outside the gate
and not the right to demand that the ditch be kept full by the municipality regardless of the water supply."

"With your permission, an important point." Ali spoke without
any hesitation in spite of the hubbub of students commenting to
each other on the teacher's commentary. He felt that the teacher

had been looking sideways at him, waiting for him to speak, and, in fact, after saying "ditch outside the gate," the teacher had half turned to Ali's side of the semicircle. "Your explanation was exactly to the point, but might the example be inexact? A dwelling is not a piece of ground and a building. The word 'building' may imply only the structure, but the word 'home' or 'dwelling' implies a building in which you reside and sleep and live." (Ali, in imitation of his teacher, at this point seized his book and raised it slightly.) "So the concept of a 'dwelling' or 'home' includes right of access and right to drinking water directly, by *'denotation'* and not indirectly by 'connotation' or 'implication.' "

At this point virtually all the students were nodding in agreement, and Ali had the feeling that if this had been the state school the teacher would have said "Bravo" and written "Bravo" in his record book. As it was, the Azerbaijani teacher's black eyebrows jutted forward and his brown eyes shone with approval. "Good, very good. For a change someone's criticism doesn't come from the commentaries in the margins. As we shall explain later, a lot of difficulties arise when an abstract concept gets mixed up with one of its points of reference in the outside world—what we call in Arabic 'mixture of the concept with the referent.' But in its abstract sense the concept of 'dwelling' is simply the concept of a residence, a place to stay.

"In the outside world, of course, it is different. In Azerbaijan to own a 'dwelling' or 'home' implies the right to sweep the snow from your roof into the meter between houses called 'the snow heap.' In Yazd, where heavy snows are as rare as palm trees would be in Azerbaijan, houses don't have a meter called a 'snow heap.' In fact, they sometimes don't have rights to the water in the ditch outside, since water comes to the cellars of most houses in underground irrigation channels from the surrounding hills. So 'dwelling' is the same abstract concept for houses in Azerbaijan and Yazd, but its connotation is different.

"If I tell you, 'Bring me a pen,' the pen denotes just this." (The teacher lifted his pen case from his pocket and took out a pen with a broad steel nib.) "But if I were to ask you to bring me a pen so that I can write a message, by connotation I would mean, 'Bring me the inkwell also and anything else in the pen case that you

need to make the pen work.' Now, if I asked you to tell me what a
pen is, you would not describe an inkwell to me. The word 'pen'
denotes this"—and the teacher waved his pen over his head in an
arc twice—"but can also connote this"—and he pointed inside his
pen case, presumably at an inkwell.

Ali had been nodding through most of this speech, much of
which he had really expected anyway. At the end he suddenly
realized that if his elder brother gave him a fountain pen, as
promised, he would make sure to keep his old pen case for the
time when he taught this chapter of *Mullah Abdollah's Commentary;*
it would provide a handsome example for him to use one day with
his own students.

· · ·

Modern Iranian secular education was planted in the nineteenth century in obedience to the formal decrees of royal government and then fed in the twentieth with the giant allocations of
state budgets. In contrast, when classical Islamic education began
over a millennium earlier, it grew almost unnoticed by any government, in the informality of the home and the mosque. Only
after several centuries of this largely self-sustained growth did
early Islamic education catch the eye of Islamic governments and
reveal itself to kings and ministers as an instrument they could
formalize, grasp, and use.

In the seventh century, simultaneously with the rise of Islam itself, Islamic education first arose from the bare necessities of religious belief. Muslims had a written scripture, the Koran, meant to
be read aloud. They also had sacred history, accounts of how the
Prophet Mohammed had received the revelation of the Koran and
how he had interpreted the Koran in the affairs of his growing religious community. Therefore Islamic education needed at the
very least to pass on the correct writing and reading of scripture,
the events surrounding its revelation, and its authoritative interpretation and use by the Prophet.

Within a generation of the Prophet's death, Islamic education
received its next great impetus from the new contacts Muslims
had with the educational traditions of Egypt and Western Asia.
After the great initial expansion of Islam in the seventh century,
the Islamic state found under its protection a whole variety of

educational institutions, from the academies of Alexandria to the law school of Beirut, the rabbinic schools of southern Iraq, and the great medical school in the southern Iranian town of Jonday-shapur. By and large the confrontation between the Islamic government and these institutions was one of disregard or neglect. Islam lived in peace with Judaism, Christianity, and Zoroastrianism, but early Muslims saw neither intellectual nor moral virtue in the subtle theological differences with which earlier religions and sects had armed themselves to fight each other in the pre-Islamic Middle East. As for the academies, they mostly survived. Some flourished as never before because they no longer had to contend with a Persian or Byzantine emperor who dictated what orthodox belief should be; others languished because the support of such emperors had been essential to their financial health and prestige.

It was not long before Muslims acquired an intellectual curiosity about these schools and also acquired some converts from among their graduates. A great age of translation opened, for Arabic soon became a lingua franca used by Jewish, Christian, and Muslim scholars alike. The large fragments left from the learning of antiquity (and, to a lesser extent, of the learning of ancient Iran and India as well) were salvaged, tidied up, and presented in Arabic to an audience that often examined them with a keenness of insight and, even more often, with an enthusiasm that these fragments had not inspired for many centuries in the blasé audiences of the Middle East.

Typical of such enthusiasts was the caliph Mamun, supreme ruler of the Muslims in the early ninth century and a lavish patron of translations into Arabic of ancient texts, especially the texts of Greek philosophy. Mamun said that one night in a dream he saw sitting on his bed a man "white in color, with a ruddy complexion, broad forehead, joined eyebrows, bald head and bloodshot eyes." Mamun, not surprisingly, was "filled with fear." "Who are you?" he asked, and the man replied, "I am Aristotle." "Then I was delighted," explained Mamun, "and said, 'Sage, may I ask you a question?' He said, 'Ask it.' Then I asked, 'What is good?' " And they proceeded to have a short but satisfying conversation that probably afforded Mamun a restful night and certainly allowed him to think that his patronage of translation was a blessing for Islam, since Aristotle had conveniently assured him that reason and revelation can be combined for the general good.

Islamic education received its impetus not only from the magnificent translations of Aristotle and Galen but also from the living technique of the many scholastic traditions that came under the protection of the Islamic government. Not that Muslims themselves lacked for theological questions; these they had in abundance, and they disputed them with growing subtlety. How, for instance, could some statements in the Koran that God caused everything be reconciled with the many statements that God rewarded good and punished evil, since God could hardly punish evil He himself had caused? To deal with these questions they found to hand a whole variety of systems of argument that had been used in the ancient world.

There was, first of all, the magnificent syllogism, that ruthless machinery of formal logic that moves in stately progress from simple figures (All logicians are boring; Lewis Carroll is a logician; therefore Lewis Carroll is boring) to its many more complicated figures, in all of which the conclusion is tightly secure if the two premises are granted. The syllogism was largely Aristotle's discovery, and a good part of the reverence for Aristotle in the two millennia following his death, including the reverence felt in the Islamic Middle East, was based on the close association of the syllogism with his name. But Aristotle had realized there were processes of reasoning in which the conclusion was a matter of opinion, not only because the premises might not be true (some logicians are, in fact, not boring) but also because a discussion had begun that, either because of circumstances or because of the nature of its raw materials (for example, observations from nature), yielded strangely qualified premises. (The logicians I have met have been boring at the times they were with me.)

Alongside these kinds of analyses of thinking the ancient world offered the Muslim controversialists highly developed theories of rhetoric from classical rhetoricians concerned not only with persuasion but also with the exact analysis of speech. They analyzed, for example, the types of similes that could occur in speech. If we say *Alice in Wonderland* is "like" a book of philosophy, do we mean that it is an "example" of a book of philosophy, or that both it and a book of philosophy share certain characteristics, or that it is a parable—a saying, in other words—about philosophy, or something yet different? These rhetorical techniques were useful to lawyers who had to persuade Roman courts both by skillful use of speech and by exacting analysis of the arguments and the law relevant to the case. They were also useful to Jews and Christians seeking to analyze the rhetoric of scripture. The Christians and the Jews, like the Muslims after them, evolved principles for this purpose partly from their own wit and partly by selectively choosing intellectual instruments from their intellectual surroundings. (The rhetorical analysis of similes in scripture is an example.) In fact, Jews and Christians added intellectual instruments, because they could bring questions of intention (especially God's intention for mankind) more prominently into play: If, according to Deuteronomy 21:33, God is troubled that the corpses of the ungodly should be exposed overnight, how much more must He be troubled by the exposure of the corpses of the godly (a kind of inference called by the Latin term *a fortiori* in the West).

The early Muslims, learning techniques of systematic discussion from their own disagreements and from their contacts with the older traditions of the eastern Mediterranean and the Middle East, found justification for such techniques in the Koran and the example of Mohammed. But some Muslims felt that no such justification existed, that these techniques were foreign to Islam and dragged the baggage of alien thoughts along with their alien methods and that therefore these techniques caused divisiveness among Muslims and should be rejected.

Although the opponents of the systematic methods of analyzing religious language never disappeared completely, and although they succeeded in excluding certain elements of the ancient traditions, by and large the proponents of such systematic discussion won. The disputation, in which some form of systematic reasoning had its place, became so much a part of the style of learning in the Islamic Middle East and North Africa that theology was called "the science of talk." Hugo Sanctallensis, a medieval Christian Spaniard who translated an Arabic text on the art of disputation into Latin, complained that the Muslims plainly gave more attention to the formal structure of their theology than to its content, something he intended to avoid by not writing his book in the "Arabic" style of the dialogue between opponents.

The triumph among Muslim thinkers of systematic methods of discussion, and especially of the methods of Aristotle, was above all the work of one man, the eleventh-century philosopher Avicenna. Abu Ali Ibn Sina (or Avicenna, as the medieval Latin translators rendered the last two parts of his name) was, perhaps, the first Muslim to make the logical traditions of the classical world thoroughly his own. They became so much his own that in his treatises, as thought through, presented, and sometimes improved by his ingenious mind, these traditions no longer seemed a slightly clumsy and foreign invention but an authentic child of the Islamic tradition itself. And in recognition of what he had done the Islamic tradition has ever since called him "the master and leader."

Avicenna accomplished this triumph at the culmination of the early Islamic period of informal learning that passed from person to person in the home and mosque. Avicenna left a fragment of an autobiography (completed by his closest pupil) that shows how this individualistic tradition of learning was experienced by one of its most brilliant spirits. He was born in 980, in the far northeast of the Iranian cultural area, to a middle-level official, who provided for Avicenna's elementary education, as would most fathers in similar circumstances at that time. He hired a teacher of the Koran and a teacher of literature for his son. Avicenna, in the tradition of so many premodern writers who saw intellectual modesty as appropriate only for the intellectually modest, says that by the age of nine "I had finished the Koran and many works of literature, so that people were greatly amazed at me." His father, as befitted an administrator, wanted his son to learn the newest methods of calculation and bookkeeping and so sent his son to "a vegetable seller who used the Indian calculation" system of the numerals (along with the arithmetic operations they simplified), which were some centuries later passed to Europe and called Arabic numerals.

Then, Avicenna relates, a man came to the provincial capital where he and his family lived who claimed to know philosophy, "so my father had him stay in our house, and he devoted himself to educating me." Avicenna had already studied some Islamic law and learned the dialectic techniques its specialists gloried in, and consequently he had become "one of the nimblest of questioners." He turned this technique on philosophy, as, in fact, the Islamic tradition itself had done and would continue to do. With his philosophy teacher he read the *Isagoge*, that wonderfully clear introduction to Aristotelian logic that a Syrian philosopher, Porphyry, had written in Greek six hundred years earlier and that had proved a favorite elementary schoolbook in the Middle Ages at both ends of the ancient world in its Latin and Arabic translations. Avicenna says that whatever problem his teacher posed "I conceptualized better than he, so he advised my father against my taking up any occupation other than learning."

While he continued to study simpler parts of logic with his teacher he turned to books to learn its "deeper intricacies," and from commentaries on books like the *Isagoge* he mastered traditional logic. Then he proceeded on his own to master Euclid's geometry, Ptolemy's great astronomical work, the *Almagest*, and then began to study the rest of the natural and metaphysical sciences available in books; and, as he says, "the gates of knowledge began to open before me." To these subjects he added medicine, a somewhat easier subject, in which "I excelled in a very short time," to Avicenna's great good fortune, since he found that people in the eleventh—as in the twentieth century—paid far more for medical than for philosophic advice. He also frequented circles devoted to disputing questions of Islamic law, even though he was only fifteen years old.

Very soon after this the young physician Avicenna fell into a sort of fever of philosophy that gripped him for a year and a half.

> During this time I did not sleep completely through a single night or devote myself to anything else [but philosophy and logic] by day. I compiled a set of files for myself, and for each proof that I examined, I entered into the files its syllogistic premises, their classification and what might follow from them. I pondered over the conditions that might apply to their premises, until I had verified this question for myself. . . . Whenever sleep overcame me or I became conscious of weakening, I would turn aside to drink a cup

of wine, so that my strength would return to me. And whenever sleep seized me I would see those very problems in my dreams; and many questions became clear to me in my sleep. I continued in this until all of the sciences were deeply rooted within me and I understood them as far as is humanly possible. Everything which I knew at that time is just as I know it now; I have not added anything to it to this day.

Avicenna's growing reputation as a physician gave him an opportunity to cure the local ruler, who, in gratitude, opened the royal library to his young doctor. And Avicenna, finding each room of the library devoted to a different science, studied the catalogue and devoured the books he had not yet seen. At about the age of twenty he felt ready to write his first compendium of knowledge. He was now a welcome figure at the courts of the rich and powerful, and, wearing the dress of a scholar of Islamic law, "with a fold of his headdress under the chin," traveled around eastern Iran like a young Mozart of philosophy, to be met and admired by the discriminating. One manuscript of this biography adds: "It is said that as a young man he was one of the handsomest people of his time and that on Friday, when he left his house to go to the mosque, the people used to crowd together in the streets and roads in order to catch a glimpse of his perfection and beauty."

Avicenna eventually reached central Iran, just in time to treat the king of Rayy, a great city that lies very close to the site of modern Tehran. This king was suffering from the delusion that he had been transformed into a cow, and "All the day he would cry out to this one and that, 'Kill me, so that a good stew may be prepared from my flesh.' " Meanwhile, as the king-cow refused to eat, he was wasting away (and hence was diagnosed as "melancholic"). The royal physicians, in despair, called Avicenna in on the case. He immediately sent a message to the king: "Give good tidings to the patient, and say, 'The butcher is coming to kill you,' " at which news the deluded king is supposed to have rejoiced. Then Avicenna, knife in hand, came to the king and ordered two men to bring "the cow" to the middle of the room, to bind him hand and foot, and throw him down. On hearing this the patient cheerfully threw himself down and was bound. Avicenna sat next to him and "placed his hand on the patient's ribs as is the custom of butchers. 'Oh, what a lean cow!' said he. 'It is not fit to be killed; give it fodder until it grows fat.' " Avicenna ordered them to unbind him and set food before him. And from this time on, whenever they gave the king the draughts and drugs Avicenna prescribed, the royal physicians said, "Eat well, for this is a fine fattener for cows." A month of this treatment cured the king completely.

After his successful treatment of the melancholic cow-king, Avicenna's soaring reputation as a royal physician gave him political opportunities that few court physicians have ever had. A short time later, when Avicenna cured the king of Hamadan, a large city in western Iran, of a mere colic, the king made him an official boon companion, and, at a point of some danger to the kingdom, the court urged the king to make Avicenna his vizier, or first minister. But the troops mutinied; and to save Avicenna's life, the king sent him into exile. Forty days later the king had another attack of colic, and this time the troops acquiesced, Avicenna returned, and he was rewarded for his cure by the vizierate. "Indeed," says one medieval Iranian author, "since Alexander the Great, whose minister was Aristotle, no king has had such a minister as Avicenna." Finally this king died of a third attack of colic (complicated by other ailments), all of which seized him, says Avicenna's pupil, because the king seldom followed his doctor's orders.

Avicenna, hesitating between two royal offers to appoint him vizier and judging the political situation uncertain, went into hiding in the house of a druggist, where, working without notes, he tried to complete the *Shifa* (literally, "The Healing"), his great *summa* of learning. He had never stopped writing even when he was the leading official of the state. "He used to rise every morning before dawn," one of his students reported, "and write a couple of pages of the *Shifa*. Then, when true dawn appeared, he used to give audience to his students. . . . We used to continue our studies until the morning grew bright, and then perform our prayers behind him. As soon as we came forth we were met at the gate of his house by a thousand mounted men, comprising the dignitaries and notables, as well as such as had boons to crave or were in difficulties"; and Avicenna gave himself over to affairs of state. Now, in hiding with the druggist and freed from affairs of state, he wrote fifty pages every day until he had finished the chapters on physics and metaphysics and had begun the chapter on logic. At this point he was found, arrested, and confined in a castle for four months.

This episode seems to have cured kings of any further interest in naming Avicenna as a philosopher-vizier, and from this time he was supported by his patrons merely as a physician and an ornament of learning. He lived on in the city of Isfahan, in the center of Iran, until he fell ill at about the age of fifty-six, when, ever the decisive diagnostician, he decided that "the [inner] governor who used to govern my body is now incapable of government; so treatment is no longer of any use." Refusing medicine, he died a few days later in Hamadan.

Avicenna's reputation was first established and survived longest in the field of medicine. His major medical book, *The Canon*, soon spread throughout the East. In the West, from its translation into Latin in the twelfth century until the rise of experimental medicine in the sixteenth and seventeenth centuries, its philosophically conceived and systematic codification of the medical experience of the Greek and Islamic worlds made it a favorite of European doctors and medical schools alike. If *The Canon* passed on many useful treatments and some of the misleading anatomical and physiological information found in ancient authors such as Galen, it also contributed new information, such as the contagious nature of tuberculosis and the role of contaminated water in spreading disease. Perhaps it was the medical reputation of Avicenna, together with his ingenuity in inventing astronomical instruments, that accounts for his reputation in Persian folklore as the wizard, the master magician who could do anything.

Yet both in the East and the West, Avicenna had far more influence on the narrow world of higher learning as a philosopher than as a physician. In the Islamic philosophical tradition, he provided the classic language and classical articulation of many fundamental ideas. At the end of the thirteenth century, when Roger Bacon, a sort of brother wizard of the Western tradition, summed up the state of philosophical knowledge in western Europe in his time, he wrote that the greatness of Aristotle had been recovered principally through the Arabs, "and in particular Avicenna, Aristotle's imitator, who completed philosophy as far as he could." Avicenna's influence owes a lot to his ability to assimilate the ideas of his predecessors and present them as his own with a clarity and comprehensiveness that his predecessors had lacked. He was the Islamic philosopher who best understood the deep wisdom of Oscar Wilde's opinion that talent imitates while genius steals. The distinction in Taftazani between the word translated as "concept" or "apprehension" and the word translated as "assent" or "affirmation," a distinction accepted in East and West as fundamental to the philosophy of logic for centuries after Avicenna, had been anticipated by the Greeks and by one of the great Islamic philosophers antecedent to Avicenna. But only in Avicenna did the distinction become a clear-cut either-or distinction, that apparently accounted for all the alternatives.

Avicenna made a similarly clear-cut distinction between "essence" and "existence," two terms previously held by many philosophers to be necessarily linked. An "essence" is what makes something what it is, and in the absence of this "essence" the thing no longer is what it was; while an "accident" can be removed and the thing retains its essence and still is what it was. Thus a "laughing" man can stop laughing and still be a man, so "laughing" is an "accident"; but a man cannot be a man without his humanness. Some philosophers had held that the reasoning that proves something is an essence proves that it exists; Avicenna argued convincingly that it only proves that if this essence is possible, it might exist.

From this distinction Avicenna created a new argument for the existence of God, whose existence according to this argument is "necessary," given that other essences are only "possible." The argument (in much simplified form) begins by saying that the actual, realized existence of any possibly existent essence must be caused either by another possibly existent essence or by a necessarily existent essence. Some essences do actually exist; unless we assume an infinite regress of possibly existent essences causing each other—and Avicenna has a highly original argument *against* holding that existent essences are an endless succession of dependencies of "possibles"—there must be a necessary being. The care and ingenuity with which Avicenna worked out this original argument made it one of that small number of arguments, or "proofs," for the existence of God that have subsisted, even though much battered, over the centuries. It was adopted by Maimonides and Aquinas, influenced Spinoza, may well have influenced the remarkably similar "proof" of Leibniz, and still has its supporters in the twentieth century.

The method by which Avicenna argues his proof breathes the atmosphere of his age and circumstances. For example, at one point he states: "Everything that exists is either necessary or possible. On the first assumption, it has immediately been established that there is something necessarily existent. . . . On the second assumption, we must show that the existence of the possible ends at the necessarily existent." The ancients had recognized the neatness of arguing by contradictories. ("Lewis Carroll is boring" and "Lewis Carroll is not boring" are contradictories; while "Lewis Carroll was blond" and "Lewis Carroll was brunet" are contraries, since they do not exhaust the possibilities—maybe he was a redhead.) Muslim thinkers loved to argue by using contraries (which meant developing and memorizing exhaustive lists of possible alternatives), but they loved even more to argue by contradictories, as Avicenna did above. Surely the cultivation of informal circles of debate, sometimes including Jews, Christians, and Zoroastrians but consisting more often of just Muslims, goes a long way toward explaining this preference for contradictories in philosophy and theology, since contradictories propel the rhetoric of argument so efficiently. And the spoken style "You say . . . but I say" is a preferred dialectical style of Muslim thinkers in their written works from the earliest times to the present day. At least half of the textbooks of Qom and Najaf are written in this style.

Avicenna's biographer, the philosopher Juzajani, who completed the autobiographical fragment Avicenna left on his earlier life, makes a remarkable confession about another aspect of Avicenna's intellectual style: "For the twenty-five years that I was his companion and servant, I did not once see him, when he came across a new book, examine it from beginning to end. Rather, he would go directly to its difficult passages and intricate problems and look at what its author had to say about them." He did so not only because by twenty-one he felt that there was no knowledge but he knew it, and not only because he was a master plagiarist working at breakneck speed while running governments and treating kings, but also because by his time Arabic books had begun to assume a predictable order in which subjects were treated in the same sequence as they had been dealt with in the previous standard book in the field. In a manuscript culture, in which indices were an extreme rarity (after all, every manuscript copy would have different pagination), such predictability in the order of subjects made it possible to disembowel books without complete readings. The very compendia that Avicenna wrote contributed to this tendency. When the *madresehs*, the first formal, long-lived Islamic schools, were founded, a generation after Avicenna's death, their choice of school texts set a final stamp on this tendency toward the use of a prescribed order in basic texts.

With the appearance of the *madreseh*, the old style of learning that Avicenna describes—the wandering from teacher to teacher, the informal discussion circle, the debates of learned men thrust into each other's presence by a bored or curious monarch—did not disappear from the Islamic Near East. Physicians in particular usually passed on the art of medicine in the old, informal, individualistic manner, along with a great deal of philosophy and astronomy that were supposed to explain the principles of medicine. Also, interest in less strictly Muslim subjects such as philosophy (and even the less "practical" aspects of astronomy) was suspect in the new formal institutions. The physician, with his court connections and his independent educational tradition, was one of the few transmitters of written culture relatively unaffected by the appearance of the new *madresehs*. Nevertheless *madresehs* came to dominate learning in the Islamic Middle East as much as universities do in the contemporary West.

The *madresehs* made their definitive appearance (after a century of uncertain and largely unsuccessful attempts to appear) in the late eleventh century, at least a hundred years before their Western counterparts, the European universities. For the Islamic world *madresehs* really were something new: schools founded on sub-

stantial charitable trusts that had been given in perpetuity for the
teaching of a specific kind of curriculum. The founders of these
madresehs, often viziers and sultans, by the size of their endowments and the stipulations in their deeds of gift, guaranteed that
these new schools would last long and take in a large number of
students (often as boarders), whom they would attempt to teach a
fairly uniform curriculum under the supervision of paid teachers.

The curricula varied, of course, not only according to the stipulations of the founders but also according to the wishes of the
teachers and directors of the *madresehs*. The *madreseh* was not expected to give its students basic literacy or an elementary knowledge of arithmetic. Either private tutors, such as Avicenna's
teachers of Koran and literature and the vegetable seller who
taught him "Indian calculation," or small, unendowed neighborhood Koran schools, which lived on the fees they collected, still
provided the very beginnings of education. What the *madreseh* was
expected to give was a basic education in Islamic religious law. At
the same time, from the very beginning it was intended that the
madreseh should teach the student the relation of law to its sources,
especially to the Koran and the accounts of what Mohammed said
and did.

Very soon the sciences of language—in particular, grammar
and rhetoric—became firmly established in the *madreseh* curriculum. How could one analyze the raw material of the law unless
one accurately understood the Koran and the accounts of what the
perfect Muslim, the Prophet Mohammed, did and said, and knew
how to analyze the similes and other figures of speech used in this
raw material? But, then, a set of systematic principles for deriving
the law from its sources was also needed, a science that would
sharpen the ability to make strict and consistent use of such instruments of reasoning as the syllogism and the argument *a fortiori*.

This science was jurisprudence, and its presence in the higher
stages of *madreseh* learning encouraged the introduction of treatises on logic at earlier stages in the curriculum. Logic could then
be used at the higher level of study, which showed the consistency
of the law (at least in its relation to its sources and in the relation
of its different parts). And, of course, the full meaning of law

could be fully understood only through a systematic study of the Creator's intentions for his creation; so scholastic theology in turn moved into what became its firmly held position in these new fortresses of learning.

The new *madresehs* in fact were not unlike fortresses. They were great enclosed spaces and became almost as predictable a part of an Islamic town of consequence as were the mosque and bazaar. Like fortresses, they were seen and saw themselves as the primary focus of attempts to preserve learning and defend orthodoxy. In many cases they also became a part of the armamentarium of the government, in that they produced highly literate graduates in numbers large enough to supply the bureaucracies of governments as well as the positions more or less reserved for the religiously learned, the *ulema* or mullahs, as the Iranians called them. The patronage of *madresehs* even provided the government with a vital piece of ideological armor. Although the mullahs avoided saying that any specific regime was sanctioned by God, they did say that the populace was well advised to obey any regime that protected true religion, and there was no more eloquent way to protect true religion than to found *madresehs* and foster their graduates.

For these very reasons, in the first thousand years of Islamic Near Eastern history Shiah learning had a very hard time of it. Most of the regimes in this first thousand years were Sunni, and in the view of Sunni regimes Shiah learning was not "true religion"; only Sunni Islam qualified as "true." There had, in fact, been a few Shiah dynasties a generation before the spread of the *madreseh*, in the time of Avicenna, who had preferred the patronage of Shiah kings (even ones who thought they were cows) to that of the Sunnis. About twenty years after Avicenna's death, when a Sunni dynasty had taken over Baghdad and established a large Sunni *madreseh* there, Tusi, a great Shiah scholar, left Baghdad and moved south to the solidly Shiah town of Najaf. Here he established his own school, which may have been a proper Shiah *madreseh*, on the model of the new Sunni *madreseh* in Baghdad, although we have only a hazy idea of the early history of the Najaf school. It does seem certain, however, that he established a curriculum, in part based on his own texts, and the scholars of the Shiah *madresehs* of Najaf in our time believe themselves to be descended from Tusi through a continuous line of teachers which stretches from the eleventh century to the twentieth.

Tusi's establishment of a school of Shiah learning in Najaf marks the maturity of Shi'ism as a developed system of Islamic thought. To both the friends and foes of Shi'ism the political distinction between the Shiah and the Sunnis had been clear-cut from the start. The Shiah, or "partisans" (of Ali), were those members of the Islamic community who held that the leadership of that community had been left by the Prophet Mohammed to Ali and his descendants (often called "the House of Mohammed"). The Sunnis disagreed; they held that political leadership among Muslims should be determined by some means other than heredity and that Mohammed had not designated Ali as his successor. The Sunnis achieved a virtual monopoly of political power from the seventh to the ninth centuries, the first three centuries of Islam, and they remain the majority among the Muslims until this day.

Nevertheless, the Shiah minority, which accepted specific designation and heredity as the basis for leadership, believed they knew which descendants of Mohammed living among them *should* be accepted as the actual political leaders of all Muslims, even if these figures whom they revered were living in obscurity. And many of these descendants of the Prophet did live in relative obscurity until one of them, the twelfth leader in the succession from Ali, disappeared in 873. The Shiah believed that this twelfth leader, whom they called and call "the Imam of the Age," had disappeared only to reappear in the fullness of time as a messianic leader who would create the perfect Islamic political community. The Sunnis thought that the Shiah, in clinging to specific designation and heredity as indicators of political leadership, had worked themselves into a trap, because their leader had died without leaving any issue.

Gradually the legal and theological differences between Shi'ism and Sunnism became as clear as the political differences. The Shiah differed from the Sunnis about some points of substantive law; for example, Shiah law gave women greater rights to inheritance of property and contained a larger list of objects and situations that made a Muslim ritually unclean. But the most significant differences appeared in their contrasting intellectual approaches. The Shiah in general believed that human ways of reasoning were not essentially different from God's ways of reasoning and that humans could therefore decode much of the reasoning behind the construction of the natural and moral world. Most Sunnis disagreed and charged that it would limit God to say that He should be expected to conform to even the best determinations of right and wrong or possible and impossible of which human reason was capable.

In the absence of Shiah dynasties the survival of Shiah learning remained precarious and dependent on the scattered Shiah communities in places such as Najaf, in southern Iraq, until the great religious revolution brought to Iran by the Safavi dynasty in the early 1500s. Until then Shi'ism had been a minority belief in Iran, a distinguishing characteristic of a few provincial areas and towns such as Qom. Then, at the beginning of the sixteenth century, the Safavis, drawing their support from the Shiah Turkoman tribes of Azerbaijan, the northwest province of Iran, imposed Shi'ism on almost all parts of the Iranian nation. Not all Iranians accepted Shi'ism easily. But the nearly simultaneous rise of two mighty Sunni empires, the Ottomans of Turkey on the West and the Moghuls of India on the East, along with the continuing threat from Sunnis in Central Asia, seems to have made the imposition of a distinctive official religion somewhat more palatable to Iranians; it gave a religious basis to the desire of Iranians to withstand the rule of these powerful neighbors. Iranians were particularly determined to resist conquest by the Ottoman Turks, even if this meant that the Safavi king, or "Sophi," as Milton called him, could at times carry on such resistance only by scorching the earth of Iran to discourage the Ottomans' advance. In the seventeenth century Milton (who was a contemporary of both the Safavis and the Ottomans) described in *Paradise Lost* how:

> . . . *Bactrian Sophi, from the horns*
> *Of Turkish crescent, leaves all waste beyond*
> *The realm of Aladuk, in his retreat*
> *To Tauris and Casbeen.*

If, to protect the Iranian homeland the Safavi, or "Sophi," had to leave the very lands he saved scorched and wasted, he was a nurturing rain for the Shiah learned men, the mullahs. Before the Safavis, the Iranian Shiah had not had a strong tradition of learning, and therefore at the beginning of the sixteenth century there were more Shiah learned men in Iraq and in Lebanon than in Iran. The Safavis founded Shiah *madresehs* in numbers in which they had never existed before. And the attraction of these *madresehs* and of royal patronage in general drew a stream of Shiah learned men from other parts of the Islamic world to Iran. Shi'ism was by no means an "Iranian religion," but Iran was emphatically a Shiah kingdom, usually the only Shiah kingdom. And from the sixteenth century to the present the weight of Iran among the Shiah, whether in India, the Arabian Peninsula, Syria, eastern Turkey, or Iraq, has continued to be enormous.

One Shiah mullah, Sayyed Nematollah Jazayeri, born in 1640 in an Arabic-speaking village in southern Iraq near the Persian Gulf, has left us a touching memoir of his struggles from his earliest education until he was appointed as a "lecturer" in a recently founded Iranian Shiah *madreseh*. A lachrymose and self-pitying man, he appropriately begins: "In this brief life, how many afflictions have befallen me." He remembered that at the age of five he was sitting and playing with a little friend when his father came and said: "Little son, come with me and we will go to the teacher so that you can learn to read and write and attain a high station." "I wept at these words and refused but it was no use." Soon Sayyed Nematollah thought of a new stratagem: he would finish his course of study as soon as possible so he could return to his games, and in a short time he finished reading the Koran and some classical Arabic poems as well. He now asked his father to release him to play with his friend, but instead his father proposed to send him to yet another teacher to learn the paradigms of the Arabic verb with all its contortions and spiky eccentricities. Sayyed Nematollah cried again, and this time his father, to teach him his place, sent him to a blind teacher, who required the young sayyed to act as his guide as well as his pupil. By the time he completed his course of study with the blind teacher, Sayyed Nematollah had become curious and wanted to read a serious book on Arabic grammar. The next teacher he found, one of his relatives, would teach him only after he had compelled his pupil to pick mulberry leaves each day for his silkworms and to cut fodder for his livestock. And the little sayyed began to grow bald from carrying bales of hay and mulberry leaves on his head.

He soon reached a point at which he had to go to a neighboring village to study the next grammar book in the curriculum. From there he went to the town of Hovayzeh, in the swamp country near the Tigris in southern Iraq, because he had heard that there was an extremely learned man there whose presence would make worthwhile the journey through narrow waterways filled with mosquitoes, "each as large as a wasp." The teacher in Hovayzeh, however, laid an even heavier burden of labor on his pupils than had the cattle and silkworm owner. The learned man of Hovayzeh required not only agricultural "service" from his pupils, he also laid down a rule that if they went to the nearby waterway to relieve themselves, they had to carry back two stones or two bricks from an abandoned fort there for the teacher's house.

The town of Hovayzeh not only had a distinguished teacher, it also had a *madreseh*, which these pupils attended until noon in order to discuss and dispute in the classical manner; the rest of the day they spent struggling to stay alive and to learn their lessons. Afternoons they gathered melon skins, which they washed to discover if any edible fragments of melon still stuck to them. Nights when there was moonlight they tried to study; when there was no moonlight they recited to each other those texts they knew by heart.

The young sayyed now wanted to go to Iran to a *madreseh* in the important southwestern Iranian city of Shiraz, and, after a visit home, he started out for Shiraz against his father's will. He stripped off his clothes and waded into the river, then hid behind the rudder of a boat on the first part of his journey so that no one should see him and bring him back. His father tried to catch up with him at the port city of Basra, but when he heard that his father had reached Basra, the young sayyed quickly found a ship and left for Shiraz. By now, at eleven years of age, he was well launched on an academic game that he was determined not to let his father interrupt.

Barefoot, he and his older brother, who had joined him, crossed the mountains that stood between the Persian Gulf port near Shiraz and that city. A fellow passenger had taught them their first Persian sentence: "We want the Mansuriyeh *madreseh*," and although each of them could remember only half the sentence, they found their way to the great *madreseh*. Here they studied for a number of years, and Sayyed Nematollah barely managed to subsist by copying books while undergoing privations that, while probably real enough, he contrives to describe with loving emphasis on every one of his "afflictions." He wants, of course, to convey that sense of learning won through many ordeals which provided a background much admired in a successful mullah. On winter mornings, after the first prayer, when his hand bled slightly with cold as he wrote marginal notes in his text, he was probably well aware that someday—if he ever made it—he would (as he did) write: "From the violence of the cold my hand ran with blood."

He was now attending the courses of important teachers, many of them, like himself, of Arab origin. One day news of the death of a relative caused him to miss the class of one of these Arab teachers, the distinguished sheikh Jaafar Bahrani. The next day when the young sayyed appeared, the sheikh said: "God curse your father and mother if I teach you again. . . . After class go away and mourn for yourself." Sayyed Nematollah swore to Sheikh Bahrani that he would never again, whatever misfortunes might befall him, miss class.

Eventually the sheikh had more than his student's exemplary attendance record to admire. A very difficult problem arose in the sheikh's class on jurisprudence, which he set as a question for them all to answer orally. The next day when the chance came, Sayyed Nematollah gave an explanation that was so far superior to all others that Sheikh Bahrani not only said that the sayyed was right but asked him to repeat his explanation so that he, the teacher, could write it in the margin of his text. After this he ordered the other students to carry the sayyed on their shoulders one by one in recognition of his superiority. To top it all, the sheikh invited him home and offered him the hand of his daughter. But Sayyed Nematollah was aware that he had now won a place in the *madreseh* system even without a marriage alliance, and anyway he wanted to be free to move on and gather yet more credentials. He had become a "traveling" scholar, a figure every bit as honored in the Islamic tradition as in the medieval European and nineteenth-century German traditions. He excused himself and said, "God willing . . . after I have completed my studies and have become a learned man I will marry," and continued living in comparative poverty in his second-floor room in the Mansuriyeh Madreseh.

After several years he went to Isfahan, capital of the Safavi government and site of many *madresehs* of the Safavid period whose outward finish of gloriously colored tiles with arabesque designs give an impression of continuity and harmony of architectural and painted space unrivaled anywhere in the world. Sayyed Nematollah, however, did not make it into one of these graceful *madresehs* right away; instead he ended up in the most miserable *madreseh* in town. It had only four small dormitory rooms, and if one of the students got up at night to relieve himself he could not avoid waking up everyone else in the room as he left.

Then suddenly everything changed; he attracted the attention of Mohammed Bagher Majlesi, who was on his way to becoming the most influential mullah of his time, and Majlesi made room for Sayyed Nematollah in his house for four years. In the Safavi period important mullahs were men of enormous power who could call kings to account and who sometimes controlled wealth that rivaled the wealth of the king himself. Through his connection to Majlesi the sayyed was appointed a lecturer at a newly founded *madreseh,* where he taught for eight years. But by this time the weakness of sight that he first experienced when reading by moonlight in Hovayzeh became a serious hindrance to his work. He sought professional help, but the sayyed, who was apparently not bedazzled by Avicennian medicine, says these "cures" only increased his pain.

Sayyed Nematollah resigned his post and resumed his travels, and now that he was a somebody, in most places he was received with honor. Predictably, he stumbled into all sorts of "afflictions" of which he complains, including a battle between the Safavis and the Ottomans. Finally he settled as a teacher, respected by the students and the authorities, in Shushtar, a town near Iraq in the southwest corner of Iran, where he wrote his autobiography in 1678. At the end of this strange document he confesses that the thought of all the afflictions of his life (which afflictions, in summing up, he classifies in seven large categories) still oppresses him. Somehow, in spite of the wealth and power that the Iranian Shiah *madreseh* system offered to a successful mullah, Sayyed Nematollah's stratagem had finally failed; he was never able to complete the game he was snatched away from at the age of five and never found satisfactions that could adequately make up for its loss.

Another and far more jaundiced view of Shiah Islamic education is given by Ahmad Kasravi, known to present-day Iranians as the most outspoken intellectual opponent of established Shi'ism in modern Iranian history. Avicenna's autobiography depicts the virtuoso—creating, fabricating, and, with every expedient available in his fertile mind, shifting for himself in an uninstitutionalized world of learning with individually hired teachers and quirky patrons. Sayyed Nematollah's autobiography shows us a man thrust into a far more institutionalized system of education, which became so much an accustomed home that it never occurred to him that he could escape it, no matter how near suffocation he may have felt. Ahmad Kasravi seems the sternest of the three, a courageous but irritable moralist who assumed that he not only had a mission but also had an innate ability to judge all the forms of learning that came his way, including his long *madreseh* education.

It is not surprising that Ahmad Kasravi thought he had a mission. His grandfather had been a respected mullah who built a mosque, which he then supervised. When Kasravi was born, in Tabriz, in 1890, he was not only named after this grandfather but was expected to succeed eventually to his grandfather's inheritable "mosque and law court." For this reason, Kasravi writes, "I was brought up with a respect that few children have. . . . My mother forbade me to go into the street and mix with other children; in fact, she even kept me from playing."

Kasravi's father, a merchant, though pious, disapproved of many of the religious practices of his time. He disliked the way different factions of mullahs involved great masses of the population in their quarrels to the extent that the factions within Shi'ism would not intermarry and would sometimes even riot against each other. He thought that it was a waste to give money to *rowzeh-khans*, those preachers who specialized in giving recitals (for pay) of the sufferings of the sacred figures of Shi'ism, especially Hosain; and, very uncharacteristically of his time and class, he refused to let *rowzeh-khans* in his house.

When Kasravi was five and complained that he could not read the letters his father wrote home while traveling, Kasravi's parents sent him to a Koran school, the only elementary education that existed. The mullah who ran the school knew only the Koran and very little Persian. (After all, they lived in Tabriz, Milton's "Tauris," the capital of the Turkish-speaking province of Azerbaijan.) Furthermore, the mullah had lost all his teeth and was extremely hard to understand. This mullah's only accomplishment, according to Kasravi, was a certain skill in beating his pupils on their hands and feet, to the satisfaction of most of the pupils' fathers, who considered beating an even more important part of education than learning to read.

Kasravi was a quick study. He progressed through the Koran far more rapidly than the other students. As was customary, when Kasravi officially finished reading the Koran, he brought a tray of sweets and money to class; and, when he reached a certain point in reading out loud, a sort of general celebration took place in the little school. After the Koran, Kasravi started to read some books in Persian, which for him—as a Turkish-speaking Iranian—was a completely foreign language. In four years at this Koran school he waded through these texts, many of them models of the intricate style of bombastic Persian that his teacher (with his scant knowledge of Persian of any kind) could not really explain to him. Without his father's help, Kasravi says, he would have been completely lost—which is precisely where most of his fellow pupils remained.

His teacher next started Kasravi on the elementary Arabic grammar used in both Koran schools and *madresehs*. But as the mullah did not really know Arabic, he simply forced the students to memorize the text, so that the students learned to say that the

Arabic word *daraba* was the "masculine singular past, and means
that an unnamed person struck at a time past," instead of learning
that it meant "he hit."

Then suddenly his father died, and Kasravi, though only twelve
or thirteen, tried to help keep the family business alive. After an
interruption of about three years he decided he really wanted
more education, which in his time in a provincial Iranian city such
as Tabriz meant going to a *madreseh*. The first stages of this period
of his education were unpleasant. A mullah-teacher discovered
that Kasravi understood the assigned text on Arabic grammar as
well as he did and—according to Kasravi—in revenge caned
Kasravi on the hands for his bad handwriting. At another school
the students, who normally took two years to finish a certain text,
jealously ridiculed Kasravi for finishing the book in four or five
months.

Kasravi then transferred to the greatest of the *madresehs* of Tabriz, the Talebiyeh. Again he found aspects of *madreseh* life he
disliked; for example, the *madreseh* was dominated by a gang of
talabehs, or student mullahs from the Caucasus, who considered
themselves the guardians of Islamic law, and, just on being told
that a young man had looked at or touched a woman, they would
rush out and beat the supposed offender. Nevertheless, in the Talebiyeh *madreseh* he found things to like. On the first day he went
there he was immediately enchanted to see that there was a study
group assembled in each corner of the *madreseh*, and he came close
enough to one of them to hear for the first time one of his future
intellectual heroes, a progressive mullah named Khiyabani, lecturing on astronomy (still, as in the time of Avicenna, associated
with the name of Ptolemy).

On the first day he also found a friend of his own intellectual
caliber who became his study partner. Every class day they would
meet and—in the classic pattern encouraged by the *madreseh* tradition—dispute the assigned texts they were currently studying;
then they ate lunch together. "Thirty-odd years later," writes
Kasravi, "I still remember those days with pleasure." They took
turns going out of their way to walk each other home; they put
their allowances completely at each other's disposal. Two other
outstanding students soon became part of their group, and,

whether discussing books still beyond them in the curriculum or trying to stump each other on abstruse points of Arabic grammar, the four came to be inseparable, carrying their arguments after class to the fields and flower beds of the public parks of Tabriz.

The events of 1906 gave their conversations a new focus. The Constitutional Revolution could not make them quarrel openly with each other, but it pulled them apart. The day the constitutional movement started in Tabriz, people closed the bazaar and went to the British consulate and to the mosque of Samsam Khan. Kasravi, who had never heard the word "constitution" before, followed the crowds to the consulate, where a speaker explained that a constitution meant that "there should be a law on the basis of which men live; the king should not be allowed to follow his whim; and an assembly should be established to conduct affairs."

Kasravi was instantly won over. His study partner also became an enthusiastic supporter of the constitution. But soon the majority of the mullahs of Tabriz emerged as opponents of the constitution, and the other two talabehs of their hitherto inseparable foursome preferred the views of their mullah teachers and ridiculed the mojahedin, "the strivers," as the supporters of the constitution were called.

In this period an unexpected disappointment came to the young Kasravi; his guardian temporarily gave the mosque and law court Kasravi expected to inherit to another mullah. This mullah apparently knew that he would eventually have to surrender his position to Kasravi, so he tried to undermine Kasravi's position with his family by saying that Kasravi had become "an open enthusiast for the Constitution; and, besides, he reads newspapers. I fear his religious belief has been corrupted." An immediate result was that Kasravi's family, many of them anticonstitutionalists, tried to prevent him from reading newspapers; a deeper result was Kasravi's increased distrust of mullah morality.

Nevertheless he continued his studies at the madreseh and finished the standard books of grammar, rhetoric, and logic that formed the "preliminary texts," the groundwork of all madreseh education. In fact, he had started the middle level by reading the standard compendium of Islamic law, at which point a talabeh was considered qualified to take charge of a neighborhood or village mosque. But the civil war between the opponents and supporters of the constitution had changed the whole atmosphere. His study partner withdrew from the *madreseh*, started studying physics and "the new sciences," and after a while became a Baha'i, a member of a new religion, founded in nineteenth-century Iran partly in answer to the Shiah expectation of the messianic return of the twelfth Imam. Another of the foursome had joined one of the new state schools as a teacher.

The middle level of *madreseh* study consisted of reading and disputing in class prescribed texts on Arabic, Islamic law, logic, philosophical theology, and jurisprudence. Strangely, Kasravi found the first two useful and the last three useless and sometimes harmful. Ever the practical son of a merchant, he thought that reasonable men already possessed logic and that the study of formal logic only confused them in using a natural faculty. Jurisprudence, the attempt to use logic, *a fortiori* arguments, and other methods to explain why the law was (or should be) a certain way seemed to him a tissue of elaborately woven, tendentious conclusions. The conclusions were, in fact, so far divorced from what Kasravi believed were the simple principles of jurisprudence that it took a student an unnecessary ten to twenty years to master the arguments that supported them. For all the vigor with which Kasravi in his simple, elegant style denounces the "fanciful" fabrications of jurisprudence, he, like so many serious *madreseh* students, seems to have been intrigued by its complexity; he calls it "all in all a rather large and deep pit" that he was glad to escape from. He had, in fact, studied all the texts on the subject taught in Tabriz; the next step was to go to a place such as Najaf or Qom and try to become a *mojtahed*, one of the few hundred authoritative doctors of the law.

His guardian now urged him to take over his grandfather's mosque and law court, and his relatives offered hints as to how he should enlarge his turban, wear green or yellow mullah-style shoes, walk slowly, and in other ways assume an imposing mullah dignity that was beyond his mere twenty years. No doubt some of his teachers urged him to go to Najaf. But Kasravi wanted to be a merchant. Hadn't his merchant father, although generous to mullahs, said: "The bread earned from being a mullah is not the bread of a man who worships the one God to the exclusion of all others.

A mullah has to behave so as to please people so that they will give him money."

Then, in the summer of 1910, Halley's comet appeared in the sky over Tabriz. In the long history of conversions, from Paul's visionary encounter with Jesus on the road to Damascus to Ernest Renan's instantaneous decision that the Book of Daniel was apocryphal and therefore everything the church had taught him might be apocryphal, no conversion is more remarkable than Kasravi's conversion by Halley's comet. Tabriz was still the scene of violent battles in which the enemies of the constitution, that symbol Kasravi still loved, now often had the upper hand. And Kasravi was still the captive of his neighbors' expectations that he would remain a mullah. Yet every night he went to the roof to watch this comet, perhaps enjoying such moments of freedom from thoughts of his political and social powerlessness to determine his own future. Then he read an article in Arabic in an Egyptian magazine which explained that European science had shown the comet to have an orbit that brought it by the earth at regular intervals; it had last been seen in 1836.

Kasravi knew that he had seen nothing in "the astronomy of Ptolemy" that he had studied in his *madreseh* that explained the regularities in the behavior of comets. The "star with a tail," as a comet is called in Persian, converted him. "It obliged me," he writes, "to search for European learning," which, quick study that he was, he did rapidly and efficiently. He immediately got a translation of a good European popular work on astronomy and found he could master its ideas. "I was pleased and happy that in Europe knowledge had fallen into such a lucid path."

Clearly, for Kasravi this was a discovery of intellectual power; assertions of social and personal power soon followed. He now openly associated with the constitutionalists, no matter what his family or the people of his quarter thought. The mullahs of Tabriz denounced Kasravi as an unbeliever and encouraged their followers to find every opportunity to give him a bad name. Unpleasant as this may have been, it was also a relief; "People, having become disappointed with me, removed their [importuning] hands from my collar. In this way the chains of the mullah profession were removed from my neck." Finally he was his own man.

The change in Kasravi really was a conversion; he became a

true anticleric, a mullah turned inside out. Skepticism seems to
have lived a secret half-life throughout the history of the Iranian
Islamic tradition. The poetry of the eleventh-century Iranian poet
and mathematician Omar Khayyam is a classic expression of this
skeptical underworld. Quiet unbelievers were tolerated as long as
they publicly conformed with religion or at least did not publicly
challenge it. Kasravi was something new: he was a noisy unbeliever, a preacher whose texts were secularism, the triumph of science, and the superiority of constitutional democracy. Many
shared some of his beliefs, but he was impatient with those who
would not share them all. Eventually, to become one of the small
but enthusiastic band of Kasravi followers was like becoming a
member of a small, nearly sectarian group. His followers even
called themselves "The Pure in Religion." Kasravi's autobiography, for all his interest in "scientific history," is in some ways sectarian history in which the role of progressive mullahs, essential
to the success of the first phase of the constitutional movement, is
noticeably played down.

Kasravi was a great pamphleteer, and his pamphlets—sometimes printed openly but often printed clandestinely by his followers—attacked "wrong" belief with a directness that thrilled as
well as infuriated his readers. He wrote satires on Shiah beliefs
and practices such as: *What Is the Religion of the Hajis with Ware-
houses?*, *Ramazan the Shoemaker Has Returned from a Session with the
Rowzeh-khans*, and, to make sure the mullahs knew the quality of
their opponent, he wrote his most systematic attack on Shi'ism in
their language of learning, Arabic. He wrote an attack on the
Baha'is to show that this seeming religious alternative to Shi'ism
was as much a "wrong" belief as any other form of religion available in Iran. In pamphlets such as *Hasan Is Burning His Book of
Hafez* he attacked the cult of Persian poetry, since he felt that Iranians used poetic quotations to avoid serious thinking. Anyway,
Persian poetry was imbued with qualities he detested—flattery of
patrons, fatalism and mysticism antithetical to science—so he in-
stituted a "book-burning festival" for his followers at the winter
solstice. And when he wrote to praise, even the heavy seriousness
of his titles testifies to his inverse piety; one pamphlet is entitled
*The Best Form of Government Is Constitutional—The Latest Result in the
Thinking of Mankind.*

Kasravi was able to support himself while he spread his message, thanks to the new education and the new legal system. He taught Arabic grammar in the first state high school in Tabriz, and thereafter he worked at intervals for the Ministry of Education and the Ministry of Justice for the rest of his life. Kasravi, like Isa Sadiq, never forgot the democratic ideals of his youth, but like him he had to turn to the new secular structures built by the autocrat Reza Shah to survive.

In the 1940s, in that curious period in which Iran seemed to have no government because the Allies had not yet given the very young Mohammed Reza Shah real power, a *talabeh*, who had adopted the *nom de guerre* of Navvab-e Safavi to identify himself with the founders of Iran's greatest Shiah state, created an organization called the Devotees of Islam to fight "all forms of irreligion." In April 1945 one of the Devotees tried to kill Kasravi but succeeded only in wounding him. In 1946 official charges of "slander against Islam" were brought against Kasravi. On March 11, 1946, in Tehran, in the last session of hearings in the court of first instance at the Palace of Justice, the Devotees shot Kasravi dead in open court. Safavi and some other Devotees were arrested, but no one would testify against them and they were acquitted.

Many centuries as well as wide differences in character separate Avicenna, Sayyed Nematollah, and Kasravi. By the time of Kasravi the free-floating world of scholars and thinkers that Avicenna knew as the only serious intellectual world of the Islamic East had nearly disappeared. The pre-*madreseh* tradition of apprenticeship education still survived among the upper bureaucrats of the government, and royal courts still fostered circles in which the traditions of the physician and the astrologer-astronomer were passed on. But even the physician, the astronomer, and the bureaucrat were likely to have spent some time in a Koran school and at a *madreseh*. With their huge endowments and their wide acceptance as the citadels of true knowledge and correct belief, *madresehs* usually dominated and often monopolized the world of Iranian education. In the Shiah Islamic world they had surprisingly uniform curricula and methods—something unthinkable in the time of Avicenna—and they therefore dominated the content and methods of education as well.

Yet all three men share some remarkable similarities of style.

All three had a love affair with the Arabic language, that strong and flexible instrument that centuries of use had made into a finely tuned language of theoretical as well as practical thought. Sayyed Nematollah was, of course, an Arab. But it took him years of study as well as long travels from the marshes of southern Iraq to the heart of the Iranian plateau to transform his knowledge of a spoken Arabic dialect into a mastery of all the intricacies of classical Arabic recorded by early Arab grammarians—as long a journey as a modern Italian would have to travel to master the intricacies of classical Latin. Kasravi, who taught Arabic for years after he had given up his turban and aba, considered Arabic one of the few useful things he learned in *madreseh*, and its utility was proved when he found the scientific explanation of Halley's comet in an Arabic periodical. Avicenna, the philosopher who in his whole life traveled only within Persian-speaking areas, might seem the least likely of the three to love Arabic. In his fifty-odd years he had traveled from the borders of Central Asia, where he was born, over a thousand miles to Hamadan, an Iranian city near the borders of Iraq, but had never been in a country where Arabic was spoken. But not only did he write most of his work in Arabic and thereby establish a significant part of the standard Arabic philosophical vocabulary, he also (perhaps while in hiding and separated from his books) wrote one of the most brilliant works on Arabic phonology, *The Point of Articulation of Arabic Letters*, an entirely original work for which he needed only a supple mouth, an attentive ear, and an ingenious mind.

The techniques of argument that had been refined in the disputations so well loved in the intellectual world of the early Muslims influenced the intellectual style of all three of these men. Sayyed Nematollah, like so many *madreseh* teachers, perpetuated this tradition through commentaries. Such commentaries were of two types: that in which there are actually two speakers, and the commentator quotes the text piecemeal, preceding each quote with "He says" and following it with "But I say"; and that in which the basic text is called a "rectification" or "gist" or "epitome," in which the subject is conveyed as completely yet as briefly as possible, so that the basic text (often a poem), while convenient to memorize, is almost unintelligible without the long paraphrases

of the commentaries ("which is to say . . ."), paraphrases sometimes written by the very author of the epitome.

Not only is there an internal dialogue of several voices within
the texts but the texts also anticipate an external dialogue, the
actual disputations of teacher and pupils in the private study
circle or *madreseh*. Such disputations are likely to take place at
established points, nodes of difficulty about which there has
been a centuries-long consensus to disagree. To create and establish a new node of difficulty in the teaching of a subject is a
difficult task, something only great scholars with intellectually
forceful personalities have been able to do. Of course, if the pupil
believes that he has found too many unrecognized and unresolv-
able difficulties in the texts, his only real choice is to leave the
system.

As we have seen above, when an argument reaches a crossroads, its future movement can be viewed as restricted to two exclusive paths that mutually exhaust all possibilities (Lewis Carroll
is boring; Lewis Carroll is not boring) or to several exclusive
paths, no two of which exhaust all the possibilities (Lewis Carroll
was a blond, Lewis Carroll was a brunet, and so on). The disputations of the Islamic *madresehs* and the books written by *madreseh*
teachers used both methods. The second, the use of contraries
(blond, brunet, and so forth) involved the student in mastering
lists of mutually exclusive alternatives that had developed around
the established nodes of difficulty in the text, a method especially
favored in the law. The first, the use of contradictories, was much
more clear-cut, in that it closed the argument at each juncture (as
Avicenna said, something was either contingent or necessary). But
in order to exhaust all possibilities in a clear-cut division of things
into two contradictories, this method created categories often artificial and sometimes amusing. (As Robert Benchley said, "There
are two categories of people in the world, those who constantly
divide the people of the world into two classes, and those who do
not.") However funny or artificial its procedures, this method was
favored by philosophers and theologians, since it seemed to produce new necessary truths from known necessary truths. Therefore the *madreseh* textbooks on theology and kindred subjects turn
to this method with relish and train the student to use or object to

arguments through contradictories when such arguments appear possible.

These highly developed techniques tended to homogenize learning and to encourage arguments (and technical vocabulary) to cross over from one field into another—for example, from philosophy to rhetoric to grammar to law and back to philosophy. In this way even the various disciplines were brought into disputations with each other. And as part of this training, the student learned to construct premises about the reasoning of the text (for example, the text presumes that every absolute command in the Koran is an unqualified law for Muslims) that he will modify as he reads further (it now seems the text presumes that every absolute command in the Koran not abrogated by a verse of the Koran revealed subsequently is an unqualified law for Muslims) and further (it now seems that in verses such as that in which God says to sinners: "Be you lowly apes!" the Koran uses a rhetorical device and does not offer a real command). In this way students learned to construct a kind of intellectual arabesque that could twine and divide and retwine until it seemed logically to embrace everything in the text before them. And in the intellectual efforts to create this arabesque students engaged in the rough and tumble of debate that had as much excitement for its young devotees as the most challenging forms of physical sport.

In the study of the law there were early books of substantive law that gave, for example, the inheritance shares that different relations are entitled to; and later discussions dared not set these books aside. The Shiah student of law, in attempting to reconstruct the subtext of premises and methods of reasoning that underlie these earlier books, is really attempting to reconstruct the mental process of their authors and, ultimately, to read the minds of their inspirer, the true Legislator, God. The study of the law at this level was the queen of the sciences, the ultimate goal of the whole educational system. It aimed at creating a theoretical science of law from the books of actual religious laws and at disclosing the Creator's moral intention for mankind.

The mullahs who have climbed into the higher reaches of this activity felt and feel themselves to have entered a charmed circle of related fields of knowledge which leads them to the best approximation of the certainty they most desire: an exact knowledge of God's law. To the masses, this charmed circle of sciences possessed by the mullahs and transferred through the *madresehs* is something of a mystery but something that must be real nevertheless; otherwise why would the learned mullahs have gone through this ordeal (bleeding hands, drastic lack of sleep, caned feet, and so forth) of which so many such as Sayyed Nematollah speak? For men of the new education like Isa Sadiq it was a closed circle, whose centripetal revolutions had not allowed the penetration of any new sciences for centuries, a closed circle that could not tolerate a significant interruption of its tradition of consensus on the limited number of doubts and difficulties considered permissible to discuss. For mullahs turned inside out, like Kasravi, it was not only a closed circle but a circle whose members, in their arrogant pride in their largely useless learning, deluded themselves into thinking that they had something useful to say about the urgent tasks of the time—the economic, the intellectual, and, above all, the political regeneration of Iran.

Yet all three—Avicenna, Sayyed Nematollah, and even Kasravi —remembered with a special excitement the first time they proved themselves masters of their texts in disputations in a study circle or before a teacher. After Avicenna, when the *madresehs* were established, these new institutions owed much of their vigor to the openness and energy with which one generation of *talabehs* after another sought by disputation to deconstruct and reconstruct the books set before them. For the clever, the intellectual ordeal was greatly exhilarating, even if the associated physical ordeals were not; and this ordeal built a camaraderie among the clever which, even when they became atheists and anticlerics, they looked back at with a certain affection. As much as Kasravi thought that most of this learning was useless and harmful, he expressed the feelings of virtually all students who had passed successfully through the disputation classes of the higher levels of *madreseh* study when he wrote, "I still remember those days with pleasure."

CHAPTER FOUR

IN THE next few years the courtyard of the *madreseh* became almost as familiar to Ali as the courtyard of the *biruni* at home. It was not that the students and teachers constituted some sort of larger family; a family so given to formal disputations and so lacking in mothers and sisters would be hard to imagine. But the *madreseh* lay somewhere between the large public world of the bazaar, with its openly discussed reputations, and the private world of the *biruni* at home, in which individual values and evaluations were mutually assumed and largely unspoken. In the *madreseh*, in contrast, there was a sense of apprenticeship (or, for teachers, of mastery) in a way of thinking that really could be only guessed at by outsiders. No wonder *madreseh* students were called *talabehs*, "seekers"; they had entered on a "quest" that distinguished them from all the uninitiated.

Ali arranged to skip some of his classes in the state school or to attend the afternoon or evening adult-education sessions in order to make room for his classes at the *madreseh*. He found that for many of the nonscientific courses in the state school, if he read the assigned textbooks carefully, he could take the exams and pass with high marks. But if he had read the books of the *madreseh* curriculum by himself he would have missed all the knowledge that went, as they said in Persian, "from chest to chest." Without this knowledge he would have made a fool of himself when he went to the class for the next book in the curriculum, not least because he hadn't heard how the previous book had been attacked and defended by his fellow students and by the teachers.

By his fourteenth year Ali had fallen into the pattern of studying each *madreseh* lesson at least three times, as did all the serious students. Like the great majority of *talabehs*, he had a study partner, a sayyed from Yazd (who confirmed that in his house, as in many others in Yazd, water did, in fact, come from the cellar and not from any outside ditch). After studying the lesson by himself at home Ali would meet his partner before class and they would dispute with each other the meaning of the text, and usually that evening before reading the next lesson, Ali would reread the text to make sure he understood all the points the teacher had made. Once or twice he had stayed after class to watch one of the better students reteach the slower-witted students, but as he understood the text at least as well as the student teacher, he decided that these postmortems were of no use to him.

His study partner lived in one of the apartments in the walls of the Faiziyeh, and through him Ali became more involved in the life of the students of the *madreseh*. As early as his first month at the Faiziyeh, Ali had made himself something of a hero to his classmates newly arrived in Qom whom he led on tours of the city complete with highly colored and even quickly manufactured histories of the monuments. His low point as a guide was the visit to the icehouse, a somewhat squat and sinister domed building of unbaked brick. Ali explained to his audience of boys in frock coats and small black abas that ice was excavated from the pit under the icehouse with shovels and pickaxes. He then went through the low entrance door by himself and, once down the first short flight of steps, stood in terror on a narrow landing of cold mud that led to a second flight of steps. A thud from some region deep under the icehouse finally saved him. He shouted: "A cave-in! The icehouse is caving in on the men with pickaxes!" and they all ran after Ali to a nearby orchard, where with many a "Praise be to God" they congratulated themselves on their narrow escape.

Ali had as much to learn from his study partner from Yazd and the other boarders as they had to learn from him. Like the flocks of migrating finches that passed through Qom, *talabehs* tended to stick to students from their own provinces who shared some local language: Kurds with Kurds, Azerbaijani Turks with Azerbaijani Turks, and so on. They were, however, all curious to know the other people in their classes, and Ali, as an unusually young and clever student, was approached with respectful curiosity. Ali found that these older students were not only more aware of Iran as a country as varied in its people as in its landscape and climate but were also more aware of world politics and, in particular, of the struggle of Muslims in regions Ali had barely heard of.

Among *talabehs* discussions of politics were a sort of frenzied farewell to the day. It was widely believed that it was harmful to read in the light of the last forty-five minutes before sunset, so during the last hour of sunlight the students whose rooms formed the walls of the Faiziyeh left their books and poured into the courtyard to join and talk with students who congregated there from all the *madresehs* of Qom, after which they would pray together when the sun had finally set and they heard the call for evening prayer. About an hour before sunset the servants of the *madreseh* spread blue-and-white throw rugs around the courtyard for the students to sit cross-legged on, and when these were filled with students, the remaining students spread their black cloaks on the ground and formed circles not only on the paved walks but also near the tubular pines. As the hour grew nearer to sunset, flights of starlings appeared, and their chatter, mixed with the excited conversation of several hundred students, produced a roaring noise that made students who wanted to be crowd-pleasers almost shout to be heard in the larger circles. Students came with the national newspapers that had arrived in mid-afternoon from Tehran, and some students read these newspapers aloud, with many interruptions by listeners who wanted to give their interpretation of events. Listening to these students was the beginning of Ali's political education.

No time in this education was more filled with emotion than the evening Ali heard that hundreds of Muslim freedom fighters had been burned alive in a cave in the Algerian desert. Until this evening Ali had been largely silent in the circles he joined. To speculate, as his colleagues did, about the hidden motives of Eisenhower and Khrushchev and their secret designs on Iran seemed to him about as useless as staring contests with storks. But this night was different. In his class on rhetoric Ali had been reading poetry about the Arabian desert and the bravery of the ancient Arabs ("like the lions of the thicket"). From the moment his study partner read the headline ("Hundreds Die in the Algerian Desert") the whole scene was alive with the heroism of the fierce but impulsively generous men of the desert who fourteen centuries ago had created the Arabic poetry analyzed in his book. Ali was also aware that this evening he was looking at the news through four pairs of eyes: Parviz had turned up with a first cousin who was studying at the Faiziyeh. When Parviz and his cousin had joined their circle, Ali and Parviz with great shared amusement had made reverential bows to each other as if they had been respected ancient ayatollahs. Even Parviz, who was being very quiet, became noticeably different and exchanged his squint for a blank stare as the student began to read the article on Algeria.

They had all followed the Algerian war with close and concerned attention. In Algeria, in their opposition to a mass of colonial settlers and the tremendous power of a European state, Muslims had refused to count the danger, had refused to become imitation Frenchmen, and had gambled their lives and the lives of their friends for their freedom. Ali's study partner began to read the article: "The Freedom Movement of the Algerian people announced that yesterday French troops operating in the Sahara surprised several hundred Algerian freedom fighters in a cave in the desert. After the freedom fighters unanimously rejected the call to surrender, the French troops poured an inflammable liquid into the cave and stood by as the hundreds of Algerians who had taken refuge in the cave, including women and children, were burned alive."

Ali couldn't listen to the rest of the article. "For the French a Muslim is not a human being; they don't care if they kill one or one thousand. The Koran says: 'Those who oppress will soon know with what kind of returning they will return to God.' God punish them! The success of the Algerians will be the example that will make all Muslims burn with a kind of fire they will never forget."

Parviz's cousin put his hand on Ali's sleeve. "Mowlana in one poem says of God:

> *When you have known the rapture of burning you will never again be*
> *   patient even to keep from the fire;*
> *Even if water from the Fountain of Eternal Life appears, it will not*
> *   tempt you from the flame."*

Ali was furious. "Don't console me by telling me they're saved. They were burned for God, but God didn't burn them. No one has a right to punish with fire except God. God curse these men who play the role of God in the very act of oppressing us."

To everyone's surprise, Parviz, the only outsider in the group of *talabehs*, spoke: "Nasser has helped the Algerian Freedom Movement with men, with money, and with diplomacy. Egyptians act; the Iranians, as usual, confine themselves to weeping. If Mossadegh were still prime minister and we had freedom to act, Iran would do more than Egypt. Remember Mowlana said:

> *In one hand the wine cup, in the other, the tresses of the Beloved—*
> *Such a dance in the midst of the marketplace is my desire.*
> *My heart is weary of these weak-spirited traveling companions;*
> *I desire the Lion of God and Rostam, the son of Zal.*

We had a Rostam, a genuine lion. The Iranians, who consistently excel only at weeping, let the English and Americans take him away. The shame is ours as much as anybody else's."

Ali's study partner spoke with the frequent hesitations of someone who knows that he is saying something unpopular: "When the Soviets took over the Caucasus, they rounded up mullahs and dropped them from planes into the Caspian. Mossadegh allowed the Communists to join his government when he didn't need them. He had no true belief in religion. He was a man who loved his European education but never loved our education. He was

not a Lion of God like Imam Ali, the Commander of the Faithful,
or a purehearted hero like Rostam."

Parviz said, "Excuse me," and began walking toward the gate to
the street. Ali knew he could take no more of this discussion and
said, "I am going to the shrine and will stay there until the call to
prayer—excuse me," and, looking at the ground, he walked toward the inside gate leading from the Faiziyeh to the shrine.

In retrospect, Ali finds it amazing that such an important
change in his thinking should have taken place in a few minutes.
The fire burning in the Algerian desert kindled a fierce burning
inside him, and from this time on the Algerians' struggle became
Ali's struggle. Now he often brought the paper to read to his circle
of friends. He never completely rejected what his study partner
had said—that the secular Iranians of the new education in
Tehran who had supported Mossadegh could sometimes be
friends of the Communists but could never be true friends of the
mullahs. But the urgency of what Parviz said pressed like a weight
on his heart—that Iran and the Islamic world needed a champion
against the Europeans, or else no one would pay for the lives con-
sumed in Algeria and everywhere else where people struggled
against oppression. He longed to believe that freedom movements
everywhere, among Muslims and non-Muslims, were part of a
divine plan for which Islam must form the final goal; and he encouraged other people to believe so in spite of his silent hesitations. He began to seek out groups of *talabehs* who were highly
political: first, a group that admired Nasser; then, after the Muslim
Brothers attempted to kill Nasser and Nasser suppressed them, a
group that was affiliated with the Muslim Brothers in the Arab
world. And he mourned the failure of his father's generation to
support Mossadegh fully. He felt, with sorrow, that in Iran another such chance might never come in his lifetime.

• • •

For his many admirers Mossadegh was unquestionably a lion of
God and a hero like Rostam, the son of Zal. But for all Iranians—
admirers and deprecators—he was more: he was the lodestone,
the magnetic field, the lightning rod that lay both chronologically
and intellectually at the center of Iranian politics of the twentieth
century. Nearly everyone was pulled or pushed, attracted into or

repelled out of his orbit. Virtually no one passed through the period of his influence unaffected by his presence. He was among both the first students and the first Iranian professors at the new Iranian School of Political Sciences, a specialist in European political institutions who, forty years after graduation, would take over mid-twentieth-century Iran to teach his slightly idiosyncratic interpretation of the constitution he had loved in his youth. He, the aristocrat, the descendant of the Qajar dynasty, would come closer than anyone else ever came before 1978 to ending the Iranian tradition of monarchy. A man whose intellectual formation had been completed well before Reza Shah, Mossadegh was the ultimate product, the last and most impressive issue of the liberal and nationalistic tradition of the nineteenth-century reformers.

Mossadegh had been born in 1882 in the heart of court life in the old regime, a son of a high bureaucrat and a great-granddaughter of the Qajar king Fath-Ali Shah. It is not really a paradox that this partisan of European liberal institutions should be a descendant of the Qajar kings of nineteenth- and early twentieth-century Iran. The new education had been designed for the sons of the government elite, and for the first half of the twentieth century Iranian politics, especially parliamentary politics, often had the character of a squabble in a vast family of landlords, courtiers, and high bureaucrats who were all ultimately related as remote cousins. Ideology drove them apart (or at least gave them high-minded excuses to quarrel with each other); blood kept them together. More than once Mossadegh's half brother Heshmat od-Dowleh, a courtier and a staunch royalist, was glad to help when Mossadegh was in danger for his support of the constitution. Until the very end, when everything blew up in the Constitutional Revolution of 1906, pressure for reform came as much from within the Qajar establishment as from without it.

Heshmat od-Dowleh's first opportunity to help came when Mossadegh wanted to go to Europe and continue the studies he had egun as an auditor at that new School of Political Sciences in Tehran, whose members had turned the grounds of the British legation into "one vast open-air school of political science" in 1906. Mossadegh came to his subject almost by heredity. His father's family had been financial experts in the central administration of

Iranian governments since the mid-eighteenth century and his father had been a treasurer general. Mossadegh was only about ten when his father died of cholera, and barely five years later the shah appointed Mossadegh treasurer of the enormous province of Khorasan. According to the ancient Iranian bureaucratic custom, he was supposed, under the tutelage of the officials assigned to help him, to learn how to apply the extensive training he had received at home in the intricate nineteenth-century Iranian methods of bookkeeping, which only government officials and great merchants thoroughly understood.

As a member of one of the voluntary societies to support the constitution, Mossadegh would have had trouble getting a passport to go to Europe from Mohammed Ali Shah, the reactionary ruler of Iran from 1907 to 1909, who spent his brief reign trying to undo the constitution granted by his father and predecessor and who was finally deposed by the constitutionalists for this very reason. But thanks in part to his brother's help, Mossadegh was able to leave Tehran in 1909, the same year Isa Sadiq entered the Polytechnic. In fact, Mossadegh had a keen sense that his early immersion in the mysteries of Iranian higher administration had caused him to miss out on the new learning, and in Iran he had attended classes and hired tutors not only for the political sciences but also for other subjects, including anatomy, which seems to have encouraged his lifelong interest in medicine.

When he arrived in Paris and entered the Ecole des Sciences Politiques, he applied himself so diligently that, as he would later explain, "the constitutional indisposition that I have had for my whole life is the result of the enormous amount of work that I did during my years of study in Paris." Mossadegh seems, in fact, to have suffered from ulcers and was bedridden for a long time during his stay. Never averse to describing the drama of his illnesses, he tells his readers with something like pride that a "well-known French physiologist" had told him that he had never seen gastric secretions as "irregular and disorderly" as Mossadegh's. In the end he found that he could not regain his health in French surroundings, and he returned to Iran to recuperate.

By 1910 he was well enough to try again, but this time, after passing a qualifying exam in Paris in November, he went to study law in the more healthful Swiss climate of Neuchâtel. Here he found that European learning, like Oriental bookkeeping, had its useless intricacies designed to keep outsiders where they belonged; to his annoyance the Swiss forced him to study Roman law in Latin. Nevertheless in 1914 he got his Swiss doctorate in law, and, after completing a period of probation by working in an attorney's office and attending trials, he was admitted to the bar. From now on he would be known to Iranians (and, consequently, to European diplomats) as Dr. Mossadegh.

His thesis, published in the year after its acceptance, made up for its modest length by its enormous title: *The Will in Muslim Law (Shiah Sect) Preceded by an Introduction on the Sources of Muslim Law.* Surely his Swiss professors would have accepted such an oddly constructed thesis only from an esoteric foreigner. There is hardly a single footnote in the whole work, and only a little over half the thesis is related to wills and testaments. The sections on wills and testaments are, in fact, not badly done, if one remembers that Mossadegh had to create everything—the European equivalents of the Islamic terms and the reorganization of his materials—in a way that would make its arguments clear to a European lawyer. Shiah Islamic law was an unheard-of subject in the French-speaking world on the eve of the First World War, and even Sunni Islamic law was generally a matter of interest only to French colonial administrators in North Africa.

The very strangeness of his subject, however, gave Mossadegh a chance to discuss such things as legal reform, which really concerned him. This discussion took place against an assumed Shiah cultural nationalism: Iran was a Shiah nation, Mossadegh was proud of his Iranian heritage, and any future development of Iran must take the Shiah culture of Iranians into consideration. Mossadegh's friends in France and Switzerland, who included such women admirers as the "saintly" Mademoiselle Thérèse, who nursed him back to health on *crème renversée*, probably did not tease him about his "many wives," as Isa Sadiq's schoolmates in his lycée had done at the same period; Mossadegh was, after all, a grown man. But Mossadegh felt some of the same embarrassment and need to explain; he devotes long and somewhat irrelevant asides to the institutions of polygamy and slavery in Islamic law.

Of polygamy he says: "In our opinion, Christianity has no right to reproach Islam in any way in matters concerning its conception of marriage"; after which he proves to his satisfaction that Muslim arguments for polygamy contradict the spirit of the Koran.

In this, as in other discussions in the book, Mossadegh leans heavily on "reason" and on social custom. He lays the groundwork for such an approach in his long (and not very accurate) description of the sources of law according to Shiah jurisprudence: the Koran, the sayings and conduct of the Prophet and the Imams, reason, and so forth. But Mossadegh often disregards the relative importance given to these elements by Shiah jurisconsults of the preceding thousand years. If Shiah jurisconsults accepted reason as the ideal means to elaborate the raw material of the law as given in the Koran, the "sayings" and the "example," or if they saw reason as a means to reconcile seeming contradictions in the raw material of the law or to make explicit its implicit premises, they regarded reason only as a potential and seldom as an actual source for any matter of law already mentioned in these raw materials. For if, in theory, one could reach many of the precepts that were given in a saying of the Prophet by sheer "reasoning," in practice it was much more reliable (and usually much less difficult) to reason from the revealed precept to its legal application. Mossadegh, after a little self-contradiction and a lot of backing and filling, declares the weight of reason superior to all other sources of the law. Is not the keystone of Islamic law, he argues, the existence of God, and do we not accept this because of rational argument and not because of consensus (there are, after all, atheists)? Therefore should not reason prevail over all the other principal sources, which, after all, consider questions much less important than God's existence?

Mossadegh, though not a profound student of Islamic law, was perfectly aware that he was running against a thousand years of Shiah thought in asserting the superiority of reason to other sources of the law, and he developed a historical scheme that completely justified his turning the tradition upside down. From the time of Mohammed until 934, he said, Muslims lived in the epoch of revelation and inspiration, in that they received direct guidance from God and infallible interpretation from His Prophet and His divinely appointed Imams until the twelfth Imam disappeared from contact with men at the end of this period. From 938 to 1906 Shiah Muslims lived in the "formalist epoch," in which Shiah jurisconsults kept themselves within the restraints of the law as elaborated up to 938, and "law remained stationary." But, he declared, with the revolution they have reached "the positivist epoch," in which laws can be made again, although all such laws should heed the Shiah legal tradition and must, according to the constitution, be examined by five jurisconsults "of the highest order" to assure that they are in conformity with religion.

That legislators "made" laws was as alien to Shiah jurisprudence in Mossadegh's period as it was to English jurisprudence in the time of Chaucer. Lawyers, even if united in some sort of consultative body, "discovered" the law, whether they "found" it in accepted "custom" (in England) or by weighing proofs as to the intention of the Divine Legislator (in Shiah Iran). Mossadegh argues that the Iranian parliament could proceed in a way different from any jurisconsult of the "formalist" epoch: it could pick and choose whatever it considered appropriate among the sources of Islamic law. To the traditional jurisconsults this shapeless and "irrational" procedure would imply that the Legislator had laid out a smorgasbord of moral and ethical rules to be tasted at pleasure, with no guidance as to the precedence, order, and purpose intended for the guest.

Although Mossadegh was aware of such conflict, he was indifferent to it; he believed that if the laws were adapted to the needs of Iran, they would conform with religion, reason, and custom. The equality of all people before the law, as laid down in the constitution, was not based on Islam, he admits; it was based on reason, since all who assume equal burdens under the law (including equal taxes) must, according to reason, have an equal standing before the law (a principle, he notes, disregarded by the French in their treatment of their Algerian subjects). But, he adds, Islam allows reason as a source of law, so we need not be disturbed by the absence of any Islamic precept to support the article on equality in the constitution.

In fact, it seems that for Mossadegh it was the specific "habits" and "resources" of Iranians that legislators must keep in mind rather than some search for a reading of God's mind detached from cultural and social circumstances. And he saw Shiah Islam as one of the most important parts of the cultural and social world of Iranians, especially as "the intensity of religious feeling of the followers of Islam is incontestably superior to that which prevails in other religions." This regard for context also explains why Iranian laws "must conform to the true interests of the country" and not be "set aside on the pretext of imitating Europe." Inappropriate European laws, if applied, often produced contrary effects in an Iranian setting; and if not carried out, gave European nations an excuse for intervention in the name of enforcing local laws.

Mossadegh, the son of a treasurer general of the old regime, ultimately takes the practical view of a high bureaucrat toward the problem of law, religion, and reform. Iranians need Iranian solutions to make them an effective polity. He argues that Iranian solutions must take heed of Shiah beliefs to be as effective as possible among Iranians, rather than arguing that Shiah beliefs are able in themselves to produce the most effective laws. Shi'ism is a natural part of the landscape in the country he loved and regarded as the natural arena for his talents, but it should be a flexible and not a rigid aspect of that landscape, yielding to the overall needs of the nation. In his thesis, as in his later books and speeches, Mossadegh the aristocrat, endlessly fascinated with his own health, turns to a medical analogy to explain the therapeutic situation of Iran. Wine is forbidden to Muslims, but in a case of necessity, Islamic law permits wine to the ill because protection of life takes precedence over all other considerations. In more general terms, the Divine Legislator, like the physician, gives general instructions to the patient and lets him work out the details according to "reason" and his interests.

For the next few years Mossadegh was forced to stay in his "ailing" homeland, because the First World War had made Europe the victim of a far more savage illness. He drifted into the politics of the always dying but never dead constitutional movement. He had been elected to the very first Iranian parliament but had not been allowed to take his seat as he was under thirty. His continuing loyalty to the ideals of 1906 had not been forgotten. The old constitutionalists now discovered that this European-trained lawyer could beat some of their enemies at their own games; in particular, he could expose certain European officials who had a stranglehold on Iranian finances. These officials and some of their Iranian associates were sometimes corrupt, often incompetent, and almost always obedient to outside powers, such as the Russians, who used them as surrogate agents to control Iran. Mossadegh, himself a financial official even before he had studied the "new" political science, understood the practical side of government as few of his high-minded liberal friends could have.

Mossadegh the "national physician" had returned to teach as well as treat the patient, and he accepted a post at the same School of Political Sciences at which he had been a student. He also taught through his books, which he and a few friends distributed free through a charitable trust he established. His books of this period include a translation of his thesis; *Iran and Capitulations of Rights to Non-Iranians* (1914); *Civil Procedure in Iran* (1914); *The Limited Stock Company in Europe* (1915); and, somewhat later, *Fiscal Principles and Laws Abroad and in Iran: I. The Budget* (1926). All of these books had the same practical thrust that Mossadegh's thesis had shown: they were carefully organized and clear expositions of new Iranian laws and practices (for example, in collecting taxes) or introductory texts on legal ideas previously alien to Iran (for example, the joint stock company). They always displayed the same practical concern for finding institutions that would work in the Iranian context and helping the Iranian "patient."

The patient, however, was about to receive a frontal lobotomy. After the Bolshevik revolution the Russians ceded the inside track in controlling the Tehran government to the British, and Iranians favorable to the British (including Mossadegh's very wealthy maternal uncle) agreed to a treaty making Iran virtually a British protectorate in exchange for a loan of two million pounds. Mossadegh was incensed; after helping to get rid of Belgian tax officials, he saw no need for Iranians to turn the finances and army of Iran over to British officials. He went to Switzerland, had a rubber stamp made reading "Comité résistance des nations," and began writing in the hope of catching the attention of the Allies, then negotiating the Versailles Treaty. One day Mossadegh, living

alone in his single room on the third floor of his pension in Neuchâtel, was approached by a "chic, tall, beautiful woman" who
said, "Est-ce que vous voulez fumer ce soir?" to which he replied,
"Pardon, madame. Je suis malade." Mossadegh decided (perhaps
correctly) that the Allies wanted to get information from him, and
he felt his suspicions were confirmed when the same woman
turned up at his ski resort shortly after. But ultimately the English
had no need for the "chic, tall, beautiful woman" because the
other Allies accepted the principle that as a nonbelligerent (even
though partly occupied by the Russians, the British, and the Ottoman Turks during the war) Iran had no right to present its case at
Versailles. Mossadegh felt totally defeated and briefly considered
settling in Switzerland and cutting his ties with an Iran that
seemed to have sold itself to Europeans who had now fully exposed their double standard. He was, like Ho Chi Minh, one of
the seminal leaders of the mid-twentieth century in whom the
Versailles Conference had created hopes it did not fulfill.

Mossadegh returned to an Iran in which the parliamentary opposition to the Anglo-Iranian treaty had prevented its ratification
even though the Iranian Cabinet had accepted it. Mossadegh's nationalistic friends had formed a new Cabinet. For the next six
years he held the highest posts: he was at various times minister
of justice, finance, foreign affairs, and governor of two of Iran's
most important provinces. He took special pleasure in his role in
the abolition of "capitulations," those treaties that gave non-Iranians special legal rights, including some rights of extraterritoriality,
while present on Iranian soil. Mossadegh, in his book of 1914, had
seen these capitulations as the ultimate humiliation that had been
imposed on Iran, since they denied Iranians control of law and
administration, the instruments of national well-being he most
cared about: "For a government to be independent it must govern
all those residing in its territory. . . . In the final analysis, a government which does not govern either its own citizens or foreigners is
no government and will become the dependency of another government that possesses this position [of full sovereignty]." Iran
had been able to cancel these "capitulations" in large part because, from 1921, when he occupied Tehran, the minister of war
had been Reza Khan, who had possessed the means to coerce obe-

dience and again make the Tehran government the effective government of the entire nation.

Then, on October 31, 1925, Mossadegh was summoned to an extraordinary meeting of the parliament and immediately noticed that the police and military officers had replaced the usual spectators in the gallery. A bill was proposed abolishing the first article of the constitution which recognized the Qajars as hereditary monarchs of Iran. Everyone recognized this bill as a preliminary to establishing the monarchy of Reza Khan. Mossadegh may have been of Qajar descent, but it was not out of concern for his own family's honor that he opposed the new bill. As the debate began, Mossadegh left the session for a bit, "because my health was very poor." But he returned, took the floor, and led the attack on the bill: "So the Prime Minister [Reza Khan] is to become the ruler. . . . Today, in the twentieth century can anyone say that a government that is constitutional has a king who rules? . . . If we take this retrograde step and say he is king, prime minister, ruler, everything, this is nothing but reaction and autocracy." The step was taken; only three members voted with Mossadegh against the bill.

Mossadegh's relations with Reza Shah entered on a downward spiral, leading to periods of imprisonment and house arrest at his estate in Ahmadabad. He had spent most of his inheritance on his education in Europe, but by the 1920s his finances had improved somewhat and he was able to buy Ahmadabad, a classical Iranian village of about a hundred and fifty families, surrounded by a wall and irrigated by the enormous, long underground water conduits Iranians call *qanats*. Hounded out of public life, in those periods during the 1930s in which he was not in jail he turned to his village as the only focus for his enormous energy (however ill he may have thought himself). In the thirties he won prizes for sugarbeet cultivation and in the forties drilled wells and started a primary school in the garden of the estate. But his greatest enthusiasm was the health of the villagers. Even though his own house was furnished very simply and had little planted around it except for a few elm trees for shade, he had a large and extremely well-stocked dispensary, which he personally ran until one of his sons qualified as a doctor and was called in weekly to help him. Lucky was the guest to Ahmadabad who was not forced by Dr. Mossadegh to swallow a spoonful of a bitter extract of boiled juniper berries, which he believed cleared the system.

When the unthinkable happened on August 25, 1941, and, to assure a corridor for aid to Russia, both British and Russian forces attacked Iran and forced Reza Shah, after token resistance, to abdicate in favor of his son, Mossadegh emerged from house arrest a hero. He was in his sixties, a man who, according to Iranian standards, had been proven "pure" in motive by his consistency through long life experience. He had long fulfilled an essential need in the moral drama that Iranians expect to see performed on the political stage. This drama allows Iranians to obey, and sometimes even to admire, the ruling autocrat, but requires that somewhere there be a man of standing who selflessly and tenaciously says "no" to the autocrat. Many Iranians believe that as long as they quietly, almost surreptitiously, admire the antihero, they need not feel that their inner soul has been bought by power, and they hope that the autocrat, aware of this hidden division of allegiances, will be more cautious in dealing with his subjects. Mossadegh had emerged as such a person; he was now a Lion of God.

As befitted a leader proved "pure" through the testing of time, Mossadegh refused to form a party, and after elections remarkably free by Iranian standards, he entered the parliament officially as a member for Tehran. His platform called for adoption of a "negative equilibrium," the playing of Russia and Britain against each other, at times by looking for support from a "third force," such as Germany, France, or the United States. He called for the transfer of the armed forces from the control of the Shah to the Cabinet, answerable to the parliament; it was, he claimed, the only way to prevent a return of the dictatorship of Reza Shah. Finally, he called for a reform of the electoral system, so that the landlords and provincial officials could no longer pack the parliament.

While Mossadegh was elaborating this platform, one of the "third forces," the United States, in a hopeful and naïve mood, saw itself as moving to guarantee the "negative equilibrium" that Mossadegh was advocating. Churchill, Stalin, and Roosevelt gathered in Tehran in 1943 to discuss the alliance and the shape of the postwar world. But Roosevelt, vaguely interested in Iran (as he had told Isa Sadiq) through his relatives such as Amory, now began to take a personal interest in its future. (In 1943 Isa Sadiq sent a note reminding Roosevelt of their earlier meeting, but he was never given an audience.) At Roosevelt's request, Arthur Millspaugh, an American who had had some earlier experience in advising the Iranian government, outlined a program in agreement with what Roosevelt and Harry Hopkins, his special assistant, had in mind: "that Iran . . . is (or can be made) something in the nature of a clinic—an experiment station—for the President's post-war policies—his aims to develop and stabilize backward areas." And it could all be done in Iran, he explained, "with negligible cost and risk to the United States." General Patrick Hurley, Roosevelt's envoy to the Middle East, told the President that Iran could develop into a pattern of "self-government and free enterprise." Roosevelt sent Hurley's letter on to the secretary of state with the remark, "I was rather thrilled with the idea of using Iran as an example of what we could do by an unselfish American policy. We could not take on a more difficult nation than Iran," a nation that he saw as dominated by "the worst form of feudalism." Only the United States, he felt, could provide the help that would change all this and protect Iran from Britain and Russia.

Mossadegh was soon to want the United States to provide more significant help than a handful of technical advisers; he wanted their diplomatic support against the British. On December 2, 1944, Mossadegh introduced a bill into the parliament forbidding the Cabinet even to discuss oil concessions with foreigners and allowing the Cabinet to sell oil (even without concessions) only if the parliament was kept informed throughout. The bill was passed with a large majority. Mossadegh, the ancient enemy of capitulations, unnecessary foreign experts, and foreign laws too expensive to Iran, the man who had had his hand on the fiscal pulse of Iran since he was a teenager, knew where wealth that could change Iran really was—it was in oil.

The events that carried Mossadegh from 1944 to his election as prime minister in 1951 and his term in that office from 1951 to 1953 are as much part of world history as the history of Iran. For the two years of his premiership his picture in the newsreels and on the front pages of newspapers made him the best known leader of the Third World. His fame was, of course, based on what he did. By nationalizing Iranian oil, which had up to that point been controlled by the British, he became one of the first Third World leaders to reclaim a great national resource with relative impunity. He was also the first Middle Eastern leader to create a vast following by using the radio; tens, sometimes even hundreds of thousands of Iranians poured into the street when he summoned them. Nasser, in both the nationalization of the Suez Canal and his use of the radio, was Mossadegh's pupil.

Yet Mossadegh's fame was based almost as much on how he did things as on what he did. The mannerisms of the tall, stooping aristocrat with the prominent teeth, the kindly brown eyes, and the warm smile enchanted Iranians every bit as much as they infuriated Westerners. He complained endlessly of ill health and preferred to conduct business, including business with foreign ministers, in gray woolen pajamas at the side of his plain iron bed. He wept publicly when deeply moved; he had fainting fits; yet he was strong enough to rip the arm off a chair in the chamber of the parliament when, in the passion of a speech, he wanted something to wave in the air at an opponent. He represented his political activity as a continuing triumph of his will and nationalistic feeling (and, perhaps, by extension, the country's will and nationalism) over constitutional ill health. In one speech to parliament during his term as prime minister he told of an incident in his youth when somebody slanderously associated him with a group of deputies alleged to have bought votes. "This news so worried me that I was taken ill with fever. My mother, who came to see me, told me after being informed of the cause of my sickness that I, who lacked any resistance, had better take up medicine and absolutely avoid politics. 'You should know,' my mother said, 'that anybody's integrity in society depends on the hardships he endures for the sake of the public.' "

The English were appalled, the Americans confused. Shortly after the news of the nationalization of Iran's oil, Harold Macmillan noted in his diary: "I do not like the news from Persia; still less the rather unfriendly American attitude. Acheson appeals to Britain and Persia to keep calm! As if we were two Balkan countries being lectured in 1911 by Sir Edward Gray!"—to which he adds in his memoirs: "Meanwhile Dr. Mossadegh raved and ranted like a lunatic." It was potentially a great blow to the British economy, heavily dependent on Iranian oil, but it was also a great political blow that could (and did) produce cracks in the British position in all parts of the world.

Macmillan's superior, Anthony Eden, was more sympathetic. Eden had studied Persian at Oxford, where he had read the odes of Hafez "for glorious reward" after laboring through the ancient and early medieval Persian set texts on the syllabus. Sympathy, however, did not disguise for him the seriousness of Iran's actions for Britain. "Now, as a result of events in Iran, Egypt became ebullient . . . This was the lowering prospect I contemplated on the day I took over at the Foreign Office [in 1951]. We were out of Iran; we had lost [the British refinery in the Iranian city of] Abadan; our authority throughout the Middle East had been violently shaken; the outbreaks in Egypt foreshadowed further upheavals." Eden's view—that this was the beginning of the end for Britain in the Middle East—was shared by the Labour party. Herbert Morrison, Attlee's foreign secretary, said of the nationalization: "It was a shocking example of modern diplomacy, or lack of diplomacy, of which the subsequent nationalizing of the Suez Canal in defiance of treaties was another."

The Americans now saw that their chosen "clinic," which, after fifteen to twenty years of treatment at negligible cost, was supposed to emerge from the "worst sort of feudalism" into a healthy country with an FBI, TVAs, and all sorts of "progressive" institutions, had instead demanded its wealth immediately and had proposed to get it by quarreling with America's nearest ally. Truman sent Averell Harriman to Iran. He seemed at first to make progress by classic American methods: advocating good will and offering an increase in aid. But gradually the intractability of both sides wore down the Americans; in any case, they became alarmed at the growing strength of the Persian Communist party, which had acted as Mossadegh's ally.

In August 1953, after an unsuccessful attempt to replace Mossadegh as prime minister, the shah fled Iran. Some were shocked at the shah's departure, others had been shocked when, a month earlier, Mossadegh had bypassed the parliament, or Majles, and got approval for the dissolution of parliament through a general referendum. The referendum was a strange dodge for a constitutionalist of such long standing, but it was a dodge not inconsistent with Mossadegh's understanding of the pragmatic populism that had made the whole constitutional experiment worthwhile. As he told the parliament on April 12, 1952 (in the official translation):

Among my professors in Switzerland there was one, who, from the standpoint of education, had divided the nations of the world into three groups: learned, ignorant, and mediocre nations. He applied the term "learned" to a nation that is capable of discerning good from bad, and has the will-power to carry out its discernments; and "ignorant" he nicknamed a nation easily misguided by individuals or other nations; and, finally, he used the term "mediocre" in relation with a nation who possesses the ability to discern but lacks the will-power to carry it out.

At the beginning of the establishment of Constitutionalism, a few well-wishing people guided the nation in directions they believed to be to their benefit; as a result despotism was abolished and a constitutional régime was adopted.

During the term of the Third Parliament, when after graduation I returned from Switzerland, I found a good example for the professor's hypothesis: the people were neither wanting in discernment, so as to be guided by others, nor were they powerful in will so as to carry out their discernment.

But before the Elections for the Sixteenth Parliament were begun, it became obvious, when I called my dear fellow countrymen to submit a supplication to the Imperial Court, that the people possess an excellent ability to discern.

From these premises I wish to infer that you are elected by a people who discerns good from bad, and that you represent a nation whose acumen no one challenges. Accordingly, you can well find out the difficulties and can easily procure means to remove them.

In any case, the British recognized that after the referendum, the shah's departure, and the new demonstrations of strength by the Iranian Communist party the atmosphere was right for a coup against Mossadegh; yet they were glad to defer to the Americans.

Coups were expensive, and if this one failed, it was just as well for Americans to take the blame (and, perhaps, learn that "clinics" were not so easily organized as these newcomers imagined). The coup succeeded with a speed that surprised its supporters almost as much as its opponents. It was largely organized by Teddy Roosevelt's grandson Kermit Roosevelt, according to Kermit's account. (American negotiators during the oil crisis had included Herbert Hoover, Jr., and Douglas MacArthur, Jr.; there was nepotism in American politics, too.) On August 18, 1953, the Iranian army, angry that the demonstrations mounted by the Iranian Communists seemed to imply that with the shah's departure the Communists were calling the tune, put down these demonstrations with a heavy hand and with loud expressions of support for the shah. On the morning of August 19 a crowd, bought in southern Tehran for only $100,000 by Roosevelt's men—a crowd that included professional bazaar toughs, prostitutes, some religious leaders, and even some sincere secular royalists—marched toward the center of the city and attacked Mossadegh's office. The aged and ailing prime minister went to the back of the garden, leaped over the wall, and went into hiding. Suddenly there were signs of pro-American and pro-shah sentiment everywhere, and Kermit Roosevelt still had $900,000 of undistributed funds in a safe. A few days later the Americans announced a grant of $45 million to the Iranian government and promised further aid. The coup had been cheap, but the Americans never did learn how to run a "clinic" at "negligible cost," much less at negligible risk.

For the mullahs the episode of Mossadegh presented a tangle of questions from which they never completely or unambiguously disengaged themselves. They had defended Iran against foreigners in the name of defending Islam against non-Muslims. Mossadegh, on the contrary, defended Shiah Islam at most as something Iranian, as part and parcel of his pride in Iran. A powerful ayatollah, Abol Qasem Kashani, who had been arrested in 1943 for contact with Nazi agents in Iran, emerged in 1945 from prison as a minor hero among the mullahs for his strong anti-English stand. Kashani continued to espouse popular causes, including the nationalization of oil, and in the intervals between his succeeding imprisonments and exiles organized a considerable following. This following included the Devotees of Islam, who became a force in Iranian politics after they killed Kasravi. Although he never publicly acknowledged a direct link with them, Kashani protected them and actually obtained the pardon of a Devotee who, in March 1951, shot Razmara, an Iranian prime minister opposed to the nationalization of oil.

Kashani led large numbers of traditionally religious people into the National Front, the umbrella organization of supporters of Mossadegh, who himself continued to refuse affiliation with any party. But Kashani and Mossadegh agreed only on what they did not want—manipulation by foreigners and foreign control of Iran's wealth. Otherwise Kashani was interested in restoring the role of Islamic law and in Pan-Islamic interests, including what he saw as the shared Muslim interests in recovering Palestine from Zionism. When Kashani and Mossadegh became aware of how much separated them, they quarreled in 1953, and Kashani was able to lead out of the National Front only a fraction of those he had led in. He and Behbahani, a leading ayatollah of the poor areas of southern Tehran, sent their followers to help form the nucleus of the crowd that set out on August 19 for Mossadegh's office.

The attitude of the truly learned mullahs in Qom to Mossadegh is far less clear. Certainly they thought Kashani an intellectually shallow, crowd-pleasing mullah, but they recognized that, as a group, mullahs benefited from the existence of a few politically active mullahs, however shallow they might be. Yet the supreme leader of the Shiah at the time, Ayatollah Borujerdi, was a master at avoiding political confrontation and public statements on political issues. From the unclear evidence available it seems that Borujerdi and the senior mullahs distrusted Mossadegh. "Doctor" Mossadegh was certainly not a conventionally religious man, and he was a great respecter of his own Western political education; worst of all, he accepted the support of Communists, who were enemies of religion. But they did not speak openly against him— so many of the young *talabehs* admired him, as did so many of the bazaar merchants, whose financial support was important even to the greatest ayatollahs. Kashani might be shallow, but they found his ideas immediately recognizable and, on the whole, sound. The

great ayatollahs of Qom may even have been instrumental in Kashani's strategic withdrawal from the National Front. The young
talabehs, however, and even some of their elders, understood that
Egypt and Algeria had inherited Iran's role as the champion of the
Islamic world's resistance to "imperialism," and for many years
after Mossadegh's fall felt that Nasser and the Algerian revolution
stood at the emotional center of world politics.

Mossadegh's attitude to Shiah Islam and the mullahs is somewhat easier to discern. Almost from childhood Mossadegh was an
administrator, a man interested in getting things done. He was
also a nationalist, a person who wanted things done effectively at
the national level for the national good. European political science
displayed a whole new set of mechanisms for getting things done,
including mechanisms for mobilizing the nation through elective
institutions. In his view such mechanisms should be borrowed
only when appropriate to Iranian resources and "habits" because
only then could they make Iran strong and able to maintain its
policy of "negative equilibrium" among powerful nations eager to
impose their self-interested laws on Iran. As he said in opposition
to a bill supported by Reza Shah: "Every honorable person, insofar as he is able, must defend his country on the basis of two
principles and not submit himself to any power. One of those two
principles is being Muslim, the other is nationalism."

Mossadegh's attitude to mullahs was as pragmatic as his attitude toward Islamic law: you accepted the friendship of the good
(that is, helpful) ones and you lured away the followers of the bad
ones. He had seen a powerful mullah such as Ayatollah Fazlollah
Nuri, who had stirred up large crowds against the constitution in
its early years because Nuri regarded it as an offense to Islam to
talk about "legislating" when the Prime Legislator had already
spoken. He had seen such a mullah as Hasan Modarres, a true believer in the constitution and one of the few men to stand beside
him in the debate in the Majles when he opposed the abolition of
the Qajar monarchy. Finally, he had experienced Kashani.

Yet Mossadegh's contact with Shi'ism was more profound than
his acceptance or rejection of Shiah law and its experts. His was,
in the end, a religious drama. In the last two days of his premiership he could have appealed on the radio for help, as he had so

many times before, and tens of thousands would have filled the streets, cut off the oddly assorted throng from south Tehran, and defended his cause. But he did not. Sources in his inner circle say that after two days of silence while hiding in a cellar with two of his ministers after the countercoup, one of these ministers (a university professor with a French doctorate) said, "How badly it all turned out, how badly!" To which Mossadegh responded, "And at the same time how really well it turned out, how really well!" For Mossadegh was not only the battling hero Rostam, the son of Zal, and the brilliant commander Ali, the Lion of God, he was also Hosain, the Prince of Martyrs.

The government put him on trial, and—old, stooping—he defended himself with the great fire and intellectual capacity that befitted an ingenious lawyer and experienced parliamentarian. The trial confirmed his standing as a martyr. He was imprisoned, then kept under house arrest in his estate in Ahmadabad, and Iranians saw rare pictures of the same man, weak but unbroken, sitting at his bedside, that they had known as prime minister. He was eighty-five years old in 1967 when, weakened by the radium treatment for throat cancer that he had received in the hospital founded by his mother, he finally died of the stomach ulcers he had developed as a young student.

CHAPTER FIVE

ALI HASHEMI's interest in mysticism grew within him in the same slow way that he himself grew to be an adult. As a sixteen-year-old in 1959 he was moderately tall; he had a dark-brown beard that was long enough to need trimming; and he had come to sense that his father's mature understanding of Islam came not only from books but also from a mystical understanding of the world.

In a way, much of the theology that Ali had studied had prepared him for a training in mysticism. He accepted the teaching that knowledge of something does not imply the separate existence of that thing in the knower's mind: Kazem, the servant of Ali, does not exist as a separate little creature, a kind of ghost, trapped in Ali's head. Instead, as his books of philosophy taught him, the moment he saw Kazem in his head, the idea of Kazem *was* Ali's mind, or at least part of Ali's mind. And if a person (Ali, for example) is what he knows, then he may have to know certain things that exist but have not yet become part of his mind for his mental existence to become something different (which transformation may, of course, allow him to know still other things). The perfection of the mind would therefore be its complete transformation by a complete knowledge of all that exists.

Mysticism was a method clearing a road to knowing things that transformed one's existence, but despite the mystical implications of much theology, mysticism had many opponents in the *madresehs* of Qom. The way of the Sufis, of collective repetition of the name and attributes of God, sometimes with music and dance, was condemned by almost every mullah Ali had ever met. Many mullahs even thought that the mystical "knowledge of the true world," *erfan,* which seemed to grow so naturally from certain ideas in theology and the general admiration for ascetic practices, was a danger, especially to *talabehs.* After all, they said, filled with the sense of immediate "knowledge" that *erfan* claimed to give, *talabehs* had been known to talk and act like the Sufi who said, "A Sufi is defiled by nothing and purifies everything"—after which a Sufi might feel superior not only to Islamic laws of purity but to whatever laws bound other people.

Ali saw the danger, but in his interest in asceticism he had already felt movements of the heart and premonitions of the mystical ecstasy that Persian poets spoke of. These intimations came to Ali especially during his nighttime prayers. The Koranic verses that promised Paradise to those "who were used to passing little of the night in sleep; and in the hours of early dawn were found asking forgiveness" called Ali (as they did so many other *talabehs*) to follow the example set by leading mullahs in the past and present. These men were said by their relatives or closest pupils to pray much of the night and also to fast from sunrise to sunset even apart from Ramazan, the month of fasting. For most religious leaders these acts of piety were personal and private (and sometimes just as privately doubted by rival mullahs).

There was no doubt in Ali's mind about the nighttime prayers of Ayatollah Marashi. Marashi was a "model" (*marja*), a title acquired by a mullah who had gained acceptance by a significant number of mullahs and others as a pattern to be imitated. Followers imitated a "model" because the learning the "model" possessed enabled him to give an authoritative opinion on disputed questions, questions in which lesser men were well advised *not* to follow their own opinions. But Ali knew that Marashi's followers appreciated their "model" not just as a paragon of learning but also as a man of engaging nobility. Marashi was a sayyed from a princely family, and he had the ease and effortless generosity of someone who felt his noble origins. He was a handsome man, short, with a luxuriant white beard, but his clothes were always a bit in disorder—his turban, in particular, usually looked as if it had been knocked a little askew in running pell-mell down some back alley. He was also a great tease.

When Ali first went to the shrine two hours before sunrise for extra prayers he found Marashi already there, leaning on his walking stick, waiting for the gate to be opened and teasing other mullahs as they turned up. As a mullah nicknamed Haj Amu, "Pilgrim Uncle," famous for the private museum of rosaries and antlers that he had installed in the long entrance hall of his house, joined his circle, Marashi assumed a very dignified air and said, "I hope you and your family and all the honorable mountain goats and stags are in the best of health." This was the occasion for a lot of giggling, even from Haj Amu, who enjoyed this sort of joke.

When the two servants of the shrine opened the gates and threw on the lights in the courtyard, everyone followed Marashi, first to the grave, then to the rooms neighboring the shrine. As Marashi recited the prayer he eventually wept, as the prayerbook recommended, and his prayer lasted longer than most others because he followed the example of the fourth Imam, the great-grandson of the Prophet, who had taken time in his prayers to cry "Forgiveness!" three hundred times. In the months before joining Marashi at the shrine Ali had recited these prayers at home two hours before dawn. But if he was always glad to have performed this prayer, his performance of it at home had often been stiff and distracted by the need to count on his rosary the phrases that had to be repeated three, seventy, and—in the case of "Forgiveness!" —even three hundred times.

This time it was different. His fingers kept count while his tongue said each repetition with more meaning; it was as if he were stripping away the external coating of the repeated word or phrase and getting nearer its reality with each repetition. Perhaps it was the nearness of the grave of Fatemeh; certainly it was in part the example of Marashi, weeping, with his cheek to the ground.

When the light of dawn became clear in the sky and someone gave the call to prayer through a loudspeaker, the light and sound poured into Ali as if they too had been stripped down to their underlying and essential meaning; they were things at once very familiar and very new and newly understood to be very ancient.

Not long after praying with Marashi, Ali asked his father if he could study mysticism with a "guide," as a teacher in mysticism is called. His father recommended a man who was a regular teacher of assigned texts but not someone Ali had studied with. He went to the teacher's house on Friday, the day of rest, at a time suggested by his father. He found the house more than modest, almost mean, but scrupulously clean. When he entered the teacher's reception room he recognized him by sight from the *madreseh:* a sayyed of middle height, always wearing thick black-rimmed eyeglasses but in no other way especially memorable. A patterned curtain was spread on his floor and around it were blankets with very clean sheets laid on them, all instead of the carpets he could not afford. He asked Ali simple questions: How do you see people? How do you see the Imams? What do you think of God? Ali felt encouraged to talk, and the teacher by a few nods and occasional words gave the impression that he enjoyed listening.

After Ali had answered questions for about half an hour the teacher took out his Koran and opened it at random to take an omen before accepting Ali as a pupil. He read the first verse that met his eye: "My two fellow prisoners, are many lords differing among themselves better, or God, the One, the Irresistible?" The teacher looked up from the Koran and recited the next verse: "If not Him, those you worship are nothing but names that you and your fathers have named, and for which God has sent down no authority. Judgment is God's alone. He has commanded you to worship none but Him. This is right religion—yet most men do not know it." Ali knew that these were the words spoken by the prophet Joseph to his fellow prisoners in Egypt, and he knew that he was a welcome pupil after an omen so auspicious, in its reference to the unity of God that transcends the clamorous diversity of man-created names of phantom realities "for which God has sent down no authority."

The teacher began to speak as he put the Koran back in a

pocket inside his cloak. "The basis of *erfan* is that you should see every person as a sign of God. Perform the nighttime prayers. Every time you prostrate yourself as part of prayer, stay prostrate until you have asked God for the spiritual qualities you want. Don't sleep after midnight on Thursday nights; you may sleep only after the dawn prayer. For the next forty days continually say to yourself: 'There is no might and no power except in God.' Everything, absolutely everything you have seen or will see is empty, blank, devoid of all qualities except that it exists; and existence is God. As you come to see things as pure existence you will come to respect all existence as you respect God, then to love all existence as you love God. Be anxiously aware and watch for God. Watch! Watch!"

Ali knew he was supposed to leave. He stood, bowed respectfully with his hand on his breast, and picked up his shoes near the door. He did as he was told. He said, "There is no might and no power save in God" every waking moment except when preparing his lessons or when he was in a public place—and, in fact, he found that without confusing himself he could smuggle this phrase in between his thoughts even while studying. At first he felt people would notice the change in him and say something. His fellow students had always enjoyed teasing him from the days long ago when he had acted as the local guide. And a few months before his interest in mysticism, when he had caught cold in his back and had come to class standing very upright and walking slowly with a cane, one student shouted, "Hey, Ali, congratulations! You've become an ayatollah!"—which made Ali laugh and then yelp, because he had moved too quickly. But now no one asked him if he was studying mysticism or remarked that he had become thoughtful or even distracted—which was just as well, since he was not supposed to tell anyone that he was studying mysticism. Still, it was a little disappointing to seem so much the same on the outside.

When he visited the teacher of *erfan* on the next Friday, the teacher began reading mystical poetry to him. Sometimes the teacher discussed the meaning, sometimes he would just read and repeat a line or even a word after a pause. On this and all succeeding Fridays toward the end of the session he would recite the famous lines of Mowlana:

> I died as mineral and became a plant,
> I died as plant and rose as an animal,
> I died as animal and I was Man.
> Why should I fear? When was I less by dying?
> Yet once more I shall die as Man to soar
> With angels blest; but even from angelhood
> I must pass on: "All save the face of God doth perish."
> When I have sacrificed my angelic soul,
> I shall become what no mind has ever conceived.
> Oh, let me not exist! for nonexistence
> Proclaims in organ tones: "To Him shall we return."

After each recitation the teacher repeated the poem's two quotations from the Koran several times, then remained silent for a few minutes. At these times Ali felt a strong desire to speak, to at least repeat these phrases himself or to say aloud the phrase he had been saying to himself at the teacher's instruction. After a silence the teacher pronounced Ali's own assigned phrase slowly three times, and, with great relief, Ali joined him and murmured the phrase in time with his teacher. This time the teacher ended the session by saying, "Watch! Watch! You will see the light."

Ali knew that seeing light was an important part of training in *erfan*. He also knew that so far he had not seen anything, even if he had felt a great deal. On the last meeting before the forty days were up the teacher said: "For the next forty days you will continually say to yourself, 'O He, O he who is He, O he who is naught but He!' " Ali understood that this sentence emphasized that any person, in fact anything that could be addressed as an individual, was ultimately He—that is, God. Still, he went home a little discouraged at hearing something that sounded so much like the singing and dancing Sufi dervish mysticism that his mullah teachers despised. He was so discouraged, in fact, that he forgot to say the old phrase about God's power for almost half a day.

He woke up on the forty-first day two hours before dawn. He did his ablutions in the pool in the center of the garden at home, then went to perform the night prayer under a short mulberry tree. He felt a new interest in what he was doing because he knew that from this time he would try to be mindful of the new phrase "O He, O he who is He, O he who is naught but He!" Ali started to say the phrase, and it happened: he saw the light. It was not a slowly rising light like that of the dawn; it was not an isolated light like that of the moon or a spotlight. It was everywhere; in fact, it was everything. The pool glowed with light, the garden beds glowed, the sky glowed, the very walls and arches around the courtyard were made of light. He looked up at the mulberry tree: its trunk, branches, twigs, leaves, and fruit were light. He soon saw that as the objects themselves were light, distances between them could not be judged by any kind of shading—each object glowed with equal distinctness. Then he discovered that the light was also inside of him and he could no longer judge his own distance from objects.

A reddish yellow dawn slowly replaced the glowing light with a more ordinary kind of illumination that gave objects shading and distance and quietly replaced the light inside Ali as well. But the experience of the light continued as a faint humming, a subtle vibration that rang through every part of his body for the rest of the day. Ali felt more clearly than before that he did not wish to talk about his experience with others. The experience spilled over to others, it washed around every object he saw; and not only the people but even the objects, according to their capacity, understood what he had felt. As he walked down the alley from his home he saw the blank walls lining both sides as "signs of God," as he himself was a "sign of God." On the inner being of the walls was a message, or perhaps many messages, written in a difficult but decipherable hand, with the deepest and most significant meaning. As he tried to read the message of the walls Ali felt the walls were trying to read the message in him, and with a sudden joy felt half certain that all these messages were the same.

The following Friday the teacher listened to the news of the light with interest but without comment. He began to read poetry by Hafez as well as Mowlana, and Ali was a little surprised. Ali had always loved Hafez as the greatest Persian lyric poet, but Hafez had seemed the very type of the sophisticated yet half wild and frenzied Sufi, a poet whose talk of wine and human beauty had too much personal warmth to be all allegory. When Hafez said, "Stain your prayer rug with wine if the Zoroastrian Elder tells you to," it might be very well to claim that he meant that it was internal religion that really mattered and that the Elder referred to was a master of *erfan*, not a Zoroastrian in the normal sense of a fire worshiper. But Hafez seemed never to find the words to praise such real guardians of religious law as mullahs. During the next week the light appeared most mornings, but Ali did not feel betrayed when it did not appear; he carried confidence in the light inside himself. The month of Moharram had begun, the first ten days of which were devoted to remembering the story of the thrilling and horrifying ten days in which the Imam Hosain defended his family and followers "on the plain of sorrow and misfortune" at Kerbela, in Iraq. This year, however, Ali had been in a meditative mood and had avoided the plays and even the many religious processions of men carrying banners or the small groups of men beating themselves with chains. But on the tenth day, the anniversary of the actual martyrdom of Hosain, Ali went to perform the noonday prayer at the Faiziyeh, and afterward walked up the flight of steps that joined the interior of the *madreseh* to the shrine. In the courtyard of the shrine the play representing the martyrdom of Hosain was in progress, and Ali went out into the courtyard with the fondness of someone visiting a childhood school.

The scene had reached the point at which Hosain had finished his heartrending partings from each of his kin, most of whom would be killed by the surrounding enemy immediately after leaving him or even in his arms. He now stood alone, wounded many times by arrows but still untouched by sword or spear, since the numerous host of his enemies feared his brilliant skill at arms, his bravery, and his sanctity as the only living grandson of the Prophet Mohammed. At this point Shemr, a captain of the enemy, rode in through the central gate of the shrine on a black horse and galloped twice in a wide circle around Hosain. Ali could hear only fragments of the lines of verse that the actors declaimed because people around him, along with the rest of the audience, were commenting on the play with intense emotion and some were even cursing Shemr. The minute Ali caught some words of Shemr—"I am a wretched man, son of a wretched man"—he recognized that Shemr was being played by the young corner grocer of his neighborhood. The whole theatrical troupe, in fact, were from his neighborhood, one of the Hosainiyehs, or religious clubs, that put on such plays.

Yet what a Shemr the grocer was! Even if he declaimed his lines of poetry in the somewhat stiff manner of these plays, his voice came out black like his clothes, his horse, and the charcoal on his face. Ali could just make out an occasional phrase in the conversation between Hosain and Shemr, but when Hosain said, "My father told me that someone like a dog would kill me," the black face of Shemr seemed to burn with pride and anger. As Shemr began to strike Hosain, the crowd cried in horror and pressed inward toward the scene. But they were held back by the presence of twenty or so policemen who had been sent to protect Shemr. When Ali's father had been a youth the crowd had killed an unlucky Shemr.

Shemr tried to strike at Hosain's throat, but when his blows hit the front and sides of Hosain's neck, places where Hosain's grandfather, the Prophet, had kissed him, they were without effect. Then Shemr struck Hosain from behind, and Hosain fell dead, his head severed. A wail went up from the crowd, and people around Ali began to strike themselves on the head and chest. Shemr galloped toward the tents of Hosain's kin and set them on fire; he then wheeled his horse around and started galloping toward that part of the crowd where Ali stood.

As Ali looked at Shemr he realized that he was not just revisiting a favorite scene of his childhood; he was beginning to understand Hosain and Shemr. The terrifying man galloping toward him was pure darkness, the absence of good, a total vacuum. Hosain had known he would be killed. His grandfather, the Prophet, had appeared to him in a vision and had forewarned him. Nevertheless Hosain had set out to claim his right as the leader of the Islamic community: he was pure goodness, and he chose to expose himself to the overwhelmingly superior force of tyrants because the martyrdom of pure goodness at the hands of pure evil would be a "sign," an unambiguous lesson from God that men of all succeeding ages could understand. Like everything else during that forty days, the passion play was a message, the meaning of which *erfan* could disclose in an unexpected way.

When Ali came near the end of his forty days of saying "O He,

O he who is He, O he who is naught but He," his teacher gave him a new phrase to repeat. The phrase was, simply, "O He!" When the forty-first day came and Ali began to repeat it, the light appeared, but something new appeared inside him as well. The humming inside him was nearly in tune with the humming of the world around him, and he knew that his slight separation from this world was the only barrier between him and pure existence. Like Hosain, he was willing to die, but Ali did not want to wait for Shemr; he longed to throw himself in the glowing pool in the middle of the courtyard and to exist entirely as part of the He that was the existence of everything.

When he told his teacher of his new indifference to life, the teacher said, "We're stopping here. This has been enough for you." The teacher began to recite a poem of Hafez:

> I behold the green expanse of the sky and the sickle of the new moon:
> I was reminded both of the field I myself had sown and of the time of reaping.
> I said: "Fortune, you have slept, and the sun has burst forth into the sky;"
> I was told: "In spite of all of this do not abandon hope for what has passed.
> If like Jesus, stripped of all and pure, you ascend to heaven's sphere,
> From your lantern a hundred rays will reach to light the sun itself."

The lines cut into Ali's soul with the knifelike sharpness of the sickle in the poem. It was true homage to the sun to carry one's own lantern to heaven, and the sun itself would accept the lantern's rays; it was not true homage to extinguish one's lantern and let one's harvest rot in the field. His teacher was telling him to remember that although Ali could retravel the mystical path as far as he had gone, he should go no farther; his mission was different: it was intellectual and moral. He recited some passages from Mowlana, then gave Ali his parting advice: "For fifteen minutes before going to sleep envisage everything you have seen during the day and decide which things were good and which things bad. Thank God for your success in everything that was good, and resolve not to repeat anything that was bad. Come talk to me sometimes and continue to be mindful of God in all the moments when you are able to give your thought direction. Go with God's blessing."

Ali went, but the light never completely left him. After a while he no longer saw the light in the outside world, even if he performed the predawn prayers and repeated one of the three sentences his teacher had taught him. He accepted what he understood to be the implication of his teacher's words: that his vocation was for scholarship and the search for good. But the memory of the light continued to shine inside him. It was something that he could mentally reach for, and when he touched it he felt a certain joy. And the remembrance that he had seen things empty of all qualities except existence came to help him at moments of danger. He too would not fear an encounter with Shemr.

• • •

Mysticism, the ambiguity of poetry, belief in the many-faced subtlety of evil, and the never fully resolved choice between the roles of hedonistic cynic and selfless devotee have created the great interior spaces in which the Iranian soul has breathed and survived over at least half a millennium. The first of these, Islamic mysticism, is in fact far older than half a millennium; in one sense it is as old as the Koran. Later Muslim mystics had no doubt of the mystical intent of the Koran when it says: "To God belong the East and the West; wherever you turn, there is the face of God— for God is All-pervading, All-knowing." To the Muslim mystics this version of the world as a place in which the face of God was to be found behind the veil of all appearances promised the immediate and universal presence of God. He was present even within themselves, for, as the Koran said, God was "closer" to each man "than the jugular vein" of his neck.

Yet, however much mysticism might have been foreshadowed in scripture, a specifically "Islamic" tradition of mysticism did not spring up full grown with the appearance of the Koran. Like Islamic education, the Islamic tradition of mysticism was at first a shy plant, cultivated by the efforts of individual believers, who attracted only occasional interest from the early scholars, caliphs, and kings of the Islamic world.

The first soil in which this shy plant grew was the asceticism encouraged by the Koran. Some of the early Muslims, like the early Christians, lived in daily expectation of the Day of Judgment. Night prayers, holy poverty, and fasting in addition to that during the prescribed month of the fast seemed to them the only possible attitude for a watchful soul that felt the nearness of the day when "men will be like scattered moths and the mountains will be like carded wool." Asceticism was a means, an instrument, for that constant "mindfulness" of God that the Koran repeatedly enjoins. The Koranic word for this mindfulness, zekr, combines in its meaning both "mention" and "memory" in a way that would shape all the central spiritual exercises of all Muslim mystics.

A few of the early Muslim ascetics found themselves striving for something more than mere preparedness for the sudden judgment. Like Christian mystics, they wanted to collapse eschatology, the doctrine of final things, and experience in this life the "meeting of God" that the Koran promised in the hereafter. They believed that when the Koran spoke of a people "He will love as they love Him," it was speaking of those who, through their special devotion of love, could meet the Divine Beloved in the present world. Night is the cover of the secret lover, and the metaphor of the Divine Lover soon entered the vocabulary of these devotees of nighttime prayers. Soon they claimed they loved and obeyed the Beloved for His beauty and not simply from fear of judgment and hell. They also collapsed eschatology when they claimed that their intoxication with His beauty was like the intoxication of Paradise, where true Muslims, in the parable given by the Koran, although forbidden wine in this world, are promised a bliss as if surrounded by "rivers of wine, a joy to those who drink."

Slowly mysticism moved from the fringes of the Islamic intellectual world to the center. A strange role was played in this movement by Sohravardi, an Iranian of the twelfth century whose odd and dramatic life matched the odd and dramatic qualities of his ideas. His interpretation of true knowledge as "illumination" won him a permanent place in Eastern Islamic thought as "the master of illumination," and as such he created a stream of mystical thought whose currents and eddies still move through the world of modern Shiah mullahs.

Islamic mysticism did not have to wait for Sohravardi to find popular acceptance. By the twelfth century, Muslim mystics, now called Sufis, or "wearers of wool," because of the hair-shirt asceticism of some of the founders of the movement, had already spread to nearly every part of the Muslim world and among nearly every category of Muslims. They had created a vivid form of spirituality that grasped the imagination not only of Muslims but also of non-Muslims; and conversion to Islam both within the lands ruled by Muslims and in lands far beyond, whether in Central Asia, Central Africa, or elsewhere, took place more often through the efforts of Sufis than through those of any other representatives of Islam.

The conversion by Sufis of the Turks of Central Asia came, in fact, just in time to avert a disaster. In the mid-eleventh century, a generation after Avicenna's death, hordes of Turkish-speaking nomads moved from Central Asia into the Muslim Middle East and swept away the crazy quilt of petty kings whose ailments the great Avicenna had tried to cure. These Turkish conquerors had recently become Muslims, largely though the missionary activities of Sufis; so they did not try to change the religion of the Middle East. But they did introduce changes so profound that the appearance of the Turks ranks in importance in the history of the Islamic Middle East only after the emergence of Islam itself in the seventh century and the challenge of the West in the nineteenth and twentieth centuries. These Turkish invaders were the first wave of a succession of migrations of Turkish peoples from the Central Asian steppes which would continue until the beginning of the sixteenth century. The invasions introduced large numbers of Turkish-speaking pastoralists with their flocks of sheep into the Middle East. These pastoralists and their Turkish cousins who remained in Central Asia formed a new military class that would also supply most of the rulers of the Middle East in general and Iran in particular until such non-Turks as Reza Shah and King Saud appeared at the head of Iranian and Arab states in the twentieth century. When Reza Shah assumed the style of a monarch in 1925, his admirers did not fail to point out that Iran now had a king who, unlike the Turkish Qajars or so many other rulers of Iran, came from stock assumed always to have spoken Persian or a related dialect.

In bringing Turkish armies with Turkish rulers to the Middle East, these invasions widened the already considerable gulf that separated Middle Eastern rulers from the non-Turkish-speaking peoples they ruled. This distance both frightened these non-Turkish-speaking peoples and threw them back on their own resources. The sense of fright constricted the area of allowable intellectual speculation and ended the buzzing but fertile confusion of the age of Avicenna, when philosophers, theologians, dualists, and even thoroughgoing skeptics attacked each other with comparative abandon.

In their desire to secure Islam from the vagaries of foreign rulers and dangers of a socially less stable and predictable world, Arab and Iranian Muslims began to organize religious and social life to a degree that earlier generations of Muslims had thought unnecessary. One such form of organization was the *madreseh*. As we have seen, these colleges of religious learning appeared in the late eleventh century, founded in most cases by Iranian civil servants who worked in high positions for the Turkish sultans and their generals. But simultaneous with or shortly after this time great numbers of "fraternal" associations sprang up in the Islamic Middle East, self-chosen associations of men who realized that they could not count on anyone but themselves to preserve their interests. Some of these fraternal organizations were paramilitary affairs such as youth gangs; some were spiritual brotherhoods such as the Sufi orders.

Sufism, with its initiation of the disciple into a mystical understanding of religion and the world and its new and stirring interest in the inward and immediate apprehension of religious reality by the initiated, was an immense success as a self-created organization of Islamic spiritual life that gave meaning and cohesion to the confused world created by distant and unstable Turkish regimes. Not that the Turks were uninterested in Sufism; some of them had been converted by Sufis, and Sufis resembled the priestly men of their pre-Islamic traditions. In fact, there evolved many "orders" of Sufis, appealing to different categories of society, from the simple Sufism of the peasant chanting the name and epithets of God to the intellectually elaborate pantheistic Sufism of some philosophers.

All these organized forms of Sufism had ceremonies called *zekrs* in which, as the word *zekr* implied, God and his epithets were mentioned repeatedly according to a prescribed pattern, much as the Hindu mystic recites a mantra or the Christian monk on Mount Athos continually repeats, "Lord Jesus Christ, Son of God, have mercy upon me." The prescribed pattern was handed down by someone called variously a "master," an "elder" or a "guide"; and the spiritual genealogy of these masters was a central part of their authority. A great many of these genealogies extended back to Mohammed through his family, as he was presumed to have taught and interpreted to his family a spiritual exercise that had such efficacy. Some genealogies even went back through Mohammed to Adam. As in the genealogies of transmitters of the sayings of Mohammed, such intellectual and spiritual genealogies, vertical links tying men together over the generations, were the characteristic Islamic Middle Eastern image for institutionalization, much as modern Europeans see themselves in groups whose solidarity grows from the crisscrossing of horizontal claims among contemporaries.

Sufis found supporters in all parts of society, even among *madresehs*; but the *madresehs* also produced their most bitter and determined enemies. The teachers and students in *madresehs* recognized in the Sufi a person who claimed spiritual authority without passing through their long curriculum of knowledge, and therefore, some of them said, an amateur and an imposter as an interpreter of Islam. A Sufi story meant to combat the contempt of the mullahs is told of Baba Taher, a Sufi and vastly popular folk poet of Hamadan, who lived in that city around the time the Turks first entered western Iran, a generation after Avicenna attended a local king there. Baba Taher, passing a *madreseh*, asked the students to show him how they acquired knowledge, and as a joke the students told him to spend a winter's night in the freezing pool in the courtyard of the *madreseh*. Baba Taher promptly complied and, after climbing out of the pool in the morning, showed total mastery of all the *madreseh* sciences, declaring in elegant Arabic, "I started the night a Kurd [a country bumpkin], and I entered on the morning as an Arab [a master of book learning]." The mullahs had another, less intellectual reason to distrust the Sufis: Sufi "guides" were an alternate spiritual elite, sometimes in direct competition with themselves for the money and loyalty of both the Muslim masses and the Turkish rulers.

Sohravardi was born in the mid-twelfth century, a century after Baba Taher, in a town not far from Hamadan. He seems to have received a *madreseh* education since his books show thorough mastery of the subjects taught in *madresehs*, although his disciple and biographer says only that "he traveled in his early years in search of learning" and was learned in Islamic law and jurisprudence. He also associated with Sufis and imitated their practices of solitary retreat and fasting, supposedly limiting himself at one period to one meal of a few ounces per week. According to the biographer of Sohravardi, who tells us this, he became a man whose outward behavior was overwhelmingly concerned with "hunger, sleeplessness, and meditation on the divine worlds. He was little inclined to pay attention to people, as he adhered to silence and inward preoccupations, and loved to listen to musical performances and tunes. And he was a man who was granted marvels and signs of God's favor."

Although he traveled constantly in search of an associate with whom he could share his spiritual world, he failed to find one, and at the end of one of his books he wrote: "Here I am, a man nearly thirty, and I have spent most of my life in travel and enquiry in order to search for an associate informed of the real sciences. But I have found no one who had any information of the 'noble sciences,' nor anyone who believed in them."

Sohravardi was by now as thoroughly eccentric in his appearance and actions as in his highly original system of mystical thought. He dressed sometimes as a Muslim learned man in a mantle and a formal tall red hat, sometimes "in the style of the Sufis," and at still other times he dressed more like a ragpicker, with a patched cloak that he pulled up as a hood, at least at those times when he had not twisted a towel around his head. He wrote ecstatic mystical poetry that shocked the anti-Sufi *madreseh* professors with its images of wine and the union of lovers. One of his Arabic poems—he wrote such poems in Persian as well—begins:

> Souls will always yearn for you in tender longing;
>   meeting you as lover is for them the wine and the
>   fragrant herb of greeting.

When Sohravardi's wanderings took him to Aleppo, in Syria, he found that his reputation as a heretic "who believed in the system of the philosophers among the ancients" had preceded him. The Muslim doctors of the law, the Sunni equivalents of the mullahs, issued a legal opinion that he might be killed with impunity, but the governor of the city, a son of the famous Saladin, chose to protect his eccentric guest. Then the doctors of the law turned to Saladin himself. Saladin had just spent the previous twenty-one years trying to unite the confused jumble of Muslim kingdoms in Syria and Egypt into one state capable of defeating the Christian crusading states of Palestine, which he had, in fact, decisively defeated a few years earlier. He had reoccupied Jerusalem, founded *madresehs*, and established an extraordinary degree of moral authority among the feuding Muslims of the Levant as a champion of Islam in general and of Islamic orthodoxy in particular. He now faced a Christian counteroffensive to recapture Jerusalem. In his hard (and ultimately successful) fight against the Christians he did find time for the chivalry that charmed the leaders of this counteroffensive such as England's Richard the Lion-Hearted. He had no time, however, for a Muslim eccentric who displeased the religiously learned Muslims of Syria. He ordered Sohravardi's execution. In late July 1191, Sohravardi, then at most thirty-eight years of age, was killed.

Sohravardi may, as he said, have found no "associate" of his own time who shared his understanding of the sciences, but he claimed as his spiritual ancestors an extraordinarily large number of the "ancient" thinkers known to the Muslims of his time. He saw himself as an heir to Empedocles, Pythagoras, and Plato as well as to the Iranian prophet Zoroaster and a host of culture heroes mentioned in the pre-Islamic Iranian tradition; they were the representatives of what Sohravardi called "the eternal leaven" that animated all true sages. In the Islamic period Sohravardi saw some of the great Sufis as men in whom this leaven was clearly at work. Toward Avicenna, however, who was his true intellectual parent, he had more ambiguous feelings, and with good reason.

Avicenna saw his own synthesis of philosophical thought as within the Aristotelian tradition, and many of his later Muslim followers called themselves Peripatetics, just as the Aristotelians had been called among the Greeks. The Sufis saw Avicenna as the archrationalist, someone deluded by his ingenuity in the use of conventional modes of reasoning. Yet Avicenna had never been fully satisfied with any of his several syntheses and kept writing new *summas* until the end of his life. For one thing, he wanted to take into account the mystical heritage of Neoplatonism, and in particular a summary of Plotinus misattributed, in its Arabic translation, to Aristotle. Toward the end of his life Avicenna conceived the project of an "Eastern philosophy"—Eastern not only because he distinguished his version of philosophy from the more slavish interpreters of Aristotelian philosophy in the Western Islamic world but also because the sun rose in the East and an "illumination" of the soul by a truth inaccessible to the conventional reason was fundamental to this philosophy. The project was never completed; after the master's death the Avicennian tradition flew apart and scholastic tradition seized on the Peripatetic half as the more coherent.

Sohravardi seized the other half. Avicenna, while accepting an Aristotelian physical universe of cause and effect, had seen the human soul as a temporary prisoner of the darkness into which it had descended from a world of light. In an Arabic poem Avicenna wrote of the soul:

> *A dove, both noble and proud, has descended to you*
> *from the most exalted of places . . .*
> *She mourns when she recalls her years in the hunting park,*
> *with tears that pour forth and do not stop. . . .*

Using the same rhyme and general style as in Avicenna's poem, Sohravardi wrote his own poem on the soul as dove, this time represented as triumphing over the grief of separation:

> *She has cast off her bodily frame at the sandy hill*
> *of the hunting park and rushed ardently forward to her*
> *ancient home . . .*
> *It is as if a flash of lightning had shone through the park,*
> *then rolled away as if it had never flashed.*

Sohravardi believed that the dove's triumph came through its contact with the "pre-eternal leaven," the wisdom that in his view must have existed in the world from the very first man, since God would not fail to provide hope of escape. In fact, Sohravardi traced his full spiritual genealogy back to Adam, the first beneficiary of the "illumination" this leaven could give.

Avicenna had already said that the soul could ascend from darkness back to light by knowledge; but such knowledge was not just the understanding that Peripatetic philosophy offered. It was, in addition, the illumination of the soul by its understanding of the symbolic meaning of things quite apart from their formal causes—that is, of the message placed for men by God in anything that men were capable of contemplating. In several short allegories, one composed in a period of imprisonment near Hamadan, Avicenna describes the journey of the soul, in one case led by an angelic guide, in another by a bird, to its forgotten home. Again Sohravardi followed Avicenna's example. But Sohravardi found fault with Avicenna for not going far enough; he criticized Avicenna's allegory because he found it "lacking in the illuminations of understanding concerning the 'supreme experience,' that which [the Koran calls] 'the Great Overwhelming.'" Sohravardi's version takes the soul on a much stranger journey, one that ends on Mount Sinai when the protagonist meets a wise man "from the effulgence of whose light the heavens and the earth almost split." The soul is, however, told that, unlike Avicenna's traveler, it is still far from God.

Sohravardi also found fault with Avicenna for not going far enough in another area: the master's critique of the nonmystical logicians of the Islamic world. In Avicenna's time these nonmystical logicians lived to the west of Iran, and therefore Avicenna called them "Westerners" to indicate not only their geographical location (from Baghdad to Spain) but also their unfortunate lack of interest in the "illumination" offered by the eastern rising of the mystical sun. Aristotle (who seems to have done a lot to improve the dream life of Islamic thinkers of these centuries) appeared to Sohravardi in a quasi dream and confirmed that the mystical and visionary strain of thought was the only true philosophy. In this quasi dream Aristotle—whom Sohravardi calls not only by his usual title, "the First Teacher," but also "the succor of souls, and the guide of wisdom"—first gave Sohravardi a long, rather scholastic lecture on essence and existence, then "praised his teacher the divine Plato in a way that amazed me. Then [continues Sohravardi] I asked him: 'Has any one of the philosophers of Islam attained to his rank?' He answered: 'No, not to a thousandth part of his rank.' Then I enumerated a group I knew about and he paid no attention to them. Then I mentioned [the Sufis] Bistami and Tustari and their like and it was as if he rejoiced. He said: 'It is these who are truly the philosophers and sages! They did not stop at formal knowledge but went on to participatory, unitive, experiential knowledge ... They spoke what we have spoken.' Then he departed from me and left me to weep at his departure."

Sohravardi had studied the philosophers valued at one thousandth of the divine Plato, and his critique of them is ingenious if not always convincing. He tried to demonstrate in their own terms that formal, rational knowledge raises many insoluble problems that fall into infinite regresses or vicious circles. He sought to prove, for example, that "existence" is not a quality properly ascribed to any object if we use conventional rational methods to discuss that object. He therefore proposed another, quite independent kind of knowledge, "illumination," through which we can know of such things as "existence." In advocating knowledge through "illumination" he was accurate in seeing himself as a continuator of the "divine Plato." In the *Republic* Plato compares men to prisoners in an underground cave seeing the shadows of objects cast by a sun that they cannot see but that, as the source of all men's vision, is the one thing without which nothing else could be seen to exist. Sohravardi went further and said that the source of light was also the source of existence. Existence is different from such categories as "circularity" or "redness," which we find ready at hand for actual objects we encounter; we *cannot* "picture" being, and yet it is omnipresent. "Existence" cannot (in Sohravardi's view) be defined or enclosed by rational expressions, yet we all grasp it, and this grasping of it is a shared elemental piece of knowledge through "illumination." Light is like "being" or "existence" in that it is not an object; it has no contours, and, like

"being," light can be said to stop only where it is absent through
interruptions that create shadows. To Sohravardi this similarity
suggests that Being is a spiritual light, the source of which is the
Light of Lights, from which all lesser illumination and attenuated
forms of being emanate.

Light mysticism is no stranger to the Islamic religious tradition;
one of the best loved verses of the Koran, inscribed on thousands
of buildings and memorized in its entirety by millions, declares:
"God is the light of the heavens and the earth; and His light resembles a niche in which is a lamp; and the lamp is within a crystal glass, and the crystal is as if it were a bright star; it is lit from a
blessed tree, an olive, neither of the East nor the West, whose oil
nearly casts its own light, even had fire not touched it. Light upon
light! God guides to His light whom he wishes. God sets forth parables for men, and God knows all things."

The magnificence of this Koranic parable suggested that the
"promised meeting of God" could best be described in terms of
light. Moreover, Mohammed's "Ascent" to the throne of God
under the guidance of the angel Gabriel, a visionary experience
recorded in all his biographies, does in all these accounts culminate in an experience of light.

The clearest Western parallel to the fully elaborated narrative
of Mohammed's "Ascent" is Dante's *Paradiso*, where, at the sum-
mit of Paradise, Saint Bernard urges Dante to look at the "Eternal
Light," and Dante prays to the Light to be returned to his senses
so that he can tell others about it: "O Light supreme that is so far
exalted above world conceiving, grant to my mind again a little of
what you appeared, and give my tongue such power that it may
leave but a gleam of Your power to the people to come. For by
somewhat returning to my memory, and by making these verses
to sound a little, Your victory will be better conceived." In both
Dante's and Mohammed's "Ascent" to heaven, God is the focus
of the most vivid lights, surrounded by nine concentric circles
formed by close files of angels emitting light, and all nine circles
revolve ceaselessly in a movement about the Divine Focus.

Dante may have been influenced by the "Ascent" narratives of
the Muslims, many of which are (wrongly) ascribed by Islamic
tradition to Avicenna, and a few (also wrongly) to Sohravardi.
Dante had a certain knowledge of and respect for Islamic learn-

ing, and he places Avicenna (and Saladin) in Limbo even if he feels obliged to put the Prophet Mohammed and Ali in Hell. But in one respect light and more particularly "the Light of Lights" in Sohravardi and the Divine Focus of Dante and the Muslim visionaries who wrote the narratives of "Ascent" are different. Dante and these visionaries spoke of the light allegorically, while for Sohravardi, as for so many pre-Islamic Iranians, such as the Zoroastrians, light really *was* a being. Some went even further and said that the source of being really *was* the most luminous of objects (and, Sohravardi would add, the farther things were from this Light of Lights the dimmer they became in their degree of being and of luminosity).

Zoroastrianism, *the* Iranian religion for at least a thousand years before Islam, had been the classic focus of dualism in the ancient Near East. For the majority of Zoroastrians the universe was the battleground between Light and Darkness, which were synonyms for Good and Evil. The two forces were engaged in a more or less fair fight, except that Zoroaster foretold the coming of a Savior under whom the forces of Light would win a complete victory. Perhaps it is not an accident that Satan, who hardly plays any role in the early books of the Old Testament, begins to be important to the Jews (and hence, to the Christians) only after the Babylonian exile, which put the Jews into contact with adherents of dualistic religions such as that of ancient Iranians.

Sohravardi, much as he shared the Zoroastrian equation of light and goodness, rejected the Zoroastrian belief in a force of evil nearly equal in its power to the force of good; as a sincere Muslim, he could hardly have done otherwise. And, as a mystic, he also rejected the objectification of evil. Evil was merely the absence of goodness and light; it was, therefore, darkness. But even if we grant that somehow the light has allowed objects to exist that cast shadows and create darkness, how is the badly lit sphere of the material world connected with the blinding brightness of the Light of Lights?

Sohravardi's answer was within the tradition of light mysticism of the ancient world, but, as befitted so original a man, it had an original twist to it. In agreement with the philosophy of earlier light mystics, Sohravardi saw the soul as a focus of luminosity more intense than its surroundings, a distant but recognizable flash from the original and supreme light. The soul was also "concentric" with Being itself, moving in a circle (the perfect figure) around the Light of Lights, yet capable through Illumination of finding within itself the Divine Center of all circular motion. Sohravardi also accepted the theory of the light mystics that the physical universe was connected to its source through emanations of light progressively more distant and attenuated as they spread outward from their source. This theory allowed the universe to remain a ruptureless whole from its most debased material objects to its luminous source. It was also a theory that satisfied the need to account for the apparent connectedness of things, a desire the mystics not only felt but thought philosophically necessary because things share in certain categories such as time which make them part of a whole.

The eccentric twist was that Sohravardi peopled the intermediate worlds between the Light of Lights and our world with angels, who acted, among other things, as the Platonic "ideas," the universals whose existence makes it possible for us to recognize that a specific circle belongs to the category "circularity" or that Lewis Carroll belongs to the category "man." Sohravardi peopled these intermediate worlds not just with a few angels but with masses of angels, to whom he gave ancient Iranian names and whom he arranged in hierarchies on Zoroastrian models, since Zoroastrianism had perhaps the most extravagant and elaborate system of angels among the religions of the pre-Islamic Middle East.

• • •

Sohravardi's desire to add an Iranian dimension to cosmology was consonant with the intellectual atmosphere of his time. Compositions in the Persian language and references to a sense of Iranianness had appeared timidly in the ninth century and their number had grown steadily ever since. Sohravardi's masses of Zoroastrian angels were yet another ancient set of Iranian motifs introduced successfully into the world of Iranian Islam. Sohravardi's occasional use of the Persian language was also an instance of the importance of Sufism and heterodox religious sentiment in general in the widespread revival of Persian as a vehicle for written literature. As a language of written literature, Persian, in one or another of its many forms, had been used for at least twelve hundred years before the rise of Islam. Then for two centuries after the spread of Islam in the seventh century, Persian fell silent, struck dumb by the defeat of the Iranians and the total disappearance of their Zoroastrian state.

In the ninth century an occasional brave soul among the masses of Iranians who wrote in Arabic would actually write down a couplet or stanza in the Persian language he spoke. By the tenth and eleventh centuries things had changed. Many parts of Iran were ruled by Persian-speaking kings who understood Arabic with difficulty, and patterns of patronage changed correspondingly. Avicenna, all of whose royal patrons spoke some dialect of Persian, composed several of his works in Persian so that these patrons would know what they were paying for, and, with characteristic brilliance, he invented a part of the philosophical vocabulary of Persian in doing so. The survival of English after the conquest of England by the French-speaking Normans, and the role of the English language in creating a separate English identity, offers an arresting parallel.

Poetry was the first literary voice in which the new Persian language spoke, and it always remained its strongest voice. The first expressions in this new voice often had little to do with Islam. In fact, the oldest extant fragment of poetry in new Persian is a poem by a Manichaean, therefore a follower of that Iranian dualist heresy of Zoroastrianism which attracted Saint Augustine in his youth before he became a Christian (and a Christian of a markedly Neoplatonic cast).

The largest and by far the greatest early production of new Persian poetry is *The Book of Kings*, completed by Ferdowsi about 1010. *The Book of Kings*, while by no means the product of a Manichaean, bears an ambiguous relation to Islam. Ferdowsi was a Muslim, and he endows some of the heroes of his poem with Muslim values, but the book is unmistakably a celebration of the history of Iran before Islam. It is a huge poetic epic, a pageant of Iranian kings from the time when, in a newly created world, an Iranian culture hero for the first time "invented crown and throne, and was a shah" until the Muslim Arabs defeated the Zoroastrian Iranians and "the throne became the pulpit." The thread that ties the epic together across this span of more than a millennium is the struggle of Iranians—led (but sometimes betrayed) by their kings—against non-Iranians, whose attempts to conquer Iran are acts of "evil." For, as Ferdowsi tells us at the outset, the only enemy of the first Iranian king was Ahriman, the name given by Zoroastrians to the personification of the force of evil whose cosmic battle with good constituted history. *The Book of Kings* is written in a military meter, suggestive of marching and of the rhythmic exercise of men who are preparing to fight this cosmic battle.

The sixty thousand-odd lines of *The Book of Kings* do, in fact, celebrate the heroism of nonroyal champions of good, and kings are sometimes as troublesome to these champions as Agamemnon was to Achilles. Tucked within the giant folds of the royal history are long cycles of stories about the adventures of several of these champions, who combat dragons, witches, and fearsome non-Iranian warriors in distant lands. The greatest of these champions is Rostam. Ferdowsi portrays Rostam as a man who, though undefeatable in battle, has whims, humor, and flaws and knows the sorrow of self-defeat. Perhaps the most moving episode of self-defeat occurs when Rostam unwittingly kills his son, Sohrab, who presented himself for single combat as the champion of the non-Iranians. Even in a flat French translation Matthew Arnold recognized this as a "noble and excellent" story of the kind of "naïve" poetry that he (like Schiller) considered very unlike "sentimental" poetry in that it could "animate," as that of Homer and Shakespeare "animates." In imitation of it, Arnold wrote his poem "Sohrab and Rustum," in which Rostam tells his dying son how he longs that

> ... *I might die, not thou;*
> *And I, not thou, be borne to Seistan ...*
> *But now in blood and battles was my youth,*
> *And full of blood and battles is my age,*
> *And I shall never end this life of blood.*

The lament, in its power and fatalism, is faithful to Ferdowsi.

Persian epic poetry may have been suspect because it found its first voice in the thoroughly non-Muslim desire to celebrate Iran's pagan pre-Islamic past. If so, Persian lyric poetry was far more suspect because—both in legend and fact—the modern Persian lyric was associated with the archheretics, the Manichaeans. From its foundation in the mid-third century until its disappearance in the late Middle Ages, Manichaeanism was an object of horror and fascination for the Zoroastrian, the Christian, and, finally, the Muslim world. The Iranian prophet Mani preached a form of Gnosticism, a belief in salvation through the acquisition of a body of revealed knowledge. And like the Gnostics in the centuries immediately before him, he preached a dualistic religion in which the material world was evil and revealed knowledge was a method for releasing the soul from its imprisonment in matter. But Mani put these ideas together in a new and powerful way: his was a universal religion, destined eventually to convert the whole world, unlike earlier Gnostic faiths that were meant only for the "elect"; and it was also the culmination of all previous religious traditions in the world, including the fledgling religion of Christianity. Manichaeanism invited everyone to enter with an intimacy and fearlessness that terrified and transformed the religions with which it came into contact.

The connection between Manichaeanism and literature grew directly out of Mani's new ideas as to what "scripture" was. The founders of other religions, he said, had not themselves written down the truths they revealed; he not only wrote the revelations he received but did so in books of great beauty, using an alphabet of his own devising. He thereby created the idea of "canon," the closed, authoritative, and metaphysically unique body of writing that later scripturalist religions felt naked without. In competition, Zoroastrians, Christians, and even the Jews (at that time not fully agreed on what was scripture beyond the Torah) were compelled over the next few centuries to define their "canons." The pedestrian Roman notebook, the "codex" of rectangular pages sewn on one side—in its humble utilitarianism so unlike the aristocratic scroll—had achieved its apotheosis through the new, exclusive universalistic religions, all of which preserved their scriptures in rectangular codices. By the fourth century the codex had the world of the written word largely to itself; the magic of saying that the truth was "between these two covers" was too powerful to withstand.

After universality and canonicity Manichaeanism offered a third, related, and equally seductive challenge to the world of religion. Mani, willing to accept so many religious traditions as forerunners of his revelation, was willing to accept many languages as vehicles of scripture, and himself translated the holy books he wrote. Most religions have been stubbornly attached to the language in which God spoke to them and in which their public services—their liturgy—were conducted. Mani himself not only wrote the same scripture in several languages, he encouraged the composition and singing of hymns in all the spoken languages of his followers. And wherever Manichaeanism went it was accompanied by a great burst of vernacular literature—the hymns, prayers, and psalms that the Manichaeans wrote for the many festivals and services that filled the calendar of their religious year.

The dialect of Persian spoken before the Islamic conquest did not remain unaffected by this outburst of song. In content some of these Manichaean psalms, which speak of the sun and moon "shining and glittering from the trunk of a tree" while "flashing birds strut with joy," seem only a step away from the description of nature as it appears in the early lyric poetry of Islamic Iran. From the ninth century, in a period when verse in the new Persian of the Muslims was making its first, timid appearances, we have a manuscript of a Manichaean poem in the same new Persian and using one of the newly invented metrical schemes of that language, certainly the oldest manuscript of such poetry and among the earliest extended examples of the new language. The poem, in typical Manichaean fashion, draws without embarrassment on the reservoir of Islamic imagery well established in Arabic Islamic literature: Noah, Joseph, and the sword of Ali all appear in the space of seven lines. The poem is an angry lament put in the mouth of a man already dead and buried, who complains bitterly that his companions have abandoned him to the arklike coffin and the pitlike grave:

> They put me, like Noah, into an ark by force—that ark
>   which is cast down helplessly on the shallows;
> They throw me, like Joseph, with violence into the pit—that pit
>   whence I shall arise only at the time of the Reckoning.

The enthusiasm with which Manichaeans took to verse in both the older dialect of Persian and the new Islamic Persian and the abandon with which they used the imagery of other religions contributed to the taint of heresy that Persian verse never fully overcame. In the thirteenth century Shams-e Qays, arguably the greatest technical critic of Persian verse in premodern Iran, wrote:

> I have read in some of the books of the Persians that the religiously learned men of the time of [the pre-Islamic king] Bahram [who ruled Iran from 428 to 438] saw nothing to disapprove of in his character and circumstances except the composition of poetry. So when he came to the throne Azorpat came before him and offered this advice: "O king, know that the composition of poetry is one of the gravest faults of kings and the vilest habits of sovereigns, because . . . its basis is foul exaggeration and extravagant excess. Consequently the great philosophers of religion . . . have considered poets among the causes of the destruction of preceding kingdoms and past nations. . . . All the Manichaean heretics and the deniers of the prophets have fallen into the vain fantasies of criticizing the revealed books and the divinely sent prophets only by means of putting speech into verse. . . . The first creature who praised himself in verse and vaunted himself over others was Satan, be he cursed!" Bahram changed his ways and never again spoke poetry.

By the eleventh century it was too late for Iranians to change their ways. The taint of heresy and the pagan subjects of the national epic could not deter Muslim Iranians from making poetry the central icon of their culture, the focus of emotion in which every speaker of Persian felt he or she could see something essential of himself or herself. As Persian poetry grew in volume and variety it extended its influence even to the illiterate population of Iran, who knew and know by heart lines of Hafez and Saadi and Mowlana Jalal ad-Din Rumi and used and still use them in their speech the way speakers of other languages use proverbs. The cultural power of Persian literature and Persian poetry in particular was shown when the Turks of Anatolia and of Central Asia, the Muslims of India and even of areas farther east, in Malaysia and Indonesia, turned to Persian models when they created literature in their own languages. This vast area, from Turkey to Indonesia, which had received an Islamic cultural mode with a

distinctly Persian flavor, continued for centuries to look to Iran as
a model of high culture; and for them (as for Iranians) the most
vivid proof of this cultural preeminence was Persian poetry.

Not unnaturally, Iranian Muslims used a poetry very emotionally intimate and very widely shared to express their Islamic religious beliefs, and after a few centuries, it is hard to find a
significant Persian poem that, like *The Book of Kings*, contains little
overt reference to Islam and, in particular, to Islamic imagery. But
if Persian poetry was not un-Islamic, great quantities of it were
not properly Islamic either. The "pagan" and Manichaean elements had a hand in setting this not quite Islamic tone for Persian
poetry; the Sufis completed their work. Sufism shared with Manichaeanism the desire to celebrate religion in the spoken language
of its communities, and Iranian Sufis turned to writing Sufi literature in Persian with the same enthusiasm that later gave Urdu,
Pashto, and a host of the other languages of Muslims such a large
body of Sufi literature.

Persian, however, was the first linguistic experiment of the
Sufis outside Arabic. And the Sufis, who had already established
their seemingly heterodox convention of describing the mystical
experience as intoxication, and the presence of God as the union
of lovers, found that Persian, already used allegorically by the
Manichaeans, already used in a "pagan" spirit by Ferdowsi to celebrate drinking bouts, romances, and battles, lent itself to even
more extravagant metaphors and allegories about the mystical
life than did Arabic. In a typical poem Attar, usually counted as
one of the more "orthodox" poets of the Persian Sufi tradition,
writes:

> Muslims, I am that ancient Zoroastrian who built the temple of
>   idolatry;
> Stepping on its roof, I gave my proclamation to the world.
> I gave to you the call to pray for impious disbelief, oh Muslims,
> Saying: "I have restored these ancient temples to their former
>   luster."
> If they should burn poor Attar in this fire of theirs,
> Then be my witness, brave men, that it is I who gave my life as
>   sacrifice.

Commentators explained away the shocking paganism of this poem (as they would subsequently explain away similar poems by Hafez and a hundred other Persian poets) by saying that the "idolatry" of the Zoroastrian represented the interiorized faith of the true believer, in contrast to the hypocrisy of the men whose shamming outward obedience to Islam cloaked their inner disbelief. All this translation of images into Sufi philosophy is faithful to what we are almost sure was Attar's fairly orthodox Sufi belief.

Yet Attar certainly did not want his readers to think that he was *merely* writing an allegory. The thrill of the poem was the suggestion that the poet might just believe some of the blasphemous things he was saying, might just believe that the old religion was nobler or that antinomianism—the rejection of all religiously sanctioned law—was true piety. Ghaleb, an Indian Persian poet of the nineteenth century, made fun of the triumph of this mad mixture of Zoroastrians, fire temples, Christian bishops, Hindu Brahmins, vintners, and taverns in Persian poetry when he said in one of his poems: "The Moslem has not dominated in any age; no sooner does the Zoroastrian leave the tavern than the Christian enters!" It was as if the established idiom of religious poetry among pious Christians was replete with images from the Song of Solomon, all apparently allegorical yet all so mixed with references to pagan symbols of erotic love and physical ecstasy, such as Aphrodite and Dionysus, that the reader could never dismiss the image of worldly love and worldly intoxication from his mind while reading it.

By the same token, even when Persian poets such as Hafez seem to speak most realistically and lovingly of the material world, they can almost never avoid using Islamic imagery, as in the poem by Hafez that begins:

> *Hair disheveled, sweating, laughing-lipped and drunk;*
> *Shirt torn, singing poems, a cup of wine in hand . . .*
> *Midnight last night to my pillow he came and sat . . .*
> *He said: Old love of mine, are you sound asleep?*

Later in this poem Hafez refers to "the day of: 'Am I not your Lord,'" the day when—according to the Koran—newly created mankind answered this question with a resounding "yes" and accepted moral responsibility ever after. The one-eyed, single-minded interpreter could always insist that this Islamic imagery proved that this poetry was nothing but religious allegory, even though any two-eyed interpreter could see that it had to be something more.

In fact, Persian poetry came to be the emotional home in which the ambiguity that was at the heart of Iranian culture lived most freely and openly. What Persian poetry expressed was not an enigma to be solved but an enigma that was unsolvable. In Persian poetry of any worth nothing was *merely* something else; the inner space of the spirit in which Persian poetry underwent its thousand transformations was ultimately a place where this ambiguous language reached a private emotional value that had to remain private, because to decode it as mere allegory, to reexpress it in any form of explanatory paraphrase would be to place it back in the public domain and, therefore, in the realm in which it was intended to remain ambiguous.

It is tempting to see the origins of this kaleidoscopic world of meaningful ambiguity in the early enigma of Iranian culture after the Arab conquest. Unlike the Egyptians and the Mesopotamians, who lost virtually all identity with the four millennia of their history that preceded the Islamic conquest, and whose ancient languages lived on only in obscure villages and in the liturgies of local Christians while the universal spoken language of Egypt and Mesopotamia became Arabic, Iranians retained their language and a fierce pride in their continuity with their pagan pre-Islamic ancestors. Iranians did so even though their culture (unlike the cultures of Christianity and Judaism) barely rated a mention in the Koran. From a strict Islamic point of view pre-Islamic Iranian culture was just one of the many polytheistic cultures, superseded by all monotheisms in general and by Islam in particular, that could safely be confided to the moral trash heap of pre-Islamic "ignorance." The enigma was real; nothing in the historical record casts doubt on the sincerity with which the majority of Iranians accepted Islam or the spontaneous pleasure that the majority of Iranians took in telling and retelling in their own language the long history of their pagan past.

The love of ambiguity had deeper and stronger reasons. It was also the register in which the Persian-speaking Iranians could talk and yet keep an emotional distance from the Turk and the Mongol who ruled them. In fact, it allowed them to keep a distance from the generations of rapacious and parasitical rulers, Iranian as well as non-Iranian, who had held power by standing on the necks of their Iranian subjects. But this ambiguity meant even more. It was the dimension in which the two great and ultimately contradictory spiritual visions of Western Asia could be simultaneously accepted without having to be resolved: the Gnostic and Neoplatonic vision of the movement possible in the life of any historical person from time into the eternal, as Sohravardi's bird escaped the hunting park; and the vision of Zoroastrianism, Judaism, Christianity, and Islam in which history is a drama of salvation that stretches through all human time from creation to the Resurrection.

This love of ambiguity was even reflected in the attitude toward Satan. In Zoroastrianism there had been nothing ambiguous about God, called Ahura-Mazda, and Satan, who was called Ahriman. In a Zoroastrian catechism that any boy or girl must know when he or she reaches fifteen and joins the world of religious adults, the catechumen says: "I must have no doubt but that there are two first principles, one the Creator and the other the Destroyer. The Creator is Ahura-Mazda, who is all goodness and all light; and the Destroyer is the accursed Destructive Spirit, who is all wickedness and full of death, a liar and a deceiver." For the Manichaeans he was not only evilness and death, he was "matter," the sticky pitch that has ensnared our souls and from which we seek to escape.

In Islam, Satan often appears very much as he appears in Christianity: that figure of false pride, of rebellion against God, that the theologians may take as a personification of evil or even—in a Neoplatonic vein—as the absence of good, but a figure that the ordinary believer recognizes as the wily plotter who tempts and provokes mankind into evil thoughts and actions. No ceremony in the pilgrimage to Mecca is more dangerous to the believers than the ceremony in which they throng around a stone column and throw pebbles at it as a symbol of the hated Satan, a hatred so vividly expressed that the participants sometimes hit each other with their pebbles in the abstraction of their emotion. Popular Islamic thought even creates—alongside a guardian angel—an attendant personal satan for every person, who thereby becomes a microcosmic battlefield of good and evil somewhat in the style in which Zoroastrianism represents the battle of good and evil in the macrocosm.

Yet Satan emerges as a remarkably complex personality in Islam, perhaps more complex than the Satan of Zoroastrianism, Judaism, and Christianity. The tradition that Satan invented poetry, mentioned by Shams-e Qays, is in part inspired by an ancient Arabian notion that personal "satans," much like the "demons" of the ancient Greeks, were responsible for creative impulses. A far more important source of the complex personality of Satan in Islam is the Koranic story of Satan's first disobedience. According to the Koran, after God molded man from clay and breathed life into him, He ordered the angels to bow before man, and one among the angels—Satan—refused and declared, "I am better than he; You created me from fire and You created him from earth." And for this God expelled and cursed Satan. Satan, however, asked and was granted a respite from God's judgment until the day of the Resurrection, and Satan said, "Then, by Your power I will surely lead them all astray, except for Your servants among them, those pure in heart."

Satan's independence among the angels, God's willingness to give him a respite, and Satan's obedient acknowledgment that he was the instrument of God's power suggested a more interesting Prince of Darkness than a mere "personification of evil," however full-bloodedly evil this personification might seem in some Koranic passages. The Sufis gazed at the possibilities of this complex Satan with fascination and, especially in the Persian-speaking Eastern Islamic world, they developed an alternate Satan. This Satan was the ultimate monotheist, the angel whose worship of God was so single-hearted that he refused to bow to man because he would bow only to God, the "lover" whose love was so unreserved that he accepted a role of alienation from the Divine Beloved because of his loving obedience to the divine command. The morally rehabilitated Satan is, in fact, a kind of martyr. In the poetry of Attar, Satan explains his motives, his suffering, and his understanding of God's secret purpose in casting him out:

> Far off stood I, yet I cannot abide that for even a moment anyone else
>   except me behold that Face . . .
> Far off stood I, in a state of gloom from separation,
>   because I do not have the radiance of that union's intimacy.
> Although I have been banished from His threshold,
>   I do not turn my head a jot from His path.
> From the moment I set my foot in the Beloved's alley
>   I have not looked in any direction but His;
> Since I am now the intimate companion to the secret's meaning,
>   I shall not look—not even the slightest bit—at anyone else.

And yet Attar, like every master of Persian poetry, exercises his right to ambiguity and at times presents us with the other Satan:

> Satan said: "I am better than Adam!" Without doubt
>   he is accursed until Resurrection Day. . . .
> Satan was banished because of his overweening pride;
>   Adam was welcomed because he sought forgiveness.

No wonder a generation later Saadi, who, despite his very moving Sufi lyrical poems, is better known for his worldly-wise books of counsel, poked gentle fun at his contemporaries' projections of character onto the mystery that was Satan:

> I don't know where I saw it in a book,
>   that a certain man saw Satan in a dream;
> He had the noble stature of a fir, the comely beauty of the houris,
>   And light streamed from his face as from the sun.
> He went up to Satan and said: "How amazing, is this you?
>   Or might you rather be an angel with such beauty? . . .
> They imagined you to be a man of dreadful face
>   when in the bathhouse they painted you so foul."
> Satan said: "O lucky man, this shape you saw is not mine;
>   The pen that paints me is in the hand of the enemy."

. . .

The hand that painted the devil in such contradictory fashions had a complementary ability to paint contradictory self-portraits of itself. The Persian poet, even the folk poet, overwhelmingly preferred to paint himself at the far ends of the moral spectrum, appearing sometimes as the hedonistic cynic and sometimes as the selfless devotee. Of the two the hedonistic cynic was once the best known outside Iran itself because its brilliant expression in the quatrains of Omar Khayyam found a brilliant English interpreter in Edward FitzGerald. We have reliable versions of the mathematical and astronomical works of Omar Khayyam that show him to be one of the most gifted men of his day; among other things, he is generally credited with the first solution of the quadratic equation. But Omar the poet is a shadowy figure; while there seems no reason to doubt that he wrote quatrains, no quatrain can be ascribed to him with certainty.

Persian quatrains form a powerful current that runs under the respectable surface of Persian literature. The quatrain is a poetical form that never quite achieved the respectability of the epic or lyric but came so easily and naturally to the Persian tongue that anonymous quatrains appear on medieval Iranian pottery bowls and on the flyleaves of medieval books. Quatrains are ascribed to Ferdowsi, Attar, Saadi, Hafez, Mowlana, and a host of other Persian poets as well as to such "wise men" as Avicenna, Sohravardi, and—most particularly—Baba Taher (who spent the night in the freezing pool). But these quatrains, sometimes of unimpeachable authenticity, rarely appear in the respectable collected works of these authors which were prepared in premodern Iran.

Some authors of these quatrains have a strong Sufi cast and are without doubt meant to be understood in a Sufi sense. And indeed there were and are one-eyed interpreters of the large body of Omarian quatrains, the quatrains of hedonistic and cynical spirit, who use the fully developed Perso-Islamic poetic idiom that Omar Khayyam employed as an excuse to allegorize all of these quatrains into Sufi lessons. But FitzGerald got it right when he spoke of "Omar's Epicurean audacity of thought." And Fitz-Gerald's contemporary Matthew Arnold, who thought the true subject of poetry was the moral question of how to live, was right to be shocked by the appeal of Omar's hedonism: "We find attraction, at times, even in a poetry of revolt against [morals]; in a poetry that might take for its motto Omar Khayyam's words: 'Let us make up in the tavern for the time we have wasted in the mosque.' "

Some of the air of world-weariness that pervades the Omarian quatrains derives from a common theme in Persian poetry: the futility of all human desires in the face of inevitable death:

> *They say the Lion and the Lizard keep*
> *The Courts where Jamshyd gloried and drank deep:*
> *And Bahram, that great Hunter—The Wild Ass*
> *Stamps o'er his Head, but cannot break his Sleep.*

The sentiment is not far from "Ozymandias." It is a sentiment so well known throughout the cultural sphere of Persian poetry that Mehmet, the Ottoman sultan, is said to have recited kindred lines from Saadi when, in 1453, he rode into Aya Sofia, the cathedral church of Constantinople, which he had just conquered from the last of the Byzantine Roman emperors:

> *The spider is the chamberlain in the palace of the Caesars*
> *The owl is the trumpeter on the battlements of Afrasiyab.*

The Omarian quatrains sound another note not entirely unknown in Persian Sufi poetry: the complaint against a God who has dropped humans into an inexplicable world (and enmeshed them in a web of responsibilities to which they have not agreed):

> *Into this Universe, and why not knowing*
> *Nor whence, like water willy-nilly flowing;*
> *And out of it, as Wind along the Waste,*
> *I know not whither, willy-nilly blowing.*

(The Persian original begins: "He first brought me in confusion into existence"—which lays the blame squarely on God.) But the true Omarian cynicism, the pose that convinced one medieval biographer that Omar was "an unhappy philosopher, an atheist and materialist," is expressed in quatrains such as:

Oh, come with old Khayyam, and leave the Wise
To talk: one thing is certain, that Life flies;
One thing is certain, and the Rest is Lies:
The Flower that once has blown for ever dies.

No one intimate with Persian life could fail to recognize the Omarian self-portrait as a hedonistic cynic for what it is: a pose, but a recurrent pose that has frequently been the inspiration for a private but nonetheless fervent cynicism and hedonism in real life.

The more public poetic pose of the selfless devotee is more problematical; its translation into real life would seem to involve a degree of sacrifice beyond the normal endurance of the poseur. Yet to understand it one can turn to an arena in which the portrait as devotee is a dramatic pose adopted self-consciously: the Persian passion play, which is as characteristic an expression of the Iranian spirit as the cynical quatrain. The passion play of the Shiah world is the only indigenous theater of the Muslims. It is as clearly of religious origin as the drama of ancient Greece that grew from choric hymns to Dionysus or the medieval miracle, morality, and mystery plays that grew from accretions to the gestures of the Mass.

Its origins lie in the historical drama that made Iran a Shiah country and in the process gave Shi'ism an Iranian cast. Until the sixteenth century Shi'ism was the majority belief in only a few areas of Iran, including, of course, Qom. The intellectually important centers of Shi'ism were in the Arab world, in the security of the mountains of southern Lebanon, where the exchange of polemical books and pamphlets with their Sunni neighbors kept alive a vigorous tradition of learning among the Lebanese Shiah, and in southern Iraq, where the Shiah *madreseh* founded in Najaf in the eleventh century somehow lived on through dozens of changes of regimes.

Some time around 1500 the Muslim world began to be aware of a new center of Shi'ism in the Turkish-speaking northwestern province of Iran, Azerbaijan. Sufism propelled these Azerbaijani Shiah as much as Shi'ism; they were led by a Turkish-speaking family of hereditary leaders of a Gnostic Sufi brotherhood who called themselves (on uncertain evidence, first challenged by Kasravi) descendants of Ali. The authority of these Safavi leaders, these supposed descendants of Ali, over their disciples was practically total, as the rules of some Sufi orders require. As their disciples included some of the warlike semi-nomadic Turkoman tribes of Azerbaijan and the surrounding provinces, this spiritual authority was eventually translated into political sovereignty. After a few generations as Sufi leaders they had intermarried with the noblest Turkoman ruling houses, and they were also obeyed as Turkoman princes of royal blood.

In 1501, after subduing all of Azerbaijan, the leader of the Safavi order, Esma'il, assumed the title of "shah." He was, as a contemporary Italian traveler tells us, "loved and reverenced by his people as a god, and especially by his soldiers, many of whom enter into battle without armor." At the same time he decreed that all public expression of Islam in his realm would be Shiah. As he explained, "I am committed to this action; God and the Immaculate Imams are with me, and I fear no one; if the people utter one word of protest, by God's help I will draw the sword and leave not one of them alive." In the next few years his ecstatic votaries proved with skill that they could draw the sword on his behalf; by 1510 all of the Iranian plateau was under his control.

The unification of Iran into a single state for the first time since the Arab Muslim conquests of the 740s helped to perpetuate what Shah Esma'il had created as a strong and stable state. Even many of the Turkish-speaking inhabitants of Iran saw themselves as "Iranian" in that they lived in and guarded "the soil of Iran," as it was called in *The Book of Kings* (which book, incidentally, owed its popularity as much to the interest of Turkish rulers as to Persian readers). This unification took place at the same time as the unification of the rest of the Middle East under the control of the Ottoman Turks, who were staunch Sunnis. Shi'ism now became intertwined with the independent political existence of the "soil of Iran." The Ottoman sultan Selim invaded Iran with a view to crushing this heretic, and in 1514 the sultan, who, with his superb cannons and enormous resources probably had the most powerful land army in Europe or Western Asia, gave Shah Esma'il a punishing defeat. The defeat was not decisive. The loyalty of Esma'il's Iranian subjects enabled him to follow a scorched-earth policy, which eventually obliged the Ottomans to give up their conquests in Iran.

Nevertheless the bloom was off Shah Esma'il's reputation of invincibility. The bloom was also off the flower of ecstatic devotion to the Safavi Sufi leader as the "perfect master." In part Shah Esma'il conspired in this change, because, unlike most of his votaries, he was aware that there was something more to Shi'ism than devotion to the Imams and hatred for their enemies. A Persian chronicle of the 1570s says (undoubtedly with some exaggeration) that when in 1501 he proclaimed Shi'ism the state religion he could find only one of the many Shiah books of laws in his capital, and of that one, only the first volume. The Iraqi and Lebanese Shiah had the books and the learning to understand them; Shah Esma'il and his successors welcomed them.

The shah's embrace was something of a puzzlement for the Shiah mullahs, who were in no sense ecstatic votaries of the Safavi Sufi order. The learned Shiah tradition held that six and a quarter centuries before Shah Esma'il made Shi'ism the official religion of Iran the twelfth in the line of Imams recognized as infallible by the Shiah community had been "withdrawn" from the eyes of men. The Shiahs believed that he still existed; the continual presence of an infallible Imam was a mercy that—in their view—God could not fail to provide for his community. But the Imam would be actively present in the world of men only when he returned as the Lord of the Age, as the Shiah call him, the Messiah who will bring an age of justice followed by the Judgment. In the meantime all governments were necessarily makeshift and stopgap measures to prevent anarchy.

Shah Esma'il and his followers, as they charged the famous cannon of the Ottoman Turks who threatened them from the west, and drove back the hordes of Central Asian Turks from the east, never stopped to ask about the juridical standing of their government in the absence of the Imam. Shah Esma'il in the poetry attributed to him alternates between Sufi-like expressions of personal near-identification with God ("I am the Absolute Truth") and self-depiction as the instrument of past imams:

> *We are Hosain's men, and this is our epoch.*
> *In devotion we are the slaves of the Imam;*
> *Our name is "zealot" and our title "martyr."*

For the mullahs, however, matters were not so easy. In the view of the majority of them, those high mullah jurisconsults called *mojtaheds* had the exclusive right to interpret right and wrong in matters of personal, social, and political morality during the absence of the twelfth Imam. Insofar as there could be Shiah government, it should be government that was in some way under the supervision of these jurisconsults. Yet some of the mullahs argued that it was pointless, perhaps even sacrilegious, to set up a government avowedly Shiah in character before the return of the twelfth Imam. By either interpretation the Safavis were unacceptable. However much they gloried in calling themselves "the dogs of the threshold of Ali," the Safavis made the dubious claim that they had established a truly Shiah state on behalf of the Imam in his absence; and they were not jurisconsults. Some conscientious Shiah jurisconsults and lesser divines disregarded the general invitation issued by the Safavis and chose to stay at home.

Many, however, could not resist the opportunity. This was a militant Shiah government, something virtually unprecedented, for the few earlier Shiah governments—those of the eleventh century, for example, when Najaf first became a center of learning—had never tried to coerce their subjects into being Shiah Muslims. The Safavis not only coerced their subjects but allotted a vast proportion of their revenues for the support of mullahs and *madresehs*. Men such as the lachrymose sayyed Nematollah struggled for recognition within the religious establishment because the rewards were enormous. And the Safavis saw to it that there really was a religious establishment. Shah Esma'il appointed an official as head of the religious class who was in charge of all public religious duties, all pious endowments, and the appointment of all Islamic judges.

On one issue the Safavis and the mullahs could embrace in enthusiastic agreement: they both wanted to implant a deeper commitment to Shi'ism in the Iranian masses. In the passion of Hosain they found their means. The passion constituted by the suffering and martyrdom of heroes was a resonant theme in the Iranian tradition long before the Safavis. Two of the heroes of the national epic, *The Book of Kings*, are killed treacherously and are bitterly lamented, and the death of one of these heroes was the focus of a cult of public mourning that Iranian minstrels ornamented with cycles of songs called "the weeping of the magi" (the magi being the priests of Zoroastrianism).

As early as the tenth century the Iranian Shiah introduced ceremonies for Ashura, the anniversary of Hosain's death, in which women went into the market "with their hair disheveled, beating their faces and wailing over Hosain, son of Ali." These sentiments found their authentic private Persian voice, however, only centuries later when—just as the Safavis were coming to power—an Iranian wrote *The Garden of the Martyrs*, an account of the sufferings of the Imams and especially "the Lord of the Martyrs," Hosain. "Garden" in the title is *rowzeh;* and the book was and is the inspiration for a large category of preachers called *rowzeh-khans*— that is, "*rowzeh* readers"—who have specialized in recitation from this book and some of its imitations such as *The Deluge of Weeping* and *The Mysteries of Martyrdom*. The *rowzeh-khans* give recitations (for which they are generously paid) throughout the year in private homes as well as on such sanctified holidays as Ashura; Iranians grant them access to the private quarters of their homes, the *andarunis,* which no other group in society has.

In the Safavi period the narratives of Hosain's martyrdom and the processions of public mourning came together. A Turkish traveler to Iran in 1640 describes the climax of a vast public mourning on Ashura held before "the nobles and notables and all the people of the city, great and small":

> When the reader of the book [on the martyrdom of Hosain] reaches the part describing the manner in which the accursed Shemr killed the oppressed Imam Hosain, at that very moment, they bring out to the field . . . mock representations of the bodies of the dead children of the Imam. Upon seeing this spectacle shouts and screams and wailings of "Alas, Hosain" mount from the people to the heavens and all spectators weep and wail. Hundreds of Hosain's devotees beat and wound their heads, faces and bodies with swords and knives. For the love of Imam Hosain they

make their blood flow. The green grassy field becomes bloodied and looks like a field of poppies. Then the mock dead are carried from the field and the reading of the story of Imam Hosain's martyrdom is completed.

Sometimes Ashura processions in the Safavi period also included *tableaux vivants* of butchered martyrs smeared with blood which were moved along on wheeled platforms. The European medieval theater of the Stations of the Cross, with its fixed tableaux and moving viewer-penitents, had been an antecedent to the full theater of the latter Middle Ages; and the Ashura celebrations of Safavi Iran are only a step away from the full-blown modern Shiah theater of martyrdom.

Self-mutilation in emulation of the "passion" of heroes who are human yet divine is no stranger to the West: flagellants who whipped themselves both in penance and in remembrance of the scourging and crucifixion of Jesus appeared in almost every western European country in the Middle Ages, sometimes with the disapproval of the church. Sometimes, like the group of flagellants who at the opening of the fifteenth century followed Saint Vincent Ferrer on his journey to preach the need of repentance and the coming of the Judgment, they were at the very heart of what conscientious churchmen most admired. Flagellation survives in Spain and in many parts of the Hispanic world. It survives, in fact, in the United States in New Mexico, where, in spite of a century of horrified disapproval by Protestants and non-Hispanic Catholics, the brotherhoods of Penitentes commemorate the passion of Jesus by flagellation, the carrying of heavy wooden crosses, and many other forms of discipline, physical and spiritual. The resemblance of the form of Penitente religiosity to Shiah practices extends to tableaux from the life of Jesus and even to the drama of a simulated crucifixion.

The resemblance in psychological content is even more striking: both the Shiah and the New Mexican Penitentes are using violation of physical self-integrity as a means to enter an altered state of awareness in which ordinary restraints of prudence are removed and the penitent loses not only his sense of self-protection but also his sense of separateness. By sharing his "discipline" the penitent has broken the boundary between himself and his fellow penitents and even—to some extent—between himself and the spiritual model he seeks to imitate; as the Penitentes say, the "Brothers of Blood" become "Brothers of Light." At bottom, both are forms of folk mysticism.

In the eighteenth century Iranian Shi'ism needed folk mysticism to stay alive. The Safavi state collapsed at the beginning of the century in the face of Sunni Afghan invaders, and for the better part of the eighteenth century Iran lived in disorder and in fear of its Sunni neighbors. Sufism, the established Islamic mysticism, even though it had given birth to the Safavi government, was anathema to the overwhelming majority of the mullahs, especially in the eighteenth century. (One famous mullah of the early nineteenth century gained the epithet "Sufi-killer" for his vigorous attempts to exterminate Sufis.) Somehow, in this confused environment the ceremony of mourning for Hosain continued to develop and emerged as full-fledged drama.

The first indisputable account of such drama was written by an Englishman in the 1780s:

> All the various events are represented by the Persians during the first days of Moharram. . . . Each day some particular action of the story is represented by people selected for the purpose of performing those concerned in it. . . . Among the most affecting representations is the marriage of young Qasem, the son of Hasan, and a nephew of Hosain, with his daughter; but this was never consummated, as Qasem was killed in a skirmish on the banks of the Euphrates, on the 7th of Moharram. On this occasion, a boy represents the bride, decorated in her wedding garment, and attended by the females of the family chanting a mourning elegy, in which are related the circumstances of her betrothed husband being cut off by infidels (for that is the term by which Shiah speak of Sunnis). The parting between her and her husband is also represented, when on his going to the field she takes an affectionate leave of him, and on his quitting her presents him with a burial vest, which she puts round his neck.

Clearly William Francklin had seen the full cycle of plays that culminate with the death of Hosain on the tenth of Moharram. With characteristic inventiveness Iranians have written and rewritten these cycles of plays right down to the present, and professional troupes travel to remote villages to perform the plays throughout the year. Every play has a reference to the fate of Hosain, and the plays performed on Ashura by amateurs and professionals throughout Iran are devoted entirely to his martyrdom, the only subject imaginable on that date. But the other plays can have remote connection with the actual events of Ashura: one, for example, concerns Solomon and the Queen of Sheba, who at one point in their romance, apropos of nothing, together cross the plain where Hosain will be killed and give speeches on the melancholy nature of the spot. Usually the heroes speak verse, the villains prose; the protagonists wear green and white, the antagonists wear red. For the last few generations warriors have worn British officers' jackets instead of coats of mail, and for over a century one of the stock plays revolves around the "Ambassador of the Europeans," who, with magnificent disregard for chronology, appears at the court of Yazid, the oppressor of Hosain, in order to plead for his life. Learned characters often wear reading glasses and, recently, bad characters wear sunglasses.

In fact, the passion play, or *taaziyeh*, is not—and in no sense wants to be—illusionistic theater. A bowl of water represents the Euphrates; if the angel Gabriel carries an umbrella, the audience knows he has just descended from heaven. Again Matthew Arnold got it right. In his essay "A Persian Passion Play," written in 1871, he compared accounts of these plays given by a European traveler to the passion play of Oberammergau, and he noticed that in this kind of theater "the power of the actors is in their genuine sense of the seriousness of the business they are engaged in. They are, like the public around them, penetrated with this." It is exactly the community of emotion and the absence of any fixed barrier between the actors and the audience that give these plays their force; actors and audience flow over one another the way text and miniature flow onto each other in a Persian manuscript. Nowadays when the marriage is performed in the play about Qasem which Francklin described two hundred years ago, cookies are passed among the audience while festive music is played. Then suddenly the riderless horse of Hosain's eldest son, who has been defending the small band during the marriage, enters the joyous scene. Everyone freezes in position. Qasem passes through the audience (since this is theater in the round) to reach "the battlefield," and he quickly returns at the head of a procession that carries the slain son of Hosain on shields. The whole audience rises to its feet and weeps, as at a real funeral procession. And, as it is a mark of respect to the deceased to carry the coffin, even those far from the procession raise their hands in the air as if to support it. The body is laid on the stage, and funeral music is played while the exuberant wedding music is resumed. The audience finds itself both laughing and weeping as the conflicting scenes continue onstage. Throughout these proceedings the director has been walking around the stage reciting bits of narrative and beating his breast with emotion at moments of sadness.

Matthew Arnold noticed that the actors in such dramas could not properly be said to "act" their parts—and, one could add, such theater is not "theater" in any ordinary sense of the word. The actors are not supposed to "identify" with the persons they represent; in any case, to do so is theologically forbidden, although it is widely believed that only a good person can play Hosain effectively and only a bad man can make a convincing Shemr, the killer of Hosain. Instead the actors and the audience share in a joy and a horror that such events took place; in fact, some actors describe themselves as transformed by the emotion of the audience. The emotion of the audience is called forth by signals indicating the emotional content of the events portrayed. And since this is not a theater of suspense, since everyone knows the events in advance, the climaxes do not necessarily come when crucial events occur; they come when crucial signals appear. The climax of the play on Ashura does not occur when Hosain is killed onstage; it occurs when he puts on his white shroud. Hosain has gone to Kerbela knowing of the prophesies that he would be killed there; as he says in one play, "Men travel by night and their destinies travel toward them." The crowning symbol of his choice of martyrdom is that he puts on his own shroud. Emotions of horror and sorrow reach a climax not because the audience has "empathy" for the "character" the actor portrays but because they feel the drama of the role of martyrdom of which he reminds them. For all its high seriousness, this theater of roles rather than characters is a distant cousin of the poetic theater of the skeptical, the God-reproaching and the hedonistic roles that were played by Omar Khayyam and his imitators. The actor in the passion play, like the speaker of Omarian skeptical quatrains, has temporarily resolved the ambiguities of the Iranian tradition: he is the role.

• • •

The mullahs remained uncertain about how to evaluate this theater of folk mystical experience. Some condoned it as a powerful means to remind the masses of the meaning of Hosain's mission, for did not the Lord of the Martyrs say, "I am killed so that they will weep"? Others condemned it as a crude attempt to represent people so sanctified that any representation of them would falsify and thereby do them a dishonor. But on the issue of the overt mystical practices of the Sufis the overwhelming majority of mullahs agreed: Sufism was wrong. Sufism with a strong Shiah orientation survived in Iran and had occasional mullah supporters. The really significant way in which Sufism survived, however, was in the individualistic and highly philosophical form called *erfan*, mystical "knowledge."

The domestication of mysticism among the Shiah mullahs was largely the achievement of Mullah Sadra, although when he died in 1640 he probably had more mullah detractors than mullah admirers. He was a man who, after a formal *madreseh* education and informal study with the leading Shiah divines of his time, withdrew to a village near Qom to spend fifteen years of ascetic devotion and self-purification until he achieved the "direct" vision of the intelligible world. To see directly the reality of the world that philosophy revealed indirectly was to see through "illumination." In his interest in illumination he is clearly a follower of Sohravardi, and for all the significant differences between the two thinkers, Mullah Sadra is the true heir of Sohravardi's ingenious and esoteric speculations about perception, which Mullah Sadra revised and presented in a rigorous scholastic fashion. The deeply mystical nature of this philosophy did not escape the notice of numerous mullahs who suspected all mysticism (and philosophy) and who consequently denounced Mullah Sadra publicly, but he had his supporters, including a Safavi provincial governor, who founded a *madreseh* where Mullah Sadra taught for the remainder of his life. In the century after his death his ideas came to dominate the teaching of philosophy in the Shiah world, and they continue to do so down to the present.

Because the esoteric aspects of this philosophy (in the view of its followers) require an experience of insight to be fully grasped, its experiental aspects are best learned under a master who has himself experienced what he teaches. Muslim scholars visualized the transmission of most learning in genealogical terms, with chains of transmitters stretching back across the generations; *erfan* could hardly have been seen in any other way. The victory of Mullah Sadra's philosophy helped to create an esoteric and unseen bond among the mullahs which gave them cohesion as a group and fostered their sense that they were a spiritual elite.

Mysticism also had important practical implications for the sexual and political life of mullahs. The great majority of beginning *talabehs* in Qom and Najaf, the Shiah seats of higher learning, are adolescents living away from home for the first time. They are in a highly male environment, for, although there are some women students, these study only with women teachers (or with male members of their family), and their number is in any case fairly small. Anticlerical Iranians (and the anticlerical strain of Iranian thought that even some devoted Shiah adopt on occasion) depict the private life of *talabehs* as one long covert surrender to forbidden sexuality. Anticlericalists see the *madreseh* dormitories as hives of homosexual activity and detect homosexual undertones in the strong ties that bind a master pupil to a master teacher. And anticlericalists consider temporary marriage, although an institution fully sanctioned by Shiah law, to be nothing but prostitution. When in a mood to ridicule mullahs, no Iranian has any doubt what Hafez meant when he wrote:

> *Those preachers who in prayer-arch and pulpit imposingly parade,*
> *When they to their chamber go—another kind of act perform.*
> *A problem, sir! Please ask the assembly's learned man:*
> *Why do those who command us to repent so seldom themselves*
>   *repentance make?*
> *You might say they put no faith in the Day of Judgment*
> *Since when they act for the "Judge," they employ all this*
>   *deceit and fraud.*

Talabehs and former *talabehs* do not deny their sexual struggle. But they claim that—whatever the secularists may say—the vast majority of *talabehs* do not surrender to sexual temptation. The sexual struggle, however, is only the centerpiece of a more general struggle for "purity," a struggle that directs a significant part of the intellectual effort of *madreseh* learning toward discovering what is "clean" and what is "unclean." Emotionally this struggle is seen as a struggle against Satanic temptation. And whether philosophically understood as a principle or imaginatively understood as a presence, Satan's master role in the inner personal drama is that of the tempter to impurity. The Koranic Satan, as a preliminary to seducing Adam and Eve into eating from the forbidden tree, gives the primal pair a conscious awareness of their own sexuality: "And Satan began to whisper suggestions to the two of them, so that he might expose to them their private parts which had been hidden from them." From this moment on Satan assumes his God-given mission to whisper in the hearts of men.

No culture is without concern for purity. "Filth" is, by definition, something repellently out of place according to a culturally determined view of housekeeping, food, language, or whatever. But in a culture that is concerned with clear boundaries between the sacred and the profane, the "pollution" by filth becomes a vital question because it precludes all human means of access to the sacred. Satan recognizes that the prescribed daily prayers are powerful means of access to God and that such prayers are not acceptable before God if the person who performs the prayer has not made himself or herself ritually clean, which involves a major ablution in ritually clean water or sand even after an involuntary defilement, such as a wet dream (sometimes called "a Satanic pollution").

Every Iranian knows the story of the mullah who, on his way to the mosque for morning prayers, was splashed by a dog shaking itself in a drainage ditch. The mullah, who knew he did not have time to change his clothes before prayers, refused to look squarely at the animal that had sprayed water on him and rushed on, muttering, "God willing, it's a goat." (Water from dogs is polluting while water from goats is not.) "God willing, it's a goat" is shorthand in Persian conversation for "Let's let things pass and not look too closely." It represents the determination of religious people to maintain agreement as to the boundaries between clean and unclean, and hence sacred and profane, without being obsessively finicky. Sometimes, in the mouth of an anticlerical Iranian, it also represents a contempt for a religious style in which a pious person is supposed to be watchfully concerned with a welter of details about the liquids he drinks, the liquids he excretes from any opening in his or her body, and so forth.

For mullahs the story of the struggle of *talabehs* with the whisperings of temptation is overwhelmingly a story of Satan's defeat. The *talabeh* has two important practical stratagems to use in this struggle: the temporary marriage and *erfan* mysticism. The temporary marriage is contracted for a specific period on the condition of the payment of a specific sum to the temporary wife. The temporary wife must have had her period three times since any previous marriage (to avoid disputes about paternity) and should not be a woman "addicted to fornication." Sunnis (who forbid such temporary marriages) as well as anticlericalists claim that Shiah shrine towns are full of de facto prostitutes. These are women who give false testimony about their past sexual relations in order to contract marriages of a day or a week with pilgrims and, sometimes, with *talabehs,* who, in the spirit of "God willing, it's a goat," don't inquire too scrupulously about the background of their temporary wives. Mullahs, on the contrary, defend the temporary marriage as an institution sanctioned by the Prophet and used conscientiously by scrupulous Shiah Moslems, including, of course, the mullahs. They strongly deny that more than a handful of women who are unscrupulous by the standards of Shiah law are to be found in Shiah shrine towns.

The second method of dealing with sexual temptations, the individually transmitted form of mysticism called *erfan,* is not a subject of dispute or even of discussion between the world of mullahs and outsiders. An initiate is not supposed to reveal the name of his teacher in *erfan,* and few outsiders are aware of the honeycomb of ties of *erfan* that run through the community of mullahs in Qom. Also, *erfan* has many enemies among the mullahs themselves; it survives without scandal by being discreet. *Erfan* has been cultivated by thousands of devotees over hundreds of years, and its complex intellectual heritage cannot be reduced to any one meaning, but one of its meanings for the adolescent *ta-labehs* is heightened self-control at a time of sexual awakening. Not all *talabehs* can afford a dowry for a wife or the cost of a temporary marriage; *erfan* is free.

In the Western context, in which mysticism is so often associated with quietism, it may seem surprising that *erfan* had far-reaching political implications, but in the Islamic context it is not. Sufi mysticism had been a key element in the radical commitment that created the Shiah Safavi state. Similarly, the mystical system called *erfan* had a hand in creating the all-or-nothing political style of the two most political Iranian religious figures of the last two centuries, Jamal ad-Din, called al-Afghani ("the Afghan") and Ruhollah Khomeini. The very heart of *erfan* is the destruction of the distinction between subject and object—an experience of the world in which seer and seen are one. And teachers of *erfan* seek to impart to their students a sense of the fearlessness toward everything external, including all the seemingly coercive political powers of the world, which true masters of *erfan* should have.

Jamal ad-Din, "the Afghan," was actually born in Iran in the late 1830s but later pretended that he had been born in Afghanistan, a Sunni country, in order to be more acceptable to his Sunni disciples in Cairo and Istanbul. He had a *madreseh* education in both Iran and Iraq. He also acquired training in *erfan* from an Iranian teacher and himself wrote a treatise on Islamic mysticism. From then on he shifted from country to country and role to role in an attempt to revive Islam as a political force. At the court of the Ottoman emperor, the Egyptian khedive, in exile in Paris or British India or czarist Russia, he proved a tireless and fearless adopter of roles and philosophies, to many of which he proved inconstant: he was at various times a Scottish freemason, a defender of Islam against European materialism, an advocate of parliamentary government within Islam, and an admirer of the messianic Islamic politics of the mahdi of the Sudan.

Jamal ad-Din (a very different man from the Jamal ad-Din met by Isa Sadiq) was invited by the shah to come to Iran and advise on affairs of government, but when in short order he fell from favor he took sanctuary in the shrine near Tehran where the mullahs and merchants were to take sanctuary in 1905 at the start of

the Iranian revolution. For seven months he preached to admirers
in his sanctuary. Then, in 1891, the shah's troops removed him
and dumped him across the border in Iraq. Jamal ad-Din, who
quarreled with most of his patrons, reserved his strongest hatred
for the shah. From Iraq he accused the shah of squandering public
moneys gained through economic concessions to Europeans—including a recent concession to a British firm to distribute tobacco
in Iran—to the advantage of the enemies of Islam. The Iranian
public and the mullahs were ready to listen; an eminent jurisconsult issued a legal opinion that prohibited Muslims from using
tobacco until the concession was canceled. The government gave
in, but Jamal ad-Din was implacable. He continued his attacks on
the shah and was one of the fountainheads of antigovernment
protest that led to the Constitutional Revolution at the start of the
next century.

The depth of Jamal ad-Din's religious belief is questionable; he
never married but picked up female companionship when he
wanted it without any show of religious scruples. But this lack of
scrupulosity does not mean that his earlier training was subsequently forgotten; his recklessness and unwillingness to count the
cost of his actions had its origin in his training in *erfan* as well as in
his own temperament. His association with Islamic men of learning also convinced him that they were the bulwark of Islam
against the foreigners, and a desire to give Muslims heart in opposing the encroachment of foreigners was one of the very few
common themes of his life. Almost all the major movements of
intellectual and political reform in the Islamic Middle East count
Jamal ad-Din as their ancestor.

Ruhollah Khomeini was also dumped across the border by a
shah when he fearlessly criticized the Iranian regime. He also
proved an implacable foe who tirelessly attacked the regime while
in exile. He also developed close ties with an inner coterie of
pupils wherever he went. He also believed that Western encroachment was the great *moral* insult to the Islamic world and
that (in the case of the Shiah world) the mullahs were the one
bulwark that could withstand this encroachment. Jamal ad-Din's
teacher of *erfan*, Hosain Qoli Hamadani, was the teacher of Javad
Maleki Darjazini, the teacher of Khomeini.

In many ways Jamal ad-Din and Khomeini are radically different. On the scene of Middle Eastern and European politics, with a masterful show of conviction for every one of his parts, Jamal ad-Din played out the "theater of roles" from the Omarian free-thinker to the suffering martyr. Khomeini has chosen the role of devotee and stuck by it; Satanic moral corruption is his enemy, and he will not compromise. But in their heedlessness and perseverance both Jamal ad-Din and Khomeini are true students of *erfan* and direct descendants of Sohravardi.

CHAPTER SIX

In 1966 Ali arrived at Najaf in southern Iraq with an introduction, for to come unintroduced to the only seat of Shiah learning to rival Qom would cost him time in establishing his credentials as a serious scholar. But he was a little anxious that his introduction, which was to Ayatollah Shahrudi, might not do its job completely. The ayatollah was one of the four "models" of learning then living in Najaf and reputed to be a hundred and five years old. It was not easy to find Shahrudi's house. Najaf was a shrine town like Qom and was dominated by the imposing gold dome over the tomb of the Commander of the Faithful, Ali ibn Abi Taleb, the cousin and son-in-law of the Prophet and the father of the martyred Hosain. But the twisting lanes of Najaf were much easier to get lost in, partly because the houses had projecting second stories with wooden lattice windows which kept the street level in a state of semidarkness.

When he finally found Shahrudi's house he was shown into a reception room where an elderly sayyed, ancient even if not one hundred and five years old, was eating sugared lupine beans with relish. He nodded to Ali to sit down and said: "I knew your father when he came here as a student. Welcome, welcome. I'm glad Qomis still think we have something to teach them. Is your father well?" Now Ali was subjected to a long interrogation about the health and activities of the ancient ayatollah's acquaintances in Qom, at the end of which he said: "I like these beans" (which was clear enough, as he had eaten about ten of them since Ali entered). "Here, have one. You know, I don't give them to just anybody; I gave you one because your father is my friend. I suppose you will attend the advanced classes of the younger 'models' while you are here. It can't do you any harm. Study hard and be a credit to all of us."

Ali had already decided to study with two "models," Ayatollah Kho'i and Ayatollah Khomeini. Kho'i had been in Iraq for years and was regarded as the leading teacher of the city. Khomeini had just arrived a few months before, in the fall of 1965, but because of his reputation as a teacher in Qom and because of his political activities, which had forced him out of Iran, he had immediately attracted an impressive following. Ali had come to Najaf in part because he wanted the esteem given to someone who had made his mark in both of the great centers of Shiah learning. But he had come at this moment because he wanted to study with Khomeini.

Khomeini had already played a brief but dramatic role in Ali's life. When Ali was growing up he had known Khomeini from a distance. Even Khomeini's close associates seemed to know him only from a distance. He was a forbidding man who never offered more than a smile in public to express his pleasure in anybody or anything. He was thought to be one of the most intelligent teachers in Qom; but he kept his master classes (which were in slightly suspect subjects such as the relationship of philosophy to *erfan*) for a chosen few. For several years he had given the "class in morality" on Thursday afternoons. This was a class that students traditionally attended only for inspiration, since there was no examination associated with it. Required or not, it was widely attended and was one of the few times when all the *talabehs* in Qom were encouraged to listen to a single teacher.

Khomeini's supporters among the mullahs said that his moving speeches in these classes showed his selflessness and other-worldliness, which was confirmed by his refusal to let his followers address him by any extraordinary titles even in print. And his lack of interest in mullah leadership was shown by his refusal to publish a handbook of basic religious conduct, an essential prerequisite to becoming a "model." His opponents said that he was an unbending man full of his own importance, who, while he taught his class in morality in a resplendent cloak of the most expensive kind was nevertheless stingy both to his family and to needy *talabehs*. He was, they said, stingy even with his presence, as he limited himself to the bare minimum in exchanging visits with the leading mullahs of Qom, an exchange that was part of the weekly round of any leader of his rank. These opponents thought it natural that Khomeini had fallen into a certain eclipse in the last years of Ayatollah Borujerdi, who had been the "model" accepted by the great majority of mullahs from 1946 until his death on March 30, 1961. With Borujerdi in Qom it was hard to fit Khomeini into a subordinate position that was to the mutual satisfaction of both ayatollahs.

In 1963 Khomeini changed for Ali from shadow into substance. It seemed to Ali that the logic of the events of March of that year had set him in a foreordained place in an immense movement of people with Khomeini at its head. The first of these events Ali knew only secondhand. He had been at home on March 22 and only a half hour after the fact had become aware that the excited noise of a distant crowd that had penetrated to his garden at home came from the raid on the Faiziyeh, in which police and government agents had entered the *madreseh* and had arrested some *talabehs*, beaten many, and killed two. Khomeini's had been the first and loudest voice condemning this act. Forty days after a death Shiah Muslims gather to mourn the dead, and on the fortieth day after the raid Ali joined scores of other *talabehs* and went to Khomeini's class in the Great Mosque opposite the shrine because they knew that he intended to pronounce judgment on the raid and to mourn those killed.

For the first half hour Khomeini conducted his advanced class on law without the slightest reference to contemporary politics. He then talked politics as no mullah had done in public in many years. He associated the raid with Reza Shah's attack on the shrine in Mashhad in 1935. He did not blame the shah's agents or his minister; he did not say (as the formula permitted in extreme circumstances) that the shah was misled. He said that the shah himself should be held responsible unless he openly repudiated these acts. The speech went on to explain that the actions of the regime were the result of its friendship with Jews and non-Muslim Iranians. But it was Khomeini's open attack on the shah that made Ali and hundreds of others who had gathered for Khomeini's class that day feel that at last the mullahs had a political leader.

Ali drew closer to the circle of Khomeini and they accepted his commitment to their cause. They informed him that on the afternoon of June 3, Ashura, or the tenth day of Moharram, after the passion plays in which Shemr killed Hosain were finished, Khomeini would preach in the Faiziyeh. Ali arrived well in advance at Khomeini's house and took his assigned place with a group of sayyeds and practiced the lines his group would shout—a rhyming chant reminiscent of a *nowheh*, an elegiac poem of mourning for the death of Hosain, traditionally recited in processions on the day of Ashura. Khomeini appeared, surrounded by protectors, and sat in the back seat of an open light-green Volkswagen beetle. As the procession toward the Faiziyeh began, the group in front of the Volkswagen shouted:

> The grand Ayatollah Khomeini, leader of the Moslems, the glory of the Believers;
> May your head be safe—your ancestor was killed!

Then Ali's group, walking behind the Volkswagen, recited:

> In mourning the talabehs of the Faiziyeh, killed for religion by the hand of the disbelievers,
> May your head be safe—your ancestor was killed!

After which the front group would repeat their lines, and so on by turns.

Ali was frightened but determined. When they reached the Faiziyeh he took up a position relatively near to Khomeini but not

too far from one of the exits he would race for if government
troops turned up. The crowd filled the courtyards of the shrine
and a neighboring building and that of the Faiziyeh, and a public
address system had been set up. Khomeini sat in the large arch-
way with the two peacocks. As a sign of deep mourning he un-
loosed the three feet of cloth that were the outside folds of his
turban and draped the loose cloth under his chin and over the opposite shoulder. As he began to speak, the government cut off
electricity to all of Qom, but Khomeini's followers had prepared
for this and they hooked up the public address system to an emer-
gency generator. Khomeini began to speak again:

> It is now the afternoon of Ashura. Sometimes when I recall the
> events of Ashura, a question occurs to me: If the Omayyad dynasty
> ... [and in particular their leader] Yazid wished to make war on
> Hosain, why did they commit such savage and inhuman crimes
> against defenseless women and innocent children? ... It seems to
> me that the Omayyads had a far more basic aim: they were op-
> posed to the very existence of the family of the Prophet. ...
>
> A similar question occurs to me now. If the tyrannical regime of
> Iran simply wished to wage war on the "models" and to oppose the
> mullahs, what business did it have tearing the Koran to shreds on
> the day it attacked the Faiziyeh madreseh? ... We come to the con-
> clusion that this regime also has a more basic aim: they are funda-
> mentally opposed to Islam itself and to the existence of the
> religious class. They do not wish this institution to exist; they do
> not wish any of us to exist, the great and the small alike.
>
> Israel does not wish the Koran to exist in this country. Israel
> does not wish the mullahs to exist in this country. ... It was Israel
> that assaulted the Faiziyeh madreseh by means of its sinister agents.
> It is still assaulting us, and assaulting you, the nation; it wishes to
> seize your economy ... to appropriate your wealth ... The reli-
> gious scholars are blocking [Israel's] path; they must be eliminated.
> ...
>
> Respected people of Qom! On the day that mendacious, that
> scandalous referendum [on the shah's "White Revolution"] took
> place ... you witnessed a gang of hooligans and ruffians prowling
> around Qom ... shouting: "Your days of parasitism are at an end!"
> ... Now, these students of the religious sciences, who spend the
> best and most active part of their lives in these narrow cells and

whose monthly income is somewhere between forty and one hundred tomans—are they parasites? . . . Are the mullahs parasites . . . and those who have filled foreign banks with the wealth produced by the toil of our poverty-stricken people . . . not parasites?

Let me give you some advice Mr. Shah! Dear Mr. Shah, I advise you to desist . . . I don't want the people to offer up thanks if your [foreign] master should decide one day that you must leave. I don't want you to become like your father . . . During World War II the Soviet Union, Britain and America invaded Iran and occupied our country. The property of the people was exposed and their honor was imperiled. But God knows, everyone was happy because [Reza Shah] the Pahlavi had gone! . . . Don't you know that if one day some uproar occurs and the tables are turned, none of these people around you will be your friends?

Every minute throughout the speech Ali expected troops to come. Khomeini had explained the shah's war against the mullahs through his alliance with Israel. He had told the shah that if he did not act as a Muslim he would be expelled. Most provocative of all, he had implicitly compared the shah to Yazid, the ruler on whose orders Shemr had killed Hosain and the children of Hosain and therefore the worst leader that any Shiah could imagine.

Nothing happened that day or the following day, the eleventh of Moharram. When Ali woke up on the twelfth of Moharram he was aware of the sound of large numbers of people in the neighborhood of the shrine and of the Faiziyeh. He dressed quickly and went into the streets. People were milling about aimlessly, stunned at the news that Khomeini had been arrested before dawn. The shops stayed closed, as they would for another two weeks. Later that morning as Ali was walking on the side of the river away from his house he saw a tank followed by some troop carriers approaching the nearest bridge. He grabbed the bottom of his robe and ran to the bridge before the tank reached it; he was across the bridge and home with a speed that almost lost him his turban.

Within a year Khomeini was in exile in Turkey, and a few months after that he turned up in Najaf. He was no longer the somewhat unapproachable expert in philosophy and jurisprudence known only to the more academic mullahs. He was now a

national figure, known to peasants as well as to *talabehs* as a man
who had dared to publicly oppose the shah. For Ali, who had become (as Parviz had been, when they had discussed Algeria so
many years ago) "weary of these weak-spirited traveling companions" in the poem of Mowlana, Khomeini had become the
Lion of God.

In Najaf, Ali went to Khomeini's lectures for students who had
finished the set texts. The lectures were held in a large mosque
near the shrine; they dealt with commercial law, a favorite subject
of advanced study for about a century. Khomeini sat on the top
step of a three-step staircase and spoke into a standing micro-
phone, which he never touched. He still seemed distant, seldom
fixing his gaze on this audience of several hundred *talabehs* but
keenly aware of their presence.

> I seek refuge in God from Satan, the cursed. In the name of God,
> the Merciful, the Beneficent.
> We are discussing the requirements that must be met if the
> terms or conditions of a contract are to be lawful and valid. As has
> been said repeatedly, the requirements are eight. A condition must
> be within the powers of the contractee; therefore one cannot buy a
> flowering plant on the condition that it subsequently bear fruit—
> an act God alone can guarantee. A condition must be lawful by its
> nature; so there cannot be a condition to make grapes into wine, an
> action by its nature unlawful. A condition must serve a purpose
> that reasonable men can understand. A condition must not be
> against the teaching of the Koran and the example of the Prophet
> and the Imams: a wife, for example, cannot put a condition in her
> marriage contract that divorce should be her right and not her
> husband's. Unlike conditions unlawful by nature, such a condition
> would be lawful but invalid. A condition must not go against the
> requirements of the contract itself. A condition must not be ambig-
> uous and therefore risk uncertainty. A condition must not involve
> things that are logically impossible. Finally, a condition must come
> within the text of the contract itself and not be a mere promise
> given outside the contract and therefore without any expectation
> of some consideration in return.
> We are now discussing the fifth requirement: that a condition
> must not be against the requirements of the contract itself, and the
> application of this principle to partnership. The late Mirza Na'ini

had something to say on this subject. The question arises whether there can be a condition in a contract of partnership to profit or suffer loss disproportionately to the proportions of original capital invested in the partnership, or even to be completely free of loss. Every increase in the capital of partnership might be assumed to accrue equally to all parts of the capital, since, from the inception of the partnership, the capital of the partners is assumed to be inextricably mixed. The growth and decrease of this capital, therefore, can be judged to belong to each partner *only* in the proportions in which they contributed to the mixed capital. This is not a requirement of partnership fixed by law. It is a requirement decided by the nature of the subject, since the very meaning of partnership is the mixing of capital, and partnership can therefore come into existence even without a contract of partnership. Contracts of partnership, however, do have some utility in that they can regulate the possibly differing rights of disposal of the mixed capital by the different partners; whether or not, for example, one of the partners has the right to sell a jointly owned house without the permission of the other.

But consider these possible criticisms of Na'ini's view, which will be discussed tomorrow. Might the definition of partnership imply only the *fact* of the mixture of capital and imply nothing about proportionality in loss and gain? Could it not be possible for partnership? to be brought into existence by mixture of capital and yet for conditions to be set in the contract of partnership for different proportions of profit to be given to each partner, depending on the final price of sale of the mixed capital?

"With your permission, Agha." A student in his early twenties, speaking Persian with a thick Arabic accent, sat up very straight in order to be noticed and addressed Khomeini. "Might not some implication of proportionality still reside in the very definition of partnership? Otherwise, a condition in the contract of partnership could state that, for example, one partner receive nothing or, conversely, receive the entire profit. But could any Islamic jurist accept the validity of a contract entailing total loss or total profit for one of the partners?"

Khomeini answered in the somewhat distant way he had lectured: "The point made is clear enough. But the important question is the legal basis of the difference that makes disproportionality possible but not total profit or loss for any true partner. This is the subject of discussion for tomorrow."

Khomeini rose and the students immediately stood. He walked out to a waiting car. Two months before he and his son had arrived in Najaf virtually empty-handed. A little over two years before he had been a respected scholar but hardly a leader among the mullahs, most especially in Najaf, the great intellectual rival of Qom. Now he was one of the handful of "models," imitated by hundreds of thousands of Shiah, who sent him generous contributions from all over Iran. He was a leader and a hero to many of the mullahs in Iran, and through his teaching and his easy assumption of the new respect shown him he had begun to put his intellectual stamp on the teaching of mullahs in Iran.

In Najaf, Ali Hashemi himself had begun to teach. The introduction from his father prepared the way for him; the intelligence with which he followed the classes of Khomeini and Kho'i caught the attention of the leading Najafi mullahs. He was given a theological text to teach, and for the first time Ali taught in Arabic. Khomeini could teach in Persian, his native language, in disregard of the spoken language of Najaf, because of his eminence. Ali, on the contrary, wanted to reach out not only to his fellow Iranian students but also to the mixture of Arab Shiah students who came to Najaf from the borders of Turkey, the hills of Lebanon, and the baked mud plains of southern Iraq.

He also wanted to prove the mastery of Arabic that years of studying Arabic grammar, rhetoric, and texts written in Arabic had given him. For Ali the Arabic language was like the names and genealogies of his near and remote cousins: something he could recall with utmost ease, the relations between whom he could explain perfectly and follow perfectly when his grandmother launched into one of her interminable lectures on the excellence of his blood lines. Ali prayed in Arabic without thinking, he read religious books in Arabic as easily as in Persian, he had written letters and student treatises in Arabic, he had even held conversations in his dreams in Arabic. But when he tried to talk Arabic extempore it was like trying to explain extempore how all his remote cousins were related; before each statement he would hesitate for a brief moment to make sure he had got it right. The dozens of dialects of Arabic with their marked peculiarities of grammars and pronunciations and the multitude of new (and often evanescent) Arabic words for such things as "automatic turntable" or "personnel management" made him yet more uncomfortable.

He had first been in an Arabic-speaking environment when he went on the pilgrimage to Mecca as a fourteen-year-old boy with his mother, and his two strongest memories of the trip itself were of his mother's indignation at the background music on the plane (as she said, they didn't even have the courtesy of cab drivers in Iran, who turned down the radio when a mullah stepped into their cab, since most mullahs disapproved of music) and of his difficulty in speaking Arabic in the transit lounge in Kuwait. He was desperate to find a men's room, and when the Kuwaiti official motioned him back from Passport Control to a men's room he had already tried and found locked, Ali, to his terror, found his Arabic dried up completely, and the best he could do was recite a bit of dialogue between Potiphar's wife and the prophet Joseph in the Koran: "She fastened the doors and said: 'Come thou!' He said: 'God forbid! Truly [your husband] is my lord! He made my sojourn agreeable!' " After which the Kuwaiti official had emitted a shout of laughter and waved him through to the men's room in the main hall of the terminal.

Now, to his pleasure, he found he could explain himself in Arabic and even handle disputation with his students. But something happened to him that was almost as bad as hysterical loss of his Arabic: for the first and only time in his life he admitted to his students that he couldn't answer a question. He was explaining why God's direct creation is a single thing, that as a single being He cannot create a plurality; He can create only another single thing (which is, of course, existence). To illustrate the necessary unity of nature between cause and effect he quoted (in Persian, followed by his own Arabic translation) the lines of Mowlana:

> Have you ever seen a horse give birth to a donkey foal?
> Have you ever seen a palm tree bear apples?

"But sir," an Arab student asked, "don't some causes produce results of a different nature? Doesn't fire produce smoke, which differs from fire in its appearance and quantity?"

For some reason Ali did not say "We'll come to that point to-morrow" or use one of the other dodges that he had used (and seen his teachers use) on the rare occasions when he had been stumped in the past. He stared at the student for a minute and said, "You're right. I don't know the answer." He rose to indicate that the class was dismissed and tried to walk out of the *madreseh* with great dignity. All the Shiah treatises on learning said that it was a positive virtue, an act of worship, to honestly admit your ignorance; but no teacher ever did. A teacher who could be stumped should cede his place to the student who stumped him; admitting to ignorance might be an act of worship, but it was also virtually an act of resignation, an intellectual suicide.

Ali went directly to a family friend, Ayatollah Sahabi, who had taught theology for years with great success. Like many of the prominent teachers, Sahabi held court every day after class, and his great reputation for piety attracted not only scholars but Bedouin Arab leaders who came from the Shiah tribes of southern Iraq to get the advice of a man they believed to be spiritually close to the hidden Imam.

Ali arrived about forty minutes before one of these sessions and was shown into Sahabi's sitting room. He was touched that this saintly man, his elder, should half rise from his old-fashioned water pipe to arrange some cushions for Ali to lean on. Ali apologized for coming before the proper time for an audience with Sahabi and then explained his question. The answer was simple, and Ali could not think why he had missed it. As Sahabi explained, there was a difference between the sufficient cause of a thing, which by itself can produce a result (which is necessarily of the same nature, since the cause produces the result by itself out of itself), and the material cause which contributes to the stuff or substance of the result but by itself would not be sufficient to produce the result. The fire is not sufficient to produce smoke; fire acts with wood and air to produce smoke, just as one needs brick and plaster and a mason to build a house, but no one of these elements is a "sufficient" cause.

Ali felt embarrassed and said so. Ayatollah Sahabi said: "Don't worry. I know you were taught these things and I know you are one of the best students in Najaf. Maybe there is a deep and 'sufficient' cause for your sudden willingness to say to the students 'I don't know.' " Sahabi took several meditative puffs on his water pipe and looked at Ali sideways out of one eye, rather in the fashion of the stork that had tried to stare Ali down on his first day of the *madreseh* in Qom. Finally he began to speak: "Maybe your deep and sufficient reason for admitting you don't know is because you're intelligent enough to realize that no one knows. Maybe you're wondering whether we can find a 'sufficient' cause for anything, much less a 'First Cause' and a God. For twelve hundred years mullahs have been writing proofs of the existence of God. Believe me, I've taught theology for a long time—none of them is real proof. The only real proof can come through illumination. You're an intelligent young man—don't waste your life as a slave to superstition."

"But you pray, you fast, you're famous for your piety." Ali was sure that Sahabi was trying to test him, to see if he was a secret skeptic.

"When I discovered that there was no rational proof of the existence of God I tried to stop praying. I became ill; I couldn't eat and couldn't keep my balance. Then I discovered another way to believe. I pray, and you should pray. Most important of all, you should require the people around you to pray. Do you think that the people around you would leave anything in its proper place if they knew there was no life after this life? One puff and all order in society would blow away like a house of straw. You're a good boy and intelligent. You've studied *erfan* and have enough strength to hear what I just told you. Now go before other people arrive."

Ali left, but he felt as if he had left a stain of blood on the straw mat where he had been sitting in Sahabi's house. Sahabi, who radiated sanctity, an unbeliever in reason as a basis for theology? As the shock wore off, it became possible for Ali to admire Sahabi again. He still found some of the proofs of God he had been taught convincing, but since other proofs really proved nothing, might not a man "in good faith" try and fail, however mistakenly, to convince himself of all the proofs? Then what should he do? "Stain his prayer rug with wine," as Hafez said, throw away twenty years of study, and become an example of moral corruption to young *talabehs*? Maybe Sahabi's sanctity was real. He had faced choices, each "more bitter," as the Arabs say, "than senility and disease," and had then made the best choice his conscience allowed. He had stayed and taught the traditional books in the traditional way. Ali was not sure that he would have made the same choice.

. . .

Willingness to conform to Islamic law, even in the face of doubt, spiritual aridity, and dark nights of the soul, is the mark of a serious Muslim. Mohammed is reported to have said: "God most blessed and most high says: 'Nothing brings men near to Me like the performance of what I have made obligatory for them; and through works of supererogation My servant comes ever nearer to Me until I love him, and when I have bestowed My love on him, I become his hearing with which he hears, his sight with which he sees, his tongue with which he speaks, his hand with which he grasps, and his foot with which he walks.' " Success in conforming to the law makes the believer both literally and metaphorically an instrument of God.

Formally the law regulated external behavior alone, although the majority of Muslim moral theologians as well as Sufis contended that God would be satisfied only if the heart as well as the external actions of the believer conformed to the Divine Will. But even the moral theologians and Sufis who emphasized the inner aspect of the law agreed that, whatever the believer's heart might feel, he must begin by making his limbs obey the Law.

Nowhere is the case for external obedience put more eloquently than in the writings of Ghazzali, the lawyer, theologian, and Sufi who is, perhaps, the greatest moral thinker of the Islamic tradition. Ghazzali was born in the mid-eleventh century in northwest Iran, in Tus, the town in which Ferdowsi had been born a century earlier. In 1091 Ghazzali's brilliance gained him a professorship at the great *madreseh* of Baghdad, where he achieved the same intellectual dominance over his colleagues as he had exercised in Iran. But a few years later he entered a crisis of doubt that led him to question not only the possibility of certain knowledge in matters of religion but also the possibility of certain knowledge of any kind, even certain knowledge of the soundness of one's own senses: "The disease was baffling, and lasted almost two months, during which I was a skeptic in fact though not in theory or outward expression."

Gradually Ghazzali regained the belief that he could accept some truths as necessary, not through "systematic demonstration or marshaled argument" but through a mystical experience, "a light that God most high cast into my breast." For Ghazzali this light was the real experience of knowledge which only mysticism could give. And although he continued until his death, in 1111, to write highly scholastic discussions of philosophy, theology, ethics, and jurisprudence, all these works have a decidedly Sufi cast. But Ghazzali now experienced another inner crisis, because, to his understanding, if he were to follow the Sufi path, he should renounce his worldly attachments. Yet Satan kept whispering to him, "This is a passing mood; do not yield to it."

Then, in July 1095, "the matter ceased to be one of choice and became one of compulsion," for Ghazzali experienced an illness strangely similar to the "pain of the chest" that gripped Saint Augustine during the summer of his conversion to Christianity and so affected Augustine's voice that it prevented him from continuing his career as a public speaker. Ghazzali writes: "God caused my tongue to dry up so that I was prevented from lecturing in the *madreseh*. One particular day I would make an effort to lecture in order to gratify the ears of my following, but my tongue would not utter a single word nor could I accomplish anything. . . . I could hardly swallow or digest a single mouthful of food." Ghazzali left Baghdad, spent ten years wandering without attachments, then returned to teaching. He became the most influential Muslim critic of a dry legal formalism: merely to fulfill God's commandments was not the goal of the law, since God watches the hearts as well as the limbs of men.

Yet even for Ghazzali the law is the indispensable beginning; and, when completely internalized, the law also becomes an integral part of the end toward which the spiritual quest is directed. Ghazzali writes: "Know that the beginning of guidance is outward piety and the end of guidance is inward piety. . . . Piety designates carrying out the commands of God most high and turning aside from what He prohibits, and thus has two parts. . . . The commands of God most high prescribe obligatory works and supererogatory works. The obligatory work is the capital on which the trade is based and through which man comes to salvation." Antinomians—people who said true piety disregarded the law—did exist in the Islamic world, but they were exceedingly rare. As Ghazzali indicated, for Sufi or non-Sufi to bet on salvation without the law was as pointless as an attempt to trade without any goods; in fact, it was fraud.

If, then, the learned tradition of the Islamic world agreed with the psalmist that "The law of the Lord is perfect" and "The statutes of the Lord are right," nothing could be more important than discovering the law. Learning existed in the first instance to discover the law, and in the first instance the learned justified their profession to the masses by offering authoritative opinions on the law. The modern Western tradition of law deals, by and large, only with those matters for which the community imposes sanctions: punishment, restriction, or nullity (the last, for example, in the case of an improper will). By contrast, in the Islamic tradition, law is, at least in theory, all-embracing: it comprises all the commands, prohibitions, and recommendations given by God in respect to human conduct, and includes on an equal footing rules for prayer and rules for contract, matters punishable by death and matters punishable by inner contrition. Its sanctions are as much otherworldly as of this world, and it sometimes even specifies the proportion of otherworldly reward given for meritorious acts.

The problem was and is: Granted the law exists in its full glory in the mind of the Divine Legislator, how do we, mere humans, discover what the Legislator knows? As a scriptural religion Islam quite naturally turned first to the Koran, the speech of God. But was there a difference between the written, physical Koran and the speaking of God? Was there a difference between God's speaking, as an act, and God's speech, which, as the totality of what he had to say to mankind, might then always exist alongside Him like His justice or His mercy? If God's speech was of the same nature as His justice and mercy, then was it uncreated and external? And, if uncreated and external, didn't this imply polytheism, just as Muslims saw Christianity threatened by polytheism through its claim that "In the beginning was the Word, and the Word was with God"?

In the Islamic world these debates are almost as old as Islam itself. It was partially to resolve these debates and partially to resolve the standing of an enormous body of law actually in force in
the Islamic world that, in the second century after the appearance
of the Koran, scholars began to collect the sayings of (and about)
the Prophet Mohammed. Surely in the words and exemplary life
of the perfect Muslim there was guidance for the interpretation of
the Koran and for the assessment of the very large area of law
about which the Koran spoke very little or not at all. Collection of
such material (called "the traditions") continued in earnest for
many more centuries, and very soon the Prophetic sayings alone
far exceeded the amount any man could have said in one lifetime.

Almost from the beginning Muslim scholars recognized that
extraneous material had been introduced into these sayings. The
science of source criticism they developed to deal with forgeries
reflects the highly personal character of early Muslim scholarship
and its emphasis on quasi-genealogical ties. Which of the transmitters of the traditions were "truthful" men, the critics asked,
and did the known dates of the lifetimes of the transmitters,
linked in a chain of authorities that extended back to the Prophet,
allow these transmitters to have met? A tradition that was transmitted through several alternate chains of authorities was judged
to be more likely authentic than one transmitted through a single
chain—and so on.

Whatever the merits of such criticism, it left an enormous body
of these traditions as possible sources for law. By and large, although some traditions were judged "stronger" or more likely
than others, even weak traditions were not thrown out until found
flagrantly guilty. In any case the traditions extended the raw material of the Law several times over.

Shi'ism and Sunnism came to very different conclusions as to
how this raw material should be sifted and further extended. For
Sunnis the legal technique par excellence was reasoning by analogy. The Koran lays down the rule that the punishment of a slave
woman shall be half the punishment of a free woman. If we decide that in this case the explanatory reason for the difference is
slavery, then, by analogy, the punishment for a male slave should
be half the punishment for a free male. Immediately a host of
problems present themselves. How do you determine decisively

what is the explanatory reason? Can we make a further analogy
based on a ruling obtained by analogy? And so forth. Sunni jurisprudence devotes much of its most rigorous discussion to the examination of analogy.

The Shiah, by contrast, elevated "reason" to the rank of a fundamental principle of law. The respect for reason accounts for the
major emphasis on Aristotelian deductive logic in the curriculum
of the Shiah *madreseh*, so one of the tasks of the jurists is to establish the major premises that exist in the law (intoxicating sub-
stances are forbidden) so that subsidiary rules can be derived
from them. (Brandy is an intoxicating substance; brandy—although not explicitly mentioned in the Koran or the traditions—is
forbidden.) But reason is one of the notorious weasel words of all
languages; it appears to designate a sanitized, universal area of
discourse and yet in practice turns out to be as culturally determined and idiosyncratic as most of our ideas. Reason has been
used to cover a whole range of ideas from the faculty that recognizes truths and abstract things (the shared roundness of round
things) to the faculty that moves the mind from premises to conclusions, not only through syllogisms but also, for example, from
observation (the sun has risen every morning so far, so the sun
will rise tomorrow morning).

Shiah thinkers, while in general giving "reason" a high status—
it was, they almost all seem to agree, one of the sources for firm
belief in religion—disagreed not only with the Sunnis about its
uses but also disagreed among themselves. In general they did not
accept the probative value of analogy as something supported by
reason. For the Shiah, analogy—when used by itself—can produce diversity of opinion and can falsely link dissimilar cases.
The Shiah saw reason in the process by which people knew the
difference between good and evil; by which people recognized the
harmony of a mathematical system; and by which a "reasonable"
man made a contract to sell his house for fair value, while a man
without reason might sell it for a watermelon seed. Mullahs properly trained by their teachers to use reason to give an authoritative
opinion of the law were called *mojtaheds*, jurisconsults. And only a
man with reason had the intellectual instruments needed to determine if another man had reason in the same degree; only a

jurisconsult could appoint another jurisconsult—still another quasi-genealogical tie.

Some of the Shiah, however, rejected a major role for reason in the law. In the heart of the Safavi period a certain mullah, Mohammed Amin, from Astarabad in northeastern Iran, decided to boot reason out of its position of honor and elevate the "traditions" to fill its place. Mullah Mohammed Amin was a clever man; he discerned exactly the points at which the jurisprudence of the jurisconsult school was most vulnerable. Syllogistic reasoning, he said, was the manipulation of tautologies (which is true) and does not produce any result not anticipated when the syllogism is set up (which may or may not be true). Anyway, formal reasoning when applied to different raw materials in the law could produce contradictory results. (And this criticism was not so different from the criticism that the Shiah made of the Sunni use of analogical reasoning.) Moreover, the elaboration of the law achieved by the jurisconsults produced only "likely suppositions," by the admission of the jurisconsults themselves. And wasn't a reliable tradition as to the opinion of the Prophet or one of the twelve infallible Imams superior to a likely supposition? In a way this last criticism was a distant echo of the skepticism that had provoked a crisis in the inner life of Ghazzali six centuries earlier.

Mullah Mohammed Amin discerned something else, which was perhaps more telling than the intellectual objections he raised to the jurisconsult school: he discerned the spiritual malaise of the mullahs of the mid-Safavi period. They knew that true sovereignty belonged to the absent Imam, the expected messianic Lord of the Age, and yet many of them, such as the sayyed Nematollah Jazayeri, whose hands had "run with blood" while studying at the *madreseh* in Shiraz, scrambled for the honor, wealth, and power that the Safavi state could confer on them. At various times in their two hundred-odd years of rule the Safavis had an official chaplain called *mullah-bashi*, or "top mullah"; they appointed mullahs as heads of the religious establishment in every major city, and they appointed an overall supervisor of the religious establishment, whose duties included supervision of the vast economic wealth tied up in religious endowments. When Mullah

Mohammed Amin proposed to turn Shiah jurisprudence on its head some mullahs may have responded to its implied attack on *all* hierarchy within the community of mullahs, for, in the opinion of the school of traditions, any person with a proper training in Arabic could be his own jurisconsult.

A mild version of the school of traditions established by Mullah Mohammed Amin flourished in the latter part of the seventeenth century, and a far more violent one appeared in the eighteenth. In fact, in the eighteenth century Shi'ism had convincing reasons to disestablish its own hierarchy. Shah Soltan Hosain, the Safavi who had succeeded to the throne in 1694, fulfilled all the hopes of the court eunuchs who had secured his election. He was extravagantly interested in his harem and in his wine cellar, in which interest, however, his eunuchs could not always protect him; on one occasion the mullahs had sixty thousand bottles of wine taken from the royal stores and smashed in public. And neither the eunuchs nor the mullahs could protect him from serious military threats. In the second decade of the eighteenth century Iran's Sunni Afghan neighbors to the east (theoretically subjects of the Safavi shahs) became aware that no one was minding the Safavi state. After sweeping aside the remnants of the Safavi administration and army, they besieged Shah Soltan Hosain in Isfahan, his magnificent capital of perhaps a half million inhabitants. In 1722, after a siege of a few months, the alcoholic descendant of Shah Esma'il surrendered unconditionally to the small army of Afghans surrounding him.

Iran from 1722 almost until the end of the century was as often as not in a state of anarchy. Nader Shah, the only really powerful Iranian ruler of the century, the man who finally expelled remnants of the Sunni Afghan government was—ironically—himself sympathetic to Sunnism, the good name of which he tried to reestablish among the Iranian people. He failed. But the experience of Nader Shah confirmed among the Shiah the wisdom of the more thoroughgoing eighteenth-century school of the traditionists: as long as there was a sentiment against hierarchy among the mullahs it was almost impossible, even for a ruler as powerful as Nader, to lay hold of the Shiah religious establishment.

Yet even in its eighteenth-century heyday, when mullahs of the school of traditionists persecuted the rare vocal supporters of the school of jurisconsults, the victory of the traditionists was incomplete. From the tenth century, Shiah theology had held that both the distinction between logical consistency and inconsistency and the distinction between good and evil were an incontrovertible part of the natural order and not the creations of God's whim and that both distinctions were accessible to the human intellect. It was possible to maintain, as the traditionists did, that reason could help the intellect discover theological and even ethical truth, but not legal truth. But this was improbable.

The man who said it was improbable, and made a convincing case that it was improbable, was an Iranian mullah named Vahid Behbahani who settled in Kerbela in the middle of the eighteenth century. From the rise of the Safavi dynasty at the beginning of the sixteenth century the government of Iran had tried but generally failed to establish its rule over Kerbela and Najaf, the Shiah shrine towns of southern Iraq. From 1638 to the present, southern Iraq (with brief interruptions) has remained under the control of Sunni regimes. The Sunni rulers of Iraq were not particularly kind to their Shiah subjects, but their rule offered one major advantage: from the safety of Iraq they could criticize with impunity the Shiah governments of Iran and/or the mullahs who were cosy with these governments. The wisdom of rebuilding the jurisconsult school from Iraq was brought home to Vahid Behbahani when he contemplated leaving Kerbela. The Imam Hosain, who was buried there, appeared to him in a dream and said, "I am not pleased that you should cease to be in my vicinity and my city"— and Vahid Behbahani obediently stayed.

Vahid Behbahani, while not a brilliant jurisconsult, understood two essential things: the dispute was about leadership and about what legal methods could be accepted as yielding "proofs" as to what was or was not the law. To establish his position as a leader he developed a coterie of faithful disciples, and his son, who carried on the fight for the jurisconsult school, was constantly surrounded by a group of toughs. Behbahani seems to have been able to exploit the tensions between the Arab students and those Iranian students who had studied in Isfahan, where *madreseh* learning had not become so hostile to the school of jurisconsults. No longer was anyone afraid to champion the position of the juris-consults in public.

Similarly, it required an intellectual frontal attack to beat back Mullah Mohammed Amin's objections to "likely supposition." Shi'ism, with its "natural" theology and emphasis on the need for infallible Imams to offer unquestionable truth, had generally placed a higher premium on certain knowledge than did Sunni Islam, and consequently it had generally suspected mere "opin-ion." But both Sunni and Shiah jurisprudence had developed cer-tain procedures for giving judicial opinions in situations (many of them involving ritual obligations) which by their nature do not allow the believer to be certain as to whether he or she has an ob-ligation or not. For example, does a man who has washed in the prescribed way for prayer but is genuinely uncertain whether some event thereafter might have made him ritually unclean (a chance that some drops of water suddenly splashed on him from a nearby roof may have come from an unseen dog) have an obliga-tion to wash again? No; assuming the "continuity" of a known condition—ritual cleanliness—is legally more proper than as-suming an obligation based on an uncertain point of discontinu-ity. In this case he can say with both eyes open, "God willing, it's a goat."

Behbahani took this small weapon into his hands and rushed into the enemy camp. He admitted that huge areas of the law were uncertain. He proposed to deal with these areas in two ways. He asserted the regular sources of law gave "overwhelming likeli-ness" (just as certain theological proofs could not destroy skepti-cism—as Ghazzali had seen—but could give "overwhelming likeliness") for some points of law. As for the rest, he said that the less certain areas of law had to be treated according to certain "procedural" principles (such as "continuity" in the example above) that previous jurists had used for a few necessarily uncer-tain situations (as in the case of the man known to be ritually clean who was then subjected to the uncertain possibility of pol-lution from water splashed from an unseen source).

It took two more generations to rebuild Shiah law in this way, but by the mid-nineteenth century the mullahs of Najaf had suc-ceeded. It helped that shortly after the death of Vahid Behbahani a strong and explicitly Shiah regime was founded in Iran. In 1795 the Qajar, Agha Mohammed Khan, declared himself shah by putting on a royal sword that had been consecrated at the tomb of the founder of the Safavi family. But unlike the Safavis, Qajars did not claim to rule as representatives of the absent Imam; they were rightful kings because they were "just" and because they were guardians of Shi'ism. The mullahs of the jurisconsult school in Najaf saw that the major center of Shi'ism was now open to receive them; within a generation they had won the minds of the majority of Iranian mullahs and the support of the Qajar kings. It now was both possible and intellectually defensible to construct a religious hierarchy, and they did so.

A hypertrophied example of a mullah of the new order was a certain Shafti, called by the title Hojjat al-Islam ("Proof of Islam"), a title hardly ever given to anyone in earlier Islamic history except Ghazzali. The title became increasingly common after the time of Shafti and at present is of secondary importance, merely the designation for a mullah of some learning who is not yet an ayatollah. Born near Rasht, a town in the region bordering the Caspian Sea, Shafti went to Iraq and studied with Vahid Behbahani in Najaf. He then arrived in Isfahan at the end of the eighteenth century, outstandingly learned in the new techniques of the jurisconsult school but destitute of any worldly possessions except a large piece of cloth appropriate for use as a turban or a tablecloth.

His learning and personal style eventually made him the dominant teacher and the great jurisconsult of the Isfahan region, and with time "the wealth of that great man," his biographer tells us, "perhaps passed calculation; and Almighty God revealed His power in him." He had four hundred caravansaries, more than four thousand shops, and owned whole villages in various parts of Iran. The same hypertrophy marked his personal behavior. It was said of him that from midnight till morning he continually wept, called on God, and beat his chest and head. Toward the end of his life his doctors had to forbid him to weep, because weeping was the presumed cause of the hernia that made him ill, and whenever he went to the mosque the professional narrators of the story of Hosain stayed away from the pulpit to avoid arousing tearful emotions in him.

He turned with similar zeal to the enforcement of Islamic law.

For at least a thousand years administration of justice in Islamic Iran had been a loosely sewn and frequently resewn patchwork of conflicting authority in which the different and sometimes conflicting sources for Islamic law—the jurists, the actual judges, and the non-Islamic law officials of the king—disputed with each other over the scope of their jurisdictions. Islamic law could be extremely cumbersome. For a crime such as theft, for example, Islamic law made no provision for a public prosecutor, and legal action was essentially a private suit brought by the victim. He had to be present at the trial; his case was destroyed if the thief returned the stolen object before an application for trial had taken place; his case, according to some jurists, depended in the absence of confession on the evidence of two male witnesses; and he had personally to be present at any corporal punishment (cutting off the right hand for the first theft, the left foot for the second, and imprisonment until repentance for all further thefts). According to some jurists, except for the satisfaction of witnessing these punishments, the victim could not recover any of the value of the lost object from the thief if the stolen object no longer existed. In contrast, the judges appointed by the king may not have had a body of law as elaborate as Islamic law (though a few Iranian regimes did produce summary written codes). But their justice was swift. And even if they sometimes took bribes, employed gruesome punishments, and often flew by the seat of their pants and not by the charts of the sacred law, the king's judges tended to give cases the kind of commonsensical solutions intended to preserve social equilibrium rather than satisfy any abstract ideal of divinely decreed legality.

Shafti's interest in enforcing Islamic law was nothing new. For all the ebb and flow in the power of the king's courts, some aspects of the law always remained in the hands of the mullahs, and the mullahs never surrendered their claim to a vastly extended jurisdiction. The village mullah was the natural arbiter in matters of marriage, divorce, and inheritance; and the exalted jurisconsult, in order to carry out the very function for which he was exalted, gave opinions on those matters of law on which he was consulted. In between the village mullah and the jurisconsult there were mullahs with courts which, while sometimes sanctioned by the royal government, depended for their power on the prestige of the presiding mullah judge as much or more than on the government's sanction. It was presumably a court of this nature that Kasravi was slated to inherit from his mullah grandfather.

Shafti's biographer tells the story of a woman who brought a case against the headman of her village for taking the property of her children, who were minors. Shafti summoned the headman, who denied the charges and produced fourteen rulings by fourteen mullah judges of Isfahan in his favor. Shafti looked at the rulings, piled the papers in front of himself, and said, "The headman is an upright person and what he says conforms to the rules." The woman wailed and clamored, but Shafti paid no attention and turned to the other cases before him. In the course of examining these cases he casually asked the headman if he had bought the property in question, and the headman said he had not. Then in a series of asides, in the course of trying other cases, Shafti found out that the headman could not claim that the property had been transferred to him through any of the means recognized as legal in Islamic law. "You are a usurper," declared Shafti, who tore up the fourteen previous judgments and wrote a judgment for the land to be returned to the woman.

The story, like many others, shows the great informality of procedure in the courts in spite of the elaborate development of the area of law that bore on the question at hand. It also shows that while in principle there is no appeal in Islamic law, the haziness of jurisdiction allowed people to carry on disputes even after a judgment had been handed down until (as in most cases) they came to some compromise, which all parties signed, sealed, and held to, or until they obtained the decision of someone such as Shafti, an authority so powerful that he was able and willing to use coercive force to get his ruling enforced.

Shafti, as the very model of a modern jurisconsult, had no qualms about coercion. He condemned at least seventy (according to some accounts, eighty to a hundred) people to death, and many of the executed were buried in a graveyard next to his house. There are signs that his enthusiasm for the death penalty was at first seen by the people of Isfahan as an example of distasteful hypertrophy in the use of the power of mullah courts. When he passed his first death sentence (for homosexuality) no one was willing to carry it out, so Shafti himself rose and struck the condemned man as hard a blow as he could. But as he was such a small man the blow was ineffective, and someone else had to complete the job. When Shafti then said the funeral prayers over the body he fainted with emotion—too late to impress his victim but not too late to impress his mullah biographer. He also impressed his biographer by imprisoning himself—on which occasion, however, he accepted the intercession for his own release by the Friday prayer leader of Isfahan.

With the rise of men such as Shafti a three-cornered dialectic developed between the Qajar government in Tehran, the mullahs in contact with the Shiah masses in Iran, and the mullah leaders of Shiah learning in the out-of-the-way shrine towns of southern Iraq. By the late eighteenth century, leadership in Shiah learning had moved to the circle of Vahid Behbahani in Iraq, and in the middle of the nineteenth century it found its highest expression in Sheikh Mortaza Ansari. This pious and truly original man was born in southwestern Iran at the very end of the eighteenth century virtually at the same time as the Qajar dynasty established its power. He went to the home of the revived jurisconsult school in southern Iraq to study, and once he had become an advanced pupil, he made a study tour of Iran in which he visited and studied with the prominent Iranian mullahs. But his return to Najaf in southern Iraq in about 1833 set the seal on the intellectual leadership of Najaf; the decline of Isfahan, its only rival, was nearly complete with the death of the ferocious Shafti in 1844.

Ansari's reputation for piety and generosity certainly contributed to his rise to leadership among the jurisconsults, but more than that of any mullah leader of the past two centuries, his leadership celebrated his learning. The new jurisconsult school admitted the uncertainty of much of the sacred law and emphasized that only jurisconsults could manipulate reason and tradition with the authority necessary to produce a "best guess." The rest of the believers, called "imitators," were free to choose among these best guessers but not to guess for themselves. In the generation of the students of Behbahani there were only about a half dozen such jurisconsults in Iran; at present, out of a population of about forty million, there are about two hundred.

Ansari was more than a mere jurisconsult; he was the first effective "model." The students of Vahid Behbahani (who were the
teachers of Ansari) developed Behbahani's ideas of the jurisconsult to their natural conclusion: If imitators should follow the example of a jurisconsult because it was wisest to follow the best
guess of men who were more learned, shouldn't jurisconsults
defer to the guess of the "most learned" among themselves? But
for this generation the role went begging in the absence of an acceptable player; for all their talents, the generation of Shafti never
produced a clear winner. Then came Ansari.

In his teaching and books of the 1830s, forties, and fifties
Sheikh Ansari brought the intellectual revolution of the jurisconsult school to its maturity. He showed convincingly and at length
why the procedural principles that Vahid Behbahani and his
pupils considered the jurisconsult's special tools for constructing
likely suppositions were, in fact, well justified. But, just as important, he showed convincingly and (in the view of subsequent
Shiah jurists) finally how these principles related to each other.
For example, when the jurisconsult faces a question without a
sense of the strong likelihood of one solution, then he must determine if the doubt is "primary" and "general," as is the case in
the absence of the discovery of any law supposed to be based on
reason or tradition. (No one knows whether the special Friday
noon prayer service should be held in the absence of the Twelfth
Imam, who has the only unquestionable right to lead it or to appoint its leaders.) Alternatively, the jurisconsult may determine
that the doubt is "secondary"; that is, we are *not* in doubt about
general principles and truths but are in doubt about something
related to the specific case (did the water splashed on me come
from the dog I saw on the roof?). If the doubt is primary, then the
jurisconsult can use the principle of "prudence" if certain further
conditions are fulfilled; if, for example, it is possible to perform all
the possible obligations. If it is not possible to do so, then the
principle of "option" applies: One obligation can be chosen instead of another—and so on and so forth, through a host of new
clarifications that Ansari introduced into Shiah jurisprudence.

These decision trees, organized schemes of alternate choices,
which frequently offered the binary either/or choices to the jurisconsult as in the examples above, are painstakingly worked out in

the writings of Ansari. Ansari used great subtlety and—within his tradition—originality in making new distinctions, always with an eye to the possibilities offered by a careful examination of all the conceivable meanings of words and all the permutations of "reason" (as understood in the Shiah tradition). Interestingly, as in the examples above, many of Ansari's new distinctions and classifications took the laws applying to divine worship and ritual purity as their points of departure.

The surprising thing is that Ansari's greatest book in which he showed how to apply these principles was not on the law of divine worship and ritual purity but on the law of commerce. Of course he considered questions that border on matters of purity: Is it permissible to traffic in musical instruments, since music is of doubtful legality—and so forth. And Ansari by no means threw out the Shiah law that existed; the basic applied law texts read by Shiah *talabehs* were (and still are) two texts of the thirteenth and sixteenth centuries. But he showed how to extend the analysis of law—in particular the enormous area that in Anglo-American law is considered the law of contracts—far beyond its previous limits; and this extended analysis he applied to commerce. For example, he distinguished dozens of ways in which an object sold and then returned, according to the recognized right of return, or "rescission of sale," might have changed in value, and he determined the legal obligations of the parties involved according to the principles of continuity and discontinuity, doubts primary and secondary as to its condition and legal status, and so on. Such law was largely new, and it was very useful.

Like Behbahani, Ansari, in the remote backwater of Najaf, had created an intellectual commodity that the Shiah world of Iran would eventually both need and be ready to buy. The Middle East was gradually but ineluctably being pulled into the world economy that had been emerging at least since the end of the eighteenth century (if not earlier). In 1814, within weeks of the announcement of peace between England and the United States, the price of coffee fell in the ports of Arabia (the home of mocha coffee but by then an importer of coffee) on news that the Yankee privateers were no longer raiding the Atlantic sea-lanes. Some of the carrying trade of Asia, the commerce in valuable commodities from China, India, and the Mediterranean world, had passed through Iran for centuries, but in the nineteenth century Iran became enmeshed in a trade with Europe, the pace and intensity of which was something altogether new. The beautiful silk brocades of Kashan gave way to the calicoes and chintzes of Manchester, and the Iranian potter and blacksmith slowly sank to obscurity as Russian hardware, crockery, and glassware flooded their markets. Iran increasingly became an exporter of foodstuffs, tobacco, raw silk, opium, and—the one manufactured product the foreigners never successfully imitated—rugs.

Not only was commerce with foreigners increasing but Iran itself was becoming a national market in which the prices for such commodities as rice and pocket watches were beginning to be set at a national level. The development of a national economy came partly from the integration of Iran into a world economy, which imposed collective demands on Iran, and partly as a result of changes in communications within Iran itself, the most dramatic of which was the introduction of the telegraph in the 1860s. Ansari (who can have had little contact with the practical world of commerce) demonstrated that Shiah law had within itself the principles and the method to create a law of contract capable of dealing with all the complexities and fluctuations introduced by this new commerce.

In 1849 the most prominent scholar of the generation senior to Ansari died. By now Ansari's work was known throughout the Shiah world and there was no question as to who was "the most learned" among the jurisconsults. The role had found its first full-fledged character; Ansari was accepted as the "model" for imitation by Shiahs not only in Iraq and Iran but also in India, Lebanon, and the Shiah communities scattered in the Caucasus and Afghanistan. The *sahm-e Imam,* or "portion of the Imam," the income owed by the Shiah to the mullahs through self-tithing in the absence of the Twelfth Imam, poured into Najaf from all over the Islamic world; and, according to one source, Ansari received about two hundred thousand tomans a year to redistribute. The financial recognition of this new centralization of religious authority confirmed the standing of Najaf as the center of Shiah learning. And thanks to the presence and generosity of Ansari, this was one center of Shiah learning where deserving students and teachers could count on receiving their stipends.

Ansari remained the pure scholar. His lack of interest in the world was shown by his lack of interest in personal wealth. (His children seem to have been slightly embarrassed at the near poverty in which they lived.) But his lack of interest showed itself in another way. He had always abhorred the idea of being a judge (according to one source, he was briefly a judge in his native town but fled when pressure was put on him to decide for one of the parties), and he was extremely reluctant to give *fatvas*, the answers to specific questions which only a jurisconsult was qualified to give. Ansari was probably the first "model" who, according to the principles of the newly reconstructed jurisconsult school, received the recognition of the great majority of other mullahs of that school; but he seems never to have exerted this authority actively among the Shiah community.

The extent (and limitations) of the authority of a "model" who did exert his authority became apparent in the career of one of Ansari's pupils, Sayyed Mohammed Hasan Shirazi, usually called Mirza Shirazi. Mirza Shirazi was born in 1815 in Shiraz, the city of Saadi and Hafez, where Sayyed Nematollah had studied two centuries before. From Shiraz he went to Isfahan, now in its twilight as an important center of Shiah learning, and at the age of twenty received his "permission to act as a jurisconsult" from one of the last important jurisconsults of the Isfahani school. Then, in the mid-1840s he went to Najaf, where the future of Shiah learning lay, and studied with Sheikh Ansari. When Ansari died in 1864, in the words of a mullah historian, "a group of distinguished men claimed the distinction of being 'most learned' and the succession to Sheikh Ansari, and of course the views of the students in his circle of learning played a significant role in the choice of a successor."

At first the Turkish-speaking students (presumably, in the majority, from Azerbaijan) had two candidates and the Persian-speaking students two others, including Mirza Shirazi. The loyalties of the small number of Arabs in this inner circle were divided among the four candidates, as were the revenues that came to Najaf from self-tithing and from pious endowments. But, as the same mullah historian writes, Mirza Shirazi "knew the world better than the rest"; when the muddle over who was most learned continued, Shirazi solved it by avoiding it. He moved to the nearby Iraqi shrine town of Samarra, where the Twelfth Imam had disappeared, and established a new center of Shiah learning. His students followed. In a short time he had acquired the reputation of being the founder of a new center of learning, and he was at the very least the absolutely undisputed "model" in that center of learning. From this point on, recognition of his leadership seems to have grown steadily.

Then came the event that swept away all doubts about his leadership and seemed to confirm the political significance of a single, supreme "model." In 1890 the Qajar ruler of Iran, Naser ed-Din Shah, prepared to restore his finances in the same way he had done many times in the past: he would grant an economic concession to a European company. This time, in return for fifteen thousand pounds a year, the shah gave the Imperial Tobacco Company the right to buy the entire tobacco crop of Iran, a valuable cash crop, since the Iranians cultivated a variety of tobacco not cultivated elsewhere which was much prized in foreign markets as well as in Iran itself. Sale was to be at prices mutually agreed upon between the company and the Iranian sellers; disagreements were to be settled by compulsory arbitration.

As word of the concession spread through Iran and agents of the Imperial Tobacco Company began to arrive, the sense of outrage was nearly universal. Not only the thousands who grew tobacco but also the tens of thousands of small merchants who sold tobacco and the hundreds of thousands who smoked realized that even Iranian tobacco would reach them only after it had passed through the hands of an English company. The Russians were jealous of the concession and encouraged agitation against it; the "reformers," advocates of Western-style institutions and government accountability, agitated against the concession; the merchants, who saw the government selling control of the trade on which their livelihood depended, denounced the concession; and the ordinary Iranian, who had for long suspected that the government was selling off the country to the foreigners, now saw convincing proof that his suspicions were correct.

The natural voice of a protest so nearly universal was the voice of the mullahs. They spoke in some part out of their own interests: they controlled considerable agricultural land tied up in religious endowments. They spoke also in part out of shared interests: they had close links to the men of the bazaar, who imposed taxes on themselves to support the mullahs and religious life in general and who were used to turning to mullah courts for settlement of certain kinds of disputes. But they also spoke in large part as guardians of certain values; they feared for Islam. The large-scale introduction of foreigners with non-Muslim ideas and the subjugation of Muslims to decisions by non-Muslims about their destinies were dangers to "the citadel of Islam," the protection of which—in their view—was the primary responsibility of every government.

By the end of the summer of 1891 there were open protests in Tabriz, the capital of the province of Azerbaijan: the mullahs stopped teaching in the *madresehs*, and the merchants closed the bazaar. From a sanctuary near Tehran, Sayyed Jamal ad-Din, the so-called Afghan and sometime freemason, sometime Sufi, and sometime almost everything else, had already been preaching to large audiences, including many *talabehs*, against the policies of the shah (with whom he had recently fallen out). Removed from sanctuary and dumped across the border in January 1891, Sayyed Jamal ad-Din saw the opportunity offered by the public outcry against the tobacco concession and wrote a letter to Shirazi, "the chief jurisconsult":

> This letter is an invocation of Islamic law wherever it is found and dwells, and an appeal by the people to all true souls who believe in this law . . . to the learned men in Islam. And this appeal I desire to make to all of these, although it be addressed to one in particular.
>
> Pontiff of the people, Ray of the Light of the Imams, Pillar of the edifice of Religion, Tongue attuned to the exposition of the perspicuous law, Your Reverence, Haji Mirza Mohammad Hasan Shirazi—may God protect by your means the fold of Islam, and avert the plots of the vile unbelievers!
>
> God has set you apart for this supreme vice-regency . . . to control the people in a way conformable to the most luminous law, and to protect their rights thereby, and to guard their hearts from

errors and doubts therein. . . . He has assigned you the throne of
authority and bestowed on you such supremacy over his people as
empowers you to save and defend their country . . .

This criminal has offered the provinces of the land of Iran to
auction amongst the Great Powers, and is selling the realms of
Islam and the abodes of Mohammad and his household to
foreigners. . . .

You know that the men of religious learning of Iran and its people with one accord . . . await a word from you wherein they will
behold their happiness and whereby their deliverance will be ef-
fected. How then can it beseem one on whom God has bestowed
such power as this to be so chary of using it or to retire it in abey-
ance?

The question had already occurred to Shirazi, who had spent
years gradually consolidating his position as "the most learned"
and had already received appeals from his followers in Iran, including many mullahs, to act. In September he sent a telegram to
the shah protesting the tobacco monopoly.

In the 1860s telegraph lines had been strung the length and
breadth of Iran. The shah wanted instantaneous news of provincial affairs; merchants wanted the information on prices and sup-
plies they needed to compete in the new national market; and the
English needed a continuous telegraphic link that stretched from
London to Bombay. Naturally, therefore, a significant part of
these lines was under British control, and—in the endlessly confusing world of conflicting jurisdictions that was Qajar Iran—a
British-run telegraph station acquired an air of extraterritoriality.
Simple provincials believed that telegraph lines delivered their
messages directly at the foot of the shah's throne. Even for sophisticated men the mystique of the telegraph was irresistible.
Some Iranian mullahs sent their protests to Mirza Shirazi in Samarra by telegraph not only because of its speed and dependabil-
ity but also because of its prestige. Whatever their motives, by
this period the telegraph helped create a national market in mullah opinions as well as in commodity prices.

In December 1891 a *fatva* in Shirazi's name appeared in Tehran:
"In the name of God, the Merciful, the Beneficent. Today the use
of both varieties of tobacco, in whatever fashion, is reckoned war

against [the Twelfth Imam,] the Imam of the Age—may God hasten his advent!" That—at least in this matter—Mirza Shirazi was
someone "on whom God had bestowed such power," in Sayyed
Jamal ad-Din's words, was demonstrated with marvelous speed
and thoroughness. Naser ed-Din Shah found that even those of
his wives who had been confirmed smokers put away their water
pipes. The mullahs and merchants communicated the *fatva* and
messages of their support for it not only by extensive use of the
telegraph but also by leaflets abundantly reproduced by the new
hectograph method. Then, in January 1892, when the shah saw
that the British government was waffling in its support of the Imperial Tobacco Company, he canceled the concession. On the
twenty-sixth of the same month the public crier in Tehran announced that Mirza Shirazi had issued a *fatva* permitting the use
of tobacco, and Iranians began smoking again. Mirza Shirazi died
in 1895. While he had written comparatively little, he had stun-
ningly demonstrated what events could do for the position of "the
most learned model" and what the position of the "most learned
model" could do for events.

When Mirza Shirazi moved from Najaf to Samarra, one of the
pupils who moved with him was Mohammed Kazim Khorasani.
As Mirza Shirazi wrote so little, we have to depend on his contemporaries for testimony to his learning; for Khorasani's learning
we have the testimony of his books. The greatest of these books,
The Sufficiency, ranks only after Ansari's treatise on commercial law
among the legal works written by mullahs in the last two centuries. In *The Sufficiency,* Khorasani gathered the jurisprudential
ideas such as "continuity" that Ansari had discussed in separate
treatises and had applied in his treatise to commerce. Khorasani
presented them in a yet more rigorous fashion as a unified theory
of jurisprudence, a discipline that for Muslims meant the science
for the derivation of the law.

Khorasani came from northwestern Iran; he was born in Tus,
also the birthplace of Ferdowsi and Ghazzali. He moved to Iraq in
1861, immediately recognized Mirza Shirazi as the leading teacher
of his time, and was himself as immediately recognized as the
leading candidate to succeed Shirazi after his death. Like Ansari,
he was not a sayyed (Shirazi was), and, like Ansari, he owed his

position almost purely to his intellectual accomplishments. But like Shirazi, and far beyond the example of Shirazi, he turned his position as "most learned model" to political use.

Shiah men of religion, people loosely called mullahs by Iranians, included a vast spectrum of learning, specialties, and opinion in the time of Khorasani. There were village mullahs, *rowzeh-khans*, preachers, and jurisconsults. The sons of prominent mullahs often dressed as mullahs, particularly if they could derive some respect or income from doing so (as, for example, when they inherited their fathers' courts), and yet might have almost no real learning. Both the barely literate teachers of elementary schools for boys (such as the men who so tormented the little Kasravi) and the modest merchants in the bazaar who studied privately their whole lives and attained a fair degree of sophisticated legal knowledge might to some degree assume the dress and accept the title of mullah. Even that secret skeptic, the preacher with the black eyes and wispy black beard, who preached to adoring crowds in the mosque nearby the house of the young Isa Sadiq was not really exceptional; a fair number of other secret skeptics without any self-consciousness assumed the style of mullahs in this period.

To a supreme jurisconsult this was both an opportunity and a danger. The mullahs recognized that they had a common interest and usually tried to present a fairly united front to the world, but in fact the jurisconsults thought the *rowzeh-khans* ignorant men, the secret skeptics thought the jurisconsults rigid and backward, and so on. The supreme jurisconsult had the opportunity to shape any emerging consensus among the mullahs (as Shirazi had done) and confirm the common cause of all varieties of mullahs (and the Shiah community as well), but he ran the danger that if he ran too far ahead of the consensus, his "imitators" among the mullahs (and, secondarily, among the Shiah masses) would bolt and recognize another mullah as "most learned."

By 1906 the collective resentment against the Qajars had reached such a point that it was as natural for mullahs to join the movement of protest that became the Constitutional Revolution as it was for them to support the resistance to the tobacco concession. In fact, without their support the movement would have failed. But some mullahs went further: they enthusiastically supported the idea of the European-minded reformers who said there had to be a fundamental national law fixed in writing—that is, a constitution—and an elective legislature. These constitutionalist mullahs ran the gamut from sincere and devout ayatollahs through religious men who doubted the sufficiency of the sacred law as traditionally taught, all the way to skeptics such as Isa Sadiq's preacher, men who thought that only if they posed as mullahs could they persuade the masses of the need for change.

Khorasani chose to support the constitutionalists. At first it seemed an even greater coup than the ban on the use of tobacco; the most learned "model" had not just confirmed the sentiments of his imitators, he had actually led them. The newly elected parliament was inaugurated in the presence of seventeen jurisconsults in October 1906. But then the mullahs in Iran, and especially those in Tehran, began to think more closely about what had happened. During the preceding summer, when the prominent antigovernment mullahs had withdrawn from Tehran to Qom in protest, the secular constitutionalists in Tehran had changed the name of the legislative body they were demanding from the Islamic Consultative Assembly to the National Consultative Assembly. This name had become enshrined in the royal decree granting the constitution. In fact, the Iranian constitution had been modeled in large part on the Belgian constitution, which, as the Iranian men of the new education had learned in their schools, was considered the most advanced European constitution according to contemporary European political science.

Consultation is a duty of rulership in virtually all traditions of Islamic thought, including the Shiah tradition, and its reprehensible opposite, *estebdad*, or autocracy, was the mark of a ruler who made up his mind without consultation. The work of such an assembly was to point the ruler in the direction of "justice," and therefore some of the mullahs called this consultative group a House of Justice. But did this imply a legislature that was elective and that actually made laws?

By February 1907 the newly elected Consultative Assembly, which included a large number of mullahs, began to discuss a supplement to the constitution, which was seen to lack a bill of rights. In May a prominent mullah in the Assembly, Sheikh

Fazlollah Nuri, began campaigning for a restoration of the Islamic character of the government, and he organized *talabehs* to demonstrate continually outside the Assembly in support of his initiative. To some extent he succeeded; the second clause of the supplement, passed in July, read:

> The Consultative Assembly, which has been formed by the blessing of the Imam of the Age—may God hasten his advent—and by the grace of His Majesty the Shah, and by the vigilance of the Islamic men of learning—may God increase their example—and by the Iranian nation, may at no time legislate laws that are contradictory to the sacred laws of Islam. . . . It is self-evident that it is the responsibility of the Islamic men of learning to determine and judge such contradictions. Therefore, it is officially decreed that in each legislative session a board of no less than five men, comprised of jurisconsults and devout specialists in Islamic law, who are also aware of the needs and exigencies of the time . . . be nominated by the Islamic men of learning. The Consultative Assembly shall accept this board as full members. It is their duty to study all the legislative proposals, and if they find any that contradict the sacred laws of Islam, they shall reject it. The decision of this board in this respect is binding and final. This provision of the Constitution is unalterable until the appearance of the Imam of the Age—may God hasten his advent.

Sheikh Fazlollah, however, was not satisfied. He took sanctuary with about five hundred followers in the same shrine near Tehran in which Sayyed Jamal ad-Din had taken sanctuary a generation earlier. From this sanctuary he began to issue a newspaper, the chief object of which was to attack the new parliamentarianism and the secular constitutionalists. He declared that they wanted to introduce "the customs and practices of the abode of disbelief [the non-Islamic world]," to tamper with the sacred law, to make all religious communities equal, to spread prostitution, and so forth. Sheikh Fazlollah said he did not challenge the idea of a "house of justice" convened to spread "justice" and to enforce the sacred law. But he claimed that during the events leading to the revolution of 1906 no one had heard talk of such a "National Consultative Assembly" or of a constitution.

An important voice in Najaf now spoke in support of Sheikh

Fazlollah. Sayyed Mohammed Kazem Yazdi, a jurisconsult, sent a telegram in which he ordered the Assembly to accept the limitations proposed by the circle of Sheikh Fazlollah and not to act as a parliament but as an assembly carrying out the Islamic injunction "to command the good and forbid the evil." Sheikh Fazlollah also printed a telegram supposedly sent by three constitutionalist jurisconsults in Najaf in which they demanded that the supplement to the constitution include a clause concerning heretics and the execution of divine commandments.

The history of the next twenty years of the National Assembly and the Iranian constitutional movement is so complex that it makes the history of the Continental Congress and the Articles of Confederation seem positively simple. Inevitably, external powers played a role. At first Mohammed Ali, a reactionary shah, found support in Russia, and the English favored the constitutionalists. But even the great powers failed to serve as fixed stars in the whirling heavens in which Iranian cabinets changed and provinces seceded and reaffirmed their loyalty to the government in Tehran. At one point the reactionary shah bombarded the Assembly. At another, Sheikh Fazlollah declared journalists non-Muslims for their support of the Assembly; then, in Najaf, Khorasani announced that Sheikh Fazlollah was a non-Muslim. The reactionary shah was overthrown; and in the flush of triumph Sheikh Fazlollah was tried, and on July 31, 1908, he was hanged. He behaved with great dignity; immediately before his execution he said that neither was he a reactionary nor were the two ayatollahs in Tehran most prominent in their support of the constitution true constitutionalists: "It was merely that they wished to excel me, and I them, and there was no question of 'reactionary' or 'constitutional' principles."

In a certain crude way Sheikh Fazlollah was right. The struggle over the constitution had opened up rifts among the mullahs which had previously been concealed or had not existed. It had proved difficult to duplicate the universal leadership as "most learned" that Ansari had enjoyed. Even in the time of Mirza Shirazi, despite the universal acceptance of his *fatva* against smoking tobacco, some of the Turkish-speaking circle of his predecessor, Ansari (and, following them, some Turkish-speaking

Iranians), had continued to recognize one of their own number as "the most learned." When Sheikh Fazlollah succeeded in drawing large crowds in Tehran and significant support from mullahs throughout Iran, Khorasani lost many of his followers to that opponent of parliamentarianism, Sayyed Mohammed Kazem Yazdi. Yazdi not only became a "model" for a significant number of "imitators" or followers but one of his books, a practical manual on the personal duties of a Shiah, became and remains the model for such books written by subsequent claimants to leadership as "the most learned" jurisconsult. According to Kasravi, in Najaf at the height of their rivalry only thirty-odd people still prayed behind Khorasani, while several thousand showed that they had accepted another "model" as leader by praying behind Yazdi.

It would be wrong, however, to characterize the mullahs at any period as either for or against the constitution. Before the Constitutional Revolution, while there had been mullahs, such as Ansari, who scrupulously avoided association with the government and spoke at crucial moments for the oppressed, these mullahs seldom publicly criticized their worldly fellow mullahs by name, and they maintained relations with mullahs close to the central government and with worldly mullahs who were men of great personal wealth. The great political acts of mullahs such as Mirza Shirazi were reactive, not initiatory; steps—often steps against some measure of the government—were taken by the great jurisconsults only when an emerging unity of opinion had identified a threat.

Since the mullahs were a widely diverse segment of the population of Iran, their ability to close ranks in a shared interest fell apart when the Constitutional Revolution threw them into the role of initiators. They varied among themselves in their attitudes toward the constitution from its first mention until Reza Shah established full control twenty years later. The politics of elections and rival mobs forced them to broadcast these differences far and wide, as they had seldom done since the triumph of the jurisconsult school.

In general, the mullahs drifted away from their early enthusiasm for the constitution. Many of them had entered the constitutional movement because of their opposition to Qajar autocracy, their desire for justice as traditionally defined in Shiah law, their anger at the sale of Iran to foreigners, and their fears for Islam. When, however, they saw that a constitution on a foreign model and ideas of justice not traditionally accepted in Shiah Islam had been pushed forward by the secular constitutionalists, they had reason to pause. Even Khorasani, who spoke in favor of the constitution until his death in 1911, supported Sheikh Fazlollah's demand for a supplementary clause to the constitution against heresy. After pausing, some mullahs turned against the constitution; many (perhaps the majority) remained silent; and some continued to support it. Mullahs (or at least men who dressed as mullahs) continued to make up a significant percentage of the National Assembly. One of them, for example, was the jurisconsult Sayyed Hasan Modarres, a brave and incorruptible man, perhaps the most fervent mullah supporter of true constitutional government. He was continually reelected, even when mullahs became a far smaller percentage of the Assembly. In 1925 he, like Mossadegh, spoke against the bill that paved the way for Reza Khan to become Reza Shah. In 1938 he died in mysterious circumstances.

Modarres, however, was exceptional. After the death of Khorasani in 1911, leading mullahs, especially jurisconsults, spoke less and less about constitutionalism in the abstract. Nevertheless they remained heavily involved in local politics. In a place such as Isfahan, for example, the weakness of the constitutional government allowed a local mullah named Agha Nurollah to exercise so much power that at times he seemed to be replaying the role Shafti had played a century earlier. He ran law courts, he interfered with tax collection, his followers closed a primary school for girls, he pressed the police to arrest lewd women. In some of his activities Agha Nurollah seems to have done some good; in many, he seems to have kept the pot boiling to no particular good and sometimes to the positive harm of Iranians, as when the participants in an anti-Jewish riot in October 1921 went to his home and do not seem to have been in any way discouraged by him.

A few years later Reza Shah was in firm control not only of Isfahan but of all Iran. In 1927 he dissolved the old Ministry of Justice, which had been formed in 1911 in a generally unsuccessful attempt to create national courts and national codes, and a new Ministry of Justice, largely composed of Iranians educated in Europe, was formed and ordered to produce codes of law. To have a single law code ran against thirteen centuries of Islamic—and more particularly Shiah—tradition. For Muslim jurists the law existed in its full form in the mind of the Divine Legislator, but on the human plane positive law was whatever the jurist said it was by applying his training in the law to the situation before him. For this reason, in classical Islamic law there was no appeal. One jurist's "discovery" of the ruling of law for a specific case would not have been invalidated by some other jurist's "discovery" of a different ruling for that case; only God could choose between them, and until the Resurrection (or, in the case of the Shiah, the return of the Twelfth Imam) God had left the matter to the jurists, and the first actual judgment was final, as otherwise there would have been an infinite regress of opinions without any final judgment. For the Shiah, who considered so much of the law to be in the realm of supposition and doubt, the resistance to a single written code was even stronger; the jurisconsult's right to describe the law in his own way was the very essence of the doctrine that had revived the jurisconsult school at the end of the eighteenth century.

For secular-minded Iranians all this resistance to a fixed written law was an embarrassment before foreigners and an obstacle to building a strong and unified Iranian state. For a century Europeans in Iran had been something of a law unto themselves. Most European governments had obtained treaties from Iran in which the Iranian government agreed to the presence at the trial of a European in Iran of a representative of the European's home country, and without the countersignature of this representative (usually the consul) the decision of the Iranian court could have no effect. Europeans insisted that they had these rights—called the regime of capitulations—virtually to veto the decisions of Iranian courts because no one knew what laws foreigners would be judged by. After all, there might be many Shiah law books, but where were the actual laws?

In 1914 Mossadegh wrote his first book in Persian, *Capitulations and Iran*, to criticize this humiliating and antiquated practice. He urged that Iran adopt a written code and thereby deprive the Europeans of their excuse, even if the adoption of a single code went against the grain of Shiah tradition. "Our condition," he explained, using a simile he had employed in his Swiss doctoral thesis, "is like that of a sick man whose only remedy is wine. Even though wine is forbidden, in such circumstances, for the sick man to drink wine becomes a religious obligation." Capitulations were a covert form of colonialism: "For a government to be independent it must govern all those residing in its territory. . . . In the final analysis, a government which does not govern either its own citizens or foreigners is no government and will become the dependency of another government that possesses this position [of full sovereignty]."

In the late twenties Mossadegh's then opponent, Reza Shah, accomplished this program in a few short steps. Early in 1928 the shah's newly appointed minister of justice (who, like Mossadegh, had a Swiss legal education) presented the Assembly with the first volume of the civil code and a scheme for reorganizing the courts on a hierarchical principle. On May 8, after little debate, these proposals were approved. On May 10 the new laws came into provisional operation, and on the same day the Iranian Ministry of Foreign Affairs unilaterally abolished the regime of capitulations.

It is not surprising that European governments allowed the change to take place without any outcry; it is surprising how little outcry there was from the mullahs.

True, they expected that Reza Shah, as a simple man of the people, would be pious, and for quite a long while he had played the part. He announced that his "model" was Na'ini (perhaps the only one of the jurisconsults of Najaf who understood and supported liberal democratic institutions from outside Iran to the extent that the jurisconsult Modarres did within the Assembly). Reza Shah even went so far as to walk in a Moharram procession in 1924 with straw on his bare head, followed by his military band, which, to indicate that they were mourning for Imam Hosain, played their version of Chopin's funeral march.

True, Reza Shah eventually threw off the mask and showed them who was boss in terms of sheer coercive force. In March

1928 Reza Shah's mother (or wife—accounts differ) had visited the shrine in Qom, and while in an upper gallery of the shrine, supposedly while changing from a heavy chador to a light one, had for a moment exposed her face. A mullah reproached her, and there was some stir in support of the mullah. Reza Shah arrived in Qom the next day with two armored cars and four hundred troops and walked into the shrine in his boots. He found the offending mullah and, according to one version, beat him with his riding crop, according to another, dragged him by his beard, and according to a third (and most probable), kicked him in the back. He also ordered that three criminals who had taken sanctuary in the shrine be evicted. When the old world of uncertain and overlapping jurisdictions went, rights of sanctuary went with it.

True, for all its borrowing from European law in criminal law, in matters of civil law the new code was overwhelmingly based on Shiah law, which the Swiss-trained minister worked into the code under the supervision of men well trained in the traditional system. And, in fact, throughout the reigns of Reza Shah and his son Mohammed Reza, judges and lawyers found the traditional Shiah law an important source for suggesting solutions in matters not explicitly dealt with in the existing civil (but not criminal) codes.

True, Reza Shah represented his legal reforms as tentative experiments and allowed the religious judges to keep their courts for matters such as inheritance until 1936, when the new system was made permanent and the religious courts were totally abolished.

Yet neither the shah's talent at feigning piety nor the measured pace of the change explains why there was so little outcry by the mullahs for what they had lost. Not only had they lost a lucrative source of income from the registration of legal documents (marriages, land transfers, and the like) in their registries and courts but they had also lost the last vestiges of the very central duty for which—in their view—they existed: the administration of Islamic law. Not even Reza Shah's ability to use force explained their comparative quietness. For all that he had kicked a mullah in the shrine in Qom in 1928 and that his army had shot into the crowd of protesters in the shrine in Mashhad in 1935, a man with an army of some tens of thousands cannot coerce a nation of sixteen million. The truth was that even though the majority of people considered themselves religious, a lot of them were thoroughly fed up with activist mullahs such as Agha Nurollah of Isfahan. A large number of the mullahs recognized this, and they also recognized that their activism on all sides of all issues during the Constitutional Revolution had revealed their divisions and destroyed the power of a unified leadership that had made the man acknowledged as "most learned" a figure to reckon with in the last half of the nineteenth century.

There was one man who understood the change in mood as well as Reza Shah, an ayatollah named Sheikh Abd al-Karim Ha'eri of Yazd. He was born in a village near Yazd, an important provincial center in southeastern Iran, but after completing the elementary part of his education there he continued with the intermediate and advanced levels of *madreseh* study. He studied with Mirza Shirazi and completed his training with the author of *The Sufficiency*, the great Khorasani. Ha'eri had returned to Iran to teach at a *madreseh* in the provincial town of Arak in about 1900, but in 1906, when he found out how political some of the mullahs of Arak were (they included one of the most outspoken and notorious advocates of absolute monarchy), he moved back to Najaf. Soon, however, Najaf became political, and Ha'eri moved to another Iraqi town, Kerbela. By 1913 things had cooled down among the mullahs of Iran, and Ha'eri moved back to Arak. Then in 1921 the mullahs of Qom urged Ha'eri to come to their town and act as doyen of the circles of learning that existed there. He was by now a well-known and respected teacher. He was also a good administrator who encouraged sociability among mullahs; he is remembered for having told a parsimonious mullah who was a prospective bridegroom, "Marriage without a feast is nearly adultery."

In fact, not very much in the way of formal Shiah learning did exist in Qom. Fath-Ali Shah, the second Qajar ruler, had reembellished the shrine there and built a *madreseh*, the Faiziyeh, in fulfillment of a vow; he also had his mausoleum built there, and, following his example, so did many of the later Qajars. The Faiziyeh was a respectable provincial *madreseh* but not on a level with any *madreseh* in Najaf or even Isfahan or Tehran. Ha'eri set out to make Qom a leading center of learning, and his studied disinterest in politics proved to be one of his most powerful weapons in doing so. The last Qajar, on November 1, 1923, on the eve of his departure for a European trip that would turn into permanent exile, paid a last visit to Qom and presented Ha'eri with an inlaid walking stick, which Ha'eri gracefully accepted. On March 26, 1924, Reza, then prime minister and not yet shah, visited Ha'eri in Qom; he was graciously received. Ha'eri, in the words of one contemporary mullah, "does not introduce himself into political concerns and governmental matters since he believes that in these times avoidance of such things is far preferable for someone like himself."

Ha'eri also understood the change in mood in another respect. Iranians were becoming more nationalistic, and many Iranian mullahs wanted an Iranian center of Shiah learning on a par with or superior to Najaf, in Iraq. Ha'eri had chosen the second most important shrine town in Iran; Mashhad, the first, contained an entrenched mullah establishment that had a certain sense of rivalry with the leading scholars of Najaf, and therefore was not a place to which the clever young Iranian *talabehs* in Najaf could be as easily attracted. They were attracted to Qom, and Ha'eri, by founding a hospital and putting up housing, made sure that the Qomis did not resent the large influx of students. Although some of Ha'eri's contemporaries outshone him as jurisconsults, he became the "model" for many religious Iranians.

Another of Khorasani's pupils, Sayyed Abol-Hasan Musavi Isfahani of Najaf, outlived Ha'eri (who died in 1937), and Isfahani remained the jurisconsult accepted as "the most learned" by the majority of the Shiah community until his death in 1946. Then a third student of Khorasani, a sayyed named Borujerdi, finally brought the position of "most learned model" to Iran and specifically to Qom. He accomplished this feat largely through the skillful management of his seventy-day stay in a Tehran hospital. In 1944 he went from his native town, Borujerd, where he had presided over a *madreseh* and circle of learning, to Tehran for a hernia operation. In the previous year Borujerdi, who was already accepted as a "model" by some of the seminomadic tribal people of Iran, had coerced government support for some measures proposed by one Ayatollah Qomi by sending a message to the government: "If attention is not paid to the requests of Qomi, do not have faith in the security of the south of Iran." Somehow while he was in Tehran in 1944 it became known that he might be willing to move to Qom, where the vacuum left by the death of Ha'eri had never been filled. Reams of telegrams poured into his hospital room from the mullahs and *talabehs* of Qom urging him to come, followed by delegations of solicitous Qomis. Then the young shah came.

The shah was in his early twenties and had for many years been as overawed by his father as had the whole country. Now, with his father's removal, he was overawed by his circumstances, since the Allies had virtually occupied the major arteries of Iran and controlled some of the shah's ministers. We have a photograph of the shah in the ayatollah's hospital room. A doctor in a white coat stands in the background, and a photographer is standing next to him; a thin, elderly mullah stands in the left foreground, and Borujerdi, with his black turban, full black beard, and voluminous aba, is seated in the right foreground; in the center is the shah, looking very respectful, fingers intertwined, eyes cast down to the ground, with his superb felt fedora placed on a table in front of him.

Unfortunately what we don't have is a reliable record of Borujerdi's conversation with the shah. They talked for about an hour. One account says that Borujerdi asked the shah to prevent the newspapers from treating religion disrespectfully and that the shah enthusiastically agreed. They must have said much more. They needed each other, as they were both within a year or two of assuming real power; they were both worried about the virtual occupation of parts of Iran and they both disliked the Communists. Borujerdi wanted women to have the choice of wearing the veil in public if and when they wished to do so (this choice had been totally forbidden under Reza Shah), and he wanted mullahs and Islam itself treated with more public respect. The shah wanted the tacit support of a paramount Shiah leader who would also remain apolitical in the tradition of Ha'eri. Perhaps each of them understood the other's need without hearing it expressed; in any case, the first visit was a success, and the shah occasionally visited Borujerdi for the rest of the ayatollah's life. By and large, each one lived up to what the other expected of him.

When he was ready to leave the hospital Borujerdi opened his Koran for an omen and his eye fell on a verse that convinced him he should go to Qom. He arrived in December 1944 and within two or three years became the sole "model" for imitation in the Shiah world until his death in 1961. During Ayatollah Borujerdi's long reign as supreme "model" the mullahs came as near to being a Western-style clergy as they have ever come in the fourteen centuries of their existence. A thousand years ago, in the early Islamic world, "men of religious learning" (ulema, as they are called collectively in Arabic and Persian) could not have been more unlike the modern Western idea of a clergy. They included an enormous range of people, from the jurist who worried constantly about the details of Islamic law to the shopkeeper who spent one afternoon a week memorizing and transmitting a few traditions. Of these men the majority—even the jurists—earned their living in the same way as others around them—as merchants, landlords, craftsmen, and so forth.

Then the founding of madresehs made religious learning into something of a profession, since the madresehs established minimum standards for at least some of the men (and occasional women) classified as religiously learned, in particular the jurists. And the madreseh professors were real "professionals," in the sense that the religious endowment that maintained the madreseh also provided their livelihood. But the ulema still remained a loose and baggy category of people which included those self-taught or tutored at home or somehow associated with religious institutions as well as those trained in madresehs. There was no clear boundary—comparable to the boundary between a priest with sacramental powers and a lay person—between the ulema and all others; a man of no religious learning who dressed like the men of religious learning might well be ridiculed, but there was no formal sense in which he could be defrocked.

In everyday Persian a man of religious learning came to be called a "mullah," a Persian transformation of the Arabic word mowla, which (with the marvelous contrary-mindedness of that wonderfully complex and inexhaustibly intricate language) means

in Arabic both "client" and "master." The word spread to all the
lands that lived in the penumbra of Iranian Islamic culture: Turkey, Central Asia, Afghanistan, and India. The thirteenth-century
Persian Sufi poet Jalal ad-Din Rumi is still affectionately called
Mowlana, "Our Master," or Mowlavi, "My Master," by Iranians.
"Mullah" was by no means a word used only by the Shiah; not
only did Sunni Indians call their own Sunni men of religious
learning "mullahs" but Persian-speaking Jews called their rabbis
"mullahs." The word, however, always had a touch of slang about
it (as did *akhund,* the other common Persian word for a mullah),
and when writing in Arabic (and therefore writing at their most
serious), mullahs have always avoided it and either used the Arab
original, *maula,* meaning "master," or "a learned man," or the
like.

In the Shiah tradition there was one title that defined a position
that was clearly bounded: jurisconsult. As we have seen, a jurisconsult could obtain his position in only one way—through the
"permission" or "authorization" of an existing jurisconsult; and
the first jurisconsults had obtained their permissions from the infallible Imams themselves. Naturally, the revival of the jurisconsult school in the nineteenth century made the distinctive nature
of this office a matter of even greater concern.

Nineteenth-century Iran, however, was in general a land of
blurred distinctions, ill-defined jurisdictions, and overblown rhetoric. The clarity of the designation "jurisconsult" was exceptional,
since most titles, civilian and religious, were affected by the in-
flated rhetoric and haziness of jurisdiction in the world around
them. Any official or courtier of importance had to have a title;
thus the teenage Mossadegh was granted the title "Mossadegh as-
Saltaneh," or "Confirmer of Monarchy," the first element of
which he chose for his last name. But beyond these tens of thousands of personal titles held by royal decree there were many
titles that were self-assumed or given by Iranians to one another
out of deference or in flattery. It is, incidentally, not surprising
that the title "prince" came to be applied to so many Iranian
males in the nineteenth century. The second Qajar king, perhaps
in compensation for the childlessness of his uncle the eunuch who
had founded the dynasty, had had over two hundred sons. As a
nineteenth-century Persian proverb says, Iran abounded in fleas

and princes. It also abounded in people who rightly demanded that they be addressed as "prince."

The same inflation struck religious titles. "Hojjat al-Islam," "Proof of Islam," was still a very exalted title in the time when it was applied to the ferocious Shafti; after him it sank steadily. The same inflation and consequent debasement affected the title "Ayatollah"—"Miraculous Sign of God"—an unofficial title conferred on a few of the very greatest jurisconsults at the turn of the century but now given to hundreds if not thousands.

The whole market in titles, official and unofficial, had its parallel in the confusion of jurisdictions, which, as we have seen, was so characteristic of law and administration in Qajar Iran. Nowhere is this confusion more curiously illustrated than in the Qajar concept of "sanctuary," a hazy epithet given to places in the same way that nebulous titles were given to people. The royal stables, telegraph stations, and the houses of important mullahs became "sanctuaries" by some mysterious consensus; but since the consensus varied and was not a matter of written law, its meaning was never quite certain. At one time an entire shrine might be sanctuary for serious criminals, while at another only petty thieves were safe in the outer courtyard, and the author of a significant crime had to shelter himself near the tomb itself. For a while the shadow of a very large cannon in a famous square in Tehran became sanctuary in daylight hours for petty thieves, who were to be seen slowly moving themselves around the square as the shadows shifted position throughout the day.

Informal consensus—even in its haziest manifestations—never lost its importance completely, but with the changes brought by the constitutionalists and Reza Shah its significance was drastically reduced. Formal titles had been abolished and the government no longer took any cognizance of informal titles. Everyone had been obliged to choose a fixed family surname. Soon popular usage gave way and a universal word for "mister" replaced such honorifics as "chief" and "prince," which Iranians had once so generously bestowed on each other. The jurisdiction of the Islamic courts had been circumscribed, then abolished. "Sanctuary" had become a historical memory. And "mullah" had become a legal classification.

The first step toward a legal definition of the clergy was taken in 1925. The military conscription law passed in that year exempted from military service *talabehs*, who had "no occupation other than study" and had taken yearly examinations and received certificates of status from their *madreseh* teachers. The next step was the law on uniformity of dress, passed in December 1928. It was one of the mysterious obsessions of Ataturk and Reza Shah to make the citizens of their countries dress in garments resembling European clothes. In the case of Iran, the best that can be said for this obsession was that it provided still another means to banish the world of numberless, ill-defined, and overlapping degrees of status, reinforced by variety of dress, that had existed before Reza Shah. But in exchange for this doubtful gain Reza Shah, in place of a population that wore even cast-off, threadbare clothes with some dignity, called into existence masses of Iranians who at first wore their unaccustomed brand-new clothes in a way that made them look cast off and threadbare. The new law stated that among those exempted from wearing "Western" clothes were Shiah jurisconsults and others "engaged in matters of the Holy Law" who had passed a special examination. Now you could really tell who was a mullah because, legally, to dress as one you had to be one. The tens of thousands of men who dressed as mullahs or dressed in part as mullahs faced a choice. Many of the halfhearted or even skeptical who wore mullah clothes in order to have access to the pulpits and to have the credentials to persuade the masses chose to put on Western business suits. Similarly, some of the traditionally educated who were sincere Shiahs and had dressed as mullahs now felt they could not survive economically on the fringes of the religious establishment, and they too put on Western suits and got secular qualifications as judges or schoolteachers.

In 1938, about three years before his abdication, Reza Shah tried to flatten out the few bumpy irregularities that still (in his view) marred the uniformity of the surface he sought to impose on Iranian life. A new law made even the most highly qualified mullahs of draftable age subject to two years of military service; its concession to their status was that it exempted them from recall duty.

This uniformity, insofar as it was achieved, remained largely a phenomenon of the surface. For all that the laws mentioned official examinations and examiners to be chosen by the government, the law had to accept the existing arrangements for leadership generated among the mullahs themselves, the jurisconsults, and the "models for imitation." Not only did the mullahs remain largely self-examined and self-defined, they were also in a significant degree self-financed.

Some of the mullahs' money came from religious endowments, and at first some of the circle around Reza Shah had seen these endowments as a powerful weapon to use in their campaign for secularization and control of the mullahs. In 1931 in his thesis Isa Sadiq estimated that these religious endowments generated an income of forty to fifty million krans a year, which—he said—went to "worldly priests; and it is time that these funds were allotted by law to educational purposes." And he left the reader in no doubt as to what should happen to the institutions of religious education once the government took full control: "At present, the students of religious colleges are floundering in their lessons; the clergy realizes its loss of prestige and influence; the religious colleges are utterly disorganized. It is time for the state to create centers for educating those spiritual leaders in accordance with the ideals of the Nation and the exigencies of the twentieth century."

This was one program the normally intrepid Reza Shah did not undertake or undertook only in a severely modified form. The government did take control of the religious endowments, but, then, so had the Qajars and Safavis in various degrees. Isa Sadiq's proposals were directly carried out only in one way: in some cases, where the endowment could be construed to be unrestricted, the income was disbursed by the government for elementary education. Otherwise the government seems usually to have turned over a fair proportion of the income of religious endowments to religious leaders, although under Reza Shah some of the most valuable properties were rumored to have passed to secular courtiers and even to entertainers. But the mullahs had lost the determining voice in the administration of these endowments, and most self-respecting mullahs would not speak to the Cabinet minister in charge of them, even though he was usually a man from a mullah family.

These endowments continued to support *madresehs* such as the

Faiziyeh, but the discretionary monies at the disposal of the great jurisconsults came from self-tithing by the ordinary Shiah. Through secularism, wars, and disputes over religious leadership, money from self-tithing continued to flow in. Thanks to this money, the important jurisconsults could pay the basic student stipend to the *talabehs* at Qom and other centers and could thereby maintain both the tradition of learning and the network of loyalties that they thought indispensable to their own well-being and the well-being of Islam.

Traditional Sunni higher learning entered the second half of the twentieth century dramatically changed by its environment and, above all, by the Sunni governments in the Arab world and elsewhere which controlled its institutions. For example, the curriculum of the greatest traditional Sunni university, the Azhar, has been revised repeatedly during the last century and a half by the Egyptian government. In contrast, the Shiah curriculum of Qom and Najaf has been and is dictated solely by the wishes of the mullahs themselves. *Madresehs* such as the one in Tehran, for example, where the government has dictated some revisions in the curriculum, have lost their prestige among the mullahs. In their own view the mullahs of Iran have kept a great tradition of learning alive in its pure form; in the view of their Iranian critics they have kept their curriculum hermetically sealed against the modern world.

The transformation of the mullahs into something like a clergy reached its height under the leadership of Borujerdi partly because in his time the accommodation of the government and the mullahs to each other was at its most stable. Under the new shah, mullahs were once again exempted from military service. The number of *talabehs* in Qom, perhaps a thousand toward the end of Ha'eri's life, rose to over five thousand. Also, in the time of Borujerdi there was a forcible accommodation of *madreseh* education to the success of secular education that emphasized how much more the *madreseh* had become like a "professional" school. The Koran school had died by the end of the Second World War; all *talabehs* came to Qom with an elementary education from a state school. In the state school even on the elementary level subjects such as mathematics and bits of general science were taught by teachers supposedly expert in these fields (while Islamic law and the Koran in the Arabic original were taught by mullahs paid to do so by the Ministry of Education). *Madreseh* learning had formerly been a conspectus of higher learning, with its optional courses in Ptolemaic astronomy, Avicennian medicine, and the algebra of Omar Khayyam. But now that the marvel of Halley's comet had finally been sighted in the heaven of mullah learning, even the mullahs recognized that their learning really was "religious" learning, and only a few enthusiasts studied the traditional nonreligious sciences such as the old astronomy in private. Increasingly the mullahs called themselves by the neologism used by government and intellectuals (in their politer moods): they were *rowhaniyun*—"specialists in spiritual matters."

For all the subtle exchanges of influence between the newly "clericalized" mullahs and the secular realms (and it should be remembered that the mnemonic, text-centered style of Iranian secular education had roots in the *madreseh* system), in the time of Borujerdi the two realms lived separately in peaceful coexistence. The shah showed due respect to Borujerdi throughout his lifetime, on occasion motoring down to Qom, not to display his power, as his father had done, but to pay his respects. (The Iranian newspapers of the period also dutifully published a picture of the prime minister kissing the hand of the dying Ayatollah Kashani at his bedside.)

Borujerdi kept his half of the bargain as well. In spite of a great deal of pressure from the *talabehs* who were swept up in the causes of the fifties, Borujerdi kept silent on political issues and sometimes silenced those who talked too much. The notorious "red ayatollah," Borqe'i, who openly championed the program of the Iranian Communist party, was exiled from Qom by Borujerdi (and, to everyone's amusement, some ten years later settled near the Russian embassy in Tehran). Borujerdi condemned Israel in private but never in public, in spite of enormous sympathy among the *talabehs* for Palestinian Muslims as coreligionists. There had been even greater pressures on Borujerdi from the *talabehs* swept up in the nationalistic enthusiasm that surrounded Mossadegh. However, Borujerdi not only kept silent, but was widely (and, probably, correctly) believed to have supported Kashani's strategic withdrawal of support for Mossadegh and to have been pleased at the shah's restoration in 1953.

It was partly as a reward for this support that the shah allowed Borujerdi to indulge in the one public political act of his life: persecution of the Baha'is in 1955. The Baha'i religion had been founded in the mid-nineteenth century as a fulfillment of the messianism of Shiah Islam. The Twelfth Imam had—according to Baha'i belief—reappeared and brought a message that claimed that the Baha'i religion was the fulfillment of messianic expectations not only of the Shiah but of all religious traditions. The belief of the Baha'is consequently took on a universalistic tenor, and Baha'is advocated world government, the equality of all human beings without regard to sex or race, and—especially horrifying to the mullahs—an end to the period of human history in which mankind needed specialists in religion.

To the mullahs the fundamental premise of the Baha'i religion was arrant nonsense. The Twelfth Imam would return to fulfill the law and to make clear what only supposition and conjecture had dealt with in the past, not to abrogate Islamic law as the founders of the Baha'i religion had done. As former Muslims who had left Islam for another religion, the Baha'is—in accord with a long tradition of Islamic law—were offered the choice of repentance or death. Many thousands died, including a fair number of mullah converts, for in the beginning the movement had found some of its most ardent converts among the mullahs. But the Qajar government and subsequent governments did not like the internal disorder and the bad foreign press that usually went along with killing Baha'is. Moreover, as the Baha'is throughout most of their history were a pawn that these governments played in their complex game with the mullahs, none of the governments was willing to surrender this pawn in a single move.

Tolerating the Baha'is was a way of showing mullahs who was boss. Reza Shah, in his surprise tours to examine his newly expanded army of conscripts would sometimes shout, "Whore-wife Baha'is step forward," after which he would grunt and tell them to fall back into place. As long as he did not call them "whore-mother Baha'is" they knew they were all right. Although he dissolved their schools, which had been important sources of the "new education" at preuniversity level (the master of Isa Sadiq's school was cursed because he allegedly belonged to this "heresy"), and although he refused to grant them any official standing as a religion, so that they were unable to meet in public or marry according to their religion, Reza Shah made sure that the Baha'is were left alone; to do otherwise would be to concede that the mullahs influenced his policies.

Correspondingly, allowing active persecution of the Baha'is was the low-cost pawn that could be sacrificed to the mullahs when the government was in trouble or in special need of mullah support. In 1955 the shah was indeed weak. The popularity of Mossadegh had not died with his overthrow in 1953, and as the shah was about to join the American-sponsored Baghdad Pact and had already accepted a proportion of oil revenues below the level nationalists considered respectable, the rumors that he had been restored by the Americans seemed confirmed. Both the military governor of Tehran and the chief of staff of the Iranian army joined a popular preacher, Falsafi, and a group of civilian enthusiasts in ransacking the Baha'i headquarters in Tehran and tearing down its domed roof.

On May 9, obviously with government permission, the press carried the text of two telegrams from the Ayatollah Mohammed Behbahani (sometimes called "Dollars"), who had opposed Mossadegh, one to Borujerdi and one to the shah, congratulating them on this event and urging that henceforth the day be observed as a religious holiday. The press also carried Borujerdi's letter of thanks to Falsafi, who during the preceding weeks had been allowed to preach anti-Baha'i sermons on the government radio. Borujerdi said that Falsafi had rendered service to "the independence of the nation and the preservation of the position of the monarchy." The Baha'is, Borujerdi complained, spread propaganda against Islam, "which, of course, is a cause of the unity of our national feeling." Furthermore, Baha'is secretly work against the monarchy and the state, "yet they enjoy influence in the government; so they should be purged from all government employment." Borujerdi's statements showed his strong support for the monarchy and his understanding of the vivid nationalism of modern Iranians. His appeal implied that even if secular Iranians did not share the mullahs' horror at the Baha'is as heretics, they could share their horror at the Baha'is for insisting on being "different."

After this things became a bit confused; in some places mobs attacked Baha'is, some Baha'is were killed, some Baha'i women were raped. Borujerdi was reported to favor the destruction of the Baha'i religion and the transfer of the assets of the Baha'is to *madresehs* and mosques without the shedding of blood. There were wild shouting matches in the Consultative Assembly, one in which a deputy accused the government of preferring the views of "bearded and ignorant infantiles" to the rule of law, after which other deputies had to be physically restrained from rushing to assault him. In fact, the government was embarrassed because the anti-Baha'i campaign had got out of hand, did not like the unorchestrated public disorders that had broken out, and was afraid of the consequences if antimonarchical secular and religious elements should act together.

After the government withdrew the Baha'i pawn from the board a few zealous mullahs and deputies continued to harp on the issue for a few months, but Borujerdi—always sensitive to the needs of the central government—fell silent. His one excursion into politics had been a success: it had let Iran taste the power of the Shiah establishment without hurting his alliance with the government; it had propelled the government into committing itself to more religious instruction in the schools and tighter control of cinemas and other offensive secular entertainment during Moharram; and the shah himself had appeared on the campus of the University of Tehran to break ground for a mosque. The government had not gone away empty-handed; in October of 1955 a nephew of Ayatollah Mohammed Behbahani spoke in favor of the Baghdad Pact in the Assembly, and no major mullah spoke publicly against it.

Borujerdi died in March 1961. The prime minister attended his funeral, and the shah proclaimed three days of mourning and attended a memorial service in his honor. With Borujerdi's death the principle of hierarchy among the Shiah religious leaders entered a crisis from which it has never fully recovered. Even in Borujerdi's time a large number of prominent jurisconsults of a younger generation had emerged, students of the students of

Khorasani, such as the students of Ha'eri in Qom and the students of Na'ini in Najaf. There had been an inflation of titles to accommodate the large number of jurisconsults who had distinguished themselves among this generation: they were called Grand Ayatollahs, a title that a generation earlier would have been reserved for a "model" alone.

The informal adjustment of titles was symptomatic of the continuing informality of structure in the world of mullahs. For all the examinations that had been introduced into the world of the *madreseh*, this was still a world of face-to-face relations in which the leading mullahs visited each other constantly and talked about the reputations of other mullahs and leading *talabehs* for learning, piety, and leadership. Only the titles "jurisconsult" and "model for imitation" had fixed meaning. Otherwise titles—while always explained in terms of degrees of "learnedness"—really expressed the informal consensus of mullahs as to the degree of deference they wished to show one another. A teacher in a *madreseh* might be greatly offended if a letter from a layman failed to call him "ayatollah," but he would vigorously reject the title if addressed as an ayatollah in public—vigorously, that is, until he sensed that other mullahs of his level would tolerate hearing him so addressed, at which point he would quietly let his students impose the title on him.

Not only learning but reputation for piety (is he said to pray late into the night?), heredity, age (virtually no mullah under forty could be an ayatollah), and ability to lead had significant roles in advancing a mullah through the gamut of informal titles. And even that formal and highest of titles, "model for imitation," while in theory conferred on "the most learned," clearly lived in this complex world of deference through a consensus formed by all these motives. Was that absolute and universal "model" Borujerdi, for all his learning, really "the most learned" jurisconsult of the Shiah world?

Borujerdi, alert to the end of his eighty-odd years, does not seem to have worked to form a consensus as to who his successor would be. In any case, there was no consensus, and if things did not exactly fly apart, they did not really hang together either. The Iranian government, which had gotten on so well with Borujerdi,

quite naturally hoped for more of the same. The shah sent a telegram of condolence on Borujerdi's death to the very learned Ayatollah Hakim of Najaf to indicate whom the government wanted
as supreme jurisconsult. It was a mistake. Hakim was an Arab
whose life had centered on Najaf and the school of Najaf; the
school of Qom now felt itself intellectually superior to Najaf and
preferred its own products. Until his death in 1970 Hakim had
followers, but not very many of them were in Iran. There were at
least seven other jurisconsults with considerable followings: Kho'i
and Shahrudi, like Hakim, in Najaf; Khunsari in Tehran; Shariatmadari, Golpayegani, and Marashi, in Qom; and Milani in Mashhad.

Then came the events of 1963 and 1964 that made Ruhollah
Khomeini a national figure and in the end recreated the pattern
that had existed at least from Ansari to the death of Khorasani in
1911: a thoroughly Iranian "model for imitation," with a large following in Iran, lived in Iraq free from the influence of the Iranian
government. Before 1962 Khomeini was hardly known outside
mullah circles, but he had created a genuinely distinct and independent position for himself within these circles. After a traditional religious elementary education in the small provincial town
of Khomain he had attached himself to the circle of Ha'eri very
shortly after this teacher returned to Iran. He was an exceptional
student, in both his talent and his interest in the philosophical
side of *erfan* mysticism, which had been developed in the tradition
of Mullah Sadra, the great Safavi thinker who had brought the
tradition of Sohravardi to its culmination.

As we saw earlier, for a while, in addition to his regular classes,
he taught with great success the "class on morals," an optional but
widely attended public lecture to *talabehs* given on Thursday afternoon, the end of the class week. He spoke in this class without
looking at his audience, and his aloofness while teaching was part
and parcel of the aloofness that was variously regarded with admiration, fear, or dislike by other teachers in Qom. Because of the
overtones of *erfan* that Khomeini introduced into his discussion of
morals and the Koran the *talabehs* saw these lectures as a powerful
encouragement to the self-control that most of them struggled to
exercise. To a very select group Khomeini actually taught the phi-

losophy of *erfan*, but he did so in private, particularly in the period from 1944 to 1961, during the ascendancy of Borujerdi, who disapproved of philosophy in general.

In his public teaching and writing Khomeini chose virtually the same areas of law and jurisprudence that Ansari had chosen: he wrote (in Arabic, of course) a collection of treatises on jurisprudence, especially the "procedural" principle of "continuity," and two books on commercial law: a five-volume work on the law of sale and a two-volume work on "forbidden sources of income." His admirers saw in these works the influence of the abstract turn of mind of a jurisconsult who was more than normally interested in theoretical questions.

They also saw something that the Iranian censors, for all their diligence and all their informers, at first did not see or did not think significant: a growing political activism. In his book on "forbidden sources of income," written in 1961, one chapter begins: "To assist an oppressor in his oppression is forbidden without any question"; and a substantial chapter is devoted to resistance to oppression. The activism is even more explicit in his discussion of the law of sale, written after he went to Iraq in exile. He discusses the situation of orphans, then begins the next chapter by saying, "Among the guardians over the expenditure of the wealth of one who cannot manage his own wealth is the magistrate who is the jurist who combines all the conditions necessary to issue a *fatva*. There is no harm in turning to the subject of the guardianship of the jurist"—and Khomeini turns to it with a vengeance. Islam, he explains, is not only here to establish rules for acts of worship and morality but to regulate the affairs of society, specifically financial and political affairs. Muslims should not accept anything less than a fully Islamic government, with Islamic courts and a leader who is, from the point of view of Islam, "better than any other" and is "a guardian learned in the laws." So "on this basis, the matter of guardianship reverts to the just jurist . . . so to undertake government and to shape an Islamic state is a kind of collective responsibility for just jurists."

This entire argument is conducted with reference to unnamed jurisconsults who disagreed with Khomeini's position. In fact, these jurisconsults included Ansari and Khorasani, both of whom argued against "the guardianship of the jurist." Quietly, from time to time, a Shiah jurist had advocated "the guardianship of the jurist," but before Khomeini none seems to have done so at such length or with such emphasis that the word "guardianship" (*vilayat*), which also means "rule," did in fact mean "rule." The "best" jurist (a slightly more general term than jurisconsult but meaning virtually the same thing in this context) had a responsibility to form and supervise the government.

Ha'eri and Borujerdi followed the entirely opposite theory of their teacher Khorasani, and as long as they lived, Khomeini kept his activism locked in his advanced Arabic textbooks and did not defy his superiors. With the crisis of leadership following Borujerdi's death new possibilities appeared, and Khomeini acted. In 1962 the government ordered the election of local councils. In these elections women were allowed to vote (as they had not been in elections for the National Consultative Assemblies), and in their oath of office elected councilors were to swear "by the holy book," a phrase that seemed to allow Christians, Jews, Zoroastrians, and even heretics such as the Baha'is to serve on councils alongside Muslims. Many mullahs protested. Khomeini sent a telegram to the government in which he said that the council law threatened "the Koran and Islam"; perhaps, he suggested, it had been drawn up by Zionists, who—"in the guise of Baha'is"—were threatening to take over the Iranian state and economy. The government backed down and suspended the law.

In January 1963 the shah submitted a land-reform law to a national referendum and refused Ayatollah Behbahani's request to exempt from it religious endowments in the form of income-producing land. The shah personally campaigned for the law in Qom, where he called religious opposition "black reaction." In February the shah gave women the right to vote. While Khomeini continued to be the most outspoken critic of the government, neither he nor any of the important jurisconsults publicly attacked land reform (although some disapproved in private); it was too genuinely popular.

Then the shah gave Khomeini the issues he needed. In March government security forces raided the Faiziyeh *madreseh* in Qom, and at least one *talabeh* was killed. Khomeini made a series of speeches, the climax of which was the sermon on Ashura in which the themes of grief for Hosain, for the slain *talabeh*, for the insults to men of religion, and for the government's enmity to Islam (while it loved the enemies of Islam—above all, Israel) were skillfully woven together.

Early on June 5 Khomeini was arrested and taken to Tehran. Rioting broke out in several major cities and lasted for two days; in Tehran the rioters surged northward from the slums of the city and almost took the radio station. After the army and police had regained control, the shah's helicopter landed in a village near Qom and His Majesty distributed land deeds to the local peasants. And after nine months Khomeini was released. The initiative seemed firmly in the hands of the government.

In 1964 the government handed Khomeini his second issue. In October the Iranian government, at the request of the United States, asked the parliament to approve a bill giving American military advisers, their support staffs, and their families diplomatic immunity. Even to the relatively obedient parliament it smacked of the old regime of capitulations. One deputy asked how he should reply to someone who said that even a foreign refrigerator repairman or apprentice mechanic in Iran enjoyed the same immunity that Iran's ambassador enjoyed abroad. The bill passed by seventy-four to sixty-one—not even an absolute majority of the two-hundred-member Assembly. Very shortly thereafter the Assembly voted to accept a large American loan, which was widely thought to be contingent on the grant of diplomatic immunity.

Khomeini then preached one of the most influential sermons of his career. After an apposite quote from the Koran ("Never will God give the unbelievers a way [to triumph] over the Believers") he said:

> Does the Iranian nation know what has happened in recent days in the Assembly? Does it know what crime has occurred surreptitiously and without the knowledge of the nation? Does it know that the Assembly, at the initiative of the government, has signed the document of the enslavement of Iran? It has acknowledged that Iran is a colony; it has given America a document attesting that the nation of Muslims is barbarous, it has struck out all our Islamic and national glories with a black line.
>
> By this shameful vote, if an American adviser or the servant of

an American adviser should take any liberty with one of the greatest specialists in Shiah law . . . the police would have no right to arrest the perpetrator and the courts of Iran have no right to investigate. If the Shah should run over an American dog, he would be called to account but if an American cook should run over the Shah, no one has any claims against him. . . . I proclaim that this shameful vote of the Majles is in contradiction to Islam and has no legality. . . . If the foreigners wish to misuse this filthy vote, the nation's duty will be clearly specified. . . . The misfortunes of Islamic governments have come from the interference by foreigners in their destinies. . . . It is America that considers the Koran and Islam to be harmful to itself and wishes to remove them from its way; it is America that considers Muslim men of religion a thorn in its path.

On cassettes and in clandestinely printed leaflets the sermon was distributed throughout Iran. Although there was no public stir when, a few days later, Khomeini was exiled to Turkey, his appeal spoke to the feelings of enormous numbers of Iranians, both religious and secular. As in the time of Mirza Shirazi, nationalistic and religious sentiments converged. In two years he had become one of the most famous jurisconsults. In 1965 he arrived in Najaf, to be greeted by an enthusiastic following he had attracted among the talabehs, many of whom came from Iran to study with him. It was widely said that because he had not issued a "manual of practice" on Borujerdi's death, he did not seek leadership. Nevertheless by the later sixties he was a "model for imitation" accepted by hundreds of thousands and ranked in importance alongside the six "models" who had emerged as leaders in 1961.

In a way the moral economy of Qajar Iran had been reestablished. Iranians had their own leading jurisconsults at home, but they had another leading jurisconsult, hostile to the Iranian government, in safety in nearby Iraq. By giving sidelong glances—without total commitment—to the jurisconsult in Iraq they let the Iranian government know that their obedience to the government could not be taken for granted. When they returned from pilgrimages to the holy places in Iraq they proudly told each other that they had prayed behind "Agha." In another way things had dramatically changed. In 1969 Khomeini gave a full, popular, Persian exposition to the idea of "the guardianship of the jurist" in a series of lectures that were printed and secretly distributed, especially among the Iranian *talabehs*. Khomeini now spoke openly: it was time to overthrow the shah and install the jurist. In Najaf, after nearly two centuries, Vahid Behbahani's idea that the more learned you were, the more correctly you could discover the law for others had reached its conclusion: "the most learned" was responsible not only for discovering the law for others, he was responsible for controlling its application.

CHAPTER SEVEN

FOR ALL his past travels to Mecca and other parts of the Middle East, when Ali came home in 1968 from two years in Najaf, at age twenty-five, it was different. He rode the last leg of the journey, the road from Tehran to Qom, in the car of his older brother, who had come to pick him up at the airport. After they passed the huge army base at Manzariyeh with its steel-and-barbed-wire fences running at mad angles up and down the hills, they started up the last long rise before Qom. Then, from the top of the ridge, they saw the valley with a patch of mingled green and brown at its end where their home town lay. Ali, who at the start of the trip had assumed some of the dignity he felt he had acquired through his advance in age and learning, had gradually become more talkative and "more on the boil," as one says in Persian, as they got farther away from Tehran. When they saw Qom in the distance Ali recited a favorite line from Mowlana:

> Should your journey take you even to Rome or Cathay,
> How could the love of home ever leave your heart?

His brother joined in with a line from Hafez:

Who will spread the name of Egypt's sweets in this place
Whose sweet people find no fault in their city's taste?

Ali suddenly felt he could admit to himself how alien Najaf had felt for all his success there as a student and a teacher. It wasn't the effort of teaching in Arabic and establishing his credentials to a new group of equals and superiors. It wasn't really anything about Najaf itself—its cantankerous shopkeepers and landlords, who loathed *talabehs*, especially those from Iran, or its unrelievedly flat surroundings, where seas of slow-moving sand ran into plains of sun-baked mud. In fact, Ali had found that he had liked some things about his surroundings. He had liked to swim in the enormous width of the Euphrates, which ran near Najaf, and he very much liked being near the tomb of his namesake Ali in Najaf and near the tomb of Hosain in the nearby town of Kerbela. It was just that Ali realized how very much he loved the dry hills around Qom, its rocky half-empty river, its outlying shrines, and the unexpected greenness of its orchards. Above all, he realized how very much he loved the Persian language; as the proverb said, Arabic is learning, but Persian is sugar. In Persian he could deal with people to the best of his abilities—persuade them if he were giving a sermon, smooth the turbulence between them when they were in conflict, even charm them with the Persian verses he could sometimes compose on the spot.

Homecoming was also different because Ali now tasted the delight of being a master in the house of learning in which he had been a servant. He had taught briefly in Qom before leaving for Najaf, but now he was a regular teacher in his own school, the Faiziyeh. He was also a valued participant in the advanced classes in law and jurisprudence. The long nights in the palm tree courtyards of Najaf in which he thought and read to stay on top of his courses with Kho'i and Khomeini had given him a rich intellectual capital on which to trade in the even more competitive atmosphere of Qom.

Ali established close ties with Marashi, one of the three "models" then living in Qom. Certainly some of the other five "models" then accepted in the Shiah world had more followers.

But whomever among the "models" he might accept as the most learned (and therefore his "model" to imitate on questions of law), Ali could think of no greater mullah who formed a moral "model" more appropriate for his own imitation than Marashi. Marashi was devout yet carried his piety lightly, dissolving any excessive show of reverence to himself with good-natured raillery and teasing. He was generous to a fault. Some "models" conservatively husbanded contributions to distribute to the faithful, but Marashi immediately gave away the monies he received and sometimes (to the distress of his entourage) tried to give away more than he received. And, to Ali's delight, Marashi spent a great deal of this money on scholarship, building libraries for which he bought out-of-print books and rare manuscripts.

Like the other "models," Marashi had open house in his *biruni* for two hours before he went to teach his morning class. The office of a "model" is called a "court," and for all that it lacked someone called "prince" or "king," Marashi's audiences, like those of the other "models," really were miniature courts. In outer rooms mullahs from Marashi's entourage, some with accounting ledgers, greeted you and asked your business. They led you to a large inner room where people sat on the ground along the walls, with the position of honor in the center of the wall farthest from the door reserved for Ayatollah Marashi with his magnificent white beard.

Immediately around Marashi would be a few of his close relations and some middle-aged mullahs who had been his students for years and had won his respect. These intimate counselors of the great ayatollah would speak to him in low voices, offering explanations about the missions of various visitors and advice as to how to deal with them. Some visitors were paying courtesy calls, but most had come with some business to transact. A government official, for example, who was scrupulous about the traditional Shiah injunction against working for the government (in fact, for any government until the return of the Twelfth Imam) would come forward and kiss the hand of his "model," then give him his "tainted" salary. The "model" would take the money in one hand, pass it into the other, then hand it back—the official could now keep it in good conscience since it had become a "gift" conferred of his own free will by a proper recipient of "tainted" money.

Others came to pay their *sahm-e Imam*, a religious tithe owed to the Imam but paid in his absence by the conscientious Shiah to their "models." Humble people paid *sahm-e Imam* to the mullah of their neighborhood, who forwarded most of the proceeds to his "model" at Qom, but wealthy people often insisted on coming to Qom in person once a year to pay their *sahm-e Imam* to their chosen "model" in person. They would be presented to Marashi at a distance, then confer with one of his assistants, who would calculate their *sahm-e Imam* on the basis of their profit minus religiously allowable deductions. The donor would receive a receipt on payment, and finally he would speak to Marashi, who, characteristically, said not only the perfunctory "May you be successful" but bubbled forth compliments and good wishes.

None of the visitors to Marashi's "court," however, pleased Ali as much as the delegations that came to ask for a new mullah for a village or neighborhood. Ali, being a teacher, would not normally have been present, but Marashi encouraged him to take an interest in all the public affairs of his "court." Classically, a district sent a delegation of seven people—the trustworthy man who yearly brought the district's *sahm-e Imam* to the "model," two wealthy men, two highly respected elders, and two strong and religious youths. Marashi took these delegations very seriously. He would say, "Will you support my student once he gets there? He will be like an object of value put in trust by me into your hands." Marashi was every bit as absorbed by the gravity of what he said on these occasions as he was by his own humor when he teased people. "It will take a lot of persuading, but I will try to talk one of my students into leaving his studies. Come tomorrow morning."

Later Marashi's close advisers would confer on whom to send. One of Ali's chief pleasures in these groups was the opportunity to see men from parts of Iran he had never seen or, in some cases, from villages he had never even heard of. Marashi knew everyone over a certain level studying in Qom, and if twenty mullahs called on him he would have twenty subtly different ways of greeting each of them. But to deal intelligently with all these localities in Iran needed the collective wisdom of Marashi's inner circle. Ali was impressed at how much Marashi's circle did, in fact, know about the internal life of the communities that sent these petitioners: they knew about their treatment of past mullahs, even the genealogies of their leading men. Ali, who now examined *talabehs* on behalf of Marashi's office when they had finished different prescribed texts, would be called on to suggest students for these positions. It was a foregone conclusion that the very best students would not leave Qom; but finding, for example, the *talabeh* with a tough constitution, and preferably a Kurd, to go to a Kurdish village near Kermanshah, or a man with enough eloquence and experience of the world for a middle-class neighborhood in the oil-refinery town of Abadan was not so easy. Conversations about students tended to be carried out in a code that Ali had already learned from listening to his father talk with his friends. When Ali said of a student, occasionally tilting his head sideways to emphasize how considered his opinion was, "He's not bad, really not bad. He's made some progress," that meant that the student, while not a total idiot, would be no loss to the *madreseh* and would do everyone a favor by leaving and not breaking his head on the more advanced books in the curriculum.

When the delegation appeared on the next day Marashi would have the chosen student, his eyes fixed humbly on the carpet, ready for presentation to the men of the delegation. Marashi's assistant would hand the student a written "permission" signed by the "model" himself which allowed the student to collect *sahm-e Imam* in his new home on behalf of Marashi and to keep one third of the amount collected to spend locally. Then—a signal honor—Marashi would stand, go over to the candidate, and whisper in his right ear, "God is the best guardian and He is the most merciful of those who show mercy!" Next he would whisper in his right ear, "He who ordained the Koran will bring you back at the resurrection. Say, 'My Lord knows best who it is that brings true guidance and who is in manifest error.' " Although these were very familiar verses of the Koran, the student never failed to look overwhelmed at hearing them. Then, speaking in a normal tone of voice, Marashi would conclude: "God willing, you will be successful. God willing, before God and those sanctified by God, your face will remain white"—that is, without reproach.

Marashi asked Ali's help not only to examine and recommend students but also to distribute money to deserving and indigent mullahs and their descendants. He guessed correctly that Ali, as a sayyed from a good family, would have a sense of the fragility of these men's feelings and that he would know how to give them money in a way so discreet and oblique that the recipient would feel none of the sting and burden of a gift.

One of the first times Ali distributed money for Marashi he went to call on a man he knew slightly but respected enormously, an immensely learned sayyed from Khuzestan who was writing a commentary on the Koran, a man therefore known as the Commentator. Ali found that the Commentator was living in the neighborhood of Parviz's family. As Ali went deeper into the jumble of alleys he realized that he had forgotten—or had never really taken in—how mean this neighborhood looked, with its miserable stray dogs panting in drainage ditches strewn with garbage. The Commentator's house was a little better than that of Parviz's father; although it was very small, the family of the Commentator did not share their front courtyard with anyone else, and the interior had some of the fine plasterwork details of Iranian houses of the last century. The Commentator and his son received Ali in a long narrow room which seemed to constitute the only closed part of their *biruni*. The son immediately brought in tea, and Ali, who had heard that the Commentator was losing his sight, was embarrassed by the old man's difficulty in getting his spoon into his glass. After a few sips of tea the Commentator began, as one says in Persian, "to reveal the table spread at his heart."

"I have heard you well spoken of—young men like you are our hope. Why are there so few students like you? I hear young *talabehs* say that philosophical ideas are opium and that studying them makes the mind flabby. Action, they say, teaches truth, while study trains men to deviate from the truth. You know the proverb, How easy it is to become a mullah; how difficult to become a full human being. But I prefer the version of my teacher, Ayatollah Ha'eri, who said, 'It is impossible to become a full human being; how difficult it is to become even a mullah.' If we don't maintain learning, what will become of religion? Which one of the men that God sent to renew Islam lacked learning? Some of our young *talabehs* think religion is like a melon that anyone can divide with a few quick slices and then everybody can eat his piece. I tell you, if their wishes are fulfilled we will have melons but no religion and no one even able to explain a really reasonable way to distribute the melons."

Ali had not come prepared for this, but he had not come unprepared. He had read some parts of the Commentator's first volumes on the Koran, and, after soothing him by calmly but emphatically expressing his total agreement, Ali discussed the passages he had read in a way that encouraged his host to talk about his reasons for approaching scriptural commentary in such a highly abstract way. After twenty or so minutes of absorbed conversation the Commentator again told Ali that he was one of the hopes for the future of learning at Qom, thanked him for paying a visit, and told his son to show Ali out. Ali stood, bowed slightly with his hand on his heart, and, as he put on his shoes next to the door, placed an envelope full of money from Marashi next to a water pipe in a plaster niche high on the wall.

The son walked with him across the tiny courtyard to the gate and said: "If religion were really treated as a melon given to us all by God, you wouldn't have to take the melons from the peasants and distribute them by the slice to people like us. We could take our own melons, by the slice or entire, as we needed them, which seems 'reasonable,' if we are going to worry about the role of 'reason' in such things. I'm not sure, though, that it would be reasonable to ask a peasant to trade a melon for a philosophical idea."

"As you know," said Ali, "the proverb says, The truly sweet melon falls to the lot of the hyena. You not only evaluate your father's philosophy in melons, you seem to want the hyena to inherit your father's lifetime work along with all the other melons you expect the hyena to distribute so 'reasonably.' "

Ali went away from this exchange in a fury. He truly venerated the Commentator, and he thought his son needed a good beating for the ease with which he had dismissed his father's learning. But he knew that he was also angry because the system of redistributing money in which he was involved did in fact make him feel uncomfortable. Also, he was determined to prove that no matter how reticent some old scholars had been about politics, learning was not the enemy of action and the tradition of Shiah higher education could be maintained by the kind of men who felt that, as Ferdowsi said, "Two hundred words do not amount to half a deed."

Unostentatiously Ali had already entered the arena of deeds. The skill at composing essays on set themes such as "the sea" which had made Ali "first student" in the state school had never left him. Since his return from Najaf he had begun to write provocative essays under a whole string of pseudonyms. One of the most effective of these had been an article on Islam and movements of liberation. It was printed in a religious magazine that was usually so nonpolitical in its interests that the censors passed its contents without serious examination.

At first glance the article looked as if it contained nothing objectionable to the government. It began with praise for the successful struggle of the Algerian people and a celebration of the role of Islam in arousing the Algerian masses against the French; it was laced throughout with quotations in Arabic (with their Persian translations) from the Koran and the sayings of the Prophet and the Imams; and the conclusion was a rejection of dialectical materialism as an adequate final goal for any movement of liberation. But the heart of the article was an appreciation of those ideas of Che Guevara that "agreed" with Islam. Ali had no trouble in showing that Islam from the time of the Prophet distinguished sharply between "those who strive," or, as the Koran calls them, the *mojahedin*, who "expend their wealth and their persons in the cause of God," on the one hand, and the hypocrites on the other, those who pretended to be Muslim and whose words and exteriors "are pleasing" yet whose faith is a disguise. The hypocrites, as the Koran says, are "like pieces of timber propped up," ready to fall pell-mell on each other from their unsteadiness, their hollowness, and their rottenness. Che Guevara rejected his comfortable upbringing to choose medicine in the service of the poor; he rejected medicine to choose arms; he rejected the narrow nationalism of Argentina to fight for all of Latin America; he rejected his city culture to organize the countryside. In every way he rejected the hypocrite's choice of the path of least resistance in order to choose the path of those who strive—as all Muslims should do. He had also understood that a conscientious vanguard could lead the productive forces of society to a more just society—and the mullahs, as the conscience of Islam, should form such a vanguard. He had believed not in sheepish expedient alliances but in direct struggle with the oppressors. Did not the Koran say, "And why should you not fight for the cause of God and of the oppressed— men, women and children?" Above all, was not Che Guevara's vision for the future ultimately a religious and Islamic vision? What "striving" Muslim could fail to agree with him that, as he said, "the sacred cause is the redemption of humanity through struggle," or fail to agree with his vision that men would eventually be purified by their struggle, so that they would gladly work for moral (and not material) incentives?

The day of its publication Ali had been in that state of anxiety that puts one, as Persians say, "between heaven and earth." Nothing happened. In fact, nothing happened during the next three weeks or the week after the spring classes at the *madreseh* had finished. Then they came. Ali was about to eat breakfast. He had stopped reading, picked up his glass of tea, and was looking at the bread, goat's cheese, and quince jelly when he heard Kazem clear his throat and enter.

"Sir, there is someone at the door for you, a Mr. Shirazi."

"Who's Mr. Shirazi?"

"I don't know, sir, he's from the municipality."

As soon as Ali saw the caller standing in the gatehouse his heart sank. Mr. Shirazi, a middle-sized man with a brownish complexion, wore a dark-blue suit that was too clean and dark glasses too expensive for a man from the municipality.

"Do you recognize me?" the man asked.

"No. What can I do for you?"

"Please come with us for a few minutes to talk with the SAVAK."

Ali knew the secret police kept their visitors for more than "a few minutes"; he asked if he could get some things.

"I am sorry to hurry you," said the man—his elaborate politeness and half smile had not failed him—"but the conversation won't even last a full hour. There's no need to bring anything along."

Ali had carried the huge paperback book he had been reading

to the door. He put it in his pocket and followed Mr. "Shirazi" to a car waiting at the end of the alleyway. The car then drove to the beginning of another alleyway, and another man in sunglasses, apparently intended to guard the wall of the back garden of the house, got into the front seat.

They drove to a rather plain three-story villa in the new part of town. "Shirazi" led Ali to a room on the second floor where a very polite young man took his photograph and wrote his name in a register, then nodded toward the next room. They now entered a very large and dark room, with a canvas chair next to the only lamp. "Shirazi," after telling Ali to be seated, left him. As Ali's eyes adjusted to the dimness he noticed three men in the room, one standing behind him and two seated in deck chairs behind a desk, facing him. Except for the three deck chairs, the desk, and a straw mat half rolled up against the wall, the room was empty.

One of the men behind the desk said, "Who are your friends, Mr. Hashemi?" Ali said his friends were well known; he started to list his fellow teachers, students, and relatives. The interrogator interrupted him. "But who are your friends in Iraq?" Ali was silent, then said that his friends in Iraq were people similar to those he had mentioned—students and teachers at Najaf. "That would include Mr. Khomeini, wouldn't it?" Ali said he had studied with Khomeini. "And we know that you collect money for Khomeini." Ali denied this flatly. "We enjoyed your article on Che Guevara and Islam. Why didn't you sign it with your own name?" Ali said he hadn't heard of the article, and the interrogator suddenly smiled, opened the desk drawer, and said, "I'm sorry, Mr. Hashemi, we have your handwritten copy here." Ali felt really afraid for the first time. A shock seized him high in his chest and he asked with a stutter to see the article so that he could prove that it was not his handwriting. The man closed the drawer without taking anything out. "At least you were courageous enough to sign your translation of Ayatollah Hakim's recent proclamation." Hakim was a "model" in Najaf, and Ali had in fact translated his strong anti-Israeli statement and signed the translation. To his surprise Ali was so afraid that he said that there were many Hashemis—perhaps the statement had been signed by another Hashemi. The interrogator, who had been looking at a file on the desk, looked up and said sharply, "Really, Mr. Hashemi, we're not stupid," and waved to the man standing behind Ali.

Ali was led out of the villa to a jeep and sat between two men in the back seat for the three-hour drive to Tehran. When he caught sight of the huge flight of imposing stairs that stood in front of the post office Reza Shah had built in downtown Tehran, Ali knew what prison he was going to. A block beyond the post office was the "Committee" prison, run by a joint committee of the police and the SAVAK.

Ali was conducted to a cell two meters by four meters. The cell was very high, and a coat of white paint made it seem even higher. There was a barred window to the outside very high up on one wall which barely cast enough light to read by even at midday, and at night the weak light from the single bulb hanging from the ceiling far above seemed to get lost in its downward journey, leaving the floor a pool of darkness. Yet as time passed, reading somehow became the only answer to the unexpected fear that now rose in his heart. He remembered that his teacher of *erfan* had taught him never to be afraid of death, for, as Mowlana said:

> *I died as an animal and I was a man.*
> *Why should I fear? When was I less by dying?*

But it was not death he feared. He feared forgetting what he knew, forgetting in any deep way who he was. Maybe he would become semiblank like his surroundings and be able to say only "I am Ali Hashemi" and not be able to remember anything more about himself.

He also had a more concrete fear: he feared being forgotten in prison. What, he wondered, had happened to the classes he taught, to his honored position with Marashi, to the course of master lessons he was taking with one of the "models" in Qom, where he had established himself as one of the "hopes" of the next generation? Would he emerge years later to find that his students had become ayatollahs and to find that he himself had become like a book worn and bleached by the weathering of time, with only fragments of his original learning still legible?

Only when reading did he feel real hope that he would continue to be a whole and integral copy of the former Ali Hashemi. The two books he had been carrying when arrested were his entire library: a pocket Koran and a giant paperback, the Persian translation of Jawaharlal Nehru's *Glimpses of World History*. In the Koran it was the story of Joseph he reread most often, coming to appreciate why the Koran called it "the best of stories." Ali liked the steady progression of the story, from Joseph's dreams to his betrayal by his brothers, his sale to the Egyptians, his resistance to the seduction of Potiphar's wife, his imprisonment, his interpretation of Pharaoh's dream, his position of trust with Pharaoh, his reconciliation with his brothers, his return to his father, Jacob. Ali had felt the story of Joseph had a special bearing on his life ever since the moment when, before accepting him as a pupil, his teacher of *erfan* had opened the Koran to Joseph's words to his fellow prisoners: "My two fellow prisoners, are many lords differing among themselves better, or God, the One, the Irresistible?" How keenly he felt the significance of other things that Joseph said, especially when, near the end of the story, he told his father, Jacob: "God was good to me when he took me out of prison and brought you here, even after Satan had sown enmity between me and my brothers. Truly my Lord is subtle in what he wishes. Truly it is He who is the wise, the all-knowing."

If the story of Joseph nurtured the hope of seeing the subtle wisdom of events explained in his eventual release from captivity, Nehru's broad and panoramic view of the history of the world nurtured a hope that his captivity would have a meaning, however small, in the history of mankind. When he read in the prologue that Nehru said religion "often cared little for the mind," in the margin he wrote carefully with his ball-point pen, "Not true of Shi'ism." Gradually he became aware that the only clear progress that Nehru saw was progress in man's understanding and use of nature. Nehru's vision of history was highly moral—particularly in his attacks on "exploiters"—but moral rewards were purely matters of this world; he had no interest in morals that entailed any other world. Ali's marginal arguments with Nehru intensified; it seemed impossible in an unjust world to claim that any moral system could be closed and balanced without any otherworldly dimension. But Ali also wanted to argue that religion too

progresses and that at its best it too could be the voice of the exploited.

Every bit as much space in the margins was filled with nonar-
gumentative comments, provoked by the scope of Nehru's work.
Ali was very pleased with Nehru's generally favorable treatment
of Islam and Iran (or "Persia," as Nehru in his old-fashioned way
called Iran). When Nehru said, "Let us go now to Persia, the country whose soul is said to have come to India and found a worthy
body in the Taj Mahal," Ali anticipated with delight a description
that only an Indian could write of the vast cultural influence of the
Persian language and Iranian art on the cultures of India and
Central Asia.

Yet the scope of the book raised questions that interested Ali in
other ways, for Nehru explained massive historical changes in
India and China at times when these countries were untouched by
Judaism, Christianity, and Islam. It was not enough to evaluate
such movements in terms of exploiters and exploited, as Nehru
often did, or to discuss their moral significance in terms of the
natural religion that, as a Shiah, he believed all mankind to have.
But the sense that all mankind (even in periods of history in which
distant peoples had not heard of each other) was linked in a common destiny, which was now converging in a movement to liber-
ate men everywhere, was so inspiring that Ali felt it had to be
done. When the guards switched off the overhead lights at eight-
thirty, the size of this vision made up for the tiny dimensions of
the cell, and Ali's imagination seemed to travel the centuries and
continents with an ease that made his nighttimes into bursts of
freedom hardly possible for the genies, not to mention humans.

By the third week, however, even the exhilaration of Nehru had
worn off. Ali had filled the flyleaves and margins of the book with
a minute and barely legible hand; now even the book seemed a
little imprisoned in the tight, neat commentary he had added to it.
He even tired of reading the story of Joseph. He began to daydream more—sometimes about the mulberry tree in the garden at
home, sometimes about food (including the breakfast he had never
finished), and increasingly about swimming in the Euphrates near
Najaf: he was swimming in circles, moving slowly upstream, occasionally letting his feet drop to touch the colder, swift under-
current of the river that ran nearly a meter below the surface.

Sometimes at night Ali's real dreams would end with the sounds of screams coming from someplace in the center of the prison, sounds that seemed to well up from some deep metallic pit. Ali had heard that the SAVAK tortured people in the Committee prison, and he had also heard that they sometimes played tapes of screams to break the will of their prisoners. Ali couldn't tell if the screams were real or taped, feigned or genuine; he only knew that when he heard the screams he would pull up his legs until his knees were under his chin, wrap his arms tightly around his shins, and watch the small opening of his cell to the corridor, a square patch of darkness slightly less intense than that in the rest of the cell.

After a while nothing, not the slow, pleasant, leisurely daydream of swimming in the Euphrates or the violent shock of hearing screams in the night, could give any outline or definition to the world in which Ali lived. Despite the white paint on the walls and his one shower a week, he lived in an unclean, gritty world in which the dust he used (as the sacred law allowed) in place of water for ablution before prayer seemed slowly to be fusing with his body, just as his body seemed at other times to be slowly melting into the dirt of his surroundings. Food lost almost all taste—not surprisingly, as the same basic stew, *ab-gusht*, was served for every meal; but by the third week Ali was puzzled to find that at moments he also lost all sensation in his tongue. At such times he had to chew slowly and carefully, as he was not quite sure where the food ended and his tongue began.

At the end of the third week a little relief came with the arrival of several new prisoners, who, even when separated, were so closely familiar to each other that they could have conversations just by speaking one word each in a stage whisper through their cell doors or windows. On their very first night one of them became tired of stealthful whispering and began to half sing, half recite a passage from the Iranian national epic about the successful revolt of Kaveh the blacksmith against Zahhak, a tyrant who ruled ancient Iran:

> *When Kaveh went out from the court of the king*
> *The crowd in the market came flocking around.*
> *Still loudly he cried and called out for their help,*

He summoned the whole world to justice's aid.
A long leather apron such as blacksmiths wear
To guard at the forge against hammerblows
Kaveh stuck solidly to the point of his lance.
Then throughout the bazaar dust of movement arose.
Crying out he paraded with the lance in his hand:
"Illustrious men! True worshippers of God!
Haste! For this ruler is Satan, father of lies."

Here the word for Satan was "Ahriman," the god of evil in Zoroastrianism, the religion of Iran in the pre-Islamic period that formed the subject of the epic. As everyone within earshot knew, the humble flag of Kaveh the blacksmith's apron on a lance became the flag of Iran, carried into battle by the just kings of Iran after Zahhak's overthrow and death. The reciter was calling for revolution and regicide.

Another voice began reciting a passage in which Rostam, the great hero of the national epic, "the great-bodied," "the elephant-statured," "the paladin" par excellence of the ancient Iranian tradition, is angry at the shah, Ka'us, for rebuking him unjustly:

The hero Rostam was amazed at the king:
"Do not nurse such fires in the depths of your heart!
Each one of your acts is as bad as the next:
You are clearly not worthy of true sovereignty."
He went out in a rage and mounted his steed.
"I am the killer of lions, the giver of crowns.
When I am angry, then who is this shah Ka'us?
Why does he reach for me? Who is his henchman Toos?
The earth below is my servant, and my steed, my throne;
The mace is my signet, and the helmet my crown.
I light the dark night with the thrust of my blade;
I scatter men's heads on the fields of battle.
The point of the spear and the blade are my friends;
These two arms and this heart I own as my king.
Why does he harass me? I am not his slave.
I am the slave of the one Creator alone."

One of the prisoners had begun to beat the marching, warlike rhythm of Ferdowsi's lines on the frame of his cot, the way drums are beaten while Ferdowsi is recited in "houses of strength" where wrestlers exercise. Suddenly they heard a guard coming up a staircase toward their corridor, and for a second they were silent.

Then, against the sound of advancing footsteps, a strong, steady voice recited the gentler rhythm of a poem by Mowlana:

> *Like Jacob I am uttering cries of grief,*
> *I desire the fair face of Joseph of Canaan.*
> *By God, without You the city is a prison to me;*
> *Over mountain and desert I desire to wander.*
> *In one hand the wine cup, in the other, the tresses of the Beloved,*
> *Such a dance in the marketplace is my desire.*
> *My heart is weary of these weak-spirited traveling companions;*
> *I desire the Lion of God and Rostam, the son of Zal.*

It was the voice of Parviz. The guard started to pound a stick on an iron railing and shouted, "Keep quiet, keep quiet!"

Ali suddenly didn't care what the man was saying; he knew that whatever happened, he would recite two more lines of this poem:

> *The bread and water of destiny is like a treacherous flood;*
> *I am a great fish and the sea of Oman is my desire.*
> *My soul has grown weary of Pharaoh and his tyranny;*
> *The light of the countenance of Moses, son of Imran, is my desire—*

The guard now slammed his stick on the door of Ali's cell and yelled, "What kind of fool are you? I told you—keep quiet!" and he hit the door a few times for emphasis.

Ali kept quiet, but inside him there was a kind of humming and vibration of life not unlike the humming and vibration on that day ten years before when every object in the nighttime world had glowed with light. By Pharaoh, Mowlana meant illusion and by Moses, he meant reality; and Ali had suddenly grown tired of his fear of the tyranny of illusion and cast it aside. Suddenly, because of his love for reality, he lived with hope, since the only feelings that could affect him deeply were his longing for that reality.

For the next two days he and Parviz, although about three cells apart, managed to exchange a few whispered messages, reduced to one or two words each. Some were about their experiences together—the answer to *"samanu"* was "mother's vow"; the other messages were geographical, such as "the bathhouse alley," to which the answer was "house of the pharmacist."

On the second day after Parviz arrived, shortly before the time for the evening meal, a man in a suit came to the door, ordered one of the guards accompanying him to open it, and said, "We are letting you go, Mr. Hashemi. The guard will take you to the gate." Ali, to his regret, walked down the corridor in the direction away from Parviz. When he arrived in the street he was amazed at how unreal the buses, taxis—in fact all the objects around him—seemed. It was partly the lingering vision of the insubstantiality of "Pharaonic" illusion compared to "Mosaic" reality and partly the difficulty that Ali had in reversing the conviction he had had for three and a half weeks that he would not see such objects again for many years.

The sun was low in the late-afternoon sky, and Ali, who felt sure that prison filth had transformed his appearance, stuck to the dark side of the streets as he walked the two kilometers to the shop of a friend. This friend was a Qomi and a bookseller, and Ali found him at a desk just inside the door of the shop. Characteristically, he was absorbed in reading a book held in his left hand while with his right hand he fed himself toasted watermelon seeds out of a small twist of paper laid on the corner of the desk. He looked up when Ali entered and said: "My God, I thought you wouldn't be out for months! The representative of Qom in the parliament has been running around Tehran demanding your release. I thought, with his connections with the court he'd get you out soon—but not this soon! As Saadi says, 'He who has lived with a good name has enduring good luck.' Let me get you some tea."

Ali did not want tea—he wanted to call home. But even more than that he wanted a bath. The bookseller told his assistant to close the shop, and Ali, feeling conspicuously dirty even though it was dark by now, got gingerly into his friend's car and a few minutes later got gingerly out of the car in front of a home where he had been promised a telephone, a bath, and a chance to wash his clothes.

Two days after his return to Qom his father asked him to preach the Friday sermon at a mosque where his family had a hereditary right to preach. Never, since he had finished his first complete book on Islamic law at age fifteen and his father had given him a turban, had he felt more conscious that people saw him as fulfilling a destiny thrust on him by both his descent and his learning. As he came near to the mosque he saw people stop, turn toward him in little groups, and murmur congratulations. When one person straightforwardly came up to him and said, "It's not right, a learned sayyed like you in prison," he said, "On the contrary, it's my heritage as a sayyed." Ali was embarrassed at how proud he felt. He was also embarrassed because his well-wishers didn't know that for a time in prison he had come close to despair, and he thanked God (and thanked Parviz) that he had found himself before he came out.

The crowd inside the mosque was so dense that, as one says in Persian, if you tried to stick a needle in, it wouldn't pass through. Ali was aware that he could make himself even more popular—even, perhaps, nationally famous—if he now got arrested again by preaching a sermon on one of the forbidden subjects—for example, the government's desertion of its Muslim brothers by its de facto recognition of Israel, or the government's craven capitulation in giving the right of diplomatic immunity to American technical and military advisers, or the government's approval of schools with mixed classes of boys and girls. But Ali was not interested in being provocative. He wanted to preach an intellectually difficult sermon in which the intellectually penetrating would see that he was talking about the inner experience through which he had gradually mastered being a prisoner.

He chose the Koranic story of Noah. He quoted the chapter of the Koran telling the story of Noah before the flood: how he had been sent to warn his people to worship God before a painful punishment should come to them; how, when summoned by Noah, they only increased their flight from righteousness and stopped their ears "and gave themselves up to arrogance"; how Noah urged them both publicly and privately to understand the bounties of God who had created rain, rivers, gardens, the heavens and the earth, which He had spread out "as a carpet" for them so that, in the beautiful expression of the Koran, "you may travel in its spacious roads." But they refused to listen to Noah, who then said to God that his people rejected him, refused to abandon their gods, and persisted in following "those whose wealth and children give no increase but only loss." When the flood came, Noah prayed: "My Lord! Forgive me and my parents and whoever enters my house as a believer, man or woman; but to the oppressors grant no increase except in perdition!"

Ali said that the story of the flood, like the bounties of God so often enumerated one by one in the Koran, like each individual verse of scripture, was a warning and a "sign," and the more this "sign" was properly contemplated, the more men could understand the meaning God intended them to draw from it. One sense of the story of Noah we grasp quickly: that while righteous men must summon the unrighteous to worship God, a stage is reached at which they must part company with oppressors and pray that God will remove them and purge the world of them through his flood. But there were other significances to the story of Noah which were not so readily understood. In the Koran when Noah is explaining the bounties of God both "publicly and privately" he says, "He has created you in stages," and he also says, "God has brought you forth from the earth like a plant." Surely these words could be understood in part through the lines of Mowlana:

> I died as a mineral and became a plant,
> I died as plant and rose as an animal,
> I died as animal and I was Man.

The earthiness of man was a truth that should never be forgotten. We are molded from earth by God's grace, and, as Noah says, after bringing us forth from the earth like a plant, "Then He will return you into it. And He will raise you forth from it." But the wicked who had been warned by Noah failed to be grateful for the rain and the rivers of God, and eventually, in punishment, they saw these blessings turn into the curse. They had become arrogant; they had forgotten that it is the spiritual significance of things that makes them sanctified or unclean, and through disobedience to God the very earth of which men were made ceased to be a bounty for them. They became men "whose wealth and children," as Noah said, "give no increase but only loss." The earth of their bodies, families, and possessions was washed away and dissolved by the flood.

Ali said he must mention one other way in which the story of Noah was a warning and a sign (though to the discerning there were a thousand ways). Noah's story was also the story of how a righteous man had remained righteous when severely tested. Noah spoke to his people repeatedly, but they stopped their ears, laughed at him, and clung to their gods. In another place in the Koran it says of Noah: "They charged Our servant [Noah] with falsehood and said: 'One possessed!' and he was driven out. Then he called on his Lord: 'I am overcome. Do Thou then help [me]!' "

Noah had not been found wanting when he was tested. As Hafez said:

> Be the friend of the men of God, for in Noah's ark
> There is some earth that would not purchase the deluge for a drop of water.

This was a notoriously difficult line, which commentators disagreed about. One meaning of these lines was that Noah's ark carried the handful of earth that was Noah and those who believed, those who had been "brought forth from the earth like a plant." They had been "created in stages," and at the moment when Noah was scornfully rejected by his people and "overcome," he had moved to the stage of utter reliance on God. Such was the reliance of Noah and his followers, this handful of earth, which was in fact all of believing mankind, that they would not drink or touch a drop of water, even to wash for their prayers. For the deluge, which at that moment was the entirety of the world outside the ark, was corrupted water that had forgotten its divine origin in the rain and rivers sent by God. This corrupted water was sin, self-indulgence, and uncleanness, and to accept a drop of it into the ark might mean the dissolution into the perdition of the surrounding flood of the pure earth of those who believed.

Ali was conscious that the sermon though difficult was a success. His reference to oppressors had seemed sufficiently political
for those who would be satisfied only by something political, and
his suggestion of a mystical meaning in the verse that we had been
created "in stages" had interested a few of his more speculative
listeners. But he was also conscious that in the prison in Tehran he
had himself entered a stage that could best be completed in
Tehran itself. He wanted to have a larger view of world history,
into which he could fit Nehru's *Glimpses* with more meaning. He
wanted to enjoy the new fearlessness he had felt in prison when
exchanging messages in poetry with young men of his own generation. Above all he wanted—if possible—to talk to Parviz.

CHAPTER EIGHT

PARVIZ WAS released in 1974, three years after Ali. Shortly after his arrival at the Committee prison in 1971, Parviz had been tried inside the prison and sent to Qasr, a jail for political prisoners famous for its excellent library and the freedom of contact allowed between prisoners.

In their earlier years Ali had always stayed in contact with Parviz, whose cousin continued to study in the Faiziyeh in Qom and remained a link between them. Ali and Parviz had seen each other occasionally in the sixties when Parviz returned to Qom from the university for vacations, and although they still felt close, they didn't have a great deal to talk about. Then Ali had heard almost nothing of Parviz for several years except that he had graduated as "first student" in the technical faculty of the University of Tehran and gone to Europe. When Ali returned from Najaf in 1969 he was told that Parviz had earned a Ph.D. in mathematics in near record time at a European university and had become involved in Iranian student politics in Europe. Some people said that Parviz had chosen to return to Iran for political reasons, but others said that ever since his return he had rejected politics and never expressed political opinions on anything. Then, after seven years of separation, he had heard Parviz's voice in prison calling for "the Lion of God and Rostam, the son of Zal." Shortly before his move to Tehran, Ali was told that Parviz was out of prison and had been asking about him. As soon as Ali moved to Tehran he sent a message through Parviz's cousin that on Thursdays he left the theological faculty of the University of Tehran at about two o'clock and could be found walking toward the house he rented in a lane off Safi Ali Shah Avenue.

These Thursday afternoon walks were leisurely affairs for Ali, who changed out of his mullah clothes at the faculty so that he would be less conspicuous; he wanted to capture the taste of life in Tehran as it was experienced by Tehranis. Ali certainly knew Tehran fairly well before he moved there; he had stayed there with friends either when he went to buy something important such as his car or when he used the Tehran airport. Now, after living in Tehran for a few weeks, it seemed to Ali that great parts of Tehran consisted of objects that were intimately connected with the airport. These were mainly objects that arrived at the airport and were being assembled or disassembled, and Tehranis who weren't assembling or disassembling such objects were buying, selling, or flaunting them.

Assembling objects from all kinds of imported parts, especially if assemblage required a factory setting, was called *montazh,* from the French word for "setting up," *montage;* and in joking, Tehranis called all sorts of jerry-built Iranian versions of foreign ideas true examples of Iranian *montazh.* In fact, even the social life of Tehran itself often seemed a huge unfinished *montazh.* Almost everybody came from somewhere else, and they all seemed out to prove that by wealth, piety, worldliness, and above all cleverness they had somehow welded themselves onto the never quite finished *montazh* of Tehran.

Sometimes Ali found Tehran rather depressing. He had come from a town of about a hundred and fifty thousand people to a city of millions, and the rudeness of Tehranis made him miss Qom, where people had time to say hello and to make way for each other on the streets. As a point of pride, two Tehranis would barely step aside when they were on a collision course with each other. Translated into traffic, the results were horrendous. Since all Tehranis were out to prove something, they directed their cars (often *montazh*-built) into the same intersection from all sides simultaneously, and the traffic-jam *montazhs* that resulted were creations that took hours to disassemble.

Yet for all its prefab, newfangled, ill-digested character it was an exciting place. If ideas as well as goods were unloaded at the bus stations, railroad depots, and airports of Tehran, they were far less predictable in nature than goods, and every Tehrani seemed to create a special *montazh* of these ideas peculiarly his own. Sometimes this variety resulted from the actual variety of educational backgrounds. Iranian doctors with degrees from the United States, France, and Germany brought their different versions of Western medicine to Tehran, just as old-fashioned Galenic pharmacists brought their tradition from remote towns such as Sabzevar and folk herbalists brought their traditions from remote villages. Often, however, this variety was produced after ideas arrived and not during their gestation outside of Tehran.

As a consequence Tehran was full of *dowrehs*, "circles" of men or women who met every week partly to share the pleasure of one another's company and partly to digest the ideas that were preoccupying their members. The members of a *dowreh* were men or women basically in intellectual and emotional sympathy. Their focus could be fiercely intellectual (contemporary Persian poetry, the Islamic philosophical heritage, and the like) or overwhelmingly social (its members being men or women from a single provincial town who enjoyed telling dialect jokes, for example), and *dowrehs* for gambling were notorious. The focus of most *dowrehs*, however, was somewhere in between. Discussion groups, whether called *dowrehs* or not, existed on every level of Tehran society, even in shantytown neighborhoods, where they might be led by the local mullah.

Dowrehs and similar groups were assemblages that were actually made from scratch in Iran, not simply put together from foreign parts in an Iranian *montazh*. They acted as the truly Iranian organs of rumination and taste through which Iranians, and most particularly Tehranis, chewed over the vast variety of foods presented both by *montazh* culture and by the more ancient culture of Iran. Ali had become a member of two *dowrehs* within a few weeks of his arrival in Tehran, one made up of Westernized intellectuals devoted to Islamic philosophy and the other made up of mullahs who sponsored an intellectual magazine meant to win young people back to Islam. Even the *dowreh* of mullahs, for all that it contained one or two people who struck Ali as bloodcurdling fanatics of a type he had seldom encountered in Qom, seemed affected by the atmosphere of Tehran. They usually wore trousers under their abas, unlike Qomi mullahs, and they usually sat on chairs. They were also cleaner, and they had many more friends who were not practicing Muslims.

Psychologically (and often physically) above all the confusion of Tehran, however, lay the one reality that tied the vast *montazh* of Tehran together: the presence of the central government and of the shah. In Qom, perhaps alone among towns of its size in Iran, there were no statues of the shah. The very ballast by which the Tehran *montazh* was tied to the ground consisted of the monuments, statues, and plaques commemorating Mohammed Reza Shah and his father, Reza Shah, as well as the huge buildings and compounds of the central ministries. Flying over it all, checking that it was still secured to its moorings, were the helicopters by means of which the shah, the queen, and the prime minister avoided the terrible traffic *montazhs* on the ground and went directly back and forth between landing pads next to the foreign ministry, in the gardens of palaces, and on the parade grounds of military bases.

Ali had been in Tehran for slightly over a month when Parviz caught up with him. It was a Thursday in late October, and Ali, as he left the theological faculty, was aware of someone half turned away from him leaning over a barrow of melons for sale on the other side of the street. As he approached, Parviz straightened up and, recognizing him, smiled the smile of great sweetness which, after the excessively serious face that Parviz had worn in his early years, had mysteriously blossomed in him in his twenties. Parviz was, in fact, little changed from his twenties—still rather tall and gaunt, with the squint that had lived on in the abstract look in his brown eyes. Unlike most men of his age, he still kept his black hair cut in a short brush, as he had done when he was an under-graduate. And his short hair, together with his tidy mustache and purposeful gestures, gave him the look of a rather intellectual army officer out on leave in his civilian clothes.

As soon as they embraced, Ali knew that the slight estrange-ment of their twenties had passed. There was no longer a question of sizing up the distance between them in ideas or careers. It was immediately clear that from the moment they had heard each other's voices in prison, they knew that they had both traveled equally long and difficult intellectual paths in the past fifteen years and wanted the companionship that two people could share only if they knew where each other's paths had started in early childhood.

They started walking northward, toward the mountains that they could just see above the polluted haze of the city. There were so many more women on the streets than in Qom that Ali asked if the climate of Tehran might not cause a birthrate unfavorable to men—or did the lewd Tehrani posters of women encourage the overproduction of chromosomes for females? Parviz told him that he was lucky (or unfortunate, depending on how you looked at it) to miss Tehran in the miniskirt craze of the sixties, for one hour on a principal shopping street would have provided him with enough thoughts to repent for a month and enough material to preach sermons on for a year. Despite the lack of miniskirts, how-ever, some of the scenery they passed had a lewd and disorderly quality. One was never out of sight of building construction, and while most of the buildings going up had a monotonous sameness of architecture, the scattering of construction cranes and piles of rubble intensified the city's disorderly *montazh* look. The lewdness was added to by the hand-painted movie posters they passed as they entered the lower stretch of Lalehzar Avenue—garish in color, with figures monstrously oversized, they implied that everything being shown, from children's films to Bombay-made musicals, was filled with naked-legged women in tempting posi-tions. The threatening forwardness of the posters was increased by the large number of tough and sullen-looking young men hanging around under the marquees.

Near the top of Lalehzar they came to an intersection, Mokhber ed-Dowleh, through which many share-taxis passed to the north of Tehran. They stood together shouting "Darband" at passing cabs, waiting for a taxi headed in that direction to stop for them. In the center of the intersection was a statue commemorating the coup against Mossadegh's government and the restoration of the shah, and officially the intersection had been renamed for the date of this event. The statue showed the joint efforts of a soldier with a bayonet and a worker with a club to kill a large reptile. Parviz pointed out that the soldier was in just as good a position to strike the peasant as the reptile, and Ali laughed.

A taxi stopped, and—as it was a large Mercedes Benz—Ali and Parviz both squeezed into the front in order not to trouble the woman in a chador in the back seat. Soon it started up the old Shemran road, and they entered a section of garages that advertised automobile spare parts and repairs, claims that were at least partly proved by the large number of elderly cars being actively cannibalized or left as carcasses by the mechanics working around them. Then they passed into an area of small new apartment buildings, ten or twelve stories high, with a sprinkling of expensive shops among them. The woman in a chador got out here and two soldiers got in. The road next wound past several huge compounds filled with trees: the radio broadcasting facility, a military command post with some signs in English for the American military advisory group housed there; a car-registration office; private compounds of the very wealthy, partly hidden behind a thin crust of small villagelike stores or fruit shops and shoemakers facing on the road; and finally, Sadabad, the summer palace of the shah.

When they got out at the parking area at the end of the road the weather was noticeably cold. There was an almost holiday atmosphere about the place—people were either about to hike or had just returned from hiking, and they treated each other with good humor as they passed or sat on wooden benches in the surrounding teahouses. Ali and Parviz walked along a river, then Parviz chose one of the mountain paths, and Ali, following close behind him, for the first time had a view that took in most of Tehran. For all its newness, its disorder, and its incoherence, this city of millions struck Ali as something wonderful. It was wonderful, if for

no other reason than because it had created a forest of trees along
avenues and in gardens, including varieties that didn't grow in
Qom, such as the plane tree with its handsome many-lobed
leaves. On most parts of the Iranian plateau trees existed in numbers only where people lived, and Tehran, Ali said, with its tree-
lined streets and tree-filled compounds was the largest man-made
arboretum in Iran.

Parviz said: "Now I understand why you left teaching theology
in Qom in order to come to study theology at a primary-school
level at the University of Tehran."

Ali laughed and said: "Look, dear Parviz, it's less difficult for a
man with a turban to register at the theological faculty than elsewhere in the University of Tehran, and it allows me to take
courses in the history department, the philosophy department,
and the faculty of law. Which doesn't prevent me from feeling
like a stranger when I go to these faculties. Practically every time I
attend classes there, some pretty young thing tries to get a rise out
of me and says, 'What a handsome man!' or 'I have a religious
question I need to talk over with you in private,' or 'I'm ready to
become one of your four wives.' Good thing my mother insisted I
marry a temporary wife before I left Qom. But I came to learn
something new, and I'm not going to be put off going to the other
faculties—as the proverb says, Since we're already in hell, why
not step one step deeper?"

They had diverged from the usual hikers' route and had followed a path that led them more directly uphill. They found a flat
area to sit on from which they could see not only the city but the
snow-covered volcanic cone of Mount Damavand, which, according to Ferdowsi, was the site of Rostam's victories over demons
and the site where a champion of Iran, fighting in the rebellion
begun by Kaveh, left the tyrant Zahhak to die, "hanging, his
heart's blood pouring down onto the earth."

Parviz said: "You'll be amazed to know that I, of all people,
came back to Tehran because of my interest in Islam. When I
went to Paris I was a Muslim the same way I was a Qomi; it was
simply a fact about my background and nothing I ever thought
about. What I did think about when I was an undergraduate in
Tehran was my future in an Iran where, in spite of a government

as wealthy as Alexander, most men could say, as Saadi did, 'I spent my precious life wondering: What will I have to eat each day, what will I have to wear each winter?' I fell in with a group of students who called themselves Marxists. This Marxist game was really a kind of lunar Marxism, in which we hadn't any clear idea of what we were talking about. When we talked about the difference between the labor value and the exchange value, we just meant that someone was living off the fat of the people's labor. When we spoke reverently of the dictatorship of the proletariat, we meant that the oppressed masses would come to recognize that a particular group of students—ourselves—knew what was in their best interests and would put us in charge of Iran. But we knew Iran wasn't Algeria or Cuba, and the few secret members of the Iran Communist party we contacted seemed useless—they were every bit as struck with calf love for the Soviet Union as our army officers now are struck with calf love for the United States.

"When I went to Paris as a graduate student I was still a Marxist, but I was less sure what that meant. Lots of Iranian students in Paris were Marxists, but except that we all were against the regime, we could hardly agree on anything. Every time I asked a friend why his version of Marxism was better than mine, he'd tell me to read the works of some French sociologist or English economist. And when I went to the bookstore and saw whole walls covered with these books, I'd decide to hell with it. I'm a mathematician; I'll figure all this out after I get my degree. After a certain point all I did was demonstrate in front of the embassy when someone important in the government was visiting from Iran. To my surprise, since so many of the students suspected each other of being agents of SAVAK, and I assumed the government knew everything I did, my scholarship was never cut off.

"In fact, if it hadn't been for mathematics I would have come home after a few months. After two months of eating French food it all began to taste the same. Even when they cook rice they make it taste like potatoes—and, in fact, potatoes were served to me every day in some form or other. They so completely disguise their food, I couldn't even guess if the meat in it was pork or fish or maybe something I'd never heard of. On Fridays I would go out to Belleville, where the Algerians have a Friday street market, and even the food sold by the Algerian Jews tasted more real than the food served to the French students.

"I became so uninterested in food that when one of my friends urged me to observe the fast I decided to try to regain my appetite, because I remembered how much my family and I used to be able to eat in Qom before sunrise and after sunset during the fast. One of these friends was a Qomi too, maybe the only other Qomi in Paris. He was slightly crazy and very simple—he had left Iran without ever really leaving. His father was a butcher, and his crazy son insisted on slaughtering sheep in his bathtub so that it should be permissible to eat the meat, until his landlady found out, kicked him out, and we convinced him that he could eat the meat prepared by an Algerian butcher. Anyway, he persuaded us to give him a little money each, and during the fast he made us huge predawn breakfasts and dinners after sunset. Even though I hadn't fasted for years I found it easy to fast, and I began to enjoy food again. Maybe it was easy because it was winter and the days were short. I gained three kilos during the fast.

"Unlike food, for me mathematics never lost its taste. I did well and was complimented by my teachers. At the end of my first year I had to take an important qualifying exam. I had studied hard for it and felt sure I would pass with the best. Then, five days before the exam, I received a cable that my mother was desperately ill. I went crazy. I couldn't sleep. I walked around the city for most of the night, looking straight at everyone I passed—prostitutes, black street sweepers, cab drivers parked in taxi stands. I was sure that someone had a second message to deliver to me that would somehow explain the cable. I had to have something to work on—a hint or riddle or something that I could sit down with and work on and decode.

"Then I suddenly realized that what I really wanted to do was make a vow. I suddenly understood what a vow is or, at least, could be: it was a declaration of generosity, a commitment to give, in the expectation that the world would give something back. I finally understood why my mother had made a vow; it was precisely because she was so poor and could do so little. She made a vow to distribute *samanu* to the sayyeds on the anniversary of Fatemeh's death. She said to God, 'I believe the world is generous and I am going to act on that belief.' She seized as much control as anyone can seize of things that lie just beyond our reach.

"You once told me that the essence of a vow was saying 'I intend,' because to really intend something good should change us inside. I told you that I knew how to solve problems—including difficult problems in mathematics that were at the outermost limit of my reach—without saying 'I intend.' I loved science because it was about the prediction and control of nature; and I loved mathematics most of all because it predicted and controlled itself. But my need to take the qualifying exam and my need to help my mother brought me into areas beyond prediction and control. I vowed that if, after taking the exam, I returned to Iran and found my mother well, I would go on a pilgrimage to Mashhad. I vowed I'd have a lamb slaughtered for the poor on the anniversary of the death of Fatemeh, just as you once vowed to do it if I passed my final school exam and went to the university. I vowed that I would devote my life to the Iranian people.

"I took the exam and returned. My mother was already somewhat better; by the time I had made the pilgrimage to Mashhad she was completely recovered. I heard that I had passed the exam with distinction. I think I realized for the first time that even when I said I wanted to know how to predict and control nature I was making a kind of vow, because I was working in the belief that knowing such things was 'good.' I mean, I don't know that I believed then or believe now that finding out things was an act of piety or something like that. It's just that I realized I was offering what I did in the expectation that somehow its 'goodness' would make sense in some large way. When I made the pilgrimage to the tomb of Imam Reza in Mashhad I knew I was doing something 'good' too, and I began to look inward and watch closely for the moments when my heart recognized goodness.

"Next autumn, on the morning of my flight to Paris, I got up very early with my parents and ate breakfast while it was still dark. My mother had prepared some thickened cream for me to eat on bread because she knew how much I missed this when I was abroad. When she saw how quickly I ate the huge portion she had given me, she gave me her portion too, and I finished that off and even part of another portion. I took a share-taxi to Tehran and then took the plane to Paris. I don't know how it happened, but I got airsick for the first time and spent most of the flight throwing up or praying that I would not throw up again.

"The second year in Paris was much easier than the first. The thesis topic I chose turned out to be every bit as interesting as I expected, and I made fairly steady progress on it. A group of us bought meat from a North African butcher in Belleville and cooked Iranian meals three or four nights a week, and we always prayed together on Fridays. We also began to study the Koran and the *Sermons* of Ali, the Commander of the Faithful, together. Paris no longer bothered me; by now I spoke French well enough for most purposes. And often when I was in a crowd, in the Métro or in a hall in the university or anywhere, I had a tremendous sense of elation. I was carrying a secret inside of me that these other people did not know—I had discovered that Islam was a system of 'goodness.' And every time I read the Koran and the *Sermons* of Ali, the Commander of the Faithful, I would discover yet another way in which this goodness could be applied to my life or the life of the world.

"We lived so simply that we were able to put together a little money once a month to publish an Islamic newspaper in Persian. I began to write. You remember, in school you could write an essay about anything, even things you hadn't seen, such as a storm at sea, while I would struggle until I felt I had a firm grasp on one thread of a topic and then followed that thread through. I now found that with such a book as the *Sermons* of Ali before me there was some advantage to approaching things in my way. I wrote a long essay, parts of which appeared in different issues. It was on Ali's famous sermon on rights and leadership, which begins: 'God has given me a claim over you by making me the trustee of your affairs; and you too have a claim over me like mine over you.' Ali explains that the only case in which there are claims or 'rights' that are not mutual is in the case of God. One-sided obligation is possible only with God, who has claims and rights over us for which we have no corresponding claims in return over Him.

"For me this beautiful, simple geometry suddenly made sense of what was good in Marxism and made me understand that Islam really did present the axioms from which a perfect society could be deduced. Ali ends this sermon by saying: 'I and you are slaves owned by the one true Lord. . . . He brought us from the condition we were in to a condition that was better for us, and replaced our straying with guidance, and gave us true sight after blindness.' I wrote in my essay that everything belonged to God, so ownership of anything was trusteeship, while God alone had true and absolute ownership. Therefore, any kind of human ownership implied an obligation, a claim by someone else for whom the trustee was acting. The whole world was a series of chains of such 'claims,' and a leader, such as Ali, held the ends of all the chains, which were extended to all those he led. For this reason as well as for so many others, kingship, such as we have in Iran, is totally false and un-Islamic. Unfortunately much of the opposition to the shah has grasped only half of this idea, because they reject the total ownership of God and the totally shared trusteeship of mankind. Still, one point the Marxists were right about: now personal wealth could and should cease. Science has given us the means to construct a society in which the trusteeship actually is collective. Now that we can all instantly speak to each other and hear each other, the chains of claims and obligations between men can be drawn into the perfect geometry prescribed by Ali.

"I also wrote that Marxism would never achieve this perfect geometry. Ali in his sermon says that piety and the faithfulness of the ruler and the ruled to their mutual obligation belong together, and the real reason we have to strive for this just, mutual relation is that in its absence our spirits are perverted and our sacred obligations to God are forgotten. I ended by calling for a new kind of leadership. Collective responsibility meant that once a decision was collectively made, the ruler and any member of the community obeyed it without wavering, even if they had favored something else to begin with. Informed obedience and collective centralization that came from true Islamic principles were the only means to revolution. And, Ali dear, you remember I am the son of a baker—in fact, a not very successful baker. I knew in my heart that only the words of Ali and the power of Islam could make people like me and my father think about something greater than: 'What will I have to eat each day, what will I have to wear each winter?' "

The freedom with which all this poured out of Parviz stunned

Ali. Parviz, who had always slowed his speech to the purposeful march of his thought, now let ideas stream out of himself with no hint of self-censorship or premeditation. Ali found that instead it was he who spoke with deliberate care and premeditation. "Of course you're right that for us as Muslims it is intention that is essential to the goodness of almost everything we can do, from prayer to vows; and you're right that vows are a step toward the moral resolution that changes the heart and often changes the world. It's not far from a vow to say, 'If the occasion arises, I will give my life as a martyr for the oppressed or for Islam.' But sincerity of intention is worth nothing if the object is bad: 'If the occasion arises, I will give my life to help the oppressor' is a resolution worth nothing to God or to man. That's why I've studied the law of Islam, because to infer what God the Legislator wants is not so simple. The more I study it, the more I stand in awe of the care that my teachers have taken to find the correct precepts of the law, adding new links to a meticulously constructed chain of learning stretching back fourteen centuries." Ali stopped for a minute and looked slyly at Parviz. "You know, I fulfilled my vow to have a lamb slaughtered and given to the poor for three years on the anniversary of Fatemeh's death if you passed the final school exam and went on to the university."

Parviz took Ali's hand for a minute, then, letting it go said: "Wait! Wait for the rest of my story—you're going to hear how I learned the most important things of all from a mullah. I returned to Iran with my doctorate, but my commentary on the *Sermons* had irritated someone important in the SAVAK. I was offered a job in a research institute but told that I had no chance of a regular job teaching in a university. In Tehran I found some of the friends I had met in Paris, and slowly we allowed people whose sincerity we could trust to join our circle, in which we studied the Koran and the *Sermons* of Ali. On Fridays we would go hiking in this area, and, when we were certain we were alone, one of us would read a sermon by Ali. I assure you, never will you see a Sufi as intoxicated by the poetry of Mowlana as we were with the words of Ali, the Commander of the Faithful. Whether standing with a book, sitting on a ledge, or lying on the rocks, we all shook with feeling.

"One Friday we read the sermon in which Ali says: 'Woe and

sorrow upon you now that you have become the target at which arrows are shot. You are attacked but do not attack. You are assaulted but do not assault. God is being disobeyed and yet you remain content!' We decided the time had come for us to get real weapons, which—gradually, difficult as it was—we did.

"Apparently our judgment about the sincerity of all our members was worthless; we were arrested about three months after this and brought to the Committee prison while you were there. But the elation we had felt every Friday remained with us. I was never tortured, but one of us, the only one who really knew where to get weapons worth anything, was supposed to have died under torture. I am told that he never revealed anything to them.

"After a trial in the Committee prison we were taken to Qasr. Never in Qom, Tehran, or Paris did I learn more than I learned in this prison. It was an amazing prison. You know, we say, 'In no place do things wet and dry burn together as they do in Iran.' Not only were the prisoners strangely assorted but the purposes of the jailors were even more strangely assorted. We had an excellent library, and we were allowed to talk with each other for many hours of the day. As a result the place was a nursery for every revolutionary idea that had ever existed in Iran, and many of us shifted our way through belief in several of these ideas as our terms dragged on. Maybe our jailors didn't care what we thought, since a lot of us were in for life anyway. They undoubtedly hoped that the quarrels between us would weaken the chances that we would cooperate if we were released—and they were partly right. They certainly approached me and almost everyone else in private and offered each of us early release if we became informers.

"There were three groups—really three communes—in Qasr: the mullahs and their followers, the Marxist atheists, and the group I belonged to. Members of our group were far less in agreement than were the members of either of the other groups. Some of my group hardly believed in prayer and prayed along with the mullahs in what was called 'tactical worship.' Many in our group believed that God was the 'prime mover' who put the process called 'dialectical materialism' into the fabric of the universe, after which God had no more need to interfere. They called Islam 'the highest synthesis' of the dialectical process. If I had read all those Marxist books in Paris, I'm sure I could have created a sect all my own.

"People would leave one commune and hardly speak with their former friends. When they left the mullahs' commune and joined the Marxist atheists, or vice versa, they were like the children of one father but different mothers, who have sworn eternal enmity. At least our group was somewhere in between; we talked with both of the other sides. But suspended above all of us, the one light from which we all sought illumination, was the spirit of Ayatollah Taleqani. He had been released before I went to prison, but his lectures on the Koran and the *Sermons* of Ali were in our hands, because some had been printed and many had been taken down in his classes in prison and copied by hand. Even those prisoners who were so proud of their materialistic atheism read his lectures with reverence because they had seen his faithfulness to what he believed through so many periods of exile and imprisonment, his willingness to discuss Islam with everyone and to listen as well as teach, and—most important of all—they had sensed the purity of the man.

"Every day when I prayed as a child and then, later, every day after I started praying again in Paris I had repeated the opening *surah* of the Koran and addressed God as 'Possessor of the Day of Judgment.' But the importance of saying this never came home to me until I heard what Taleqani said about it. He not only said (as I had) that God possessed everything but he explained that God had given back to us a very important thing: freedom to dispose of our actions in any way we wanted. But if we possessed our actions as a gift, God had retained possession of the world in which they took place, so He possessed the consequences of these acts both morally and physically. We can, for example, build an electric generator of our own free will, but we cannot of our own free will choose the laws of electromagnetism, nor can we choose to create the moral law that decides how good or how bad the results of building a generator might be. So our actions exist in two worlds: the world in which God has granted us control so that we can both conceive of actions and then carry them out, and the world that remains in the possession of God, in which world God decides their consequences. How can I tell you the joy with which we all recited this part of the Koran in our prayers after we had read the explanation of Taleqani?

"We had found a spiritual father, and—at least in the group I belonged to—we lived like a family. You remember the nasty spirit in the state school—these microscopes belong to the school, that pen belongs to Ahmad, this desk has been assigned to Parviz, and so on? We finally got rid of it. We shared everything—our food, our possessions, our thoughts. When anyone wrote anything, it was almost impossible to get him to sign his name to it, because if our ideas poured down different channels, they ended in one central pool that was everybody's and nobody's.

"The day before I was released from prison I was deeply depressed at leaving my spiritual family. But I kept repeating to myself 'Father' Taleqani's words: 'My message is shared consultation and martyrdom.' I knew I had to go out to lead other Iranians to take their share in the great consultation that alone could make us a people and reveal to us the true nature of Islam. And I had to go out saying to myself, 'If the occasion arises, I will accept martyrdom.' "

Ali was afraid to disturb the state of near ecstasy Parviz had reached while telling this part of his story. He noticed that Parviz's abstracted look had gradually grown to resemble his old squint as he talked, but the squint no longer made him look even slightly hungry, as it had in the past.

The late-afternoon sun was about to reach the mountains north of them, and they started back. When they came within sight of the parking area they saw that many kebab sellers had appeared, working in the light of their Coleman lanterns, and from a distance the scene looked like a cheerful nighttime street fair. Ali realized they wouldn't have much more time to talk confidentially; he wanted to be brief and he didn't want to argue; he knew how much he valued Parviz's love for him and he didn't want to drive him away.

"I'm glad you have a good opinion of at least one mullah. It's true, he's a saint. He told me that he thought the perfect death would be to die defending someone oppressed. He really is the mullah who would best understand the third part of the vow you made when your mother was sick—that you would devote your life to the people of Iran. And it's also true that he thought that the Islam he had been taught at Qom had too many things woven into it; he thought Islam was something simple, and he would approve of your efforts to discover Islam through reading the Koran, the *Sermons* of Ali, and consulting together. But studying Islam without developing systematic principles for interpreting its sources, whether they be the Koran or the sayings of Imams such as Ali or the basic rules that we use when we think, is to remain at least half ignorant. When I met Taleqani I said to him, 'You are asking people to study the calendar while refusing to let them study astronomy.' Even he grudgingly granted me two or three hundred people a generation to study what we 'ancients' teach at Qom.

"I don't doubt that all property ultimately belongs to God, but why does the Koran specify what share of an estate each relative is entitled to? What do you think will happen when two poor peasants get together to bring an abandoned piece of land into cultivation and then quarrel? Can we assure them that they will have justice and that neither of them will be oppressed if the judgment of their case comes not out of some systematic principles but out of their own reading of the Koran or some national consensus on the meaning of Ali's sermons?"

Parviz looked really delighted that Ali had taken him so seriously. He grabbed Ali's hand again and said: "Dear Ali, I'm much nearer to your fellow mullahs now than I was fifteen years ago, when the Algerian war convinced me you were all a lot of useless mumblers who lived on the backs of people like my parents. I'm not a fool. After all, I do have a French doctorate in mathematics. I've done not badly figuring things out for myself."

They found a share-taxi that was almost full. This time there was no choice—Parviz sat next to a woman in a chador in the front and Ali sat next to a man and a woman (no chador) in the back seat. The taxi driver was playing a tape of his favorite selections of Iranian popular singers. Ali was glad he was not wearing his mullah clothes, in which case, out of respect, the driver would have turned off the radio. Ali, unlike most mullahs, did not disapprove of some forms of popular music; if it was hard to argue that when premodern Persian poets talked about profane love they were always talking about God, it was just as hard to argue that all modern Persian love lyrics were purely sensual. A famous Iranian woman singer sang about moonlight, narcissus eyes, the black eyes of the woman in a white chador, and death "from the never attained happiness of holding your hand near my heart." And Ali felt that her voice and the cheerful three-piece orchestra accompanying her were the appropriate background to the growing stream of light as they descended past dimly lit front gates of the mansions of the wealthy to the busy streets of the center of Tehran, now fully illuminated and crowded with people leaving work for the Friday weekend and shopping on their way home.

Ali could see from Parviz's face that his fellow Qomi, for all his years in Paris, felt the same awe at the bigness, incompleteness, and diversity of Tehran. In Persian a peep-show is called "the city of the Franks," and when they came to the garish movie marquees, in which, thanks to spotlights, the larger-than-life figures painted on the posters now positively looked like members of some alien species, Ali leaned forward and, using a common Persian saying, whispered loudly to Parviz, "This is the city of the Franks where all sorts of things can be found." Everyone in the cab laughed.

The two of them got out at the *montazh* of cabarets, theaters, and shops a few blocks from the statue of the dying reptile. He and Parviz were going in different directions. Parviz asked him, rather shyly, if he would like to join his circle for reading the *Sermons* of Ali. Ali quoted Saadi: " 'Take the ass of Jesus on a pilgrimage and it returns an ass just the same.' I'll just inhibit the discussion. But I'll be offended if you don't come to visit me. My mother sends *sowhan* from Qom practically every week, and I desperately need help finishing it."

Parviz did come from time to time, but except to ask Ali an occasional brief question about Islamic law, he never discussed religion with him again. He occasionally talked about politics but without committing himself strongly to anything except the kind of criticism of the regime that was part of the universal grumbling that was every bit as much the background of Tehran life as was the noise of traffic. Ali knew this caution was partly from habit; Parviz had contacts that he had to protect. But he knew that it was also a suspension of judgment; he sensed a hesitation that seemed to cloud the near ecstasy that Parviz had shown on the day of their hike.

Early in 1976 Parviz came to visit rather late one evening and stayed unusually late into the night. He was in high spirits. He talked a lot about Qom and the Qomi things he missed living in Tehran. He also seemed to be more full of poetry than usual. After this Parviz didn't come at all. Ali asked Parviz's cousin and others about him; he had disappeared. His research institute was sure he had not been arrested. After a few months everyone assumed that he had gone underground.

· · ·

Of all the intellectuals who returned to religion in the sixties and seventies none was more revered by his fellow intellectuals than Jalal Al-e Ahmad. Throughout his life Al-e Ahmad seemed a bellwether figure, a man always ahead of the flock, but he was, in fact, so sensitive to others, so close to their inner feelings, and at the same time so plainly outspoken that he was less a bellwether than the first to say unambiguously and out loud what the flock had already dumbly sensed. And he said it all with a certain toughness and a great deal of self-mockery while betraying that he felt it all with great pain. He said aloud so much that was felt inwardly by so many different Iranians that in the end he seemed intellectually to be a hopelessly confused and self-contradictory man. But whatever he felt he said so well and with such evident fearlessness and honesty that nearly everyone loved to listen. Of all the Iranian writers of the twentieth century he is probably the only one who has been read with the same enthusiasm (if not always approval) by the entire spectrum of Iranian intellectuals, from the Western-educated leftists of Tehran to the older *talabehs* of Qom.

The *talabehs* had reason to think that Al-e Ahmad understood their experience; he had once been one of them. In a fragment of autobiography he wrote: "I grew up in a family of (Shiah-Muslim) clergy. My father, elder brother and the husband of one of my sisters died as clergymen. Now my brother's son and the husband of another sister are clergy. And this is only the beginning of the love affair. As for the rest of it, the entire family are religious—with the odd exception here and there. . . . My childhood passed in one of the sorts of upper-class well-being common to the clergy. That is, until the time when the Ministry of Justice under Davar [Reza Shah's minister, who rewrote the law codes] laid its hand on the registries and my father did not submit to the burden of the government's supervision, with its stick-on stamps and rubber stamps. He closed up shop and was satisfied simply to be the gentleman of the neighborhood."

After Al-e Ahmad finished primary school he was sent to earn a living in the huge bazaar of Tehran, the town of his birth and the scene of most of his life. He also attended the Marvi Madreseh for a religious education (with his father's approval, of course). But without his father's knowledge he attended night classes at the Polytechnic, which, after the founding of the university, was merely a secondary school but one of the best secondary schools in Iran. He describes himself at the time of his high school gradu-ation in 1943 as "a young man with a carnelian ring on his finger, a shaved head, about a meter and eighty centimeters in height, transferred from that religious atmosphere to the hurly-burly of the period of the Second World War. Which, for us, did not have slaughter, ruin and bombardment. But which did have famine, ty-phus, confusion and the tormenting presence of the occupying forces."

He was at that moment hesitating between the two worlds. He set out that summer to study in Beirut, presumably at the Ameri-can University, but on the way, when he stopped in Najaf at his brother's house, he felt the pull of his family tradition of religious learning and stayed for three months. Then, "in something that was virtually a flight," he rushed back to Iran, "turning my back on both my father and brother," since in his future he had seen "a snare in the shape of a cloak and an aba."

Actually he was already on his way to becoming one of the "odd exceptions" in his religious family. "In the last years of upper school," he writes, "I became acquainted with the speech and words of Ahmad Kasravi." This whiff of Kasravi seems to have banished forever the possibility that Al-e Ahmad could ever be religious in a conventional sense. His interest in Kasravi also led him to read the radical magazines that appeared out of no-where in the censor-free no-man's-land of wartime Iran. He was now living in an environment receptive to radical ideas. After his flight from Najaf he had entered the Tehran Teachers College as a literature student, and he always remembered his years there with special affection because of the sense of sharing and camaraderie he enjoyed with the students in his dormitory. He also found companionship in the Reform Society, a group that like-minded intellectuals had founded in 1941, and for this society he wrote a wall newspaper and taught free classes in Arabic. Like Kasravi, he found his *madreseh* training had left him at least one thing of value: he knew Arabic well, and he even used his Arabic to translate a book critical of the *taaziyeh* and similar practices (the entire edition of which was bought and burned by someone in the bazaar). These were years, he wrote, "when political parties grew like mushrooms," and after he and other members of the Reform Society had taken turns attending meetings of all the available parties, they chose to join the Iranian Communist party.

In 1946, when he graduated from Teachers College and became a teacher, his sharp break with his family had thrown him completely on his own resources, and he owned almost nothing except one necktie and one secondhand American suit. From this time on and throughout his life he felt a longing for a vanished sense of family. Rediscovering such things in the Iranian Communist party was not easy. What he did find was an intellectual father among its members—Khalil Maleki, a German-educated social democrat who was one of four dozen Marxists imprisoned by Reza Shah in a roundup of radicals in 1937 (most of whom were released on the shah's abdication in 1941).

Twenty years after meeting him Al-e Ahmad wrote: "I don't know why, but I know there is something which attracts me to Maleki. Because he has always been suppressed? Or is it because of his sternness and intransigeance? And, of course, he could have been my father, both from the point of view of age and personality. Perhaps I've made him a substitute for my real father. . . . Yet I don't see in Maleki a father or a hero, but a representative of intellectualism left over from the previous generation, a man who has neither submitted to the evils of cooperation with these governments, nor surrendered to silence in the face of exploiters."

Al-e Ahmad's obvious talents almost immediately won him a

place on the party's Tehran Provincial Committee and an important role in supervising party publications. The Iranian Communist party was at the height of its influence. Few significant young intellectuals dared oppose it even if they did not join. While the party's membership remained small, it had organized successful strikes in factories and was trying to organize those who worked on the oil fields, the government's most valuable property.

Al-e Ahmad and Maleki, however, were too independent for the party. They wanted more democracy in the choice of party leadership and a less nakedly pro-Soviet party program. In particular, Maleki was offended that the party had both supported a Soviet demand for oil concessions and defended the continued presence of Russian troops in the Iranian province of Azerbaijan. Maleki led a number of intellectuals, including Al-e Ahmad, out of the party. In January 1948 they founded the Socialist Society of the Iranian Masses, but a few days later, when Radio Moscow attacked them, the new organization obediently self-destructed; they were unwilling publicly to oppose what they considered the world's most progressive nation. For the national goals of the Iranian Communist party this withdrawal of a few timid intellectuals had no importance, but for other Iranian intellectuals it was a momentous event: it marked the end of the near hegemony of the party over intellectual life.

The shock of Al-e Ahmad's rapid entrance into and exit from the party set him on a road that became clearer as time passed; increasingly he saw himself as a cultural critic and not as a politician. He taught, he translated, and he traveled extensively in Iran. In 1948, on a bus from Shiraz to Tehran, he met his future wife, a talented writer from a wealthy Shiraz family. And also he wrote fiction. In fact, after the publication of three volumes of short stories between 1945 and 1948 he was generally considered the most original writer of Persian short stories to emerge after the Second World War.

His originality lay both in his approach to his subjects and in his style. His stories present themselves as fragments of autobiography (which many of them seem, in fact, to have been), and the narrator of the autobiography usually examines the events of his life with the unforced and yet unmistakable alternation of moods of one who sometimes feels deeply inside the events he describes and sometimes sees them from the outside. His style, which matured only in the fifties, displays both moods: emotional inwardness and distance. It is a style that often succeeds in displaying these moods simultaneously and not in alternation because it is the style of a man who feels deeply but speaks from a certain ironical distance from his own and others' feelings. It is a wonderfully dense style and entirely new in Persian literature.

Traditionally, Persian literature had achieved its rich density through its weight of allusions, its many oblique and overt references to the poems of Hafez, Mowlana, and comparable works of literature in the vast treasure of memory that an educated Iranian carried with him. Writers before Al-e Ahmad had reacted against this weight of allusion; Kasravi, for example, tried to write in a stripped, "pure" style (for which, with characterisic obsessiveness, he created words more "pure" than those already extant in Persian and was consequently obliged to attach glossaries to his books).

Al-e Ahmad knew classical Persian extremely well and very occasionally alludes to it, but his allusions are overwhelmingly to the living speech of Iranians, and they evoke the entire spectrum of the spoken Persian of Tehran, from the argot of the streets to the euphemisms of the educated. His allusions are presented in the most condensed form possible: he uses just enough words from the idioms and proverbs that shape his every sentence to enable an Iranian to make out what he is alluding to. Consequently the Iranian reader feels that he fully understands Al-e Ahmad precisely because he fully shares Al-e Ahmad's rich experience of living Persian; in this sense, Al-e Ahmad establishes a barely noticed sense of collusion between author and reader. Yet it is collusion with an author who speaks with self-deprecation and frequent touches of irony. Between the almost telegraphic sentences the author seems to raise his hands as if to say, "After all, you know the sort of person I'm talking about, and you know the sort of fellow I am." Under this highly condensed style of short, very idiomatic sentences there is evidence of an enormous emotional energy which the condensation of speech and self-mockery are trying to control, energy that sometimes transforms itself into anger and sometimes into euphoria.

In one of Al-e Ahmad's first short stories, "The Pilgrimage," published in 1945, well before his literary style had matured, he has already mastered this skill of presenting a narrator who seems at some times to share deeply and unselfconsciously the emotions of those around him and at others to feel himself an outsider watching those around him from an uncomfortable distance. The story (which also establishes collusion with its Iranian reader by the wide knowledge of religious folk custom it assumes) begins: "Three times I passed underneath the Koran, the water and the flour, and three times I kissed the Koran and laid it against my forehead. My relatives, breathing out their prayers and holy phrases, filled the air with an odor of mosque and sanctuary—a sanctuary from which only the smell of burning fat and the sharp tang of tallow candles were missing. Then amid the tears which streamed from the eyes of my two sisters and my younger brother I went out of the house." Outside the house, as others ask the narrator to pray for them and weep from religious feeling, the narrator suddenly feels very close to them: "Until this day . . . I had not known that this language I have in my heart is a sort of melancholy which visits everyone." In the bus on the way to the shrine towns in Iraq his slight feeling of distance from the simpleness of his fellow passengers disappears before the genuineness and depth of their emotion at going to "the holiest of places on earth." At the shrine itself he shares the emotion of the other pilgrims but can't fully make sense of it:

> Once again I fixed my gaze on the tomb and the precious stone inside the lattice of the sepulcher, and once again the hidden desires in the core of my heart stirred and boiled, and came forth in a long-drawn sigh. I don't know exactly what it was I wanted, what my need was . . . The smell of cheap cigarettes, the breath of the thousands of pilgrims passing in and out of the crowd mingled with the smell of their perspiring bodies and filled the air with a peculiar and noxious odor, which was softened by the smoke from the twigs of aloe-wood, slowly burning in every corner. Words from the Koran echoed and re-echoed beneath the lofty domes. Those Arabic words poured out like rain and charged the whole place with holiness. On doors and walls, on the friezes, on the glasswork of the ceiling which reflected in countless broken fragments the images of that vast crowd, on the fronts and backs of

Holy Books, on the prayer books in men's hands, on the threshold of the sepulcher and all around it, on the great silver padlocks of the shrine—everywhere those Arabic words were inscribed in thousands of designs and figures and scrolls, on wood and tile, on brick, on silver, on gold: everything was absorbed by their power. God knows how many years these words have been there, looking at all these hurriedly passing by, and not batting an eyelash in concern.

By now the narrator has understood that he is involved in the pilgrimage in a different way from the people around him: "Everyone was in a special state, and no one there was a spectator except me." Then, as he watches the corpses of the faithful being carried around the sepulcher in a farewell pilgrimage before burial, the narrator is drawn back from his distance. He feels in his heart that to hope for anything else for himself at the time of his own death is just not possible: "How much I long that I, too, when I die, may be treated in this way. Honestly, provided that assurance, a human being need never again fear death."

Al-e Ahmad flirted briefly with party politics again during the fifties, but the more deeply he got involved, the less his heart was in it. At first the thrill of Mossadegh's presence revived hopes he had set aside in 1948. In 1950 and 1951 he joined his intellectual father, Maleki, in organizing the Toilers' party, the basic program of which was to support Mossadegh (who, however, did not believe that political parties could be effective in Iran and was uninterested in forming his own party). Then, when this party split, Al-e Ahmad joined the faction around Maleki, which, in 1952, formed a new party called the Third Force. But Al-e Ahmad could no longer really believe that anyone was going to change anything significant by forming political parties.

Early in 1953, when he went with a group of friends to protect Mossadegh from an attack by Royalists (which failed), as the bus stopped near Mossadegh's house "and their 'excellencies,' [his friends] looking so 'terrifying,' had got out on foot, I turned to Sayyed [Javadi, another prominent writer] and said: 'Are you in the mood for a beer in place of these ceremonies?' He was ready. And we went. For me, being near power never cast its appropriate charm." In the events of this period Al-e Ahmad's movement toward political commitment, then sudden withdrawal, proved characteristic not only of Al-e Ahmad but of a great many of his fellow intellectuals. Deep down so many of them did not really believe any political movement would work—or, if it did work, would make any difference.

Then, after fighting the central committee of the Third Force over the expulsion of one of his close friends, Al-e Ahmad withdrew from party activity. A few months later Mossadegh was overthrown in the coup of August 1953. Maleki was arrested and imprisoned for several years, but Al-e Ahmad had so completely lost faith in party politics that—to the shock of the many intellectuals who held out—he joined those many others who succumbed to pressure from the regime and published a letter of "repentance" in a newspaper: "I hereby declare that I have resigned from the Third Force, and have, moreover, completely abandoned politics."

Although Al-e Ahmad remained friends with political activists, especially the circle of Maleki, he now turned entirely to the great subject of his life, the politics of culture, and to this subject he devoted much of the fiction and virtually all of the essays that he subsequently wrote. He wanted to renew his ties with the soil of Iran and the people who lived on it in order to restore himself after his disillusionment with politics. Although he remained a schoolteacher in Tehran, he spent a great deal of time over the next seven years in the countryside gathering material for three books and several essays on the world of Iranian villagers. He knew that his work was anthropologically naïve, and he called these books merely "observations." But he also knew that in the hearts of many Tehranis there was an uneasy feeling that, while they were trying to determine the fate of Iran in the fever of coup and countercoup in the capital, the real Iran might be "out there" in the tens of thousands of villages, neglected, quietly suffering, not yet seduced by a thousand foreign objects and ideas, still somehow genuinely and unembarrassedly Iranian. He spoke to their unease, and they listened.

His first subject of study was the village Owrazan, from which his ancestors had come, and the first sentence of his book on Owrazan announced his program for the whole series: "Even though, according to the present custom, politics, culture and press of our nation, a single village is in no way of the slightest account, nevertheless the essential kernel of the social organization of this land and the essential arena for any judgment concerning its civilization is, in any case, precisely these scattered villages . . ." This northern village of a few hundreds is, he says, "like thousands of other villages of Iran where the soil is ploughed and a quarrel about the division of water is always in progress; whose inhabitants rarely take a bath and drink their tea with raisins and dates." It is a village that "is not only unaware of primary schools, police stations and public health but most of whose inhabitants still light their pipes with flint and touchwood."

Al-e Ahmad also had a personal connection with the second area, Boluk-e-Zahra, where he studied two villages. His book on this area (like Owrazan, in northern Iran) begins: "When I was still very little one of my sisters (the eldest) was given to a husband who was a *talabeh* of religious learning in Qom; and it had been decided that he would soon take his father's place as the mullah of the villages of Boluk-e-Zahra." The second monograph, like the first, contained careful descriptions of agriculture, dwellings, marriage and burial customs, dialectology, and the like, but the second book was more frankly sentimental. In the preface, after explaining the happiness that thinking back to Boluk-e-Zahra in the time of his youth could bring him, he suggests that writing the book may purge him of memories that occupy him too obsessively: "When you have stepped out of your youth how much you need such mental housecleaning!"

The mental housecleaning seems to have worked to some good effect. By the time Al-e Ahmad published his third monograph and some ethnographic essays on rural Iran in the early 1960s, he was somewhat clearer as to what things he missed in contemporary Iranian society and why they were missing. In a way Al-e Ahmad's personal sense of the loss of family, created by his break with his father and nurtured by his grief at his own childlessness, had allowed him to develop a general critique of the Iranian society he lived in, its selfishness and its lack of emotional and moral authenticity. He had seen glimpses of the world of material

and emotional sharing that he yearned for—in the dormitory of
the Teachers College, for example, in an Israeli kibbutz in which
he had worked in the mid-sixties, and, above all, in the village life
of Iran, insofar as it had survived untainted by the cultural "illness" that had stricken the towns and cities of Iran.

For this illness Al-e Ahmad seized on a newly coined word, and
he made this word a rallying cry for Iranians from the sixties to
the present. The word translated literally, piece by piece, is
"West-stricken-ness," but even this clumsy translation fails to
convey the sense of the Persian original, *gharbzadegi.* "I say that
gharbzadegi," he writes, "is like cholera [or] frostbite. But no. It's at
least as bad as sawflies in the wheat fields. Have you ever seen
how they infest wheat? From within. There's a healthy skin in
places, but it's only a skin, just like the shell of a cicada on a tree."
To be "stricken" in Persian means not only to be afflicted with a
disease or to be stung by an insect but it also means to be infatuated and bedazzled; "West-stricken-ness," therefore, has sometimes been translated as "Westoxication." But a less outlandish
word, "Euromania," captures enough of the sense of the Persian
to be a passable stand-in for the nearly untranslatable Persian
original.

It is significant that Al-e Ahmad's major book on the subject,
entitled *Euromania,* started as a series of talks to the Council on the
Aims of Iranian Education in 1962. Al-e Ahmad had always taken
his role as a teacher seriously and regarded education as a primary cause for the dislocation Iranians had suffered from the
original values of their culture. Al-e Ahmad criticized modern Iranian education in his books of essays and in *Euromania,* but his
most powerful criticism was his portrayal of an Iranian school in a
semiautobiographical novella he published in 1958 under the title
The School Principal. Al-e Ahmad had himself been a principal of
an elementary school for the academic year 1955–56, and although the book was influenced by Céline's *Voyage au bout de la
nuit* and is about many things besides education, it is nevertheless
a more or less accurate account of his experiences as a principal in
that year. Wherever its inspiration came from, it is a stunning example of Al-e Ahmad's mature style—pithy, idiomatic, with lightning changes of registers and emotional lurches toward and away
from the subjects it describes. Like so much of Al-e Ahmad's

work, it often seems too raw and too chaotic, but it was so true to the experience of so many Iranians that it was enormously successful, perhaps the most successful novella of the postwar period, and its prose style (virtually impossible to translate) was imitated by a whole generation of young Iranian writers.

The narrator decides to become a school principal because he is disgusted with teaching Persian literature in the way that the Ministry of Education has prescribed: "Ten years teaching the alphabet; the stupefied faces of the children at the silliest rubbish you can imagine . . . the Khorasani and Indian styles of [Persian] poetry and the oldest Persian poem; literary devices like proverbs and anadiplosis . . ." But slowly he realizes that the school is run with total disregard for the world from which the children come. When rain turns the playground into a muddy morass, absenteeism increases tenfold, and the narrator comments: "Before this I had read lots of rubbish about what the basis of education is: teachers, blackboard cleaners, proper toilets, or a thousand other things. But here, quite simply and primarily, the basis of education was shoes."

At one point the principal looks at the projects (cardboard cupboards, doll furniture, a miniature Eiffel Tower) in the handicrafts class, a new addition to the curriculum in belated acknowledgment of the need for hands-on education that Isa Sadiq had preached over a generation before.

> How many jigsaws had been used up to produce this worthless junk? How many cut hands? What money has been taken out of the pockets of the fathers, and what quarrels at home—and for what? . . . We import jigsaws by the donkey load, along with safety pins, porcelain toilets, water piping, enema pumps, and thousands of other pieces of junk. One person in a thousand opens a frame-making shop or an inlay shop [to use his jigsaw craft] or swaps his jigsaw for a hacksaw . . . God bless the father of this education with its handicraft system so successful in increasing the number of sidewalk ice-sellers, its grades in deportment, its left-face right-face march, and its [demand for the memorization of the] borders, lakes and exports of Ethiopia . . .

Al-e Ahmad described *The School Principal* as "an eternal curse, a spit on this age," and the force of that curse is the raw energy that made his *Euromania*, and the satellite essays and short stories that revolve around it, so powerful, in spite of the confused and self-contradictory terms in which the argument is presented. Satan is the machine, the instrument of power in the hands of the industrialized countries that used machines to produce finished goods. When grafted onto unindustrialized countries, the machine enslaved them with new dependence on the makers, maintainers, and culture of the machine. "The soul of this devil 'the machine' [must be] bottled up and brought out at our disposal . . . [The Iranian people] must not be at the service of machines, trapped by them, since the machine is a means not an end."

The machine is partly responsible for turning Iran into an unproductive consumption economy. "These cities are just flea markets hawking European manufactured goods . . . [In] no time at all instead of cities and villages we'll have heaps of dilapidated machines all over the country, all of them exactly like American 'junkyards,' and every one as big as Tehran." (To drive his point home Al-e Ahmad gives a phonetic rendering of the English word "junkyard" in Persian.)

The machine had created an all-embracing world market, after which—said Al-e Ahmad—Marxist class analysis no longer explained much, for now the world was divided into the poor and the rich, "one the constructors [of machines] and the other the consumers." The appetites created by this consumption economy have gripped the townspeople throughout Iran; the towns "day by day demand more Western goods as fodder, and day by day they become more homogeneous in decline, rootlessness and ugliness." "Lacking social services, empty of libraries and of centers for social life," these towns are stripped of significant communal buildings and have only "ruined mosques, the strewn remnants of Hosainiyehs, and *taaziyeh* theaters that have become meaningless."

To Al-e Ahmad enslavement by the machine and by the market found its final and most repugnant form in the spiritual enslavement of Iranians to the alien gods that Euromania had injected into the Iranian imagination. With the economic disruption of traditional rural life and the spread of the transistor radio, the disease of Euromania, with all its feverish delusions and fanciful cravings, was no longer an exclusive possession of the large cities. Now the disease had infected every sort of Iranian, from "the villager who has fled to the city and won't ever return to the village because in the village the door-to-door barber doesn't stock brilliantine and because in the village there's no cinema and you can't buy a sandwich, to the fussy minister in the national government who has a sensitivity to earth and dust (an 'allergy'!) and roams the four corners of the earth all twelve months of the year [in search of relief]." Since nothing has any deep resonance in the Euromaniac, neither the tradition of his own culture nor his adopted Western culture, "he has no personality—he is an object with no authentic origin. Neither he, nor his home, nor what he has to say gives off any kind of odor . . . He has only fear . . . fear of the revelation that the bladder which, by way of a brain weighs down his head, is empty." Such a person acts out his Euromania with a belief in and loyalty to the principle of imitation and not to the things he does. Give him money and the Euromaniac's house "one day resembles a villa by the sea, with huge picture windows and fluorescent lights. Another day it looks like a cabaret, sparkling, shining, and full of bar stools. On yet another all the walls are the same background of multicolored triangles."

In one of his rare direct allusions to classical Persian literature Al-e Ahmad compares Iranians to the crow in a well known story in Mowlana's long Sufi epic. In this story the crow sees a partridge walk by and is amazed at the measured elegance of the partridge's gait. After long and painstaking practice the crow forgets how to walk like a crow but never learns how to walk like a partridge. "For two hundred years we've been like a crow who tries to be a partridge (if we can be sure which is the crow and which the partridge)."

As early as his first version of *Euromania* in 1962, and increasingly in later versions of this book and in the other books and essays of the sixties, Al-e Ahmad identifies one strand of Iranian life that has survived undiseased: religion. The sometime admirer of Kasravi, who in 1943 had fled Najaf because he had seen a snare in his future in the shape of a mullah's cloak, had slowly sorted through the heavy freight of ideas he had picked up over the years and found that none of it had the same weight of "authenticity" as Shiah Islam. And above all, none of it had the ability to move people that Shiah Islam had. He himself could never become fully committed to religion; but he recognized that religion was the only element in Iranian life that could call forth total commitment on the part of the majority of Iranians. Al-e Ahmad never threw all the cargo of his irreligious years overboard; he was an extremely honest man and he knew that he had been practicing the partridge strut too long to feel at home with the gait of a crow. Besides, for all his increasing admiration for mullahs, he also continued to express his dislike for what he considered to be their rigidity and superstition. Nevertheless he felt some of them were "authentic" intellectuals in a way that only a handful of "educated" Tehranis were either authentic or intellectual. He wanted to reach out to them, and he wanted to understand why, when he spoke as a Shiah Muslim, he had the sudden comfortable feeling of wearing his own skin.

Despite his break with his father and his long-term commitment to Marxism, religion probably never ceased to play an important role in Al-e Ahmad's imagination; it certainly plays an important role in the imagination of the characters of his early short stories. His experience in the Iranian countryside in his "anthropological" years confirmed the experience of his youth (on which he drew in so many of his stories throughout his career). Religion might for the moment make only a modest appearance in the "reception room" of Iranian life, but in the private quarters it reigned with its old vigor and intensity, particularly among those Iranians the government least noticed:

> At present, 90 percent of the people in this country live by religious values and criteria . . . Inevitably, they search in the sky for the good fortune they have not found in the present, just as they search in religion and the hereafter; and so much the better for them. Sometimes they even drink arrack; but they wash out their mouths with water, stand to pray and repent in the month of Ramazan—and they even offer a sacrifice at the shrine of Davud, a descendant of the Imams. Our villager, as soon as he gets a ten-seed return on the seven seeds he planted, will grab his wife and children and go on pilgrimage to Mashhad or at least to Qom . . . And all of us are waiting for the Imam of the Age. I mean we are *all*

waiting, and rightly so, because no ephemeral government has come through on the least of its promises and undertakings, and because oppression is everywhere, along with injustice, suffocation and discrimination. . . . These are the reasons why all religious structures all the way from the drinking place in the passageway [that was built with a religious endowment] and the small mosque at the end of the alley to the shrine outside of the village are covered with all variety of demonstrations of this non-confidence in the government and its works. They are filled with signs of anticipation of the advent of the promised messiah, His Excellency, the Lord of the Age, of whom we truly pray: God Almighty hasten his advent!

Such religious fervor might seem strange in a man who drank and who seldom performed his obligatory prayers. But Al-e Ahmad was no sham. He knew he couldn't fully believe, but he also knew that to him very little else seemed worthy of real belief. He was conscious that he, personally, was suspended between what was for him intellectually acceptable and what was "believable," and his struggle to be honest about it shocked as often as it disarmed his critics. In an interview with some university students he was asked if he believed in evolution or creationism, to which he answered: "Between the two—that is, between the supposition or speculation [of evolution] and the story [of creation]—I like the story. Why? Because it is poetry. And the basis for poetry. You know best for yourself. Accept whichever version you like . . . I'm from the race of Adam. Who was created from earth, and God breathed into him so that he got up on his feet and stood upright." (At which point a number of those present said "Not acceptable.")

Al-e Ahmad also believed that, historically, the intellectuals had been politically successful only when they had taken the religious authorities as allies: in the resistance to the tobacco concession, the Constitutional Revolution, the rise of Reza Shah, and the struggle led by Mossadegh to nationalize Iran's oil. Al-e Ahmad even defended the conservative (most Iranian constitutionalists would say "reactionary") jurisconsult Sheikh Fazlollah Nuri, who had attacked both parliamentarianism and any accommodation of secular ideas. Fazlollah, he writes, was "martyred because of his advocacy of a government based on the sacred law of Islam—and,

I might add, because of his advocacy of the whole idea of Shiah Islam . . . To me, the corpse of that great man hanging on the gallows is like a flag they raised over this country . . . to symbolize the ascendancy of Euromania. Now, in the shadow of that flag, we're like a nation alienated from itself, in our clothing and our homes, our food and our literature, our publications, and, most dangerously of all, our education. We affect Western training, we affect Western thinking, and we follow Western procedures to solve every problem."

If Al-e Ahmad reached out with one hand to the religious authorities as fellow intellectuals (second in their "intellectuality," he says, to only a handful of Iranian writers, inventors, and scholars), he used his other hand to hold them at arm's length. Al-e Ahmad was nobody's man, not the Communists', not the social democrats', not the clergy's. In *Euromania*, for all his praise of Shiah Islam, he wrote: "The religious establishment, with all its institutions and customs, leans on superstitions as much as it can. It seeks refuge in times long past and outdated ceremonies and is satisfied to be the gatekeeper at the graveyard." In another book, after arguing at length that *madreseh* education is a source of intellectuality, he feels compelled to explain why an intellectual who has grown up in a clergyman's family can sometimes become as insistent on his Europeanized style of intellectuality as a clergyman can be about the details of religion.

> . . . in a clerical family, the children are just the ones who have firsthand experience of the fanaticism, crudeness and ossification of the clergy, or sometimes, of their narrow-mindedness and hypocrisy behind a facade of spirituality . . . I myself, the writer of these words, was declared "irreligious" in my clerical household, at that very time when I no longer placed the clay tablet [of earth from Kerbela, the scene of Hosain's martyrdom] under my forehead during prayer, on the basis of my own opinion that—were I to do so—I would be engaged in some sort of worship of an "idol" by virtue of praying over a clay tablet. But in my father's opinion it was the beginning of "irreligion." Rest assured that when [the charge of] "irreligion" comes so easily to hand, then anyone from the race of Adam, with this experience already behind him, claims for himself the right to push on to the end.

As this passage shows, Al-e Ahmad was always aware that the psychological seeds of his distrust of "official" Shiah Islam lay in his break with his father. As the bitter taste of that break faded, he came increasingly to hope that he could accommodate the strongly religious component in his own identity and—at the same time—could bring the religious and leftist opponents of the government to cooperate. In about 1960 his father became seriously ill and eventually was paralyzed. Al-e Ahmad went to visit him in Qom, and they were reconciled; in 1962 his father died. When Khomeini arranged a memorial service in Qom, Al-e Ahmad attended and after the service visited Khomeini to thank him. Khomeini is supposed to have told Al-e Ahmad that he had read *Euromania* and admired it. (The book undoubtedly had an enormous vogue in Qom from the time of its publication.) In any case it is certain that Al-e Ahmad was electrified by the rising of March 1963, in which Khomeini was the leading figure. Al-e Ahmad is also supposed to have visited Khomeini when the ayatollah was under house arrest in Tehran before his exile in 1964, and is supposed to have said to him while shaking his hand, "If we continue to join hands we will defeat the government." Those who told the story believed it was emblematic of the growing alliance of one wing of intellectuals with religious leaders.

In 1964 Al-e Ahmad went on the pilgrimage to Mecca. It was an act completely in the style of the later Al-e Ahmad. It was an act of "commitment," of "engagement"; it was not for nothing that Al-e Ahmad was the author of several fluent (if not always accurate) translations of Camus and Sartre. It was an act of defiance to the secular intellectual who would "turn up his nose and gather up his skirt [and say:] 'A trip for the pilgrimage [to Mecca]? Can there be such a shortage of places [to go]?' " It was an act of family piety. His brother had died in Medina, where he had been the representative of Ayatollah Borujerdi and the spiritual leader of the Shiah community. It was an act of self-discovery. Having decided that, at bottom, his cultural identity lay in two things, the Persian language and Shi'ism, he wanted to test the religious half of his identity on the sounding board of his soul and, in the Al-e Ahmad manner, to hear inwardly what rang true and what false.

On the plane to Saudi Arabia he noticed that some of the crew that were taking him for his pilgrimage were "Lebanese Armenian Arabs." After which he asked himself: "And who are you? I remember in the morning in the pilgrim's area of the Tehran airport I said my prayers. After I don't know how many years. No doubt since abandoning prayer in the first year of university. . . . But the truth is now I no longer have the disposition for it. I feel it's hypocrisy. That is, it doesn't come out right. Even if it isn't hypocrisy it isn't belief. It's just to be part of the crowd."

This desire to be part of the crowd becomes the most important spiritual element of the pilgrimage for him, and correspondingly the element of Islam that the pilgrimage allowed him to take away as his own. He is aware of the divisions among the pilgrims, even among his fellow Iranians. He notices that one mullah and his followers who are staying in the same house in Mecca have become a tight group. "They have gone upstairs and we constantly hear their calls to prayer and *rowzehs* and mournful elegies. And we, who are not so rigorous, and don't consider ourselves in such need of *akhunds* and mullahs are on the middle floor." (The women were crowded together on the lower floor.) But he is also thrillingly aware of the power of abstraction inherent in the pilgrimage—one of the religiously "appointed times" in the life of a Muslim—and of the way that the individual Muslim on pilgrimage, abstracted from all divisive coloring of group, was supposed ultimately to encounter himself.

He arrived in Mecca at four-thirty in the morning, and, he says, as he waited for daylight, "Whatever poetry I knew by heart I recited . . . and looked as minutely into myself as I could until dawn. And what I saw was only a 'bit of straw' that had come to the 'appointed time,' and not a 'person' that has come to the 'appointed meeting.' And I say that 'time' was eternity, that is, it was the ocean of time; and the 'appointed time' was in each second, and every place, and only with oneself."

Even this expectation of absorption into the mass of believers is sometimes fulfilled, sometimes betrayed. Circumambulating the Kaaba, the holiest shrine of the Islamic world and the focus of the pilgrimage, he had one of those glimpses of the seamless community of shared experience that he had longed for throughout his life: "to go in one direction shoulder to shoulder with others, individually and collectively, around a single thing. That is, there's an objective and a system. You're a particle within a ray moving around a center. And, thus, attached, not released. More important, there are no encounters. You're shoulder to shoulder with others and not face-to-face. You see self-abandon only in the rapid movement of the people's bodies or hear it in what they say."

In contrast, in the second ceremony, in which the pilgrim alternately walks and runs several times between two small hills in Mecca, Al-e Ahmad saw the kind of self-abandon that was for him the most frightening face of religion. "The loud mumbling . . . the self-abandon. . . . Can you keep your wits in the middle of such self-abandon? And act as an individual? Have you ever been caught in the midst of a terrified crowd, fleeing from something? Read 'self-abandon' for 'terrified.' . . . Whatever they are, they don't seem to be human beings to whom one could turn for help." And yet, later in the day, at the sunset prayer, he had again experienced what was for him the greatest miracle: that the concerted behavior of people who shared a belief seemed meaningful in a way that individual behavior could not be. "I began my prostrations. By the time I raised my head again the entire population of the mosque [that surrounds the Kaaba] was lined up, from one end of the porticoes and rooftops to the other. The greatest assembly of human beings under this sky who came together in one place in response to a command. And, after all, there must be some meaning to this gathering."

Much of Al-e Ahmad's social, cultural, and religious analysis has a familiar ring. A painfully honest man, he never sought to disguise his sources. He was deeply interested in the West's view of itself and of the East. His pilgrim's journal has a few references to the well-loved theme of the pilgrimage in Persian literature but also includes references to the pilgrimage of Malcolm X and to the Arabian journey of the French author Paul Nizan, who had been greatly admired by Sartre. Al-e Ahmad acknowledges the influence of an Iranian professor of philosophy who invented the Persian term for Euromania to explain the relevance of an idea in Heidegger to the Iranian situation. Throughout his writings he draws extensively on the West's criticism of itself. For example, in

1953 a work by the Hungarian Tibor Mende was translated into Persian by Khalil Maleki, Al-e Ahmad's intellectual hero, and Al-e Ahmad, with a limited but orthodox Marxist-Leninist background, found in Mende's division of the world into the industrialized and the nonindustrialized one of the roots of his own division of the world into the masters and the servants of the machine.

Yet for all his western European sources of inspiration, to us Al-e Ahmad's critique has a familiar ring for another reason: it sounds Russian. It is close to a voice most recently made familiar to us by Solzhenitsyn when he spoke at the three hundred and twenty-seventh commencement exercises at Harvard:

> [The] persisting blindness of superiority continues to hold the belief that all the vast regions of the globe should develop and mature to the level of contemporary Western systems, the best in theory and the most attractive in practice; that all those other worlds are but temporarily prevented (by wicked leaders or by severe crises or by their own barbarity and incomprehension) from pursuing Western pluralistic democracy and adopting the Western way of life. Countries are judged on the merit of their progress in that direction. But in fact such a conception is a fruit of Western incomprehension of the essence of other worlds, a result of mistakenly measuring them all with a Western yardstick.

Solzhenitsyn is, of course, the heir of the nineteenth-century Slavophiles whose voices we hear in many Russian novels of that period. And, in fact, Al-e Ahmad's life in a loose way resembles the movement of the life of Nikolai Gogol, who moved in the late 1840s from gently satiric descriptions of petty bureaucrats to social criticism mixed with passionate praise of the Russian Orthodox Church, which, he said, "like a chaste virgin, has uniquely preserved itself—as though sent directly from Heaven for the Russian people ..." For Gogol the church was the deepest element of Russian identity and its ultimate arbiter: "In my opinion, it is folly to introduce any innovation into Russia outside our Church without obtaining its blessing. It would be even absurd to inoculate our thought with any kind of European ideas, so long as it has not baptized them with the light of Christ." Even the populism of Al-e Ahmad is fully developed in his Russian predecessors. The mouthpiece of Turgenev (who despised the Slavophiles) in his novella *Smoke* says: "If I were a painter I would paint this picture: an educated man standing before a peasant and bowing low to him. 'Cure me,' he is saying, 'little father peasant, I am perishing with disease.' And the peasant, in his turn, bows low to the educated man. 'Teach me,' he is saying, 'little father and master, I am perishing of ignorance.' "

Al-e Ahmad almost certainly did not know he had Russian predecessors. Although he translated Dostoevski's *The Gambler* from French into Persian in 1948, he does not seem (to his loss) to have been interested in Dostoevski's complicated relation to the belief of the Slavophiles or to religious belief in general. And after 1948 Al-e Ahmad was far more interested in French than any other foreign literature. At any rate, Al-e Ahmad was an original: everything he did had the stamp of his Iranian circumstances and his character on it, a character that came through in the pungency and freshness of his style.

Unlike *The School Principal*, which met with almost universal admiration, *Euromania* met with much severe criticism. Yet, even though *Euromania* is self-contradictory (its author declares the victory of the machine "inevitable" at the start of the book and proceeds to disagree with this conclusion in subsequent passages), and even though it is laced with wild historical fantasies (he sees the flight from "Mother India" as the origin of Euromania), it was a book on which every intelligent Iranian had an opinion; it struck a nerve. It did so partly because of the author's evident sincerity and commitment to what he was doing, but it did so even more because it spoke so directly about changes that Iranians were only just beginning to sense around them.

One change was the confusion and increasing lack of self-belief on the part of the left after the collapse of Mossadegh's government. To an outside observer the Iranian left in the late fifties and the sixties seemed very much alive—it captured the allegiance of Iranian students in Europe and America far more than any ideological movement, and both SAVAK and the CIA watched it with great apprehension. But in Iran itself, though the left was still significant, it gradually lost the central position it had held from 1943 to 1953. Every division in the Communist world, from the birth of Maoism on, was repeated tenfold in the Iranian left, whose penchant for sectarian purity sometimes resembled a similar penchant among the endlessly self-dividing communities of early Shiah Muslims. It was precisely his distaste for this sectarianism that had driven Al-e Ahmad out of politics altogether.

Al-e Ahmad was also one of the first Iranians to sense and express an even deeper weakness of the Iranian left: its distance from the masses. It might be a very fine thing for the left to dominate the intellectual *dowrehs* in Tehran, but when push had come to shove and the ayatollahs Kashani and Behbahani had come out against Mossadegh, the religious leaders were able to deliver the crowd. The mullahs proved this all over again with compound interest when in 1963 Khomeini and a few other ayatollahs mounted the first significant nationwide rebellion against the government since 1953. The left criticized itself for its inability to move the masses in the way that religion did; it never found a solution.

The left's own basis of power in the oil fields and the factories gradually melted away, in part because of government suppression but also in part because the government began to deliver some of the things that the left had said only a leftist government could deliver: job security and a more or less continual rise in real income. The Workers' Profit Sharing Law of 1963 in effect guaranteed the workers in large factories at least a month's annual bonus, and the Ministry of Labor fought effectively for their job security. For the left, however, the greatest ideological confusion was sown by the Land Reform Law of 1962, at which time 56 percent of the land was in the hands of 1 percent of the population. Land reform began in earnest immediately after the "troubles" of 1963, and when the shah (at first uncertain) became aware of the immediate demand by the peasants for its implementation, he saw to it that it was, in fact, implemented.

In he first edition of *Euromania*, in 1962, Al-e Ahmad could speak with accuracy of the 90 percent of the Iranian population in the forgotten villages and tents of the farmer and pastoralist. However, by the time of his later edition (and his writings of the later sixties in general) the countryside was no longer ignored, and he explicitly attacks land reform, as did many of the intellectuals. Some of these attacks were on target: land reform allowed a single owner to hold as much as a single village; in some places it destroyed ancient systems of cooperation (often, in effect, land and labor cooperatives based on local customary law) among peasants; and in some places it created a class of "kulaks," big peasant holders, who could be even more vicious and exploitive to small peasants than the big owners had been. But many of the attacks on land reform show a desperate need to find fault; the left had called for land reform for over twenty years, and the government—however imperfectly—had actually carried it through.

Al-e Ahmad strongly disapproved of the government's land-reform program, but by and large he chose his ground shrewdly: he objected to its cultural and moral effects. Land reform (together with a number of associated government projects for the villages, such as universal education) had extended Euromania, he claimed, to the zone of Iranian life that had remained relatively unaffected. In doing so it had created a hunger for the expensive, vacuous symbols of Euromania: signs in neon lights for the exteriors of mosques, inappropriate agricultural equipment, radio-cassette players, and the like. Moreover, the irrelevant and intrusive cultural baggage brought by the state textbooks and the state radio alongside these changes had sowed division in the villages both between the generations and within each generation. It had introduced a war of greed and envy between the large peasants and the small and had destroyed the cooperative character of village life. Sucked into the market economy and the false needs it created, stripped of their spiritual tradition and their former sense that they survived through sharing, the peasants either stayed in the countryside to quarrel or fled to the cities in the pathetic hope of finding the material paradise that would satisfy their new appetites.

In many ways it was a preposterously exaggerated picture, a projection of Al-e Ahmad's strongly romantic longing for the lost innocence of Iran before the "Fall," but there was an element of truth in it. Of course there was (and is) an element of truth in such a description of the entire Third World. But from 1962 on, as Iranian intellectuals read and reread the chapter in *Euromania* in which Al-e Ahmad says, "Look what a graveyard our nation's farmlands have become," they found his words to be prophetic.

What is far from clear, however, is that the peasants shared this grief. Al-e Ahmad, by giving a cultural and moral cast to his version of the criticism of the land reform by the Iranian left, in effect conceded that the rural peasant had accepted the dynamic in which he was caught up and therefore would not be an instrument easily grasped by political parties, including those of the left. In his last novel, *The Cursing of the Land,* published in 1967, he praises the committed hero who moves from the city to a village and struggles to preserve the values of village life. But in the end the hero, although he has done some little good for the village, leaves it as he came to it, on a truck, aware that the sickness he sees in village life is something for which he cannot prescribe a general remedy.

There were other ways (less related to the discouragement of the left) in which Al-e Ahmad's theory of Euromania spoke early but with great accuracy for feelings that after his death came to fever pitch in the Iranian consciousness. One was, paradoxically, a reflection of Iran's increasing oil wealth. Iran, he said, had been merely a nonaligned country until the discovery of oil. Now, as oil became more expensive, Western powers dictated what products Iran should buy from them, setting up a kind of enforced barter that involved huge and unnecessary purchases of arms and the dumping of Western agricultural surpluses in Iran, products Al-e Ahmad repeatedly characterizes as "chicken milk." By the last half of the seventies, when the government contracted to buy American nuclear submarines to secure its power in the Indian Ocean, and Tehran hotels were jammed with Western salesmen almost angry if the "immensely rich" Iranians did not buy, and cargo ships loaded with Danish butter, Australian lamb, and American wheat steamed in circles around the Persian Gulf because of bottlenecks in the Iranian port cities, fury gripped Iranians as they came to see themselves plundered in just the kind of enforced barter that Al-e Ahmad had described. The barter was far less enforced and—at least in the case of foodstuffs—far, far more necessary to Iran's survival than Al-e Ahmad admitted, but it had a manic and uncontrolled character that made Iranians feel powerless over their own resources in a way that they had not felt since the days of the tobacco monopoly.

Al-e Ahmad also saw and scorned the early stages of a new national cult of monarchy. Monarchy has authentic and deep roots in the Iranian tradition; it is not an accident that the national epic is called *The Book of Kings.* Some of what Al-e Ahmad scorned was, in fact, the continuation of a traditional cult of monarchy, which the Pahlavis perpetuated "with the crown jewels at the National Bank . . . and with anything, in general, that catches the eye. Fill the little man's eyes so he'll think he's great!" But the new element was the cult of the Iranian past and, in particular, the Iranian monarchy, before Islam.

Iranians felt they knew their ancient kings and heroes as intimately (sometimes more intimately) than the Iranian kings and heroes of their fourteen centuries of Islamic history. But these familiar ancient Iranians were the kings and heroes of the stylized, paradigmatic, poetic history of *The Book of Kings,* not the ancient Iranians of Xenophon and Herodotus or even the Iranian kings of the books of Isaiah and Ezra. Through school books and popular publications the young nationalists around Reza Shah sought to educate the Iranian public in this newly recovered history. Emphasis was placed particularly on the history of those early Iranians who had been called Persians by the Greeks and whose vast empire—which included Egypt, most of Western Asia, and neighboring parts of Central Asia and India—had been a looming presence to the Greeks from its foundation by Cyrus in the sixth century B.C. to its dismemberment by that brilliant (and philo-Iranian) semi-Greek adventurer, Alexander the Great, in the fourth century B.C.

From the 1930s on, middle- and upper-class Iranians, duly impressed by the role of Iran in ancient history, gave their sons such names as Cyrus and Cambyses, names that would have been outlandish and virtually meaningless to Muslim Iranians before the translation of modern European books in the nineteenth century. In fact, by the next generation, when the Cyruses of the 1930s had grown up and had named many of their children after ancient Iranians, the newly engrafted historicist cult seemed to have taken. The traditional pre-Islamic history of Iran as recorded in the national epic—a mixture of myth, real imperial history, and real local history transposed into imperial history—had been annealed in the minds of many educated Iranians with the history of the Iranians as found in the Greek classics, the Bible, the clay tablets of Mesopotamia, and the papyri of Egypt. Both versions complemented the new nationalism of twentieth-century Iran; by either account the Iranians had been one of the great peoples of the ancient world for over a millennium before the coming of Islam.

The second generation of Cyruses that worked in the civil service for the second Pahlavi shah confidently assumed that the union of the two histories was an accomplished fact, which Al-e Ahmad's "neglected" Iranians would duly accept as the spread of education brought this message to the great majority of Iranian children in the state textbooks of the postwar period. The younger Cyruses were only partly right. The third generation of Cyruses does not seem to have been significantly larger than the second: in spite of universal education, there were still an enormous number of Mohammeds, Hosains, and Fatemehs.

Something had gone sour, and, as usual, Al-e Ahmad was one of the first to sense the change in national mood and to speak for the change. In 1962, in *Euromania*, he ridiculed the government's "mania for honoring the ancient past . . . a mania for showing off in front of strangers, for competing in boasting vaingloriously and stupidly of Cyrus and Darius, and for basking proudly in Rostam's reflected glory." Among intellectuals the change grew partly from resentment at what seemed to them the exploitation of history for the advantage of the regime. The more tightly the regime wrapped itself in the newly reconstructed history, the more irrelevant ancient Iran seemed to Iranian intellectuals. Even the historical territory that both the regime and the intellectuals continued to share was interpreted at cross-purposes. *The Book of Kings* as retold in the state school books was suspiciously innocent of references to regicide, of which the eleventh-century original offers a few striking examples. Some of the intellectuals in the opposition wanted it all the other way; for them these few examples became the central theme of the national epic.

Besides, since the end of the Second World War, hundreds of thousands of Iranians from levels of the population that were more traditionally religious had become enmeshed in national life in a way their ancestors had not been. As the transistor radio and universal education asked them to join the supposed consensus as to the burden of Iranian history, the Mohammeds, Hosains, and Fatemehs from traditionally religious backgrounds felt themselves obliged to answer and thereby to take a stand, as they had never done before in that world of ambiguity between Iranianness and Islam. They knew themselves to be Muslims and also to be the cultural heirs of the Iran before Islam depicted in *The Book of Kings*. And they knew that from a strictly religious point of view, those ancient pagan rulers who had called themselves "King of Kings" were nothing to be proud of—didn't a well-known saying of the Prophet declare that "The most wicked title in my sight is 'king of kings' "? For centuries they had invoked their pre-Islamic cultural heritage in nonreligious settings and had invoked their Islamicness in religious settings. Correspondingly, Iranian Islamic rulers had flashed their traditional Iranian regalia, crowns, royal parasols, and so on when holding court for their nobles but had proclaimed their roles as protectors of Islam, patrons of the mullahs and the like in religious settings. Now the government was asking even very humble Iranians to identify themselves explicitly and uninterruptedly as heirs of Cyrus and to identify their ruler as the heir of Cyrus's monarchy.

Even this dilemma was based on an idiotic question. While *The Book of Kings* correctly identified many of the Iranian kings between the time of the invasion of Iran by Alexander the Great in the fourth century B.C. and the invasion by the Arabs in the seventh century A.D., only one of the kings before Alexander in the national epic (Darius III) corresponds to the history of that period as recorded in inscriptions and ancient Greek texts; the rest of this earliest dynasty of "epic" kings are either cultural heroes from the Zoroastrian tradition or early provincial kings whose stories have been reset in the imperial court. Persepolis and Pasargadae, those magnificent stage sets that Cyrus and his successors built for self-display, were rightly recognized by the medieval Iranian Muslim monarchs as palaces and places of ceremony for the ancient Iranian kings. And the medieval Muslim kings visited these sites and left inscriptions testifying to their respect for their pre-Islamic predecessors. But medieval Iranians knew Persepolis as "the throne of Jamshid," Jamshid being an ancient Iranian king who founded towns by the thousands and established the Iranian new year's festival. Who is the more admirable king, Jamshid or Shah Esma'il, is a possible though improbable question for Iranian culture. For hundreds of years, who is the true type of hero, Rostam or Hosain, has been a probable but carefully avoided question. But Cyrus or Hosain?

If Al-e Ahmad's critique of the glorification of an emotionally unconnected past hit home with the broad mass of Iranians, his claim that the West had with good reason lost confidence in itself was really understood only by the intellectuals—and yet this was a claim that had dim echoes in all parts of Iranian society. "Let's assume," says Al-e Ahmad, "that tomorrow we become like Switzerland." Even if this were possible (and Al-e Ahmad is convinced it isn't), who wants to be like the West? Weren't Western intellectuals the first in the West to be ashamed of colonialism, which Al-e Ahmad considers a natural outgrowth of the adventurism of the West? And isn't the literate, cultivated person in the West infatuated with African music and Eastern spirituality— which shows, at the very least, "his weariness of his environment, customs and art"?

The litter left by Al-e Ahmad's lifelong reading of Western self-criticism fills his books. He seems to be aware that he is playing with fire. If a man finds so many of the best weapons for attacking the West in the West's own arsenal, isn't he still very "West-stricken," a bedazzled Euromaniac with no indigenous standards of his own? A harsh critic might be tempted to repeat the charge leveled by Turgenev's spokesman in *Smoke:* "It wouldn't be so bad if we really did despise [the West]; but that is all talk and lies. We swear at it and abuse it, but its opinion is really the only one we value; and fundamentally it's the opinion of Parisian idiots."

Al-e Ahmad fully recognized his problem. One of the characteristics of the Euromaniac, he tells us, is that he regards Western Orientalists as the only good sources for understanding himself. The Euromaniac "has placed himself, an object of supposition, under the Orientalist's microscope, and he depends on what the Orientalist sees, not on what he himself is, feels, sees and experiences. This is the ugliest manifestation of Euromania." It was Al-e Ahmad's honesty that made it impossible for him to escape this dilemma. He might praise Sheikh Fazlollah's cultural integrity in opposing the secular constitutionalists, but he was not ready to say, "Our indigenous standard for accepting or rejecting anything is the sacred law as understood by Shiah Islam." Al-e Ahmad did not believe the solution was that simple. In any case, his point was taken; Iranian intellectuals were keenly and other Iranians were dimly aware that the West had lost its self-confidence. It was one thing to want to become a Westerner in the age when the West looked East through Kipling's *Kim*, quite another when it looked East through Hesse's *Siddhartha*.

Perhaps Al-e Ahmad's most telling criticism was in the area of life he knew best both from his own experience as a youth and through lifelong involvement: the social import of education. Here his language is not as florid and his examples not as amusing as in his criticism of the related problem of the cultural impact of education. With his impressionistic methods, buttressed by scattered and not always relevant statistics, as a sociologist of education he seemed to Iranians a lightweight. But in fact he had identified an area of Iranian life in which education had created long and seemingly pointless queues of graduates, who, a generation after *Euromania* was written, had turned into angry mobs of graduates who couldn't even find any queue to join. As he wrote:

> There's no previous plan whatsoever [in our educational system], no consideration of where schools are needed and where schools are superfluous. The concern for quantity still prevails over the wise heads in the Ministry of Education. And the ultimate aim in the Ministry of Education? As I have said, the aim is to nurture Euromania, or to place worthless certificates of employability in the hands of people who are only fit to serve as future stuffing for promotion to any position. ... We have technical and trade schools, and a legion of other kinds, but the utility of all this diversity, the reason for the existence of each of these schools, what they're cultivating, or what work their graduates take on ten years later is nowhere established or recorded.

Under Reza Shah almost all graduates of high schools who cared to could find either a government post or a position in the freshman classes of the Teachers College or the University of Tehran. The number of *talabehs* in *madresehs* had fallen, particularly after Ayatollah Ha'eri's death in 1937, from a reported 5,532 in the academic year 1929–30 to a mere 1,341 (although both the government and the religious authorities may have had reasons for underreporting the actual number toward the end of Reza Shah's reign). In any case, a sizable number of children of prominent mullahs joined the administrative elite created by the new education, as often as not with the blessing of their fathers, who thought the psychological atmosphere and economic prospects unpromising for any but the most determined and/or financially independent students of the traditional religious sciences.

The government was able to expand the number of universities (and, hence, of university places) to keep pace with the expansion of elementary and secondary education in the period immediately after the Second World War. Between 1947 and 1955 five new provincial universities were founded. But the economy expanded by fits and starts or even went flat for periods. Neither the bureaucracy nor the economy seems to have been able to accommodate the new harvest of homegrown and foreign Iranian holders of university degrees.

Nevertheless elementary and secondary education continued to reach larger and larger numbers of Iranians, but between 1955 and 1975 only two proper universities were founded, both in Tehran. Meanwhile the economy had performed at first indifferently, then well, then spectacularly. In some years Iran was one of the few really populous countries of the world to exceed Japan in its real growth rate; jobs were being created that could have absorbed all the university graduates. But as time went on there were proportionally fewer places at the universities for high school graduates. In the academic year 1961–62, out of 15,942 who passed the prestigious final high school examination (comparable to the French *baccalauréat*) 36.3 percent found places in Iranian universities; by 1975–76, only 14 percent found university places. In 1975 the government tried to whistle a dozen or so new universities into existence. It was much too late. In the year of the revolution, 1978–79, out of about 235,000 high school graduates only 12.1 percent could find university places. The high school population was still growing faster than the universities.

Not all of this mismeasurement by the government was the result of stupidity. As the population became more prosperous, it became possible for more and more families to support their children at foreign universities; and the government wanted a certain number of Iranians to study abroad. Of course these were the people Al-e Ahmad regarded as most alienated from their own culture: "It's true that we train specialists in America (and perhaps Germany), but these people are barbarians, blown in by the wind, who will be blown away by it as well. In Europe too (I mean France and England) they train this same type of specialist; but they train boasting, self-important know-it-alls." The government also wanted more technicians with practical training rather than hordes of examination-book writers, and accordingly expanded institutions of higher education, such as technical schools and schools of nursing, that did not grant B.A.'s. While in 1956–57 over 99 percent of those high school graduates who got places at institutions of higher education in Iran itself went to universities, by 1976–77 only 44.1 percent, a minority, went on to universities, and the rest went to institutions that did not give bachelor's degrees. But here the cultural prejudice that Isa Sadiq recognized and overcame in himself when he saw the self-service cafeteria at Columbia's International House in 1930 proved too strong for most Iranians of a later generation. Too many still felt that the whole purpose of education was to raise themselves above the level of people who worked with their hands. Too many of the 55.5 percent who went to the technical and vocational schools felt cheated.

In a way they were right: in Iran, the degree—domestic or foreign—made the man. Of the 4,478 people listed in the Iranian *Who's Who* of 1976, 45.6 percent had at least one degree from a foreign university and 30.7 percent had doctorates. It had not always been this way; university teachers, of course, were normally Ph.D.'s or M.D.'s, but "Doctor" Mossadegh was so called because his Swiss doctorate was an unusual distinction for a man of public affairs. When in the elections of 1943–44 nine holders of doctorates (medical and otherwise) were elected to the fourteenth Consultative Assembly, it was a record for that body of two hundred people. By the eve of the revolution the core of the Iranian government was stiff with "doctors." There were 31 "doctors" in the last Consultative Assembly before the revolution, and in the last government of Hoveyda, formed in 1975, 13 of the 27 ministers were "doctors." In 1977, of the 108 deputy ministers, 41 were Ph.D.'s or M.D.'s. In the same year, out of the 518 enormously powerful people in the top grade of the civil service 22 percent had doctorates.

Iranian education had succeeded magnificently at the bottom; it had made the majority of Iranians born in the late fifties and in the sixties literate. It had also succeeded for those who made it to the top; their degrees had given them chances that would have been enormously hard for them to get as mere clever Iranians, naked of any diplomas from institutions of higher education. But for too many Iranians between the top and the bottom it had been a bait-and-switch con game against which there was no appeal. Thousands of Iranian students, as they worked their way forward in the crowds in front of the University of Tehran when the university posted examination results and university acceptances, only to find they had not secured places, wondered what in God's name this education had been all about. Thousands of others, who returned with their Ph.D.'s from wonderfully obscure American universities to occupy civil service posts in no way connected with the learning (however limited) they had picked up in the West, must occasionally have wondered what in God's name all those years of attending graduate courses so irrelevant to their present jobs had been for. But one thing was clear to these experts "blown in by the wind." A "West-stricken" government had established an intricate and lengthy ritual, and if you were fortunate enough to have your parents or the Iranian government pay for you to "stay the course," you got as a reward a desk, a life-long stipend, and—after thirty years of service—retirement at full pay.

. . .

In 1965 Al-e Ahmad, the sometime teacher and the long-term employee of the Ministry of Education, got a chance to go back to school. The opportunity came, as Isa Sadiq's had come thirty-five years earlier, from a great American university; he had been chosen as a leading cultural figure of the younger generation to attend the Harvard International Summer Seminar directed by Henry

Kissinger (soon to be one of the rare "doctors" in an American cabinet).

For the purposes of the seminar Kissinger had chosen well. The seminar was supposed to gather together intellectually interesting political and cultural figures in their thirties and forties who were likely to become leaders in their countries. Al-e Ahmad was at the height of his powers; he was unquestionably an intellectual leader already. He was a handsome man, with a shock of gray hair that fell back from his forehead in a way that emphasized his resemblance to Faulkner, a writer he much admired. At least once a week he presided over a *dowreh* that met at the Café Firuz in what had once been the heart of elegant Tehran but now was just a bustling middle-class shopping street with an odd miscellany of stores—a Russian bakery, a large stationery store, a toy store, and a bookstore. The café was in a brick building of the style considered fashionable in Iran between the wars, with blue tiles set between the bricks. To enter, you went up three or four steps into a surprisingly spacious room, where a stout elderly man in a black suit and a bow tie led you through the columns to one of the smallish rectangular tables. From March to November you could sit at the wooden tables in the open courtyard in back, where there were evergreen trees and honeysuckle vines growing on the walls. The stout man with a bow tie let Al-e Ahmad and his circle sit hours over a cup of coffee each; he knew that Al-e Ahmad was the most talked-about intellectual of his generation.

Seated at the Café Firuz, the thin, gangly Al-e Ahmad, who was only slightly taller than average, seemed a tall man, all legs, elbows, and angles—as far as you could, in fact, see him through the cloud of smoke from the lighted cigarette he always carried. He felt he needed the angles, for although he was a bit pleased to be a guru, especially a controversial one, he was afraid of hangers-on, of the merely curious who were not committed in the way he was. He subjected newcomers to all the points of his angularity by being brusque and dismissive, but if they passed the test he was a loyal friend, because, of course, his prickly first approaches were the strategy of an extremely sensitive and sentimental man. (He was also constant in his enmities. Of two early friends in the Iranian left, one—Ehsan Tabari—went to eastern Europe to run the Moscow-aligned Iranian Communist party in exile, another—Parviz Khanlari—joined the regime and became a minister of culture. Al-e Ahmad put savage caricatures of both of them in his stories.) And, of course, to be his friend meant to hear him talk, fluently and self-mockingly, in the same wonderful elliptical style in which he wrote, changing registers between all the levels of Tehran speech, lurching emotionally away from and back toward his subject, desperate to find an opinion that was really his own on anything he touched, desperate to maintain his autonomy.

He suspected from the start that the Harvard seminar was an attempt to buy his autonomy and the autonomy of intellectuals like him. Apparently the CIA agreed, as some of the funding for the seminar came through CIA conduits. But he didn't care; his wife had been a guest at the seminar some years earlier and had told him that its intellectual content was genuine, and Al-e Ahmad was extremely eager to meet foreign intellectuals, from whom he felt cut off. (He had, in fact, been accepted for the 1964 summer seminar, but the Iranian government, which considered him a problem—he had to report once a month to a SAVAK office—had refused to give him a passport in that year.) He was also most happy to be going to school again.

A bus met him and other participants when they arrived in New York on the *Queen Mary*, and of New York, which Isa Sadiq had so admired many years before, he saw only the potholes on Amsterdam Avenue and "steam" rising from the sewers. The participants were delivered to a Harvard dormitory and introduced to the program, which Al-e Ahmad found—to his delight—would be "altogether a real lesson," with daily lectures and discussion hours. Of course there were planned trips to factories, museums, schools, and the Tanglewood Music Festival, as well as arranged invitations to various American homes, at one of which he was forced to play baseball. But Al-e Ahmad seems not to have been much interested in all this (unlike Isa Sadiq who, after his factory visit, gave a long description of the vertical integration of production in the Ford plants in Michigan). Al-e Ahmad had come to talk with intellectuals.

In this respect Henry Kissinger put on a good show. Al-e Ahmad heard Robert Coles discuss the race question from the perspective of a psychiatrist and David Riesman talk on "affluence for what?" He did his assigned reading and attended his classes in Lamont Library, where the group discussed such American "classics" as *The Naked and the Dead*. He attended a teach-in at Memorial Hall, "a building large, arresting and churchlike," where he listened to a talk by the author of this particular classic, Norman Mailer, a man "of middling stature, rotund, with his hair blown around like wheat." But best of all for him was meeting Ralph Ellison, whose *Invisible Man* he considered a kind of manifesto for blacks. Al-e Ahmad thought that Ellison had a deeper view of the race question than other writers, because he saw the American black in the context of his resentments, and that Ellison's position was like the position of Camus on Algeria. With customary prickliness, knowing that Ellison liked jazz, Al-e Ahmad (according to his own account) told him, "I believe that the problem of American blacks comes from the two refuges they have constructed for themselves: Christianity and jazz."

It would never have occurred to intellectuals of Isa Sadiq's generation to travel to Europe or America in order to explain to the oppressed in the West the cultural factors that made for oppression. But Al-e Ahmad was interested in the intellectual dynamics of oppression, not in finding the key to the success of the West; he wanted to compare experiences of liberation, not bring home Western models of social organization or production. To the mystification of the Iranians he met in Cambridge, he claimed he had discovered a working-class bar in Harvard Square where (despite his still extremely halting English) he had had several "significant" conversations with working-class Americans.

During his stay in America, Al-e Ahmad encountered even more resistance to his ideas than he had known in Iran (for all that there were a fair number of Iranians who thought him intellectually trivial). When he gave a talk on Euromania to his fellow students he was intimidated enough by the environment to modify his thesis and say that he was not worried about the disappearance of national cultures because they would all be replaced by a world culture that would be "a mixture of all cultures." Even this concession did not win over all his listeners, but although Al-e Ahmad seems to have enjoyed the arguments he occasioned, he was not noticeably influenced by the discussion. And he never again felt obliged to make any bow toward "world culture."

He also had a run-in with the Iranian student opposition. After the seminar he went to Chicago to attend a meeting of Iranian students, who told him that they believed that the opposition to the shah's regime in Iran should come into the open immediately. Al-e Ahmad told them that they didn't know what they were talking about, that there were times to fight openly and times (like the present) to fight covertly and with cunning. Again neither side seems to have persuaded the other, although Al-e Ahmad enjoyed meeting a live and vocal opposition, however unrealistic its pretensions. In fact, he had enjoyed the whole trip without being much changed by it. He had already visited the Soviet Union, which he regarded as a colonialist power that held millions of Muslims in bondage, and now he had visited the other pole of "Euromania." He could say from firsthand experience that he had found both of them pretty much as he had expected.

He was, of course, right about the late sixties not being the time to fight the regime openly. Land reform and a sustained investment of oil revenues in all sectors of the economy had given the shah a broad popular constituency for the first time, even if—as Al-e Ahmad correctly maintained—they had torn apart all sorts of traditions of social cooperation and had left areas of terrible poverty. Al-e Ahmad both in his life and in his fiction of this period of the sixties sought to put before Iranians the example of the person who could not be bought. It was the best he could offer the opposition as it struggled, and it commanded respect. But he wasn't sure where things were going. Under all his customary vigor as an essayist, a writer of fiction, and a leader of an important intellectual circle his friends saw a man who was not sure that there could ever be any solution and was grieving. In one of his novels of this period the hero (who very obviously expresses Al-e Ahmad's ideas) says: "At heart I am opposed to every government, since the necessity of each government is to use force, and then inhumanity, confiscation, execution, imprisonment and exile. Mankind has been dreaming of the government of philosophers for over two thousand years. Whereas philosophers cannot easily issue a judgment, let alone govern. From the beginning of time, government has been manipulated by thoughtless people. Governments have been manipulated by those hooligans who have supported an adventurer in order to attain their own ends."

Al-e Ahmad was grieving for many reasons. He was grieving because he had no children, a deprivation he uncharacteristically blamed on his wife in a late autobiographical essay. He was grieving for a cultural heritage that seemed irremediably doomed to extinction and that, at the same time, he could never define to his full satisfaction. He was grieving because, with his unusual empathy for other Iranians, he sensed the failed hopes of his generation of Iranian intellectuals, and because his hope was failing too. His hair had turned completely white. In August 1969 Al-e Ahmad's intellectual father, the social democrat Khalil Maleki, died; Maleki's request to be buried next to Mossadegh was denied. Fifty-eight days later, on September 8, 1969, Al-e Ahmad died of a heart attack at the age of forty-six. He was buried next to Maleki.

Had he lived, Al-e Ahmad would have seen his intellectual children, direct and collateral, in the thousands. The intellectual heritage of Avicenna split in two after his death; the far more disparate and unsystematic intellectual heritage of Al-e Ahmad split into a hundred parts espoused by a hundred groups, all of which were against Euromania but otherwise agreed on very little. A liberal left, an Islamic liberal left, an Islamic left that detested liberal institutions, and an Islamic movement that detested both liberalism and leftism all claimed Al-e Ahmad as one of their forebears or early supporters—and, to a degree, all were right.

Strangely, some of Al-e Ahmad's association with these movements came to him by descent. Al-e Ahmad's grandfather had come from the town of Taleqan and hence his family had had a long-term connection (and distant ties of kinship) with another mullah family of that town, the family of Mahmud Taleqani, the ayatollah who attracted such a large number of admirers when in Qasr prison. Taleqani's father had been a mullah who moved to Tehran and was an associate of the jurisconsult Modarres, who, as a member of parliament, had joined Mossadegh in opposing the alteration of the constitution necessary to establish the Pahlavi dynasty. Reza Shah made life difficult for the father, but he was so impressed by his integrity that, in a period in the 1930s when no religious processions were allowed, Reza Shah allowed a public funeral procession for the elder Taleqani.

The son, Ayatollah Mahmud Taleqani, studied the traditional curriculum at Qom, but early on he showed his determination to make Islam intellectually accessible to the masses and to prove that the message of Islam was relevant to their needs. In 1941, when he was about thirty, he founded a center in Tehran where he gave public lectures, and Al-e Ahmad, who knew of Taleqani from his youth, maintained a connection with him from the late forties on. The friendship was strengthened by the events of the early fifties. After Ayatollah Kashani deserted Mossadegh, Taleqani (though not very prominent in the Shiah hierarchy) was probably the highest ranking mullah in Tehran to stand by Mossadegh.

After the restoration coup of 1953 Taleqani made a special attempt to attract intellectuals, and in this effort he was helped by a professor of engineering at the University of Tehran, Mehdi Bazargan. Bazargan had been scrupulously religious as long as anyone could remember; he had embarrassed his fellow Iranian students in Paris in the early thirties by his diligence in praying at the proper times regardless of the circumstances or occasion. He had been a valued supporter of Mossadegh, and—as a professor of engineering—had been sent by Mossadegh to the Abadan refinery to oversee the transfer of authority from British to Iranian hands. At the same time he was far too religious for Mossadegh, who refused to make him minister of education for fear of what he would do to the textbooks and curriculum. Bazargan used to bring a group of like-minded intellectuals to hear Taleqani preach once a week at his mosque in Tehran. Al-e Ahmad is said to have attended some of these meetings; he certainly established contact with Bazargan in the fifties and maintained this contact throughout his life.

Taleqani had a somewhat ambiguous relation with the *madreseh* teachers in Qom. He thought that the elaborate *madreseh* education he had received was largely irrelevant and that the meaning of Islam could be understood quite directly by studying the Koran and the *Sermons* of Ali. Needless to say, the *madreseh* teachers did not agree. Taleqani wrote in support of the thesis of the early constitutionalist mullahs that Shi'ism was inherently in favor of democracy. Important jurisconsults had not spoken up for this position in years. Taleqani wrote that socialism and religion were compatible, because God had not intended for mankind to be divided into the exploiters and the exploited. This sounded very much like the dangerous talk of Mossadegh's leftist friends, the kind of talk that had convinced the religious authorities in Qom to support Ayatollah Kashani's withdrawal from Mossadegh's National Front.

Yet the religious authorities were not ready to disavow Taleqani. He had had a proper *madreseh* education; he was no fake mullah. He had been sent to prison and would be sent many more times; they respected his courage and suffering, especially in a period in which they themselves were remarkably quiet on political matters. In general, the clergy never broke ranks publicly unless they felt themselves or their principles seriously in danger. And most important of all, Taleqani was acquiring a serious following. Some of this following came from the men of the Tehran bazaar, who were pleased to find a mullah more aware of the world than the older religious authorities in Qom. But more impressive was his following among university professors such as Bazargan; it had been a long time since a mullah had held such an audience enthralled. Even more amazing, some of his following was among the Marxist students Taleqani had met in prison. And it was at this point that Al-e Ahmad's intellectual influence started to be noticeable. In his critique of the direction of Iranian society, Taleqani turned to the rhetoric of Al-e Ahmad—as did even more traditional religious authorities in their sermons in Qom or as any social critic in this period was quite naturally obliged to do.

Taleqani was kind, he was open. His message of a socially concerned and politically active Islam was something new and appealing for the politically deeply committed young Iranians he met in prison. (In fact, earlier in life his concern for political activism had even led him to close contacts with the right-wing Devotees of Islam who had shot Kasravi.) And Taleqani's message of an Islam intellectually accessible to the concerned lay reader also appealed to them, because the young members of the left were proud of their "modern" education and felt themselves intelligent enough to interpret religion without a ten-year slog through the *madreseh* curriculum. His young admirers came to call him "Father Taleqani." Al-e Ahmad had chosen a social democrat as an intellectual father, but young leftists of the generation influenced by Al-e Ahmad chose a mullah.

Until the early seventies Taleqani and his followers were nearly invisible to most Iranians. Then the full face of what Al-e Ahmad had seen in distant profile began to appear. The government felt it had found an unbeatable combination of economic policy and national ideology. No longer did memories of 1953 and 1963 make the government hesitate. In reaction, a new kind of resistance appeared, and, since in its initial phases the struggle was cultural, its rhetoric of cultural criticism was a significant part of the rhetoric of Al-e Ahmad.

In 1971 the shah decided to celebrate. By somebody's (questionable) calculation it was two thousand and five hundred years since Cyrus had founded the first Iranian empire, and the shah ordered a celebration of "two thousand five hundred years of Iranian kingship" to be held at Persepolis. The celebration was to be a triumphant declaration of the historical depth of the state's ideology, with loving emphasis on the king-emperors of ancient Iran, the builders of Persepolis and the neighboring archaeological site, Pasargadae. It would show off Iran's considerable recent achievements to the outside world and at the same time show Iranians how respectfully the outside world would treat the official ideology. The shah, incidentally, seems to have really believed in what he was doing. In the 1960s he had given himself a new title, "Light of the Aryans." The ancient Iranian king Darius had called himself Aryan in his great inscription (first read in modern times by a nineteenth-century English archaeologist), and, whatever Darius meant by the word, its later pollution by the Nazis did not deter Mohammed Reza Pahlavi.

His party at Persepolis was more or less a success. The Emperor of Japan came and Haile Selassie came, as did the kings of Belgium, Denmark, Greece, Jordan, Lesotho, Morocco, Nepal, and Norway, representatives from two dozen or so nonmonarchies,

including the then American Vice-President, Spiro Agnew, and
not only Nikolai Podgorny of the Soviet Union but also a high-
ranking official from Communist China (which cut the ground
from under the shah's Maoist critics within Iran). The guests
found Guerlain shaving preparations, Alka-Seltzer wrapped by
Fauchon of Paris, and other fancy amenities awaiting them in
their quarters; twenty-five thousand bottles of wine and all their
food (except the caviar) were flown in from France. (When France
failed to send Pompidou himself, Franco-Iranian relations were
strained for several years.)

It may not have been, as the shah had promised, "the greatest
show the world has ever seen," but it was a gala event, filled with
pageantry and important people, and it came off more or less as
planned. At the ceremony that was meant to be the symbolic
heart of the celebration, the shah stood before the tomb of Cyrus
and said, "Sleep easily, Cyrus, for we are awake." A desert wind
sprang up immediately after he spoke; an American Orientalist
present (many Orientalists came) said that this seeming spirit
wind had made the hairs on the back of his neck stand up.

Some Iranians were also impressed. A joke of the period
claimed that an Iranian office worker was so enraptured by reading these words of the shah in his newspaper that he went home
unexpectedly early to tell his wife; there he found his wife and his
neighbor, Cyrus, asleep together in his bed. Overcome by the
drama of the moment he raised his hand and said, "Sleep easily,
Cyrus, for we are awake." Many more Iranians were unim-
pressed. The whole thing had cost about three hundred million
dollars, and the shah, aware that there had been criticisms of the
expense, gave an interview on the subject in which he said, "What
am I supposed to do—serve [heads of state] bread and radishes?"
Some Iranians were horrified; it seemed the stinking blossom on
the plant that Al-e Ahmad had identified as the "mania for showing off in front of strangers, for competing in boasting vaingloriously and stupidly of Cyrus and Darius."

Among the horrified were the mullahs. They saw it as the
beginning of the end for themselves and for everything they believed. On the eve of the celebration Khomeini issued a declaration from Iraq condemning the whole affair:

Ought the people of Iran to celebrate the rule of a traitor to Islam and the interests of the Muslims who gives oil to Israel? . . . The crimes of the kings of Iran have blackened the pages of history . . . . Even those who were reputed to be "good" were vile and cruel . . . Islam is fundamentally opposed to the whole notion of monarchy . . . We who depend on Islam for our living—are we not to lift a finger for the sake of Islam and the Muslims? . . . People address themselves to us constantly from all over Iran, asking permission to use the charitable taxes demanded by Islam for the building of bathhouses, for they are without baths. What happened to all those gilded promises, those pretentious claims that Iran is progressing on the same level as the more developed countries of the world, that the people are prosperous and content? . . . If these latest excesses are not prevented, still worse misfortunes will descend upon us and we will be confronted with even more distasteful events.

This declaration did not go unnoticed among the mullahs in Iran itself. Clandestine organizations began to appear among young mullahs and *talabehs* which were dedicated not just to the reintroduction of Islam in education or legal life but to the permanent destruction of monarchy in Iran. The government's position stiffened. In August 1971 the government announced and, in 1972, actually brought into being a Religious Corps, intended to function parallel to the Literary Corps and to bring religious values to neglected Iranians. The Corps, recruited from graduates of the theology departments of state universities, was never developed to any significant size, but it was a threatening gesture to even the older clergymen: if they did not cooperate, the government would create its very own mullahs.

While there were periods of tension and of calm, from 1971 until 1977 neither side conceded an inch ideologically. The government, aware of the growth of active disloyalty on the part of some of the mullahs, wanted the "models" and other high religious leaders resident in Iran to speak against this disloyal element, and it leaned on them heavily to do so. The high religious leaders refused to comply; even if they had found that they could do so in good conscience (and they could not), they would have lost their influence with other mullahs completely. By the mid-seventies, although none of the "models" had been arrested, any self-respecting *madreseh* teacher in Qom was ashamed if he had not been arrested at least once or sent off to Zabol or some other remote town in Iran to which the government banished mullahs whom they thought "difficult."

The more inflexible the mullahs seemed to the government, the more the government felt it needed its own ideology. In the boldest gesture of all, the government changed the calendar from the Islamic era to an era based on the supposed date of the foundation of Iranian kingship by Cyrus. In 1976 Iranians found themselves no longer in 1355 of the Islamic era but in 2535 of "the era of the King of Kings." It was an act of defiance to religion that only a time like the French Revolution could produce in the West; it exceeded any fantasy Al-e Ahmad had ever had about the regime.

Another opposition was born out of desperation in 1971. On a crisp morning that winter thirteen young Iranians with rifles attacked the police post at the village of Siakal on the edge of the Caspian forests that had once hidden the forces of Kuchek Khan. They killed three policemen, freed two colleagues, and disappeared into the mountains. It was the beginning of six years of guerrilla activity carried on by several groups. Some of the guerrillas may really have expected that the "oppressed peasants" would welcome them and that the grandchildren of the troops of Kuchek Khan would form a people's army, as their grandparents had done. Most of the guerrillas, however, knew better. They were acting in the spirit of the hero of one of Al-e Ahmad's parables, who says, "The power of the Truth is in the word 'martyrs.' "

These guerrillas were not people of the masses; of the three hundred and forty-one killed between 1971 and 1977 well over three hundred could be classified as intellectuals. Not surprisingly, they came from several small groups involved in internal political struggles that produced new splits and new coalitions throughout the six years. More surprising is that several of these groups were religious. They prayed regularly, and they believed themselves to be fighting for the ideas of "Father Taleqani." Some of the young *talabehs* were impressed by the dedication of the guerrillas, even if they recognized them to be a totally alien sort of creature. Most of the ayatollahs were unsympathetic to them. But, then, they shared the guerrillas' sense of desperation. There were rumors that prominent ayatollahs sent the guerrillas money through intermediaries in order to keep alive some kind of armed opposition to the government.

The Islamic leftist guerrillas may have recognized themselves as the fulfillment of some of Al-e Ahmad's many dreams: they were committed—to the point of martyrdom; they were for radical redistribution of wealth in favor of "neglected" Iranians; and they believed in solutions that were culturally "Iranian"—which, like Al-e Ahmad, they understood to include Shiah Islam. But another kind of intellectual was emerging, who was the successor to Al-e Ahmad in a more direct way: the intellectual who called for immediate cultural revolt against the regime through a return to Islam. In the prerevolutionary period the most prominent of these was Ali Shariati, only a decade younger than Al-e Ahmad—like Al-e Ahmad, the son of a militant Muslim, but unlike him, a man who had studied in the West. After attending the University of Paris from 1960 to 1965 he got his doctorate and returned to Iran. In 1967 he became a lecturer at the Hosainiyeh of Right Guidance, a religious meeting hall financed by the Iranian representative of the Dodge Motor Company, a close friend of Taleqani and Bazargan. Shariati was a spellbinder. He combined a thoroughgoing cultural commitment to Shi'ism with a demand for economic justice. Almost everyone critical of the regime or of the tenor of Iranian life in the seventies used the word "Euromania," but in Shariati's mouth Al-e Ahmad's critique had its most vibrant and influential second life. For example, in a book entitled *The Return to Ourselves* he wrote:

> I want to turn to a fundamental question raised by intellectuals in Africa, Latin America, and Asia: the question of "return to one's roots." ... Since World War II, many intellectuals in the Third World, whether religious or nonreligious, have stressed that their societies must return to their roots and rediscover their history, their culture, and their popular language. ... Some of you may conclude that we Iranians must return to our racial roots. I categorically reject this conclusion. I oppose racism, fascism and reactionary returns. Moreover, Islamic civilization has worked like

scissors and has cut us off completely from our pre-Islamic past. The experts, such as archaeologists and ancient historians, may know a great deal about the Sassanids, the Achaemenians, and even the earlier civilizations, but our people know nothing about such things. Our people do not find their roots in these civilizations. . . . Our people remember nothing from this distant past and do not care to learn about the pre-Islamic civilizations. . . . Consequently, for us a return to our roots means not a rediscovery of pre-Islamic Iran, but a return to our Islamic, especially Shiah roots.

In the early seventies, however, all these people seemed to be on the margins of Iranian society. When the guerrilla movement began, it seemed to most Iranians a piece of insane, if noble, theater. They might disapprove of some aspects of the regime, but the shah seemed a fact of life, and life was not so very bad. In fact, the period from 1964 to 1973 was the golden autumn of Pahlavi rule. In this period the Iranian economy had grown impressively, often by over 10 percent a year, a rate matched by very few countries of the world, and until 1971 there had been comparatively little inflation. Moreover, until 1970 there had been a respectable growth in all sectors of the Iranian economy, including the traditional bazaar economy and agriculture. But from 1970 on, the income from oil, which had of course been the most sustained and important element in this growth, began to multiply at a dizzying rate. Iran's oil revenues rose from $1.1 billion in 1970 to $2.4 billion in 1972 and had reached $17.4 billion in 1974.

The Iranian government saw itself in a new light. The government would make Iran the Switzerland or, more exactly, the United States of the Third World, for, once its oil ran out, Iran would have an infrastructure of roads, education, even nuclear power plants that would be unmatched elsewhere in the Third World. Alongside this infrastructure it would have a highly educated, technologically experienced population and would be able to export technology to the Third World more cheaply than Japan or the West. Of the oil-rich countries, only Iran, with a population of about thirty-five million, would be both populous enough and rich enough to recreate its future in this way.

For the opposition it was another bad dream of Al-e Ahmad's come to life. The explosion of oil revenues from 1970 on had convinced the opposition that time was running out; the regime was going to buy everyone's loyalty and sell everyone its alien ideology. The regime also felt its time was limited; it had a plan, was banking the nation's greatest asset on it, and could not squander months or years fighting sedition. The shah felt the need for more direct government of his kingdom to accomplish his quick march to the new Iran. The SAVAK was given a freer hand, and it used an arbitrary brutality toward suspected enemies of the regime which would have been unthinkable in the sixties. And while the shah had been satisfied from 1963 on with two official (and carefully controlled) parties, a pro-government party and a "loyal opposition," in 1975 he decided that the debate between the two was a waste of time, outlawed both parties, and proclaimed a one-party state.

The economy was having fits of impatience too. At first the word was murmured privately in ministries, then spoken politely at press conferences, then shouted in newspapers and on the radio: "bottlenecks." The plans for Iran were impressive; they were usually appropriate to what Iran wanted to become and constructed with shrewd guesses as to what Iran actually was, but as is so often true, the longest way between two points was a straight line. Too many things ran into each other. Too often goods and directives for all manner of organizations, such as cooperatives, universities, and craft guilds, just would not circulate through the arteries and veins of Iranian life as planned despite the ever-growing government bureaucracy, which was reaching deeper and deeper into Iranian life. Inflation reappeared; the government guaranteed low prices for foodstuffs; farming became less profitable, and the flight from the land became noticeably more rapid. In 1976 the government called an abrupt halt; it started a "war on profiteers" and made credit harder to get. Only owners of banks could get money easily, and the merely rich began to hate the truly wealthy.

Just as bad were the human bottlenecks: people were not getting appropriate jobs or were found to be less qualified than they had looked on paper. Again Al-e Ahmad had foreseen it: "It's true that we've wearied the minds and thoughts of the children of our people for years in our schools with chemical, physical and mathematical formulas ... but to what purpose? There's no practical setting for the hypotheses and equations. We have not put theory into practice for students in any laboratory. We're still obliged to turn to some European laboratory to measure every rock, earth sample and batch of tar!" The consequence, of course, was the prominence of the foreign adviser, a figure who had never gone away but had never been obtrusive since the late Qajar period. If, Al-e Ahmad said, in the past only the British and Russian ambassadors "imposed their opinions on us ... now there are legions of Western advisers, parasites, specialists and experts ... This is the way they run a nation, a nation abandoned to the fate of machines, guided by these West-stricken intellectuals, in the hands of these seminars, conferences, Second and Third Plans ... and this ridiculous investment in rootless ancillary industries."

It seemed a replay of the late Qajar period in other ways too. Several hundred of these foreign advisers had diplomatic passports, and Iranians believed that the majority of the tens of thousands of foreigners resident in Iran, particularly the Americans, carried such passports; certainly many of the Americans behaved as if they were protected by some "regime of capitulations." It was also like the late Qajar period in that the government, try as it might to detach itself, appeared to Iranians to be as closely attached to the United States as the Qajars had been to the English and Russians.

The complex of idealism and greed that motivated these two countries, the United States and Iran, as they drifted into each other's paths, produced a tangled emotional history that both parties, like most couples angrily divorced, now falsely simplified. Without question, the United States was a generous friend to Iran in the fifties, when the U.S. gave not only substantial aid but sent a small but valuable corps of Point Four experts. Mossadegh, for all his nationalistic feelings, wanted them so badly that he let them come with semidiplomatic status. Unquestionably, in the seventies the United States saw Iran as its favorite petroleum friend, at whose establishment it most enjoyed recycling dollars. In May 1972 President Richard Nixon, accompanied by Al-e Ahmad's sometime teacher, Henry Kissinger, visited Tehran. Nixon promised to sell Iran any nonnuclear weapon in unlimited quantities, and over the next six years the shah bought accordingly.

It can be questioned who was using whom. Often the shah's desire to be a regional power exceeded any ambition the U.S. had for him and appalled his friends in Washington. It can even be questioned whether the widespread Iranian perception that the shah wanted to Americanize Iran was correct. The shah enjoyed criticizing the disorderly aspects of American life, and culturally he respected France and England far more. The twenty-four thousand Americans working in Iran were an artifact of America's technological position; the shah wanted to get the best money could buy. But it was a match—if not made in heaven—that had become psychologically extremely important to both the shah and the U.S. government, even if they sometimes quarreled, and the Iranian public had been correct insofar as it had seen this psychological need. When Harvard, Kissinger's old university, conferred an honorary doctorate on the shah in 1968, a year when the shah's friend David Rockefeller was a member of the Harvard board of Overseers, the citation by America's greatest university said what "wise" Americans believed: "His Imperial Majesty Mohammed Reza Pahlavi, Shahanshah of Iran, Doctor of Laws: A twentieth-century ruler who has found in power a constructive instrument to advance social and economic revolution in an ancient land."

The shah in his acceptance speech proposed that every country add to its educational budget the equivalent of one day in its budget for armaments. It was a disappointment for the shah that no one greeted his proposal with much enthusiasm and that no one in the audience, as he had hoped, seemed to compare his speech to General Marshall's Harvard speech of 1947, which had launched the Marshall Plan. There had been only abstracted applause, and, as the shah drifted away from the platform, most of the excitement had been generated by his secret service agents, who had rushed about him shouting "Vive Shah" and had beaten up an Iranian-looking Harvard graduate student. But disappointed or not, the shah had chosen the arena that almost inevitably seemed to him the most appropriate in the world to cut the kind of world figure he wished to be. Iranians were not altogether wrong to think that the King of Kings was psychologically a petitioner at the court of the great republic of the West.

It is enlightening to see Ayatollah Khomeini's reaction to this arena in which the shah saw himself playing a significant role. In a letter sent in 1972 from Iraq to the Muslim students of North America he said: "Never confuse the Noble Koran and the salvation-bestowing path of Islam with erroneous and elusive schools of thought that are the product of the human mind. You must be aware that as long as the people of Islam are subjected to these imperialist schools [of thought], as long as they compare divine laws with those of other schools and put them together on the same level, tranquillity and freedom will be denied to the Muslims."

It might seem a small step from Al-e Ahmad's denunciation of cultural imperialism and admiration for Shiah Islam to Khomeini's utter lack of interest in any standards but the Koran and Islam. In fact, it was an immensely long step and one that Al-e Ahmad would never have taken. After a long intellectual journey Al-e Ahmad had come to respect his Shiah Islamic roots, but he had not therefore concluded that Shiah Islamic roots were the only standard by which things were to be respected. In one of his last books he quotes a speech Khomeini gave in 1964 as proof that a "clergyman" could be a committed intellectual. But two sentences are removed from the speech, and in brackets Al-e Ahmad says: "From here I have taken out two sentences which gave forth the smell of mullah games: about male teachers in female schools and the reverse [both of which Khomeini had called causes of corruption]. These are words which diminish the value of the clergy as a religious and social guide. You will excuse me."

Al-e Ahmad was fundamentally different from all the appropriators of his rhetoric. Even Shariati, who resembled him in many ways, never outwardly showed—and perhaps never felt—the doubts that Al-e Ahmad continually had and expressed. Ultimately these doubts prevented Al-e Ahmad from pushing any single solution as the salvation of Iran; he was the master of social and cultural critique but not of social and cultural construction. This failure was a mark of his extreme loyalty to and honesty about his own feelings. He had assimilated the messages of traditional Iranian religious culture, of the Iranian left, and of the self-critical intellectuals of postwar Europe. He had found things to admire and to disdain in all of them. But he, the great Iranian advocate of the committed man, was unable in full honesty to commit himself to any program. He could never, for the sake of expediency, be silent when he thought he detected a bad "smell" issuing from any one of them.

Kasravi, a sometime *talabeh* like Al-e Ahmad, had merely turned his role inside out: from being a mullah he turned into an anti-mullah, with his dogmatic character fully intact. Another former *talabeh*, Jamal ad-Din, the so-called Afghan, never had to pause for a moment between his many roles, because he had little continuity of character except for his love of roles. Al-e Ahmad, so concerned about the reformation of society, and at moments so desperate for revolution, was a man of great but slowly changing character who searched for—but never found—a permanent role. In a way the spiritual burden of Al-e Ahmad's message was highly individual, for all the wanton energy of his critique of Iranian society. He was really the prophet of a religion whose meaning was discovered internally without reliance on external authority, and in this sense he was the forerunner of thousands of young Iranians who rediscovered Islam on their own terms with their own definitions. As Al-e Ahmad said near the end of his life: "Somewhere I wrote that for me the Imam of the Age is spread in the body of each individual. The Imam of the Age for whom we are all waiting is within each one of us."

CHAPTER NINE

In TEHRAN, Ali often thought of one of Saadi's lines: "Either choose not to make friends with elephant drivers, or build a house fit for an elephant." Basically, he had two sets of friends in Tehran, neither of which he could quite satisfy: on the one hand those, both mullahs and pious businessmen, who sought him out as an outstanding young scholar with ties to the leading men of Qom; and on the other hand, the secularized professors in the humanities and social sciences who were delighted to have a student who was also a liberal mullah. His professors found that they could talk to him and that he was witty and learned, and he had quickly been accepted as a kind of cadet member of their *dowreh* devoted to Islamic philosophy. But his association with each group slightly compromised him in the view of the other group, and he never really remodeled his life so as to provide an elephant-sized space for either group to park in.

One of the first group, a pious merchant named Bagher Vahid, was a thorn in Ali's side, and Ali would have kept his distance

from the man if he hadn't been a business associate of Ali's
brother. Bagher came from a family of local landlords of Jafarabad, a small town in the Qom region, and his one endearing trait
was his loyalty to people of this region. When he had first taken a
room in the bazaar of Tehran he sold crops grown on the family
lands around Jafarabad. Then he opened a small factory in Tehran
to produce cooking oil, most of which he sold to wholesalers in
the Qom region, including Ali's older brother. His brother begged
Ali to find time for Bagher, because the two brothers had become
deeply involved in each other's affairs. Ali might have been
trapped into some kind of contact with Bagher anyway because of
his own curiosity about and concern for the poorer Qomis who
had emigrated to Tehran. For Bagher showed his loyalty to the
Qom region and, in particular, to Jafarabad and its surrounding
villages by staffing his Tehran factory with as many competent
men from the Qom region as he could find work for.

Bagher was considered extraordinarily wealthy by Qomi standards, but by Tehran standards his factory was modest and he
himself was only well-to-do. As Ali later learned, Bagher thought
the only obstacle between himself and fabulous riches was his
difficulty in getting credit with which to buy better machinery
and, perhaps, even to buy the large farms near the Caspian where
sunflowers and soybeans were grown and where the crude oil
processed at his factory was prepared. Bagher claimed that the big
investment banks that lent money to businesses at low rates were
just lying when they said that his business did not have the record
or assets to secure a loan. They lied, he said, because everyone
knew that they kept the overwhelming majority of their loans for
about twenty giant Iranian firms.

It was Bagher's search for credit that got him together with Ali.
Bagher telephoned Ali, politely explained that they had met when
he had gone to Qom to pay his *sahm-e Imam* and had stopped to
visit Ali's brother. Then he asked if Ali would do him the honor
of visiting him in his office in the bazaar since he urgently needed
Ali's advice. Ali didn't feel like wasting the two hours such a visit
would cost him. It would take two hours partly because of the
time it would take Ali to find his way around the huge and un-
familiar bazaar area of southern Tehran and partly because of the

inevitable oceans of small talk Bagher would engage in before getting to the point. Ali said he was at Bagher's service, but if the question should be anywhere within his capacity of answering, he would almost certainly be able to answer it by phone, especially as he remembered Bagher well and respected his continuing high character among people of the Qom region. Bagher pushed a bit, offering remarks about how fortunate he was to have a religious and learned friend such as Ali, with whom he could consult on a really confidential matter. But as Ali refused to take the hint and persisted in saying that he was unworthy of such compliments, Bagher finally gave in and came to the point. He had always borrowed money in the bazaar on short-term loans because of the cash-flow difficulties in his business, and he had always taken these loans in a proper Islamic way, sometimes making the borrower a partner for the term of the loan in the equipment he bought, and so forth. He now had an opportunity to borrow a large sum on reasonable terms and to double the size of his business. Would Ali take an omen for him by opening his Koran and interpreting the first verse that his eye fell on?

Ali felt he deserved better than this. After twenty years of studying Islamic law he should at least be consulted on the fine points of contract and not be used as a mere fortune-teller. But he wanted to be polite—and, after all, he himself had benefited from the omen that his teacher of *erfan* had come across when deciding to accept him as a pupil. Ali asked Bagher to wait, took a Koran out of his pocket, and opened it at random. To his embarrassment, his eye fell on the verse "O you who believe: Do not take the Jews and Christians as friends. They are each other's friends and whoever among you turns to them is of them. God does not guide an unjust people." Ali was embarrassed, because many narrow-minded people took this verse quite literally, while he felt that it referred to the specific circumstances in which it was revealed: Mohammed's small community of Muslims was tempted to take as "official friends" (which in a tribal society meant protectors) powerful Christian and Jewish Arabs; and these people fell away from the fellowship of Islam into the company of people who scorned the new religion.

Ali never got a chance to explain any of this. As soon as he finished translating the verse Bagher burst out: "This is incredible! This is incredible! I was going to borrow the money from a Jew, and you didn't know that! This really is 'the Tongue of the Unseen' speaking! How can I express my appreciation? I will always be indebted to you for your kindness. I stand at your blessed command."

Ali already suspected that it had been a mistake to be helpful; a week later he was certain. Bagher telephoned and said that the Jewish businessman had gone bankrupt. The Jewish businessman had owed money himself, and his creditors were demanding immediate payment from everybody who had borrowed from him. Bagher would have been caught with a demand for immediate repayment had he taken out the loan. Ali felt hopelessly trapped. He knew that Bagher was convinced that Ali had a direct line to God, and that he, Ali, would now stand at Bagher's not especially blessed command to give omens for all sorts of business matters.

Ali thought of preparing for such occasions by gathering a list of verses that meant practically nothing out of context, such as: "We shall brand it on the snout" or "Except for a boiling hot fluid and a filthy fluid, intensely cold"; or else he might scare Bagher, who was a big eater, by reading a passage condemning gluttony. But in the end he was too conscientious to do anything of the sort, and, fortunately, the next three or four times Bagher called for an omen, Ali's eye fell on passages expressing pious thoughts that both of them readily understood but could not sensibly connect with Bagher's immediate problems. Finally Ali had the courage to suggest that God had used him once so that Bagher should turn to him for advice on matters that made use of Ali's more specialized training.

The change was a relief for both of them. Many of the immigrants from Jafarabad and the rest of the Qom area had settled in one neighborhood of Tehran, and Bagher had bought a piece of land in this area which he wanted to make a *vaqf*, a pious trust, and build a mosque on it. Ali was able to advise on the drafting of the deed of trust. Then, a few months later, Bagher insisted that Ali accompany him on a Thursday afternoon to visit the half-constructed mosque and advise him on the Koranic and other inscriptions that should be written in the proper places on its new walls.

Bagher arrived at Ali's house late in the afternoon in a magnificent American car driven by Bagher's nephew. They drove west through a section of small, squalid factories to a part of Tehran Ali had never seen and arrived at a slightly raised piece of ground overlooking a shallow dish-shaped depression. The houses on the raised ground looked decent and were arranged along streets that followed some sort of geometrical plan, but the crazy jumble of houses in the depression, with their façades and roofs of melting mud brick and tin, looked as if they had been washed into total disorder by Noah's flood. In fact, these seemingly flood-wracked buildings seemed so dangerously impermanent that one half wished the flood had lasted another forty days to finish off the remains.

They parked the huge American car on the raised ground in an open space near the half-built mosque. As soon as Ali got out he realized that everybody around him was speaking with thick versions of the accent of the Qom region, which he had finally managed to lose. Ali, Bagher, and the nephew walked under the central dome of the mosque, which so far consisted only of brick and poured concrete. The dome enclosed a huge area, and Ali was impressed by the expansive feel of the place and by the expansive generosity of Bagher, whom he had slightly disliked up to this moment. Bagher might be a shallow man, interested in the meaning of religion in only a very conventional and almost superstitious way, but his generosity in religious matters was on an unconventional scale.

Bagher said that the architect wanted to leave large parts of both the interior and exterior bare concrete, as they now were, in order to express the religious value of simplicity and austerity, but, Bagher said, he himself thought a mosque of plain concrete without tiles was more like an expression of nakedness than austerity. Ali, who had spent what seemed like the better part of a lifetime following colored patterns with his eye, from his first fascination with the stained-glass windows at home to the interwoven designs on the tiles of the Faiziyeh, agreed.

A crowd of neighborhood people had gathered around them. Bagher explained that this evening they had the great honor of having with them Ayatollah Hashemi, who had just become a jurisconsult and was an outstanding teacher in Qom. A bystander,

Musa, apparently the household steward for Bagher, took on the role of spokesman and kissed Ali's hand, to his embarrassment. Musa said that the arrival of Ayatollah Hashemi was an act of God—their mullah was ill, and they would be deeply honored if Ayatollah Hashemi would lead their prayers that evening. Ali said that God forbade anyone to call him an ayatollah when there were others, his seniors in learning and in every way, who deserved that title, but of course he would be glad to lead the prayer.

After the prayer Musa, who consistently addressed Bagher as "Engineer Vahid," insisted that they come to his house. It was much like the other houses in the better neighborhood on the higher ground. It was small, built of baked brick—as were most houses in the neighborhood—and jutted out at unexpected points on the second story where rooms had been enlarged in defiance of municipal building ordinances. The entrance led into a hall, which opened on two ground-floor rooms and a tiny courtyard in the rear, maybe four meters by four meters. The reception room was on the second floor, out of reach of the smell of the kerosene stove which pervaded the ground floor. Musa made an elaborate fuss, insisting that Ali shouldn't stop to look while he showed Bagher how he had installed one of Bagher's cast-off bathtubs in the bathroom with a ring of supporting bricks. The house had both electricity and running water. Bagher said he thought he had some pipes that had to be removed and that next time Musa came to work he could take them and actually hook up his newly acquired bathtub.

Ali and Bagher sat in the place of honor, and as the room began to fill, Ali realized that he was replacing the ill mullah not only as a prayer leader but also as supervisor of the *hay'at*. A *hay'at* was an informal neighborhood council with a religious purpose, which met on Thursday evenings. Ali, who had virtually no experience as a pastoral mullah, felt his heart sink, but inwardly repeated the proverb, If the water has risen above your head, what difference if it's too deep by one fathom or by one hundred? When the room had filled he recited a longish prayer in Arabic in order to decrease the time for discussion, but no one seemed deterred.

Musa spoke first. He praised Bagher for his generosity to the neighborhood and his loyalty to the people of Jafarabad and the other towns and villages near Qom. He said that even before he started building the mosque Bagher had arranged for a tent to be pitched on the property for the "breast-beating" ceremony their *hay'at* organized on every anniversary of the death of Hosain. He said he had just one question with which he would trouble the ayatollah (Ali mumbled, "I am not an ayatollah"): Was television lawful? Ali had already seen some television aerials in the neighborhood, and he immediately understood from Musa's tone of voice that his host was against television. Ali knew he was already more than a fathom in above his head. He himself had a television set and thought there was nothing unlawful about television but he also knew that some mullahs said that television was unlawful because moving images of people could be provocative and because Iranian television was controlled by ungodly people. Ali gave a long, ambiguous answer, full of quotes in Arabic and summaries in Persian, the upshot of which was that while many television programs were potentially harmful, programs changed all the time, and they should ask their regular mullah.

A young man spoke: he tried to lead the life of a good Muslim, but sometimes he had problems. He liked listening to music on the radio, but sometimes the music inflamed his thoughts and it became very difficult to keep them pure. Ali said that there was no doubt that the city was full of traps, and it needed inner strength to avoid these traps. One shouldn't listen to the music if one felt weak, and, Ali added, prayer was a source of inner strength that should never be forgotten.

A bent old man began to speak. He was the kind of man in baggy country pants who would have been as uncomfortable in Western-style trousers as he would have been in women's clothes. He spoke slowly in a dry voice, with far less apparent emotion than Musa or the young man. The ayatollah's wisdom and his understanding of the people from Qom gave him the courage as a farmer from a village near Qom to ask a question that he had not dared to ask before. His wife had died before he came to Tehran, and his eldest daughter was raising his children. He still had not found a permanent job and lived in the sunken area nearby. His daughter was very beautiful; life in Tehran was full of temptations, and a wealthy man had offered to keep her; he did not know how to make her stay home, where he needed her; yet for her to go to this man was like death to him.

As the man spoke Ali saw that, although elderly, he was not as old as he had first appeared. With the broad, shallow pockmarks on his face and the large irregular patches of white in his beard and hair he looked as if the hot sun of Qom had grabbed away pieces of his skin, had shrunk him and had left him partly dead on the surface.

Ali was appalled. He felt himself totally inadequate. Any advice he could give would be deceptive, since it would imply that this man had some kind of control over his situation, while the man was really a piece of the soil of Qom dumped by some flood in the filthy depression next door. Ali spoke of the importance of consultation, and he implied that the old man's neighbors should consult with him with a view to helping him. Then he told the story of Noah, how Noah had had to be satisfied with saving those willing to be saved. Then, realizing that he was actually sweating from embarrassment, he recited a prayer in Arabic to close the meeting and stood.

As he left the room he felt Musa slip an envelope into his pocket. He immediately handed it to Bagher's nephew and said, "If this can be spent on building the mosque, please do so." The nephew, who had started the evening in a mood of ill-concealed boredom, had become increasingly interested in Ali as the evening wore on. Ali had heard that the nephew was the "fixer" for the family business: he got government licenses to manufacture from the Ministry of Industry and Mines, got building permissions from the Tehran municipality, got permissions to import from the Ministry of Commerce, filed papers with the Ministry of Labor on wages, health benefits, and so on *ad infinitum.*

Once in the car the nephew said to Ali: "We were deeply honored to have you tonight. I was very religious when I was young, and when I was my father's assistant in the bazaar in Jafarabad I organized a group of apprentices who read the Koran under the supervision of a mullah. I admit I have not been so religious since I came to Tehran, but you have renewed my interest in religion. These people in government have no religion; no wonder everything they do comes out half-baked. Can you find time to teach us?"

Ali, who was now thoroughly soaked with sweat and felt like a victim of Noah's flood, suddenly had an inspiration. "Haji Bagher, I will telephone the offices of all the 'models,' and we will find a mullah who will be freer than I am and can visit you and your nephew frequently in the bazaar, at your factory, and at home. I regard this as almost a religious obligation."

"This is extraordinarily good of you! God recompense you. What troubles you put yourself to!" As he spoke, Bagher seemed on fire with the excitement of having an in-house mullah, and Ali, glimpsing the prospect of relief from Bagher's attention for the first time in many months, said, "What trouble? It's nothing worth mentioning." Ali was a little frightened by the slight irony in his own voice when he said this, but Bagher apparently noticed nothing. All the way back to Ali's house he bubbled with plans to find tasks and contacts for the new mullah and promised that he would be paid appropriately.

Ali devoted the next day to arranging the matter and had his brother call Bagher and personally recommend the candidate they had chosen. Although Bagher did not fade completely out of Ali's life he now became a minor annoyance, seldom heard from. Ali, who had seen scores of his students go out to become the mullahs of neighborhoods and villages, now thanked God he had the talent to remain in a life of learning, since he clearly lacked the courage—he was tempted to say audacity—to tell other people how to live their lives. He now appreciated more than ever before the Koranic verse "And similarly among men and beasts and cattle are there those of differing colors. Only the learned fear God among His servants; God is powerful and forgiving."

. . .

In the traditional Iranian city, religion lived with a particular character that could not be found in the villages. There were three indispensable features (and usually three correspondingly magnificent buildings) to a city: a seat of government, a bazaar, and a "grand," or "Friday," mosque, Friday being the day for communal prayer. Since by custom there was only one grand mosque in a city, this mosque represented the self-willed unity of the city in a way that the other two buildings could not. The prayer leader in the grand mosque had precedence among all the holders of pulpits in the mosques of the city and was understood to be in some senses the ceremonial leader of all the collective, public religious life of the city.

The relation of the mosque to the seat of government was always, in theory, problematical but often, in practice, cordial. The Safavis, or their official who acted as a sort of "minister of religion," appointed the Friday prayer leaders. After the Safavis this position was more or less hereditary in one family in each city, provided that the family could produce a son who was qualified to preach. Otherwise the Friday prayer leader would choose a deputy, who had the inside track to succeed to this position if he made a success of his temporary appointment. Some post-Safavi governments, even in the twentieth century, have issued decrees appointing Friday prayer leaders, but these decrees merely recognized what that marvelously self-regulating instrument, the informal consensus of the religious community of the city, had already decided.

On a theoretical level the relation of the mosque to the bazaar was altogether friendly, but on a practical level it too could face problems. The bazaar merchants did not always like the justice of the mullah courts (which, in turn, sometimes depended on the government for execution of their decrees). And some bazaar merchants were the patrons of forms of popular religious expression, such as the *taaziyeh*, which some great mullahs disapproved of. Nevertheless, while both the government and the mosque generally regarded cordial coexistence as a condition for their mutual survival, the mosque (in the sense of the urban religious establishment) and the bazaar actually acted to give each other shape and sustenance. To be successful, especially in commercial dealings over the long term, a bazaar merchant needed the capital of a good reputation as much as he needed material capital. If he were a Muslim, to have a good reputation he had to tithe himself and pay this tithe to a mullah, either a "model" or the representative of a "model." Correspondingly, a mullah could finance the religious life of the community in proportion to the tithes he received.

There were also ways in which religion lived in the bazaar relatively independently from the mosque as an endogenous expression of bazaar life. The most important of these endogenous bazaar expressions of religion was the *hay'at*, the "association." Alongside the groups with informal boundaries which work by consensus, such as the mullahs or the bazaar community, Iranian society has long fostered small groups of friends who meet regularly to promote shared goals or, simply, to meet. In traditional Iranian society such a group among the people of the bazaar almost inevitably took on a religious coloring; to be respectable, its meetings had to begin and end with some form of religious exhortation.

The merchants of the bazaar often belonged to *hay'ats* that met once a week in each other's homes to hear a mullah preach. In such cases men of the mosque were guests of men of the bazaar (although, of course, in traditional Iranian society there were a fair number of bazaar merchants who considered themselves to be and dressed as mullahs). The merchants of the bazaar also contributed to the *hay'ats* that their apprentices voluntarily formed in order to read the Koran under the supervision of a mullah. Contributions to the *hay'ats* of the apprentices were not only a pious act but also were a way of exercising some influence over one of the most dangerous elements in the bazaar—unmarried and unpropertied male adolescents.

In a Shiah context, *hay'ats* of people in the bazaar at the merchant, apprentice, and even lower levels of society quite naturally turned to the subject of Hosain, and some *hay'ats* existed primarily to keep the members mindful of the martyrdom of Hosain. Among the poor, both in the city and in the country, *hay'ats* of this nature, which took part in the Moharram processions commemorating the martyrdom of Hosain, were practically the only voluntary organizations that existed.

By the mid-seventies traditional Iranian cities were small islands surrounded by the newer constructions of the Pahlavi era. Al-e Ahmad's lament for the villager who "in search of work flees from the village to the town so he can drink Pepsi Cola and eat a five-kran sandwich and see a Brigitte Bardot film for two tomans," was as much prophecy as description. Between 1966—roughly when Al-e Ahmad described his villager—and 1976 the urban population increased 6 percent annually. Cities engulfed surrounding villages; at least a third of a million Iranians became city dwellers, not because they chose to live in the city but because the cities grew to enclose their villages. But of course the majority of new city dwellers, like Al-e Ahmad's peasant, had left their villages on purpose.

The trend had begun well before this period. In 1900 there were only three cities with a population of over a hundred thousand; by 1948 these were eight; by 1956, ten; by 1966, fourteen; and by 1976, twenty-three. But the giant was Tehran; by 1976 at least 13 percent of Iran's total population was living in the capital city, and over 50 percent of the population of Tehran were migrants. While the population of the countryside flowed toward the city more or less without interruption through the twentieth century, there seems to have been a big jump around 1934, when Reza Shah's regime was firmly established, and another jump in the fifties. After this, such a high rate was sustained that the urban population nearly trebled in the period from 1956 to 1976, while the rural population increased just over a third. In this last period, step migration—from village to town, then town to city—was no longer common; villagers were moving directly from communities of a few hundred to cities of over a million.

Migrants to the city were not a random ingathering of Pepsi-Cola lovers. Typically they were males between twenty and twenty-four and females between thirty-five and thirty-nine. (Probably the women came to join their husbands and brothers only when these husbands and brothers felt themselves somewhat securely established.) There were wealthy and middle-class migrants, but the great numbers came from the landless poor of the villages, the farm laborers who had been the biggest losers in the wake of land reform. And among the landless poor they tended to be the better educated, those whose literacy, however rudimentary, had freed them of the villager's terror of the city. They were the people the countryside had treated least well and who were willing to risk everything they had on the city, which they knew, for all its wealth, might treat them even worse.

The cities often did treat them worse. The least fortunate were the squatters, who lived in their huts of hammered scrap metal surrounded by seas of muck and vermin, sharing one hand-dug outhouse between ten or more families. They were a few tens of thousands in the fifties, perhaps a few hundreds of thousands in the seventies. They were largely silent in their misery; to speak would be to risk notice, and notice might mean expulsion, which would be an instant forfeit in their all-or-nothing gamble to find a niche in the life of the city.

The majority of migrants were slightly more fortunate; they found employment in the new factories and the vastly expanded service industries of the postwar era. But they had won only half their wager; they had found jobs but not decent places to live. Speculation in urban real estate has been the real winning game in Iranian history of the last forty years, and it has been a game the rich never tired of. It kept the price of houses completely outside the reach of wage earners. And in their anxiety to convert land to middle- and upper-class housing, owners often refused repairs or improvements to the lower-class renter, who could find himself living in quarters only marginally better than the squatter's, with even less security. Nevertheless most migrants thought themselves better off in the city. Despite the sentimental longing that the intellectuals had for the migrants to return to the land, most of the migrants were not interested.

Some of these migrants lived or worked near those two great institutions, the bazaar and the mosque, that had given form to the religious life of the traditional city and were drawn into their orbit. Most, however, lived far from mosque and bazaar in the oddly assorted and often ragged wrappings of new neighborhoods that surrounded the old city. And they worked as day laborers on the skeletons of huge apartment buildings, or in the enormous shedlike factories with corrugated roofs, or as peddlers and sweepers in the shadow of the high-rise banks and ministries that had replaced the mosque and the covered bazaar as the giant buildings emblematic of city life. It was not easy, often not possible for the renters in the new neighborhoods to find a point of entry into the collective life of the merchants or bazaar apprentices or into the *dowrehs* of the intellectuals or of the established bureaucrats. What they did find was that they could make something resembling *dowrehs* for themselves: they could create their own *hay'ats*.

The neighborhood *hay'ats* had a somewhat different character from the *hay'ats* formed in the bazaar. In size they were about the same, seldom made up of more than fifty people, often around thirty. But unlike the *hay'ats* of the bazaar, such as the *hay'at* of the tailors' apprentices or that of the cooking-oil wholesalers, the neighborhood *hay'ats* were formed on the basis of neighborly contact or, more often, of village and regional origin—the *hay'at* of migrants from Aliabad or from Nishapur, for example. Often, of course, these bases for membership overlapped; the people of the same village tried to settle near one another and often sought work in the same factory. In fact, many migrants would not have been able to stay without such ties. A study in Tehran in the 1970s showed that 34 percent of a sampling of migrants had received loans from relatives and friends, and the first line of friends were one's fellow villagers.

The neighborhood *hay'at* shared the character of the bazaar *hay'at* in that, while it had a strongly religious character, the mullah (if any) who attended it was the guest of the *hay'at*, which usually met not in the mullah's official terrain, the mosque, but in the houses of its members, especially in the house of its "leader." This leader emerged as such by virtue of his comparative economic success (he had the most appropriate house or apartment), his enterprise (he found the *rowzeh-khans* and other mullahs who would preach at the *hay'at*), and his trustworthiness (he gathered the contributions from the members to pay for the *rowzeh-khans* and defray other expenses). On occasion he would even be the middleman who would get a rich person to construct a mosque for the neighborhood.

A typical meeting of a *hay'at* with a clergyman present would begin with members of the *hay'at* reading verses from the Koran in sequence, while the mullah corrected their pronunciation; or, in the case of a *hay'at* of nearly illiterate or illiterate members, the mullah would himself recite the Koran in Arabic. Then the mullah would preach, and, finally, he would open the meeting to questions. Overwhelmingly the questions were about what was ritually clean or unclean, including the new temptations that the city had to offer, the Pepsi-Colas and Brigitte Bardot films which had lured Al-e Ahmad's peasant away from the countryside in the first place. Then came the *rowzeh*: the events of Hosain's martyrdom were recited by the clergyman, after which all stood and for ten to fifteen minutes beat their breasts in a rhythm to fit an elegiac poem. The head of the *hay'at* discreetly gave the mullah a contribution as he left. A *rowzeh-khan* might visit two or three such meetings in one evening.

In the later sixties a new feature was added to these more formal meetings of *hay'ats* (which, incidentally, also had less formal meetings): the playing of a cassette with a sermon by a popular preacher. The radio had conquered Iran in the fifties and early sixties, putting a powerful instrument first in the hands of Mossadegh, then of the shah; by 1965 there were approximately two million radios, with an estimated audience of ten million. In the later sixties and, especially, in the seventies Iranians learned to their delight that they could control the electronic noise in their lives: they discovered cassettes. Every self-respecting taxi had a cassette player in nearly continuous operation. And as Iran was (and is) not a member of the copyright union, Iranian entrepreneurs bought machines to duplicate foreign cassettes by the hundreds. Popular preachers, critical of the government, no longer felt their exclusion from the state-controlled radio so keenly; God had given them a new medium. Shops dealing in cassettes of religious sermons appeared in all bazaars of any significance.

Given the opportunity to choose between hundreds of sermons, Iranians became discriminating connoisseurs of preaching, especially as a cassette cost about three dollars, the equivalent of a day's worth of meals for an Iranian of the lower middle class. But cassettes were worth it; they not only gave you control of the music and the sermons you heard, they also offered you a chance to thumb your nose at the government as you listened in private to sermons obliquely critical of it, or even to those of Khomeini (smuggled from Iraq), which were directly critical. You wanted a live preacher at your *hay'at*, but, thanks to the cassette, you could also afford to listen to the best preaching around, and many *hay'ats* chose to listen to both a live and a taped preacher in one session.

There was a change in the attitude toward politics and toward mullahs in second-generation migrants which eventually affected the character of the *hay'ats*. In a small village the mullah had been a man of scant education who had to work part or full time to supplement his income as a religious leader. Even in large and prosperous villages the mullah, while respected and considered a necessity of life, was put down behind his back as a man overwhelmingly preoccupied with two subjects: his income and narrow-minded rulings of the law. A universal Iranian joke tells of the village mullah who fell into a half-dug well and, despite a circle of villagers shouting, "Give me your hand!," sat at the bottom in angry silence. Then a more experienced villager came over and told them, "Gentlemen, you never ask a mullah to give anything"; and when he said to the mullah, "Take my hand" the mullah responded and was saved.

Slowly the image of the mullah changed. The children of the migrants did not know the village mullah; they did know the activist mullah who was eager to reach the urban poor and to preach at their *hay'ats*. In the summer of 1962, when an earthquake destroyed part of the provincial city of Qazvin, the *talabehs* from Qom and elsewhere were among the first to bring help to the homeless. In the winter of 1963, one of the coldest in recent Iranian history, Khomeini, while under arrest, sent out a proclamation that the wealthy should help the poor; and, in fact, some wealthy men of the bazaar did distribute charcoal and funds.

This pattern of activism continued, especially among the *talabehs*. The mullah was no longer a slightly burdensome though necessary expense to you. Instead he now became someone whose concerns you could seriously listen to and who seemed to have your well-being at heart. Often he was present in your life because you yourself wanted him there: he came as your guest to your *hay'at* in your home. When he complained that the government neglected the needs of the masses, his and your interests seemed to coincide, and you might well feel that the harassment he claimed to suffer was something that touched you personally. The government did not seem to have any serious interest in religion. Therefore religion became something that you could provide for yourself in defiance of the government's lack of interest and that at the same time no government would have the nerve to interfere with. Further, the more you identified with the concerns of the local religious activists, the more the gulf between you and the government widened.

There was a corresponding change in the image of Hosain. In 1969 a book entitled *The Eternal Martyr* was published in which the author claimed that Hosain had not gone to Kerbela simply to be martyred but that martyrdom had been the subordinate consequence of Hosain's political activism. He had gone to Kerbela intending to overthrow an unjust government and, if possible, to win. The Shiah religious community was split: two of the "models" of Qom approved of the book, two disapproved. The religious community had usually been successful in keeping its quarrels private, but this quarrel was too violent, and in a sense too fundamental, to be hidden; one faction even killed a member of the opposite faction. Eventually the quarrel subsided with a seemingly official victory for the older, passive image of Hosain that the *rowzeh-khans* preferred, but in fact the new image continued to gain ground. It was supported by Montazeri and Meshkini, two leading *madreseh* teachers in Qom who were spokesmen for and former pupils of Khomeini. And it was a central theme of the talks of Shariati, whose cassettes had an enormous popularity among young literate men even in the villages. The seemingly insane theater of the guerrillas of the early seventies who had fought against hopeless odds began to be seen in a different light.

In general, the atmosphere grew angrier. In some years the cost of housing rose by as much as 30 percent, and the wage earner in a rented house paid accordingly and despaired accordingly of ever owning his own bit of the city. At the same time, government-sponsored adult literacy classes at factories had made almost 100 percent of the long-term employees of large factories literate, and with literacy came a new curiosity about politics. In fact, their fathers' generation, before land reform, had rather enjoyed politics, because, even if many parties were outlawed, there were often hard-fought elections between rival landlords in the countryside who courted the peasants (and especially their local mullahs) to get themselves elected. When they moved to the city, they didn't bother to vote. Nobody was offering inducements—

and anyway, after 1975 there was only one party. Their sons and daughters were far more interested in politics, but the only politics that reached the masses was the politics of the government and the implicit political message of Islam. Even the squatters, who remained the most timid and least politically active element in the population, became more visibly angry. In 1958, when a squatter settlement was bulldozed, the inhabitants ran away; in 1977 they had a five-hour pitched battle with the authorities in the course of which they killed a policeman.

The importance of religion to the urban lower and middle classes in Iran is as much an enigma for the historian of twentieth-century Iran as it is for the historian of England during the industrial revolution. At times intensified religious feeling and at times an increased disrespect for religion can seize the person who moves from the countryside to the partly industrialized city, and in early Victorian England there were signs of both. In 1844 Friedrich Engels, in his carefully observed study *The Condition of the Working-Class in England*, wrote: "[Among] the masses there prevails almost universally a total indifference to religion, or at the utmost, some trace of Deism too underdeveloped to amount to more than mere words, or a vague dread of the words infidel, atheist, etc." The religious census of 1851 confirmed the interpretation of Engels when it found that the working class was far less likely to have ties to churches than the middle or upper classes.

Al-e Ahmad had also described the growth of irreligion among the lower classes. In *Euromania* he spoke of the change in the Iranian migrant to the city: "This man, who believes in predestination, tells fortunes by opening books at random or consulting a rosary, makes holiday sacrifices and accepts soup offered as devotional charity as his due, is now involved with machines.... His brakes will engage no more quickly nor will his motor run more slowly because of his monthly sacrifices. So, when his monthly sacrifice has no effect and he keeps having accidents, he suddenly gets fed up, knuckles under, and either turns out completely apathetic and a criminal or just drifts with the wind." Even in the traditional villages there could be a traditional village agnostic. One American anthropologist describes an illiterate man in the village he studied who got fed up with all the talk of Hosain and started saying to people, "Just tell me, who is this Hosain? I don't believe he ever existed." There may have been many more such agnostics among the lower class and lower middle class of Tehran than there had been in the villages, despite all the *hay'ats* and new mosques.

Yet insofar as the migrants were religious, they were so with a new intensity in both the Iran of the sixties and seventies and the England of the industrial revolution. Chapel religion was in some measure religion that the neglected constructed for themselves in England in the eighteenth and early nineteenth centuries, and the Anglican evangelicals and the Methodists were the churchmen who reached out to them with a religion that seemed concerned with their destiny in a way that a government of the middle and upper classes was not. In 1789 John Wesley, preaching in Dublin "On the Causes of the Inefficacy of Christianity," said: "Is not the neglect of [providing for the poor] one cause why so many are still sick and weak among you; and that both in soul and in body? that they still grieve the Holy Spirit, by preferring the fashions of the world to the commands of God?" This passage also hints at another cause for the intense religiosity of the urban migrant: he needs a more self-willed belief to resist the "traps" of the city, and if—as is usually true of a member of a *hay'at*—he is the father of a family, he needs the force of religion and the image of religiosity to keep control of his family, particularly his children.

The net effect of such religion on politics is not easily measured in either historical example. One view of the English working class holds that Methodism made for social discipline and avoided revolution. Another view sees Methodism as the sterile consolation, the long-lasting lollipop that the English working class clapped into its mouth after the failure of political reform in 1815. Still another view says that chapel religion gave its members an identity, and therefore a class consciousness, which allowed them eventually to form political parties that made sophisticated demands directed at their own interests.

The burden of religion for the Iranian urban masses is no easier to make out. What is clear is that, even if statistically (which is not certain) members of *hay'ats* were a minority, they were people who cared a great deal for their *hay'ats*, and their *hay'ats* represented the only nongovernment-sponsored organization known to urban members of the lower and lower middle classes. It is clear that the urban members of these classes were becoming in some sense politically aware and aware that members of the religious establishment were concerned about them. It is also clear that they knew that enormous wealth was coming to Iran, and if they didn't understand the shah's plan of capital-intensive projects for a perpetual boom, they did understand that no one was building public housing or even the sewers and paved roads for their neighborhoods—which would have directly benefited them—except as occasional token gestures. The government kept the price of bread artificially low and forced employers to pay annual bonuses of two and even three months' wages to their employees. It wasn't enough. The migrants and their children had gambled on the city, and they felt that if only the government had done its full share, they would have won handsomely.

In 1976, 1977, and 1978, when shortages of basic commodities such as onions went on for weeks at a time and even the rich couldn't find cement to build additions to their houses, there was an impatient, often angry mood among urban Iranians. If this mood motivated a few thousand squatters to fight the Tehran municipality in 1977, it motivated hundreds of thousands of the working and lower middle classes to march in the revolutionary demonstrations of 1979. Of the angry, they were the angriest. They created neither the strategy nor the ideology of the revolution, and their opposition alone would never have cowed the regime. But they contributed the gigantic numbers before which the will of the government and the army collapsed. The mullahs, who had telephones, knew whom to contact to bring out the masses without telephones; many of those who marched came as members of their *hay'ats*. And many felt that they had internalized the fearless spirit of Hosain. As one squatter told an Iranian social scientist in the mid-seventies, "Nothing brings us together more than love for Imam Hosain."

CHAPTER TEN

EVEN THOUGH February 17, 1978, was a cold day, Ali decided to walk the one and a half kilometers from the University of Tehran to Ahmad's institute. Ahmad was the only man in Tehran he could think of who might have something useful to say about his problem. Even if he had nothing useful to say, Ahmad would at least understand the problem, because he too had been trained at Qom.

Ahmad had grown up in Kerman, and although he retained only a slight Kermani accent, he did wonderful comic imitations of Kermanis speaking a Persian only barely intelligible to Tehranis. But his parents came from Zabol, a tiny town in the province of Sistan, a province neighboring Kerman. Sistan was the homeland of the hero Rostam in the national epic, and Ali liked to imagine Rostam as an enormous version of Ahmad, who was a handsome man with warm brown eyes and a charming smile. Ahmad, in fact, was not very small, even unexpanded to the dimensions of Rostam. He was tall, and for all that he was sixty, he was a broad-shouldered and remarkably robust man, especially for a university professor.

Yet, in spite of his stature and health, Ahmad always looked slightly oppressed. Ahmad never felt that he had lived up to the promise of his youth. He came from a family of small bazaar merchants, who had sent him to the local *madreseh* as well as to the state school, and his *madreseh* teachers had been so impressed with his talent that they had arranged for him to go to Qom at thirteen. He had been an outstanding success during his first years at the Faiziyeh, but then people began to notice that he was interested only in logic, philosophy, and rhetoric, and his roommate reported that when he tried to wake him for morning prayers, Ahmad could scarcely disguise how annoyed he felt. Nevertheless Ahmad stuck it out at Qom, avoiding the advanced classes in theology, law, and jurisprudence, until he was about twenty.

Seven years after his arrival in Qom he suddenly appeared without his turban and aba and left town. At first he eked out a miserable existence in Tehran from the fees he collected for cataloguing manuscripts for booksellers and for translating modern Arabic theologians into Persian. Then a second breath of life reinflated his career: a powerful landlord from Kerman, who was also an important man in the court, "discovered" him and supported him until he took the university entrance exams. With his outstanding marks, he easily won a place at the University of Tehran. He no longer needed powerful friends; again his teachers applauded his every step forward, and he won a scholarship to do advanced work abroad. He studied philosophy in England and the United States. When his thesis on an Iranian Islamic philosopher was published to much acclaim, he had had the opportunity to take a university post somewhere in the English-speaking world. He chose to return to a post at the University of Tehran and to marry a Kermani wife. He could be heard talking with her in a thick Kermani accent, presumably more for its expressiveness than for its comic qualities.

His choice of a wife and a job seemed to have been Ahmad's last major decisions, after which, to all appearances, his capacity to decide completely left him. This loss was partly due to circumstance. After being a devoted father to his own children he had been a devoted father to the younger children of his sister, who had been widowed and left nearly destitute. Also, as a man with a deep knowledge of philosophy, history, classical Arabic, traditional rhetoric, and classical Persian, he was seized by students and colleagues with questions from the moment he appeared on the university grounds until the moment he left, and with his always kind but slightly oppressed look, he would try to help everyone.

It was to escape these people that he had accepted an office in a research institute out of reach of most (but not all) of his possible captors. Yet even Ahmad knew that he could no longer make choices in life mainly because he no longer wanted to choose. Perhaps inwardly he felt like the Rostam of legend, who, sometimes disturbed by the behavior at the court of the shah, wanted to return to his native Sistan to hunt, to brood, and above all to be left alone. Outwardly he offered a much more homely comparison: he said he sympathized with Mullah Nasreddin when this stock character of Iranian (and Turkish) folklore was acting as a judge in a lawsuit. First the plaintiff argued his case, which he stated so persuasively and eloquently that Mullah Nasreddin was moved to say, "I think you are right." Then the defendant spoke, and he argued his defense so convincingly and tellingly that Mullah Nasreddin said, "I think you are right." At this point the clerk of the court said, "But, Mullah, they can't both be right," and Mullah Nasreddin, following the perverse logic that illuminates so many of his jokes, said, "And I think you too are right."

Combined with this indecision was Ahmad's sense of being intellectually incomplete; he felt he had never really read enough and never studied enough to offer a firm opinion on anything. Privately he would assure his friends that they had no idea, they could not possibly imagine, how ignorant he was. In the semipublic arena of the *dowreh* on Islamic philosophy that he and Ali attended, when Ahmad entered the conversation he would talk brilliantly about a subject for a few minutes, then think up objections to what he had said, then think of things he should have read before he had spoken on the subject. Then, after adding several times, "What can I say? I don't really know," he would tumble into silence and, in his good-natured way, look even more

deeply oppressed than he had before he talked. It was no surprise
that Ahmad published very little, and no surprise that Ahmad,
who recognized how powerfully his choice of hesitation and indecision had worked to produce his own oppression, liked to recite the half line of Hafez: "Because I followed my fancy all my
works drew me to ill fame in the end."

The institute with Ahmad's escape office was a plain, modern
building surrounded by a small garden. When Ali entered his
room on the fourth story he found Ahmad walking around an
enormous gray steel desk with a gray linoleum top which had obviously just been delivered. Ahmad was pleased to have someone
to show his desk to, and as he pulled out the drawers one by one
he said, "Every piece of this beautiful desk was made in Iran. I
can't decide where to place it in the room. Look how easily the
drawers open and close."

Ali liked Ahmad almost as much for his pleasure in little things
and his ability to express it in front of his juniors as for his great
(even if greatly denied) learning.

" 'A table not yet laid raises hopes of a feast.' May you see the
good it can bring," Ali offered in encouragement.

Ahmad restricted his answer to saying, "God willing, God will-
ing," and sighed deeply. He drew up a chair for Ali and sat down.
He said to Ali, "I understand you had some kind of problem with
Davudi."

"It wasn't so much that I had a problem with Davudi; I inherited someone else's problem with Davudi. In his course on
Aristotle, Davudi mentioned that Mohammed is supposed to have
said that Aristotle was a prophet, and he started discussing the
degree to which the Islamic Aristotle was different from any Aristotle that could have lived three and a half centuries before Christ.
He said that Aristotle, like the people around him, believed that
there were animals that are generated spontaneously without parents, and like the people around him admired music and the
drama. At the end of class a woman student in traditional Islamic
dress, the kind of woman you people call 'a daughter of Zainab,'
came up to me and said, 'How can you let that Baha'i attack Mohammed? We were all waiting for you to answer.' I didn't object
to what Davudi said, but then some of these students went up to

him and asked him how he could speak this way in front of a mullah. Davudi said nothing and left, but one student defended him, and then another student accused his defender of being a Baha'i. I felt I couldn't go back to the class without either causing factionalism or stifling my teacher—as they say, 'Where there are two cooks, the soup is either tasteless or too salty.' I don't want to impose in any way, but since you took your turban off forty years ago and no longer smell like a mullah, perhaps you could tell Davudi that I departed for the common good."

Ahmad was already nodding and saying "With greatest pleasure" before Ali finished. "You know," he continued, "one of the things I left Qom for was to discover the Greek Aristotle. It was during the Second World War, perhaps about the time you were born. The war made me fall in love with world history; world history led me to fall in love with a whole variety of philosophies, Islamic and non-Islamic; and my ability to say 'You too are right' led me to fall in love with the indecisive character and perplexity of all human thought. As Hafez says, 'Love seemed easy at first, but then difficulties befell.'"

Ali was touched that Ahmad, so much his senior, should confide in him. Ahmad had always treated Ali as an equal, but he seemed to feel that Ali was also an intimate, a confidant who could intuitively share his inner world. Ali felt bold enough to ask a question he had never dared approach before; he asked Ahmad, "Which 'difficulties' befell you so that you left Qom?"

Ahmad smiled. "I was born with some difficulties you hardly know about; you are a sayyed and come from a wealthy family. My father was a small merchant, and for a brief time I was even an apprentice in the bazaar of Kerman." (Ali winced; he remembered a different bazaar and a different apprentice, the tailor's child assistant, whose disappearance before Ali could understand and comfort him had left a residue of unease in his soul which thirty-odd years had not removed.) "And what a bazaar it was! When I read about the great markets of Isfahan and Baghdad hundreds of years ago, I have some idea of what they were like: great places of making, moving, and storing beautiful things. Or was it just that I was a child? But it must be more than that, because in the twenties, when I was a child, that was dying. There were still silks from Yazd, Kashan, and Rasht, but they were becoming rarer and rarer. Every pot in the kitchen, every stick of furniture in the house used to be made in the bazaar, but people were beginning to buy cheap foreign-manufactured goods and had developed a taste for them, and the bazaar was shrinking and changing. That was why, for all that we hated Reza Shah, we admired him. You don't know what it meant to see the picture of an Iranian match factory in the newspaper. Maybe it was built by men carrying cement on their backs, maybe the equipment came from abroad. But Iran no longer lived on Russian matches; suddenly great quantities of Iranian-made matches appeared in our lives, and it was as if we had recaptured the fire from the hands of foreigners to light our stoves and our lamps. And the railroad! Of course, foreign engineers and foreign equipment were used to build it, but it was a legitimate child of Iran, conceived and—best of all—financed entirely by the Iranian government.

"When the Allies deposed Reza Shah, it was as if God had given us a vision of the afterlife, in which heaven and hell were so mixed that He made any worldly action seem useless. We were really free; you could say anything you felt like saying, write almost anything you felt like writing, and wear almost anything you felt like wearing. Women such as my aunt, who hadn't left her house since Reza Shah's forced unveiling of women, felt as if they had been released from prison, because they could appear in the streets in their chadors. But what could we do with our freedom? Watch the British, American and Russian soldiers who protected goods going from the Persian Gulf to the Caspian? Look at the handful of state factories, built with such difficulty, languish from mismanagement and inefficiency?

"Even though I was a *talabeh* in Qom and felt the relief of every *talabeh* that this man would no longer bully us, I didn't feel stronger. Because when Reza Shah went, it was clear how weak and poor we all really were. Weak, because other people decided at the snap of their fingers that the ruler of Iran should go; poor, because if civil order guaranteed that the bare necessities were distributed throughout Iran, and our own revenues let us build a railroad, most of us never had more than the bare necessities and never rode in a train.

"You don't know how poor a poor *talabeh* was in my time in Qom. We wore clothes cut from an incredibly rough handmade Qomi cloth that you could buy for a few pennies, and toward the end of the month, when we had spent our trifling *talabeh* stipends, we would dream at night of stews and kebabs, because we were living on bread and sesame paste.

"In spite of our poverty there was one luxury I and a few friends never gave up. There was a hotel in Qom where you could listen to the radio if you paid twice the going rate for a glass of tea. We always went for the evening news. A man with a bland voice would read the news of these titanic battles between the Americans and the Japanese or the Germans and the Russians. Sometimes the numbers of people involved were twice what was then the population of Tehran.

"I think it was the war that made me aware of the world and not my reading—but maybe I've got it backward. I was trying to teach myself something about the history of the world, reading books in Persian, in Arabic, and even—with the greatest difficulty—in English. As the proverb says, The man who wants a peacock must take the trouble of going to India. But of all the history I read, the history of the Greeks fascinated me the most. It had the names of philosophers familiar to me from Islamic philosophy—Plato, Aristotle, the Peripatetics—but all living in a world of many idols and, despite their intelligence, not feeling that abomination of idols and of assigning partners to God that we felt. So, as I told you, I took off my turban and went to Tehran—in part, at least, to find the real Aristotle."

"I'm surprised to hear that the real Aristotle was in Tehran in the forties," Ali said. "And I would have thought that when you had discovered him, you would still have found more people to talk philosophy with in Qom."

"You're right in a way," Ahmad admitted with a smile. "In terms of finding Aristotle, Tehran was a disappointment. Remember, though, philosophy was somewhat out of favor during my period in Qom. Don't misunderstand me—in many ways I loved Qom: I loved the give-and-take of discussion in the classes, the amazingly close scrutiny given to texts, and the beautifully subtle distinctions a really good teacher could make. The beauty of the distinctions added new branches and twigs to a tree, but nobody asked about the condition of its roots and trunk. In that sense, if I wanted to understand why other people grew different trees, I had to go to other places.

"You're right for another reason. In 1946 and 1947 we had a vision of heaven and hell jumbled together in a different way from the way they had appeared at the time Reza Shah abdicated. It was hell because we had a weak government, and we suspected that the competing hands of the English and the Russians were behind its every movement. Yet it was also heaven because the freedom lingered on for a few years after the war. There was an atmosphere of good will in the world, and for a while all things seemed possible. The old men of the Constitutional Revolution reappeared and said that the constitution had not been a false dawn and that the sun had continued to rise behind the clouds and would soon shine forth unobstructed. This mood captured me—or was it just my youth that captured me? I don't know."

Ahmad paused to consider his own question, then went on. "Anyway, I was in a mood of hope and of cautious trust toward the distant masses of humanity, whose gigantic battles during the war had excited my imagination. I decided that we should understand Islam in its root meaning, as the innate submission of the human spirit to God, as in the Koranic verse: 'Do they seek something other than the Religion of God while all creatures in the heavens and the earth, willingly or unwillingly, have accepted Islam from Him, and to Him shall they all return?' So my second reason for going to Tehran and then going abroad was that I counted all mankind as in some sense Muslims, and in that mood I decided there were other 'muslim' systems of thought waiting to be discovered which I couldn't find in Qom. After all, despite the beauty of the philosophy taught in Qom, fourteen hundred years after the Prophet the Shiah were a minority among Muslims, and Muslims were very much a minority in the population of the world. If Islam in this broader sense did not exist widely and deeply outside the Islamic world, how could I help but feel that God had betrayed Islam?"

" 'There is no god save God,' " Ali said in a slightly teasing way, pointedly choosing this exclamation for its content as well as its force. "I was beginning to think that your roommate slandered you when he said that much as he liked you, in all honesty he had to admit you had lost your belief. Now I'm beginning to think he was right. Revered professor, with all due respect, I'm an enlightened mullah and I believe that many non-Muslims are saved. And at the same time I believe that the revelation of the Koran is a unique event in human history, even if a majority of mankind have not yet accepted it. Anyway, many people of your generation felt God betrayed Islam because He left the Islamic world weak. Are you sure that you were worried about intellectual betrayal and not about God's political betrayal?"

"I'm nearly sure I was worried about both," Ahmad said, without any resentment at being challenged. "So my roommate remembers me with affection! Tell him that I think of him with affection too when I wake up early and hear the morning call to prayer. But in honor of all the *tas-kebabs* I cooked for the two of us in the front of our room he should admit that he is ignorant about the state of my soul then and now. I am most emphatically not a skeptic, although there are moments when I come perilously close to accepting the advice in the lines of Hafez that say:

> Untie the knot at your heart and pay no heed to the
> heavenly sphere;
> For this is a knot that the deliberation of no
> geometer has ever opened.

But I'm not decisive enough to be a skeptic. I just see everything that has ever been believed swimming in the ideas of its time and place as a fish swims in water."

"With your permission, a problem"—and Ali raised his forefinger as he began to speak. "Either all these systems of belief are understood by you in the terms of our time and place *or* you have properly understood them in the terms of the time and place in which these systems were or are believed. In the second case you have no problem, since you see these beliefs as they really are. But if you think it is impossible for someone to understand beliefs outside their contexts, then you will have to admit that you will never know any beliefs other than your own and have no way of

knowing if these other systems have differences that remain unintelligible because of their different contexts. If these undiscov-
erable differences don't exist, you will have wasted your time
looking for them; if they do exist, then your attempts to discover
them will increase your stock of misinformation."

"A good point—and God bless your fine Qomi mind!" As
Ahmad spoke, Ali noticed that his friend looked less oppressed
than at any time since they had started speaking—less oppressed,
in fact, than at any time they had ever been together. "But,"
Ahmad continued, "consider. Perhaps the differences are discov-
erable and it is possible to imagine contexts different from one's
own, but only by such hard work that although one can continue
to improve one's translation, a perfect translation is out of the
question."

"With your permission, an important point." Ali pushed his
chair back slightly before he went on. He felt that if they were
really going to dispute this question seriously there should be a
suitable distance between the two of them. "You may remember,
since you were so good at it, that at Qom we study Arabic grammar and rhetoric because, first, we can understand the Arabic of
the time of the Prophet, since we recognize that the Koranic revelation is in the language of the seventh century, and second, we
know that any translation of the Koran will be a betrayal of the
original."

Ahmad was beaming. "An interesting point," he said, "but one
that, along with my answer, will probably remain in the margin.
To translate from one time and place to another requires more
than a good grammar book and a good dictionary. When al-
Jobba'i in ninth-century Basra and Locke in eighteenth-century
London argued for free will and against determinism, most likely
they weren't talking about the same thing. Al-Jobba'i was arguing
with people who were primarily concerned with understanding
what the Koran meant when it said that God was the cause of
everything, yet men would be rewarded if they obeyed God's
commands and punished if they disobeyed. Locke was arguing for
the freedom of the will in a world in which all movement was
thought to be explained by the mechanics of Newtonian physical
law. We can't understand al-Jobba'i's Iraq of the ninth century by

subtracting buses from modern Iraq and finding a good dictionary
of ninth-century Arabic.

"Some of our Qomi teachers would argue that there is certain
knowledge, which rests on the bedrock of self-evident truths, and
so al-Jobba'i and Locke can talk to each other across the continents and the ages insofar as they have developed their systems
from self-evident truths. Even a confused man like me believes in
self-evident truths. But, you know, some ideas that are self-evident in one time and place are not self-evident in another. There
is a modern mathematics that holds that it is not self-evident that
only one parallel to a given line passes through a point off that
line. Not only is it not self-evident, sometimes it is even misleading to say so. But this was a piece of Euclid that we accepted from
the time Euclid was translated into Arabic a thousand years ago,
just as the West accepted it without question until a century ago."
Ahmad paused for a moment, then said, "Ali, may my life be a
sacrifice to you, you keep looking at your watch."

It was true, and Ali felt he had to apologize for so obviously
checking his watch. "Please excuse this slow-witted *talabeh*, who
will have to read the text and the margins several times to make
sure he gets today's lesson right. But I must get to the university
library before it closes today, so I'll try to make my last question,
as they say, 'brief and useful.' You know as well as I do that a
jurisconsult really understands how uncertain the law is and how
many opinions there can be on any one point. But when someone
has to act, he has to decide 'Yes, this is right' or 'No, this is
wrong.' How do you get from a description that says 'My best
guess is that the world is so-and-so' to 'Thou shalt not kill?'
Which is exactly why the crown of Shiah learning has been jurisprudence; by mastering jurisprudence a mullah who is a jurisconsult learns how to make the best guess as to what we should do.
No wonder the ordinary people of Iran look up to us and not to
intellectuals. Do you expect a man to sacrifice, to control his pas-
sions, even to give his life for beliefs that are floating in a sea of
possibilities and not anchored in any certain truths? Illiterate
peasant or learned jurisconsult, we all want a belief that is by its
very nature what the Koran claims to be: 'This is the very truth of
that which is certain.' "

"Honorable sayyed," Ahmad replied, "you too are right, and
the sincerity of your belief in Islam is fully accepted here. You remember that the prophet Joseph in his Egyptian prison told his
companions: 'My two fellow prisoners, are many lords differing
among themselves better, or God, the One, the Irresistible? If not
Him, those you worship are nothing but names that you and your
fathers have named, and for which God has sent down no authority. Judgment is God's alone. He has commanded you to worship none but Him. This is right religion—yet most men do not
know it.' So how do we get past the names to the irresistible truth?
I think that the text of names that our world is made of is far less
tidy than we were taught in Qom, and the copyists have added far
more errors to it than we realize. You remember, in the wonderfully orderly creed of Allameh Helli that they used when we studied theology, he argues that the proofs that Mohammed was a
prophet include his miracles, such as 'the feeding of a great multitude with a little food'? I am not a skeptic; I don't argue that this
feeding was done by a deception on the part of the Prophet—God
forbid! I don't say that the eyewitnesses misinterpreted the facts,
or that there were no eyewitnesses and the accounts were fabri-
cated. I just say that since Christians associated such an event with
the coming of a prophet and associated this miracle with Jesus,
Muslims saw Mohammed as a prophet and associated the same
miracle with Mohammed. It was the easy reading of the 'text' of
the Prophet's life, which does not make it either true or false, right
or wrong. The question is how can we get rid of the wrong readings? Not just by asking who were reliable witnesses.

"I don't know, and I really do want to know because I very
much care. Like you, I know that most men can act only out of
belief. In part I blame myself for not knowing; maybe my infatua-
tion with indecision keeps me from knowing. Some days I think
that the veil of 'names' is impenetrable and that the few self-evident things in our minds are trivial rules that reflect the ways in
which our minds are constructed. I think sometimes that in a
world of probabilities, absolute moral judgments that don't yield
to experience are like the serpents on the shoulders of the tyrant
Zahhak—they eat people with indifference. Other days I think all
the world is what it is whether we find it or not, and, as we will

never give up trying to believe that we've truly got hold of some fragment of it, and can reconstruct its shape, we might as well assume it is a place within reach, a place, Mowlana says, just beyond some barrier:

> *For in that place there is no wound: all is mercy and love;*
> *But your vain imagination is like a bar behind the door.*

Still, self-indulgent creature that I am, my vain imagination always comes back; I can't force the door permanently open. I don't know."

Ali could see the look of oppression reappear on Ahmad's face; he longed to lighten Ahmad's burden, to help him at least to live comfortably with his indecision. He said, "Ahmad, I confess that in many ways I don't know either. For the last few days I too have seen myself in some verses of Mowlana:

> *Our desert has no bound, our hearts and souls no rest.*
> *World within world has taken Form's image; which of these images*
> *   is ours?*
> *When you see a severed head in the path rolling toward our field,*
> *Ask of it, ask of it, the secrets of the heart: for you will*
> *   learn from it our hidden mystery.*

You know, I feel the burden of the jurisconsult's task precisely because I understand what you're saying even if I don't agree. As a Shiah jurisconsult I must try to construct man's moral duty from two different starting points: those things I believe to be anchored in the certainty of reason (whether you agree or not) and those things specifically prescribed in the Koran. When it says in the Koran that of the inheritance that goes to the children there goes 'to the male a portion equal to that of two females,' or when it says, 'As to the male thief and female thief, cut off their hands,' I defend the reasonableness of the law for the world in which the Koran was revealed. But I recognize the variety of human situations, and I want not just a principle that suspends the law when necessary for the general good—I have that already—I want a principle that allows us to seek the spirit and intention of the law and to apply it accordingly. This principle should be something that doesn't destroy the Koran by allowing people to read into it whatever they want, as some of our young people do. It should be a principle that preserves the substance as well as the name of religion and also preserves everything good that centuries of careful study of the law have given to us. I haven't found it. I haven't found which image is mine. I still wait, hoping that I will learn the secret from the severed head."

"Sayyed Ali!" Now Ahmad too tried to speak in a consoling tone. "You are a scholar. To fall in love is not hard: 'How easy love seemed at first, then difficulties befell.' There is no love more difficult than the love that calls us to be truly faithful to learning, it makes us learn what even the unpleasant parts of the text say in order to learn the text whole."

Ali was astonished at how genuinely happy he felt to be recognized as a man faithfully in love with learning. "It's too late for me to change," he said. "I'm supposed to be a revolutionary because I went to jail and because of my radical friends. And when I see that the shah is embarrassed before foreigners at what we are and wants to turn us into counterfeit copies of Americans, I burn. I hate to think who we'll be when the oil runs out, or what we'll be."

Ahmad interrupted: "Poorer than Bangladesh."

"Without the slightest doubt. And yet, when my friends in the bazaar ask me if they should close tomorrow, and mullahs telephone me all day to tell me of their plans to lead their followers to demonstrate, I long to return to Qom, to return to the books I haven't read carefully enough or haven't read at all."

"I wish I could return with you and eat some *sowhan*," said Ahmad, "then argue with you in your class, then talk politics with you against the chatter of birds in the courtyard of the Faiziyeh before the evening prayer. Forty years ago when I was there I didn't really belong—I was seldom fully convinced by my books—but how I loved it! I still can't read a serious book without stopping occasionally to make a speech to an imaginary audience: 'But has the author made his point correctly?' When I hear about your new *madreseh* buildings with air-conditioned classrooms and running water in every dormitory room, I despise them. We had to shake our shoes every morning, because in Qom in my day there were still plenty of scorpions."

"I'm sorry to disappoint you, but the government has managed to get rid of the scorpions and has brought running water to all the houses. I don't know if this news is going to make you more indignant at the government or more of a royalist."

"I don't know myself," Ahmad admitted with a laugh. Then with sudden concern he said, "You don't think anything serious is going to happen tomorrow?"

Ali was reluctant to repeat everything he had heard, but he felt he owed Ahmad a warning. "Tomorrow in some cities some people intend to use the forty-day mourning ceremony for the *talabehs* killed in Qom to close their shops and gather in the mosque in the bazaar to protest."

"My God," said Ahmad, "do you think I should withdraw some money from the bank? I hope I don't have something new to be undecided about."

"Dear professor, I have no fear for your safety or well-being; God takes care of the pious even if—like you—they give their piety perverse forms. Remember, Hafez says:

If, like the prophet Noah, you have patience in the distress of the flood,
Calamity turns aside, and the desire of a thousand years comes forth.

They both stood up, and Ahmad, opening the door to the hall, said to Ali: "It may need the thousand-year patience of a Noah or a Job; I suppose, for Iran, I could manage it. By the way, what would *you* do with your money if you withdrew it now from the bank?"

"Now and always—buy books."

At the government's behest on January 7, 1978, a leading Tehran newspaper published an article attacking the "imperialism, both red and black," of those who opposed the shah's reforms and accused these opponents of turning for support to "the specialists in spiritual matters." The article attacked in particular Ruhollah Khomeini as "the most intransigent and reactionary" of the agents of imperialism. It openly accused Khomeini of being a tool of reactionary landlords who opposed the shah's land reforms and sneeringly asked if there might be truth in the rumor that Khomeini was known as the "Indian Sayyed," because his family came from India, where Khomeini might have had contacts with British imperialism or because he wrote erotic poetry under the pseudonym "The Indian." (Khomeini's grandfather was a Kashmiri sayyed of Iranian origin, and Khomeini uses the pen name "The Indian" for his *erfani* poetry.) The government had thought it worthwhile to plant such a provocative article because Khomeini's name had just recently been mentioned publicly in Qom for the first time in a long time. Khomeini's eldest son, Mostafa, had died in Qom late in the fall of 1977, and on his *arba'in*—the very important memorial day observed forty days after a person's death—a few preachers had openly criticized the government and praised Mostafa's father, who then was in exile in Iraq. As U.S. President Carter was visiting the shah in Tehran on New Year's Day, 1978, and as the shah for over a year before this visit had been trying to demonstrate interest in Carter's human rights policy, the Iranian government had let the favorable references to Khomeini and his politics at the *arba'in* pass. The *talabehs* felt bolder.

The day the article was published was bright and cold, one of those winter days when Qomis sit around a charcoal brazier under a low table covered with a quilt. The Tehran papers, as usual, arrived in Qom at about three o'clock in the afternoon. It took the *talabehs* the rest of the day to get in touch with each other and decide what they wanted to do. The next day they let the people of the bazaar know very early in the morning that they wanted the bazaar closed; and from that morning until February 11, 1979, except for forty isolated days, the bazaar remained shut. Next the *talabehs* went in groups to the houses of "models" and other leading religious scholars. They wanted these scholars to issue statements denying that the Iranian clergy disapproved of Khomeini or gave approval to the "White Revolution." All of the scholars spoke in support of the *talabehs*.

By afternoon the *talabehs* had gathered near the shrine in the Khan Madreseh, the center of teaching in Qom since the government had closed the Faiziyeh some years before. The outrage of the *talabehs* had not been satisfied, and in the late afternoon a few thousand *talabehs* and sympathizers set out in a slightly belligerent mood from the Khan Madreseh to the house of a teacher who was an influential speaker and an outright supporter of Khomeini. They marched toward the hospital crossroads, which is the exit point from the shrine area to the south. When they passed the police station at this crossroads they were asked to disperse. They refused to do so, and some shouted, "We don't want the government of Yazid [the caliph who ordered the massacre of Hosain and his followers]" and "We want the return of the Ayatollah Khomeini." The police fired into the crowd. According to Qomis, at least twenty died on the spot (although much lower and much higher figures were given by outsiders) and many more were injured.

The next day, January 9, something occurred that was, as Iranians say, as rare as the sight of the "phoenix of the western climes." On the Persian Service of the BBC they heard Ayatollah Shariatmadari, one of the most important of the "models" in Qom, criticize their government. Shariatmadari had been in some measure the heir of the Ayatollah Borujerdi's policy of cautious accommodation with the government, and since his fellow Azerbaijanis almost universally accepted him as their "model," he had the largest following of any of the "models" then living in Qom and was treated by the government as the head of the religious establishment. He was notoriously cautious. Even in the mid-seventies when the government closed the Faiziyeh and sent so many *madreseh* teachers to prison or into exile in remote parts of Iran, Shariatmadari did not speak out. Then the tens of thousands of Iranians who listened to the BBC Persian Service as their most accurate source of news heard this cautious elderly man say, with his Turkish accent, that the government should take responsibility for the shooting; no warning shots had been fired, and there was every reason to assume that the crowd's intention was innocent.

The events of the next fourteen months were a bit like the *taaziyeh*, which combines the marriage of Imam Hosain's daughter to Qasem, Hosain's nephew, with the funeral of Hosain's eldest son.

At first Iranians looked on with curiosity, then—with the removal of all barriers between actors and audience—they were drawn into a community of emotion in which the shared grief for the "martyred" and the euphoria of a celebration were being powerfully mixed. Leading mullahs called on Iranians to observe the *arba'in* for the Qomis killed on January 8. While there were services held in many parts of Iran, it was in Tabriz, the capital of Shariatmadari's home province of Azerbaijan that the demonstrations on February 18 turned ugly. A mourner was shot, and thirty-six hours of rioting followed. Demonstrators attacked banks, liquor stores, sexually suggestive billboards on movie houses, and anything (including shops) displaying the blue-and-gold emblem that had been used since the Persepolis celebration to symbolize the two thousand and five hundred years of Iranian monarchy. The government sent in troops to regain control, and several demonstrators were killed.

The shah made a conciliatory gesture by dismissing some officials and sending delegations to mullahs, but the gesture was seen as weakness and not as genuine conciliation. When the forty-day mourning period for those killed in Tabriz had passed, demonstrations were held in many parts of Iran, and many ended in riots. Demonstrations and riots continued throughout the summer, in one of which the government forces attacked the house of Shariatmadari, who now found it even harder to reassume his former policy of peaceful coexistence with the government.

There was no single point at which the awe wherein dread and fear of kings reside clearly departed from Mohammed Reza Pahlavi. But gradually, step by step and—after many steps—ineluctably it did depart. The king, who in 1963 had flown to Qom and had spoken in public for his "White Revolution," who had appeared in the villages nearby after the rising in Qom in 1963 and distributed land deeds to the peasants, was confused and inconsistent. Sometimes the government reacted with great force, sometimes with unexpected and almost apologetic conciliation.

There were several events that moved great numbers of Iranians across the emotional barrier between the audience and the actors. On August 19 a fire at the Cinema Rex in Abadan killed over four hundred people. The government accused the religious conservatives of setting the fire and hinted that the inspiration came from agents sent from Iraq by Khomeini. Khomeini issued a proclamation angrily denying that any religious Muslim could be involved in such an event and accused the SAVAK of starting the fire to blacken the name of opponents of the regime. Regardless of who started the fire (perhaps no one), many people believed that the circumstances confirmed the government's guilt, and suddenly thousands of Iranians who had felt neutral and had until now thought that the struggle was only between the shah and supporters of religiously conservative mullahs felt that the government might put their own lives on the block to save itself. Suddenly, for hundreds of thousands, the movement was their own business.

The shah continued to vacillate. On August 27, during Ramazan, he installed a new prime minister, who allowed the Tehran newspapers to publish a picture of Khomeini. Late in the afternoon, as the people of Qom were going home and preparing to break their fast for that day, news of the picture spread throughout the city, and people began to blow their car horns. The always slightly festive atmosphere of a night after daytime fasting turned into a jubilant celebration.

September 4 was the end of the month of fasting, an occasion for a jubilant celebration in any year, and leading mullahs called for all Iranians to join in the communal prayers of the day. In Tehran a hundred thousand people turned out in one place, and after prayer they marched through a central avenue of the city. There were similar demonstrations elsewhere, in which, in a kind of euphoria, the marchers realized their numbers. On this day and on religious festivals throughout the autumn great numbers of villagers, including busloads of village women, came to the cities to join in marches which, for many of them, had the mixture of seriousness and excitement that a holiday visit to a shrine city might have.

The government decided enough was enough and declared martial law. The next day, Friday, September 8, demonstrators in a large square near the parliament building in Tehran, probably unaware of the martial law regulations, refused to disperse. The troops fired directly into the crowd and killed scores of people. By the time this event was known, the majority of Iranians were no longer onlookers but participants, emotionally penetrated by the significance of what they were watching.

This startling mixture of peaceful and euphoric demonstrations of hundreds of thousands with occasional violent encounters with the army—violent encounters now often sought by smaller groups eager to fight and ready to be killed—continued, as did the vacillating policy of the government. On December 2, with the beginning of Moharram, a curfew was imposed in all the cities. Nevertheless, on the evenings of the first few days of Moharram young men paraded through the streets in white burial shrouds, indicating their willingness to die, and several of them were shot. The government saw no way to stop the parades for the ninth and tenth days of Moharram, Tasu'a and Ashura, the anniversaries of the martyrdom of Hosain, and so gave the organizers of these parades permission to hold the demonstrations on the condition that they be orderly. The parades were carefully organized by the opposition, and in Tehran there was a march that lasted for eight hours in which two million are said to have participated. Pictures of Khomeini were prominent.

On January 16, 1979, the shah, carrying along a box of the soil of Iran, as his father had done in 1941, left Iran. On the first of February Khomeini returned to Iran. The army, which had been overwhelmingly loyal in the face of demonstrations of millions of their fellow Iranians, dissolved in the absence of the shah, the focus of the one deep personal loyalty they possessed. On February 11 the caretaker government set up by the shah before his departure disappeared and Ayatollah Khomeini sat in the courtyard of a high school in Tehran and took the salute from troop after troop of Iranian soldiers.

It had been a victory of "the word." Al-e Ahmad had known that if there ever were such a revolution, it would be a revolution of the "word" and that, to have this power, the "word" would have to come from men of religion. He had written: "If the clerical establishment had [only] realized—with the belief that it isn't necessary to obey leaders—what a precious jewel lay hidden in the hearts of people, like a seed for any uprising against a government of oppressors and the corrupt, and if [only] it could have shown the people the fundamental nature of these leaders by means of the media . . ." The clerics had to reach the people with their words through the media, Al-e Ahmad had written, because in Iranian history prophets, reformers, and true intellectuals are possessors of "the influence of the word."

Khomeini had sat first in Iraq, then (after October 1978) in Paris, and said, "The shah must go; the shah must go." Other leading mullahs, including some of the "models" in Qom, had been willing to compromise with the shah's government; but Khomeini had not. He spoke the word without compromise, and finally the shah left. With his success it was as if all those Arabic words Al-e Ahmad had noticed on objects at the shrine in his story "The Pilgrimage" had come to life, and "everything," as the story says, "was absorbed by their power."

EPILOGUE

Over six years have passed since the great marches of the autumn of 1978. Looking at their present situation, many Iranians could repeat with conviction Saadi's line, "I am not mounted on a camel, nor, like an ass, am I saddled with a load; I am not the lord of subject people, nor am I the slave of any monarch." Saadi meant this line to express the speaker's happiness at his freedom from real burdens and from the even heavier imagined burden of placing himself subject to or in authority over others. An Iranian, repeating the line in the winter of 1984, might see an irony in its application to his own situation, in which it is unclear to what extent he is or might hope to be the master of his own fate.

The intoxicating euphoria of those scenes in which the Iranian masses saw themselves for the first time as actors on the stage of history lasted through the first five years after the revolution. In some moods and on certain occasions it still lives vividly among the masses in this sixth year of the revolution. Neighborhood leaders turn out in large numbers for Friday prayers; tens—

and in Tehran hundreds—of thousands march on great religious holidays. In Shiah communities outside Iran, particularly in Lebanon and the Arab countries of the Gulf, the Iranian revolution inspired radical political movements that included men who, convinced they had assimilated the spirit of Imam Hosain, carried out suicide bomb attacks against the American embassy in Kuwait and the American Marine headquarters and embassy in Beirut. In Iran itself in the summer of 1984 the state television showed queues of young men approaching the doors of buses, where each would kiss the edge of a Koran held by a mullah, then touch the Koran to his forehead, and finally enter the bus to go to fight Iraq. The anger at Iraq for starting the war and the readiness for martyrdom, repeatedly praised in messages from Ayatollah Khomeini, have kept the heroic image of the fearless devotee constantly before the Iranian public in spite of the hundred and fifty thousand Iranian lives lost in that war.

The attraction to and repulsion from the heavy burden demanded by the image of the martyr is creating a drastic change in the self-conceptions of many Iranians. Among every category of Iranian there seem to be large numbers who see the love of ambiguity that gave Iranian culture a flexible exterior and a private interior as something no longer tenable, a freedom that history no longer permits. That dawn six years ago when the whole earth wore the beauty of promise and it was bliss to be alive was followed by another dawn in which Iranians saw the cultural goods and values of their two and a half millennia of history in a new and harsher light and felt an urgent longing for the open and unambiguous definitions that this new light demanded. They saw their past in the lines of Mowlana in which he describes people seeking for the *qebleh,* the direction of the Kaaba of Mecca and focus of prayer, in the dark of night:

> *Like people who diligently search about,*
>   *turning every which way they fancy the* qebleh *to be;*
> *When at dawn the Kaaba appears,*
>   *It is revealed who has actually lost his way.*
> *Or, like divers under the depth of the sea's waters,*
>   *Each one plucking something in haste . . .*

When they come from the bottom of the deep sea
It is revealed who now owns the exquisite pearl
And who has brought the little pearls
and who the tiny stones and worthless shells.

During the sixth year of the revolution many Iranians are telling each other by indirection that the heroic image of the selfless devotee is a role, even a pose, that they can no longer maintain without interruption. Not only the Iranians in exile, and royalist Iranians who remained in Iran after the revolution, and the anti-mullah revolutionary Iranians who claimed their revolution was hijacked but, also the religious, revolutionary Iranians now sometimes say, with a slight smile, when referring to a death mentioned in the newspaper, "And he died a martyr." Some of these Iranians seem to be able to shift roles from devotee to cynic without difficulty, but others shift with evident self-consciousness, or not at all. For the Iranians who shift with difficulty or not at all the inner spaces created by ambiguity no longer exist, and the attraction of ambiguity is forever dead.

In the great shifting of official cultural goods and values through the revolution, it is still far from clear who got what. The mullahs got the state cult of monarchy removed—not, of course, in favor of the older arms-length coexistence of the ethos of government and the ethos of religion—but in favor of the complete absorption of the ethos of government by religion. Some mullahs have attacked the task of bending the state to their will with a vengeance. As judges in courts, as ministers and plenipotentiary supervisors of ministries they have ordered the execution of thousands and purged tens of thousands. After all, the new constitution, in force since 1980, unambiguously established the principle of "the guardianship of the Islamic jurist," which Khomeini had been developing from its nineteenth-century sources for at least twenty years before the outbreak of the revolution.

Yet strange things have happened to the theory of "the guardianship of the jurist" on its way to enshrinement in the constitution. In his book *Islamic Government*, which Khomeini published in 1970, he roundly attacked the constitution of 1906 and asked, "What connection do all the articles of the Constitution . . . have with Islam?" He went on to explain:

> The fundamental difference between Islamic government, on the one hand, and constitutional monarchy and republics, on the other, is this: whereas the representatives of the people or the monarch in such regimes engage in legislation, in Islam the legislative power and competence to establish laws belongs exclusively to God Almighty. The Sacred Legislator of Islam is the sole legislative power. No one has the right to legislate and no law may be executed except the law of the Divine Legislator. It is for this reason that in an Islamic government, a simple planning body takes the place of the legislative assembly that is one of the three branches of government.

Nevertheless a new constitution was written, and (in seeming contradiction to the clauses that established the authority of the Islamic jurist), it declared that the source of legislative authority was "the will of the people." Moreover, it reestablished a parliament, now called (as Fazlollah Nuri had wanted) the Islamic Consultative Assembly rather than the National Consultative Assembly. While elections to this Assembly are very far from being free and open—some parties are forbidden, the media are controlled, vote counting sometimes remains in the hands of dubious local officials—they have nevertheless been hard-fought. Moreover, debate among those candidates allowed to run for election has been remarkably open. The atmosphere of open debate and of due procedure within parliament has been even more remarkable. Parliament has both debated and acted as if it has the power to make law, and the mullah speaker of the house follows the very evident will of the members that points of order (first and second readings of bills and so forth) be punctiliously observed, almost always in accordance with the procedures established by the parliament under the old constitution.

In this sense the generation of 1906 has established a victory for their constitution—so hated by Khomeini—which was never unambiguously clear under the Pahlavi shahs. The Iranian constitution of 1906 was a little over seventy years old when it was abolished. It may have been a dead letter in most of its provisions for many of those seventy years, but the mere existence of a parliament remained emotionally a very important fact for very many Iranians, and time had given this fact its own sanctity.

This sanctity is felt by many of the mullah as well as the non-mullah members of parliament, whatever Ayatollah Khomeini may have said in his book. The *talabehs* who grew up in the years of the Second World War and in the time of Mossadegh, and who avidly read the newspaper accounts of the hard and comparatively open debates of those periods, insist on a parliament of this nature without second thoughts. When the parliamentary recorders presented summaries of debates in the first sessions of the new parliament, the publishers of the official gazette told them that nothing less than full accounts of the debates had ever been proper; and parliament agreed. When, on June 28, 1981, a bomb blew up the headquarters of the Islamic Republic party (the party favored by Khomeini and the majority of politically active mullahs) and several members of parliament were killed (exactly seventy-two, the same number as were killed at Kerbela, Ayatollah Khomeini insisted), those mullah members of parliament who survived managed to leave their hospitals temporarily a few days later, some on crutches, some carried by attendants, to attend a meeting of parliament in which their votes were needed to carry a critical bill. To these mullahs a parliamentary majority seems to be as important as a closely reasoned argument about the intention of the Divine Legislator.

And yet the parliament, whatever it is called or however it is composed, is far from sovereign. The Council of Guardians, a body of jurists appointed in accordance with the constitution to judge in terms of Islamic law the legality of acts of parliament, has turned down some of the most important legislation passed on land reform and family law. Not for nothing do the faces of Ayatollah Kashani, who left the camp of Mossadegh, and Fazlollah Nuri, who opposed the Constitutional Revolution, and Navvab Safavi, who led the Devotees of Islam who shot Kasravi, now appear on postage stamps.

For that portion of the population of Iran that was culturally Shiah and vaguely religious the last six years have been a rediscovery of what Shiah Islam as taught in the *madresehs* really is. Some of this discovery has come through education. At first enthusiasts proposed that *maktabs*, the old Koran schools, be reestablished. The proposal failed, and the state school books were carefully revised to include ample information about Islam, although the rest of their contents and, in fact, the whole preuniversity state educational system, including a revised set of Persian songs, have remained much the same. Some parts of the work of the generation of Isa Sadiq proved as hard to expunge as did the idea of a parliament. Universities are in a sort of limbo, half functioning, half idle. Nevertheless university teachers who want to keep their posts are more or less obliged to go to Qom for special summer courses taught by mullahs.

On a personal level, rediscovery of the interpretation of Islam in its fully elaborated form as taught in the *madreseh* has been a shock to many middle-class Iranians. Some young Iranians have accepted the jot and tittle of the law with enthusiasm and have joined the patrols of vigilantes who go around enforcing the dress codes for women (all hair must be covered) and smelling out "corruption" wherever they can find it. But many Iranians who were laxly religious before the revolution, and who were strongly attracted by Khomeini's repeated statements that politically passive mullahs had made Islam into a religion preoccupied with ritual purity in order to avoid its political message, have since found out that, for Khomeini, Islam is most emphatically about both politics and ritual purity, a subject on which Ayatollah Khomeini has conservative views. He is, for example, one of the "models" who hold that the touch of non-Muslims is impure, requiring a major ritual washing.

This shock has been greatest among the intellectuals, who at first had loved the revolution as their own, believing that the masses under the leadership of Khomeini had finally spoken up for what they, the intellectuals, had always wanted. They soon learned otherwise. About three years ago a poem was passed hand to hand throughout the intellectual community of Tehran in which the poet exalted Zoroaster as the prophet who "never killed nor ordered anyone to be killed." The poem is addressed to "our ancient land and soil":

> *You, O ancient elder, eternally young,*
> *It is you I love if anything I love;*
> *Of Ferdowsi, that castle of legend that he raised*
> *to the heavens of might and glory I love;*
> *Of Khayyam, that anger and complaint that eternally*
> *affects the heart and soul I love.*

These words echo one of the most self-consciously dramatic episodes in the intellectual history of the nineteenth century. Ernest Renan had been trained to be a learned priest, an "Orientalist" who could study the textual evidences of Judeo-Christian origins not only in Greek and Latin but also in Hebrew, Syriac, and Arabic. Philology proved his religious undoing; he decided that the Bible had conflations and misascriptions of texts that made its divine origin intellectually untenable. In the 1860s he wrote in French a rationalist life of Jesus that was one of the storm centers of the debate of religion versus irreligion in the nineteenth century.

In his memoirs Renan describes how, while standing at the foot of the Acropolis in 1865, he suddenly realized that all the peoples he knew about—Orientals, Germans, Romans, Slavs, and Celts— were to some degree barbarians and that this Greek temple was the revelation of the only nonbarbarian beauty he believed to exist. Renan addressed to the Acropolis his famous "prayer" to "the goddess whose worship means reason and wisdom." And he confessed the difficulty of cleansing himself and others from accretions such as Christianity behind which history had half hidden the rationality once worshiped there. Quoting Saint Augustine's moving apostrophe to God in the *Confessions* almost word for word, Renan wrote: "Late have I come to love thee, beauty ever ancient and ever new." Similarly, the Iranian poet who praised Zoroaster had also come to feel that what he loved in his land, that "ancient elder, eternally young," was its partly rediscovered ancient past, which to him no longer seemed emotionally unconnected. For some Iranians, particularly among the intellectuals, this past had at last taken root; they had been forced by the dialectic of events finally to say whether the Iranian image of the hero was Cyrus or Hosain, and they had answered: Cyrus.

For the leftist intellectuals the revolution is a riddle wrapped in a mystery inside an enigma. The earth had moved, and when it settled again it seemed that—however ingeniously they sought to prove that the masses had been deceived—the masses had acquiesced in the leadership of the new elite in place of the old elite. This was an elite, because mullahs, they claimed, were more often than not the sons of mullahs, and mullahs were in disproportionate numbers sayyeds (certainly all the living "models" are sayyeds). In the view of the leftists the revolution had brought to power an old semihereditary elite, the last elite remaining after the landlords, the great men of the bazaar, and the shah's technocrats had been broken. And this elite had found its henchmen in the lumpen bourgeoisie, the disappointed, such people as the young man who had found no place at the university after completing his high school or the factory foreman who had found no political outlet after becoming the organizer of a *hay'at*. Now the lumpen bourgeois tasted power by serving the new regime as a member of a revolutionary committee or as a member of the paramilitary Revolutionary Guard. For all that there had been some redistribution of land and much nationalization of large companies, the intellectuals could not understand how a revolution so popular in origin should be so conservative in outcome.

Isa Sadiq died in 1978 surrounded by news of the enormous demonstrations and outbursts of popular emotion that would lead the revolutionary opposition to victory. He was not surprised at the demonstrations; he had grown up amidst the revolution of 1906 and knew firsthand the power of the mullah and the mosque in Iranian life, particularly in periods when no other channels of protest were available. Had he survived a few years longer, he would probably have found the orientation of the revolution less puzzling than it seemed to Iranian leftists who had come to maturity in the forties and fifties; unlike Al-e Ahmad, he had actually known men like Fazlollah Nuri and seen their impact on the course of the previous revolution.

Isa Sadiq believed that the protests of 1978 were in large part the result of the nation's failure to create the kind of educational system for which he had labored. It had created, he said, a lot of people who wanted the prestige of paper degrees in order to sit behind desks, and a lot of people who resented their lack of degrees and exclusion from desks; it had never succeeded in creating respect for working with one's hands. Moreover, the educational system had never created "the man *in* society," an idea of John Dewey's to which Isa Sadiq had remained faithful for nearly half a century. Although a loyal and veteran servant of the Pahlavi dynasty, he privately complained about the shah. The shah, he said, wanted too much Westernization, while he, Isa, wanted that never-fully-described but recurrently sighted fascination of Iranian intellectuals: a truly Iranian modernization of Iran.

In many ways Isa Sadiq was right to see the failures of the educational system as, at the very least, symptomatic of the comparative fragility of the social order that existed under the shah. Perhaps, in his appeal to the ideal of John Dewey, Isa Sadiq sensed the confusing disjunction between the communalism of Iranian family life and the different, even if imperfectly assimilated, ethic of individual possession and loyalties to state-created corporate entities that the secular educational system tried to cultivate. Perhaps he sensed that the mental geometry and discipline that secular education sought to instill in hundreds of thousands was even more unrelated to the lives of many Iranians than the more self-instilled geometry and discipline learned through reading set texts under teachers at the *madresehs*. Perhaps he sensed that the disrespect that lay just beneath the reverential obedience of students to the teachers in the state schools was somehow analogous to the disrespect that lay just beneath the awe many Iranians felt for the shah.

And yet if Isa Sadiq saw Iranian secular education as a step-child, it was a stepchild in whom he could feel much genuinely paternal pride. Not only had it made millions literate and created tens of thousands of highly trained specialists, it had also created a fair number of Isa Sadiqs. Isa Sadiq, who emerges in his *One Year in America* as a great counter of objects, foreshadowed a growing number of Iranians who discussed the future of Iranian society in terms of statistical results and probabilistic solutions. For them such considerations formed the primary source of law, which should be endlessly modified according to the changing human perceptions as to the results that laws had achieved or might be expected to achieve. For them, as for Justice Oliver Wendell Holmes, "The life of the law has not been logic: it has been experience."

The new Isa Sadiqs were not necessarily without religion, at least in their own eyes. Isa prayed regularly and did not drink; he would probably have considered Kasravi's irreligion emotionally unacceptable. But he regarded religion as a personal thing, somewhat in the manner of a Western religious secularist. Some of the tens of thousands of Isa Sadiqs are as religious as Isa, some less. The belief of the great majority of Iranians almost certainly falls somewhere between the belief of the Isa Sadiqs in a law shaped by "experience" and the belief of the Islamic jurisconsults in a law shaped according to the most "learned" surmise of divine intention. It is clear which group at present has the upper hand; it is not clear to which group, if either, belongs the future.

. . .

Sometimes, when he is in the *andaruni* of the family home in Qom, it seems to Ali that very little has changed. The cypresses in the four parterres of the *andaruni* died in the extreme cold of the winter of 1963, and four flowering ornamental pomegranate bushes have been planted in their place, but otherwise the garden looks as it always did. Now that neither of Ali's parents is alive, he shares the house with his brother, and his library has taken over his half of the *andaruni*, leaving him and his wife only two rooms, which they use as a bedroom and a sitting room. Occasionally Ali still takes a hand in the garden, and there are times when, leaning over a seedling next to a bush in the *andaruni*, Ali feels that the quiet and privacy he loved while sitting under the bush as a child has remained there undisturbed in the shade of the bush for thirty-five years.

Sometimes the world outside seems unchanged too, but mostly Ali is aware of how changed it is, how painfully unsure he is of the direction in which the change is going, and how relieved he feels when he has returned home and reentered the world of his books. Physically, of all parts of Qom, the bazaar seems least changed. Sometimes when he walks in the lane of the spice dealers and sees some of the old men nod to him from behind the open sacks of turmeric and coriander, he half expects to see his mother come around the corner and lead him to one of these shops as she did years ago. And twice a year Hamid comes around to prune the trees; he has a motor bike now, but the saw is still in his hand.

In most places, however, he notices the changes. Villagers have continued to move to Qom, as they have to every city of Iran, regardless of the revolution and the disappearance of Brigitte Bardot films, and the open fields he would cross to walk to nearby shrines are now covered with small houses. Qom also has a considerable population of refugees from Khuzestan, the southwestern province that the Iraqis partly occupied, and from Iran's neighbor, Afghanistan, where the war against the Soviet-supported regime has been especially brutal to the Shiah province in the center of the country. And there are well over ten thousand—some say fifteen thousand—*talabehs* in Qom instead of the former five thousand. Training to be a mullah, as one says in Persian and in English, 'has taken on a considerable luster.'

Teaching is much as it used to be, and the really apt and serious pupils, despite the increase in the number of *talabehs*, are just as few. His old teacher of elementary logic has remained at his job, and, while thirty years ago he looked near fifty, he looks virtually the same now that he is seventy. Marashi, who is about eighty, is much the same—generous, always eager to hear about new books even though his sight has almost failed, and a great tease. When old pupils come to him he indicates his opinion of mullahs who have gone in for government in a big way by saying to them, "Well, are you involved in the murder-and-plunder side of things or have you chosen to lead souls astray and make other people's prayers null and void by your presence?"

It is when Ali thinks about Iran outside Qom that he feels most aware of the change. Davudi is dead, Parviz may be dead, Parviz's *talabeh* cousin is a notorious "hanging" judge, and his study partner from Yazd is dead. The death of Davudi, his professor of Aristotle, is not absolutely certain; as a leading Baha'i he was among the first people arrested after the revolution. But it is hard to imagine that five years later he is alive and among the seven hundred-odd Baha'is in prison and has not been executed along with the nearly two hundred Baha'is whose executions have been acknowledged. At the end of 1984 there was a new wave of arrests of Baha'is and fourteen more executions of those already in prison. As a condition of release Baha'i prisoners are now asked to sign a statement that reads: "I, the undersigned, have undertaken not to have in my possession any book, pamphlet, document, symbol, or picture of this misguided Zionist, espionage group of Baha'is. If any of the above-mentioned articles belonging to this hated underground movement is found on my person or in my home, this will be tantamount to being of those who 'war against God' [a capital crime] and the attorney-general will be free to give a decision against me in the manner he sees fit." So far no Baha'i prisoner has chosen to sign this strange document in exchange for the flimsy protection offered. Ali holds no particular brief for the Baha'is, but he considers the vendetta of some of the mullahs against them, which has caused them to be thrown out of schools, ousted from their jobs, and in some cases even stripped of their bare possessions, a breach of the honor one owes to one's fellow Iranians.

In fact, honor and a strong distaste for violence have separated Ali and some like-minded mullahs from the mullahs who have thrown themselves, from their *giveh* shoes to their turbans, into politics and into other people's business. Ali keeps telling mullah friends who share his distaste for the purges and killings other mullahs have directed, "But I know for a fact that years ago they would walk out of their way to avoid stepping on an ant." Maybe the cousin of Parviz would still avoid stepping on an ant, but he has turned into a vindictive judge who orders flogging and execution with abandon. He was one of the vocal supporters of the reintroduction by parliament of Islamic criminal law, and he was openly pleased at the official "removal" of Shariatmadari (supposedly for treason) from his position as a "model" because Shariatmadari said the drastic punishments of the criminal law, like the chopping off of hands, were to be applied only when a perfect society was constructed so that no temptation other than the inner whisperings of Satan could be held to have misled the criminal.

The uncertain fate of Parviz has created a great vacuum in Ali's life, a hollow well into which he can reach without ever feeling its bottom. Parviz was very much in evidence during the revolution, a leader among the armed Islamic radical groups that skirmished with police and the army during the last critical months. After the return of Khomeini, Parviz had been everywhere, speaking in public and trying to organize groups in all parts of Iran. Then, in 1981, the government decided to stop the *Mojahedin* and other leftist groups from operating publicly, and these groups—believing that there was no more hope of constitutional opposition—had declared war on the government. In the violence that followed, Ali's study partner from Yazd had been killed by a bomb in his mosque. Parviz simply disappeared, like the elderly storks of Qom (who were reputed to go on pilgrimage to Mecca and die in the sand near the Holy City). He wasn't in exile, he wasn't known to be underground, he wasn't known to be among the over six thousand *Mojahedin* reportedly killed in shoot-outs or executed in prisons. Ali's prayer for him is that, if he is alive, he will have a copy of the *Sermons* of Imam Ali, which he loved so much, and pencil and paper. God willing, as a mathematician, he might not need more.

Ali sees his life as a long ascent from the world of pure learning into the world where learning and politics mix; and then, from the point of zenith he had reached at the time of his imprisonment, a slow descent back into pure learning. Ali's companions think it ironical that Ali, who had once burned with a fire of fellow-feeling for the Algerians, has steadfastly resisted the flame of the new revolution; Ali thinks it ironical that the long-awaited Iranian revolution has happened and—in one sense—nothing has happened. He is outstandingly learned now; he is a jurisconsult who has written so well and so extensively on Islamic law that everyone calls him an ayatollah. But Ali is conscious that he has worked principally to clarify and reclassify the existing tradition and has avoided writing opinions on the law because he is waiting for an innovator. He is waiting for another Ansari, who will reach deep into the Shiah legal traditions and show new points at which possible lists of contraries may be constructed and the flexibility and humanity of the law demonstrated. Otherwise the revolution, he says, may leave the Shiah community as divided as the Constitutional Revolution did, or even give birth to a new wave of anti-jurisconsult Shi'ism, as happened in the later Safavi period.

Ali desperately cares that the intellectual tradition he has so painstakingly mastered should not be lost in the storm. And because he is proud of his descent, he hopes that the innovator who can safeguard this tradition will be a sayyed. Then, he says, the famous saying of the Prophet will be fulfilled: "The likeness of the people of my family is the likeness of the ark of Noah; the one who embarks on it is saved, and the one who holds back from it will drown and sink." God willing, he says, the ark will appear before the water rises much higher.

SOURCES AND CHRONOLOGY

THE FOLLOWING note gives the sources for those matters of detail in the text (including those quotations I have cited directly) that are, so far as I can judge, not generally known to the intelligent general reader of Middle Eastern history. These sources are listed more or less in the order in which they occur in the text. I have used existing translations where possible, although I have often modified these translations to accord better with my understanding of the original text. Dates of publication are given in the Christian or Islamic eras, whichever the text itself cites.

In Chapter One the speech of the popular preacher denouncing the government is from *Iran Between Two Revolutions* by Ervand Abrahamian (Princeton: 1982), by far the fullest and most professional treatment that we have of Iranian history from the turn of the century until 1978.

Abrahamian is also the source for much of the information on the Revolution of 1906 in Chapter Two, including the description of the British legation. Hafez Farman Farmayan gives a good

summary of intellectual protest against the Qajars, including the
activities of Mostashar ad-Dowleh, in his essay "The Forces of
Modernization in Nineteenth Century Iran: A Historical Survey"
in *Beginnings of Modernization in the Middle East: The Nineteenth Century* (Chicago: 1968).

The principal sources for the life of Isa Sadiq are his books:
Yadgar-e Omr (Tehran: 1338), *Yaksal dar Amrika* (Tehran: n.d.),
and *Modern Persia and Her Education System* (New York: 1931).

The development of the techniques of dialectical discussion,
including the quote from Hugo Sanctallensis, is given in the magisterial essay by Joseph van Ess, "Disputationspraxis in der islamischen Theologie. Eine vorläufige Skizze," *Revue des études islamiques*, 44 (1967). Avicenna's autobiography and its continuation by his disciple has been translated by A. J. Arberry in *Avicenna on Theology* (London: 1951) and, more recently, by W. E. Gohlman in *The Life of Avicenna* (Albany: 1974). Further anecdotes on his career as a physician are taken from Nizami Aruzi's *Chahar Maqalah*, translated into English by E. G. Browne (London: 1921). A convenient summary of Avicenna's proof of the existence of God is given by Herbert A. Davidson in *Islamic Philosophical Theology*, edited by Parviz Morewedge (Albany: 1979). Sayyed Nematollah Jazayeri gives his autobiography at the end of his *al-Anwar an-Nu'maniya* (Tehran: 1280). The biography of Ahmad Kasravi is largely drawn from his short *Zendegani-ye man* (Tehran: 1323) with some bibliographical information from a Princeton Ph.D thesis on Kasravi by William Stalley.

The sketch of Mossadegh's life given in Chapter Four is largely
based on an oral autobiography given in *Mossadegh va Masa'el-e Hoquq*, edited by Iraj Afshar (Tehran: 1358). His two books quoted in this chapter are *Kapitulasiun va Iran* (Tehran: 1332) and *Le testament en droit musulman (secte chyite)* (Paris: 1914). Among the sources used in this chapter for the history of the postwar period are: Barry Rubin, *Paved with Good Intentions* (New York: 1980), L. P. Elwell-Sutton, *Persian Oil* (London: 1955), and the anonymous *Mossadegh va Nehzat-e Melli-ye Iran* (Tehran: 1357), which includes his speech in opposition to a bill supported by Reza Shah.

The sources for the biography of Sohravardi are given by his
principal European interpreter, Henry Corbin, in a number of

essays and translations. The parallel poems of Avicenna and Sohravardi are to be found in Ibn Khallikan's *Wafayat;* Sohravardi's quasi-dream of Aristotle is given in his *Opera metaphysica,* edited by H. Corbin (Istanbul: 1945), pp. 70–74. Asin Palacios elaborately discusses the parallels between Dante and Islamical mysticism in his *Islam and the Divine Comedy* (London: 1926), even if his case for Islamic influence is generally considered unproven. Matthew Arnold's relation to Persian literature is discussed in the essays named in the text, in *The Poems of Matthew Arnold,* edited by Kenneth Allott (London: 1965) and in his *English Literature and Irish Politics* (Ann Arbor: 1973), in which see especially p. 46. E. G. Browne, whose four-volume *A History of Persian Literature* remains after half a century the best introduction in English to the cultural history of Iran, gives in Volume Two an interesting collection of opinions of Omar Khayyam by later Iranian authors. In Volume Four he gives the standard picture of the rise of the Safavis as conveyed in later Safavi chronicles, although the brilliant research of Jean Aubin has shown the limitations of this standard account. An outstanding series of essays on the passion play have been assembled by Peter J. Chelkowski in *Ta'ziyeh* (New York: 1979). Alessandro Bausani's bravura attempt to interpret the whole range of religious experience in Iran, *Persia Religiosa* (Rome: 1959), has influenced much that I have written in this and other chapters.

The speech of Khomeini quoted in Chapter Six is from the collection of his writings used repeatedly in this book, *Islam and Revolution,* edited and annotated by Hamid Algar (Berkeley: 1981). The autobiography of Ghazzali and some of his general statements on the law are taken from W. Montgomery Watt's *The Faith and Practices of al-Ghazali* (London: 1953).

Much of the information for prominent mullahs of the nineteenth century comes out of *Qisas al-Ulema* by Tonkaboni (Tehran, n.d.), whose information is compared with other primary sources by Hamid Algar in his *Religion and State in Iran, 1785–1906* (Berkeley and Los Angeles: 1969). Abdul-Hadi Hairi gives a carefully researched description of prominent mullahs of the late nineteenth and early twentieth centuries in his *Shi'ism and Constitutionalism in Iran* (Leiden: 1977). There are also Persian biographies of Behbahani, Ansari, Khorasani, and Borujerdi—this last, by 'Alavi-Tabataba'i, containing the photograph discussed in the text. The invaluable *Hayat-e Yahya* by Yahya Dowlatabadi (Tehran: 1336) contains the description of the split in the circle of Ansari after the latter's death (I, pp. 25–26). The letter from Jamal ad-Din to Shirazi is quoted from E. G. Browne's *The Persian Revolution* (Cambridge: 1910). Much valuable material on this period is also found in S. A. Arjomand's important article, "The 'Ulama's Traditionalist Opposition to Parliamentarianism: 1907–1909," in *Middle Eastern Studies* 17 (1981). Two sources for the history of religion in twentieth-century Iran are Amin Banani, *The Modernization of Iran, 1921–1941* (Stanford: 1961) and Shahrough Akhavi, *Religion and Politics in Contemporary Iran* (Albany: 1980)—the latter being my principal source on the treatment of the Baha'is in 1955. Muhammad Mahdi al-Kazimi's *Ahsan al-Wadi'ah* (Najaf: 1928) is the source for the quote on Ha'eri's nonpolitical style (p. 268). My source for Khomeini's opposition to the election of local councils (and for many points about Iran after the Revolution of 1979) is Shaul Bakhash's outstanding book, *The Reign of the Ayatollahs* (New York: 1984). I have briefly treated the importance of the issue of diplomatic immunity to the rise of Khomeini in an article, "Iran's Foreign Devils," in *Foreign Policy*, 1980.

The materials for the biography of Al-e Ahmad given in Chapter Eight are from his *Yek Chah va Do Chaleh* (Tehran: 1343) and from the very fine Edinburgh Ph.D. thesis by Robert Wells, *Jalal Al-e Ahmad, Writer and Political Activist* (1982). Other autobiographical material, including his rejection of Najaf and his impressions of Harvard, are to be found in his *Karnameh-ye Seh-Saleh* (Tehran: 1357). The quotations from *Euromania* are based on the translation of *Gharbzadegi* by John Green and Ahmad Alizadeh (Lexington: 1982). *The School Principal* is translated in its entirety by J. K. Newton (Minneapolis: 1974). An anthology of Al-e Ahmad's writings, edited by Michael C. Hillmann in *Iranian Society* (Lexington: 1982), includes a complete translation of "The Pilgrimage" and a small fragment of his revealing memoir on the pilgrimage, *Khasi dar Miqat* (Tehran: 1966). The statistics on education were provided to me with characteristic generosity by David Menashri from his important forthcoming book, *The Role of Higher Education in the Development of Modern Iran*.

Almost all the statistics on urbanization given in Chapter Nine come out of Farhad Kazemi's *Poverty and Revolution in Iran* (New York: 1980). The case for Saint Augustine's influence on Ernest Renan is fully established (along with the original text of Renan's "prayer") in Pierre Courcelle's *Les Confessions* (Paris: 1963), p. 519. For the discussion of the Islamic view of Satan, I am indebted to Peter Awn's outstanding book *Satan's Tragedy and Redemption* (Leiden: 1983).

The reader may find the following chronology helpful:

c. 550 B.C.—The Iranian leader Cyrus the Great founds the Achaemenid empire.

486 B.C.—Darius I, builder of Persepolis, dies.

400s B.C.—Prophet Ezra is authorized by Achaemenid ruler to regulate religious matters among the Jews.

331 B.C.—Alexander defeats Darius III, last Achaemenid.

c. 1 A.D.—The Magi, Zoroastrian priests, are said to visit infant Jesus.

162—Galen, Greek authority on medicine, settles in Rome.

224—Sassanian dynasty is established; it strongly advocates the ancient Iranian religion of Zoroaster.

c. 305—Porphyry, Neo-Platonic philosopher and author of the *Isagoge*, a summary of Aristotelian logic, dies.

565—Justinian, Christian Byzantine emperor, dies. He had banned the still surviving Academy founded by Aristotle, whose members briefly found asylum with the Sassanian king.

c. 610—Mohammed, the founder of Islam, receives the first of the revelations later collected as the Koran.

632—Mohammed dies.

661—Ali ibn Abi Taleb, who moved the capital of the Muslims from Arabia to Iraq, dies. He was a first cousin of Mohammed and the husband of the Prophet's daughter, Fatemeh; the Shiah consider him the First Imam.

680—Hosain, son of Ali and Fatemeh, dies at the hands of followers of the Omayyad dynasty, which rules the Muslims from Syria.

762—Baghdad founded, returning the capital of the Muslims to Iraq.

833—Ma'mun, ruler of the Muslims and patron of Greek learning in Arabic translation, dies.

873—According to Shiah belief, the Twelfth Imam disappears; he remains the "Imam of Age" until his reappearance as a messiah.

c. 1020—Ferdowsi, author of *The Book of Kings*, the Iranian national epic, dies.

1037—Avicenna dies.

1071—Central Asian Turks, having conquered the Iranian plateau, take most of Anatolia from Byzantine control.

1111—The theologian Ghazzali dies.

1132—Omar Khayyam, mathematician and poet, dies.

1191—The mystic Sohrawardi dies.

1192—Saladin and Richard the Lion-Hearted call a truce.

1204—The Jewish philosopher Maimonides dies in Cairo.

1273—The mystic poet Mowlana Jalal ad-Din Rumi dies.

1292—Persian poet Saadi dies.

1321—Dante dies.

c. 1390—Hafez dies.

1453—Mehmet the Conquerer, the Ottoman Sultan, takes Constantinople.

c. 1500—Shah Esma'il founds the Safavi dynasty and begins to enforce Shiah Islam as the only acceptable religion for his Muslim subjects

1514—Ottoman Sultan Selim defeats the Safavis.

1624—Mullah Mohammed Amin, one of the founders of the "School of Traditions," dies.

1638—Ottomans take southern Iraq from Safavis.

1678—Sayyed Nematollah writes his autobiography.

1722—Shah Soltan Hosain, last effective ruler of the Safavi dynasty, abdicates.

c.1795—Qajar dynasty is founded in Iran.

1828—Fath Ali Shah, after repeated defeats, signs treaty of Torkamanchai with Russia.

1848–1896—Naser ed-Din Shah reigns.

1863—Baha'i religion is founded.

1864—Sheikh Mortaza Ansari, intellectual consolidator of the triumph of the "Jurisconsult School," dies.

1892—Concession to the Imperial Tobacco Company is canceled because of the opposition led by Mirza Shirazi, the first politically effective supreme "model" of the Shiah.

1897—Jamal al-Din "al-Afghani" dies in Turkey.

1905—Sugar merchants are beaten and the agitation leading to the Constitutional Revolution begins.

1906—Mozaffar ad-Din Shah grants constitution.

1907–1909—Mohammed Ali Shah reigns, supported in his hostility to the constitution by Sheikh Fazlollah Nuri.

1911—Khorasani, a leader of the mullahs favorable to the constitution, dies.

1921—Reza Khan enters Tehran; Ha'eri moves to Qom and stimulates its growth as a center of Shiah learning.

1923—Reza Khan becomes premier; the last Qajar ruler leaves for Europe.

1925—Reza Khan, proclaimed Shah, founds Pahlavi dynasty.

1928—Secular civil code and new court system are adopted.

1941—Allies force Reza Shah to abdicate in favor of his son Mohammed Reza Shah.

1946—Devotee of Islam shoots Kasravi.

1951—Devotee of Islam shoots Razmara, the prime minister.

1951—Mossadegh named prime minister and nationalizes oil.

1953—Mossadegh falls in coup d'état.

1955—Mullahs lead attack on Baha'is.

1961—Borujerdi dies without clear successor as supreme "model" of the Shiah.

1963—Riots against the Shah's government are inspired in part by Khomeini.

1964—Khomeini is exiled.

1971—Twenty-five centuries of Iranian kingship are celebrated at Persepolis.

1972—Nixon and Kissinger visit Iran, offering unlimited arms sales.

1975—Shah proclaims Iran a one-party state.

1979—After a year of riots, the Shah leaves Iran and Khomeini returns.

ACKNOWLEDGMENTS

IT WOULD NOT have been possible to write this book without the extensive help of several scholars who studied the traditional curriculum at the *madresehs* of Qom and Najaf: Sayyed Mohammed Husain Jalali, Sayyed Reza Borqe'i, Sheikh Reza Ostadi, Ayatollah Majdoddin Mahallati, Dr. Abbas Zaryab, and—above all—Dr. Hossein Modarressi, whose endless intellectual generosity really is a "miraculous sign of God" to those who, like myself, have benefitted from his vast learning.

By its very nature this book depends on the personal recollections of many Iranians of their education, upbringing and friends. Some of these Iranians wish to remain anonymous; nevertheless, I do have the pleasure of acknowledging the advice of Dr. Ali Banuazizi, who shared with me some of his unpublished material on *hay'ats*, and the patient and thoughtful help of Dr. Haleh Esfandiari. I am also deeply grateful to several Iranians who took the time to give me information about some of the figures who appear in this book: Ali Matin-Daftari, the grandson of Dr. Mohammed Mossadegh; Dr. Ehsan Yar-Shater and Dr. Majid Tehranian, friends of Jalal Al-e Ahmad; and Dr. Anushirvan Sadiq, who sent me information about his father, Dr. Isa Sadiq, through Dr. Shaul Bakhash.

Several scholars have had the great kindness to read and comment on the manuscript of this book in its entirety: the two highly gifted brothers Dr. Abbas and Mehrdad Amanat, Dr. Said Arjomand, Dr. Abdallah Hammoudi, and those two "models" so admired in the *madresehs* of Princeton, Dr. Peter Brown and Charles Issawi. Dr. Jeanette Wakin not only read and commented extensively on the manuscript, but, with that spirit of unselfish kindness that is an inspiration to her many friends, gave painstaking attention to details of style and consistency. Dr. Ahmad Ashraf also read the entire manuscript, and without his life-long professional study of Iranian social statistics and his immense knowledge of the inner history of Iranian radical groups in the sixties and seventies this book would have been considerably poorer. Dr. Andras Hamori read both early drafts and a final draft of the manuscript with the patience, support and intelligence that make him an exemplary friend. Two other scholars, Dr. Shaul Bakhash and Dr. John Gurney, also read first drafts as well as the final draft of the entire manuscript, a greater task than the seven exploits of Rostam and the seven exploits of Esfandiar put together; at every stage, what I have written has been greatly improved by their accurate and intelligent knowledge of Iranian history.

Three philosophers read part or all of the manuscript and gave me the benefit of their valuable criticism: Dr. Calvin Normore, Dr. Amelie Rorty and Dr. Eric Ormsby.

Other scholars who have helped me with encouragement and advice include: Dr. David Menashri, Dr. Ervand Abrahamian, Dr. Albert Hourani, Dr. Frank Stewart, Dr. Farhad Kazemi, Dr. Jerome Clinton, Dr. Eric Hoaglund, Dr. Roger Owen, Dr. David Burrell, Dr. John Gager, Dr. Robin Derricourt, Robert Peter Fichter, E. A. Bayne, John Cooper, Barbara Ajami, Luis Sanjurjo and John Herman.

My reference of first and last resort in all matters concerning this book has been my wife. A Persian proverb says: When the wife is satisfied and the husband is satisfied, confound the judge! A spouse with so "satisfying" a source of reference is never far from happiness.

INDEX

ABOUT THE AUTHOR

Roy Parviz Mottahedeh was born in New York City, educated at Harvard and Cambridge. An internationally recognized scholar, he is currently a professor of medieval Middle Eastern history at Harvard and has received numerous academic awards, including a Guggenheim and a MacArthur Prize Fellowship.